THIS COPY OF "THE MARVELS OF PRAYER" IS PRESENTED TO

Rev M. M. Martin's

LIBRARY

BY A FRIEND OF

The North Dutch Church,

THROUGH

G. S. PLUMLEY, PASTOR.

J. C. LANPHIER, LAY MISSIONARY.

"Sing praises to the LORD, *which dwelleth in Zion: declare among the people his doings."*

SEPTEMBER 23d, 1877, is the Twentieth Anniversary of the Fulton Street Daily Noon Prayer Meeting. The Lay Missionary, to whom it owes, under God, its origin, had no expectation of what it would grow to become, or of the results that would flow from it. He had felt it to be his duty to leave the avocations of a business man, and devote himself to the work of a city missionary. This he did under the supervision and with the countenance of the Consistory of the Reformed Protestant Dutch Church of New York, the oldest religious organization on Manhattan Island. Hence, in a record like this, it is appropriate that the illustrations appear that bring before its readers associations connected with the past and present work of the North Dutch Church, the particular Church with which the history of the Fulton Street Daily Noon Prayer-Meeting is identified. This Church still possesses a local habitation, and its interior presents, during the hour of the daily prayer-meeting, the appearance exhibited in the plate facing page 193 of this volume.

Over two hundred of the several hundred members of the Collegiate Reformed Protestant Dutch Church are represented at the North Dutch Church, and these have the ordinances and sacraments of the Church regularly administered among them. Some who read this book may, when visiting New York, wish to worship with the North Dutch Church. For their information, the following guide to its services is furnished:

Divine Service every Lord's Day, morning and evening at the usual hours.

Prayer-Meetings every week-day, at noon (including all holidays), and on Friday Evening.

Praise-Meeting every Monday Evening.

The Lord's Supper is administered on the first Sabbath of March, June, September, and December. Preparatory Sermons are preached, and

Baptism is administered on the Friday Evening previous.

To all the services all are welcome, and seats are provided for strangers who are guests of the neighboring hotels.

A list of the books that form a historical record of the Daily Noon Prayer-Meeting, shows that the twenty years of its progress have produced twenty interesting volumes. These can be procured by addressing the several Publishers, New York City.

These works are:

POWER OF PRAYER. By S. Irenæus Prime, D.D. Scribner & Co., Publishers, New York.

NOON PRAYER-MEETING. By Talbot W. Chambers, D.D.
THE LITTLE SYRACUSE BOY.
THE DRUMMER BOY.
ARMY LIFE.
LIVING WORDS.
YOUNG QUARTERMASTER.
CHRIST EVER WITH YOU.
HOSPITAL LIFE.
OUT OF DARKNESS INTO LIGHT.
HIGH MOUNTAIN APART.
FULTON STREET PRAYER-MEETING HYMN-BOOK.
HOURS OF PRAYER. By Talbot W. Chambers, D.D.

Published by the Board of Publication of the Reformed Church in America, Synod Rooms, 34 Vesey Street, cor. Church, New York.

FIVE YEARS OF PRAYER. By S. Irenæus Prime, D.D. Scribner & Co., Publishers, New York.

FIFTEEN YEARS OF PRAYER. By S. Irenæus Prime, D.D. Scribner & Co., Publishers, New York.

REMARKABLE CONVERSIONS AND REVIVAL INCIDENTS. By Wm. C. Conant. Published by Derby & Jackson, New York.

THE REVIVAL AND ITS LESSONS. By James W. Alexander, D.D. Published by Tibbals & Son, New York.

ALONE WITH JESUS. J. C. Lanphier, Compiler. Published by Tibbals & Son, New York.

MARVELS OF PRAYER. Published by Evangelical Publishing Co.

WONDERS OF PRAYER. Published by H. D. Williams.

Also, FIRST HALF HOUR of the Fulton Street Prayer-Meeting. A Steel Engraving of an interior view of the room, furniture, etc. Published by Geo. E. Perine, New York.

"Jesus Only."

MARVELS OF PRAYER,

ILLUSTRATED BY THE

Fulton Street Prayer Meeting.

WITH

LEAVES FROM THE TREE OF LIFE.

BY

MATTHEW HALE SMITH,

AUTHOR OF "MOUNT CALVARY," "SUNSHINE AND SHADOW IN NEW-YORK," "FUTURE RETRIBUTION," "SUCCESSFUL PEOPLE," ETC.

"ELIAS was a man subject to like passions as we are, and he prayed earnestly that it might not rain: and it rained not on the earth by the space of three years and six months."

New-York:

PUBLISHED BY THE EVANGELICAL PUBLISHING CO.,

FULTON STREET PRAYER MEETING BUILDING,

No. 103 FULTON STREET.

S. W. Green,
Printer & Electrotyper,
18 Jacob St., New-York.

CONTENTS.

1769.

NORTH REF. PROT. DUTCH CHURCH, COR. OF WILLIAM AND FULTON STS.

1857. *Pray without ceasing.* 1875.

"IN GOD WE TRUST."

I.

OUTLOOK.

AND I will pour upon the house of David, and upon the inhabitants of Jerusalem, the spirit of grace and of supplications: and they shall look upon me whom they have pierced, and they shall mourn for him, as one mourneth for *his* only *son*, and shall be in bitterness for him, as one that is in bitterness for *his* first born. In that day shall there be a great mourning in Jerusalem, as the mourning of Hadadrimmon in the valley of Megiddon. For these are not drunken, as ye suppose, seeing it is *but* the third hour of the day. But this is that which was spoken by the prophet Joel. And it shall come to pass in the last days, saith God, I will pour out of my Spirit upon all flesh: and your sons and your daughters shall prophesy, and your young men shall see visions, and your old men shall dream dreams.

No one claims for Fulton street that it is sacred above all other places, or that prayer is only here specially answered. The noon-day hour is sacred to prayer and praise. For this place God has manifested a gracious regard; for seventeen years he has filled the meeting with his presence, and given manifest tokens of his divine regard.

The incidents and illustrations recorded are selected from a group, equally interesting and equally authenticated. Only a small number of direct answers to prayer have been reported. As in the case of the lepers, ten were cleansed, while only one returned to give glory to God. Few who send requests to Fulton street for help in time of trouble, feel called upon to send thanksgivings for mercies received. It is estimated that a case a day of answer to prayer has been known. This would make in seventeen years over six thousand cases.

The illustrations are given without prefix or explanation, as near as possible in the style and terseness with which they were given to the meeting. No explanation or defense of what seems to be marvelous has been attempted. Those who believe in prayer need none. Those who do not, would be no better satisfied with an explanation than they would be with a simple statement. The whole drift of the meeting from its humble inception—its first half hour and solitary worshiper—through all these years, proves that the Lord of Hosts is the same ever-present help in time of trouble—the same gracious answerer of prayer that he was in the olden time, when his presence was revealed between cherubim, and when, for the defense of his people, he rode on the column of cloud and column of fire.

This title, "LEAVES FROM THE TREE OF LIFE," given to the selection of Scriptures in this book, are taken from the impressive words of Revelation: "In the midst of the street of it, and on either side of the river, was there the tree of life, which bare twelve manner of fruits, and yielded her fruit every month: and the leaves of the tree were for the healing of the nations." The variety of subjects in the Bible is simply marvelous. Every one who reads the Bible knows how difficult it is to make an appropriate selection in a hurry. Men are perplexed at prayer-meetings and at family devotions to search for Scriptures adapted to the hour. The title to each paper will usually be found in the first verse of the Scriptural selection.

II.

HOUR OF PRAYER.

AND he spake a parable unto them *to this end*, that men ought always to pray and not to faint. I will therefore that men pray everywhere, lifting up holy hands, without wrath and doubting. Not unto us, O Lord, not unto us, but unto Thy name give glory, for Thy mercy, *and* for Thy truth's sake. Finally, brethren, pray for us, that the word of the Lord may have *free* course, and be glorified, even as *it is* with you. To whom God would make known what *is* the riches of the glory of this mystery among the Gentiles ; which is Christ in you, the hope of glory. Whom we preach, warning every man, and teaching every man in all wisdom ; that we may present every man perfect in Christ Jesus. Unto me, who am less than the least of all saints, is this grace given, that I should preach among the Gentiles the unsearchable riches of Christ.

THE Fulton-street Daily Prayer-meeting, during the seventeen years of its existence, has exhibited a power the most wonderful. Some of the answers to prayer would be pronounced marvelous. A company of women and men have assembled in the Old North Church, at the hour of noon, for prayer and praise. This meeting has been continued for seventeen years, through storm and sunshine; through revival and declension; through civil war and the triumphs of peace. As the City-Hall bell booms out the hour of noon, from three to four hundred persons have gathered daily in the busiest part of New-York, at the busiest hour, day by day, from year to year, to offer prayer to God for the salvation of men. The meeting has taken on the simplest form of service; plain congregational singing, reading the word of God, with prayer and exultation, no one service exceeding five minutes. Requests for prayer—from ten to fifty—come in from every part of the land and the world; from the Pacific coast; the islands of the sea; from the old world; from the mountains of India; from the sands of Africa; from the sacred country,

> "Over whose acres walked
> Those blessed feet which,
> Eighteen hundred years ago,
> Were nailed for our advantage
> To the bitter cross."

If answers to prayer are miracles, then Fulton street is full of them. One need not visit Treves to look on the miracles of the Holy Coat; nor visit the sacred wells of the East; nor look on the sacred shrines where canes and crutches are piled, which indicate the healing power of sacred relics. At Fulton street, in answer to simple, fervent prayer, the sick have been healed, the destitute fed and clothed, the drunkards reformed, obdurate and hardened men subdued and converted, family alienations healed, prodigals brought back, business embarrassments removed, bad tempers mellowed, the very appetite for rum and tobacco changed. Men reformed and saved are in our midst; any one who wishes can lay his hands on them. Men, now eminent in the law, eloquent in the pulpit, skillful in surgery, successful in trade, reformed and pious, are among us, and stand forth, known of all men as trophies of this meeting.

III.

THE AUTHOR TO THE READER.

NOW the God of peace, that brought again from the dead our Lord Jesus, that great Shepherd of the sheep, through the blood of the everlasting covenant, make you perfect in every good work to do his will, working in you that which is well-pleasing in his sight, through Jesus Christ, to whom *be* glory for ever and ever. Amen. After this I beheld, and, lo, a great multitude, which no man could number, of all nations, and kindreds, and people, and tongues, stood before the throne, and before the Lamb, clothed with white robes, and palms in their hands ; and cried with a loud voice, saying, Salvation to our God which sitteth upon the throne, and unto the Lamb. And all the angels stood round about the throne, and *about* the elders and the four beasts, and fell before the throne on their faces, and worshiped God, saying, Amen : Blessing, and glory, and wisdom, and thanksgiving, and honour, and power, and might, *be* unto our God for ever and ever. Amen.

THE author has had ample opportunity to collect the wonderful and touching narratives running over the long period that the Fulton-street Meeting has existed. The subjoined letter of the founder of the meeting is ample testimonial. A very large number of the incidents in this book were taken down at the time they were uttered. Other pens have done the same work. These incidents have been set in a frame-work of the word of God; subjects doctrinal, experimental, and practical have been selected, suited to public and private devotion, and to every-day life. The utterances of the Holy Spirit show how eminently adapted to common practical life are the Holy Scriptures. How well fitted is the Holy Book "to make the man of God perfect, and thoroughly furnish him to every good work." It is hoped that these leaves from the Tree of Life, with illustrations, will make a book precious to all who love our Lord; a book suited to public and private devotion; a book for the pastor's table, prayer-meeting, and the Bible-class; for the fireside, Sunday-school, for daily conversation, and for the closet; a welcome companion for travel or repose.

NEW-YORK, September, 1875.

Matthew Hale Smith

North Dutch Church.

Union Prayer Meeting.

New York May 1875

I have read with great satisfaction and with pleasure, that I have not words to express. The work in manuscript; Marvels of Prayer, Illustrated in the Fulton St. Prayer Meeting, with Leaves from the Tree of Life - by Dr Matthew Hale Smith. Dr. Smith has brought to this work rare gifts and superior opportunities. He was one of the earliest friends of the Meeting, knew its history from its earliest conception to its consummation, Possessing a catholic Spirit, devoting his time and energies to Mission work among the Lowly with acknowledged gifts as an author and writer, he has contributed much to the interest and usefulness of the Daily Prayer Meeting. Taking notes of interesting incidents from year to year - he has the rare advantage of presenting fresh and otherwise unknown incidents of the Marvels of Prayer. I have personal knowledge of some of the most important facts and incidents related in this work. I know that they are not colored nor over stated. Many now in distant lands, many now living amongus, are ready to bear ample testimony to the vivid truthfulness of these statements.

I shall be disappointed if the Marvels of Prayer, do not find a cordial reception in the thousands of homes where Prayer is accepted. and the Saviour has a friend.

J. C. Lanphier.

Third Story Room in the Consistory Building.

IV.

ORIGIN OF THE FULTON-STREET MEETING.

NOW Peter and John went up together into the temple at the hour of prayer, *being* the ninth hour. As for me, I will call upon God; and the Lord shall save me. Evening, and morning, and at noon, will I pray, and cry aloud: and he shall hear my voice. And they, continuing daily with one accord in the temple, and breaking bread from house to house, did eat their meat with gladness and singleness of heart, praising God, and having favor with all the people. And the Lord added to the Church daily such as should be saved. Wherefore, Jesus also, that he might sanctify the people with his own blood, suffered without the gate. Let us go forth, therefore, unto him without the camp, bearing his reproach. For here have we no continuing city, but we seek one to come. By him, therefore, let us offer the sacrifice of praise to God continually.

FULTON-STREET MEETING was founded in no spirit of self-glorification. The missionary with whom the meeting originated, as he sat out the first half hour alone, had no thought unto what the thing would grow. Meetings of prayer and praise were no novelty, but such a meeting as Fulton street was never before known. A meeting at the hour of noon; its duration sixty minutes; no one allowed to speak or pray over five minutes; parties to come and go at pleasure; with singing crisp, copious, and abundant; without denominationalism or talk on controverted points. The founder of the meeting had, in a simple and unostentatious manner, indicated its start. He says:

"I regard the origin of the Fulton-street Prayer-Meeting an additional evidence that God delights to honor humble instrumentality. I should not have noticed any thing that might have been written or said concerning the origin of the meeting, had not efforts been made to give it consequence, and to claim for those who had no connection with it, a historic record as its founders. I consulted with no person, and no person consulted with me about that meeting, until I had determined to establish it. I applied for and obtained permission to use the room for that purpose. I then appointed a time for holding the first meeting. Immediately after, I commenced to give notice by cards, letters, and handbills. I found no encouragement from any of them. During the period which elapsed between my determination to establish the service and the first meeting, nothing occurred to give me the least hope of Christian sympathy or support. But my trust in God, and my firm reliance on him, and feeling in my inmost soul that my purpose was in this humble way of prayer to honor him, I felt that such a meeting would become the instrument of his blessing to souls of men. I had been accustomed to be in that room for prayer before the day on which the first meeting was appointed. Sometimes one or two, and once three, were with me. But on the day that the Fulton-street Meeting was established, notwithstanding the great pains I had taken to make it public, I was there alone with Jesus for half an hour before any person entered the room. During the last half hour, five other persons came in. What has followed is a matter of history.

V.

PECULIARITIES OF THE MEETING.

UNTIL the Spirit be poured upon us from on high, and the wilderness be a fruitful field, and the fruitful field be counted for a forest. Then judgment shall dwell in the wilderness, and righteousness remain in the fruitful field. Behold, the days come, saith the Lord, that the plowman shall overtake the reaper, and the treader of grapes him that soweth seed; and the mountains shall drop sweet wine, and all the hills shall melt. What is it then? I will pray with the spirit, and I will pray with the understanding also: I will sing with the spirit, and I will sing with the understanding also. Else, when thou shalt bless with the spirit, how shall he that occupieth the room of the unlearned say Amen at thy giving of thanks, seeing he understandeth not what thou sayest? And thus are the secrets of his heart made manifest; and so falling down on *his* face he will worship God, and report that God is in you of a truth.

THE Fulton-street Meeting soon outgrew the place of its origin. Men were attracted from all parts of the land and the world. It was remembered by Christians in all climes. Its remarkable story was told in every language spoken under heaven. Requests for prayer and thanksgivings came from over the seas. Merchants from a distance paused in their purchases to look on New-York at prayer at the noontide hour. Strangers to God and to his grace wondered whereto this thing would grow. It was a well-selected hour for prayer and praise. The founder, himself a merchant, knew that the hour of noon was the hour of leisure to business men. Clerks, hastily swallowing their lunch, hastened to Fulton street to join in the song of praise. The coming or going was no interruption, for it was one of the rules of the meeting that visitors could stay five or ten minutes, or the whole hour. Young men came in with bank-books in their hands, pencils behind the ear, memorandum-books peeping out of their pockets, with other marks of trade, to join in the service. Carmen and wagonmen drove their teams to the curbstone, and, with frocks on, knelt down to pray. The merchant came from his store, the mechanic from his bench, the coachman from his box, and the lawyer from his brief. The sight on each anniversary has been especially grand. The old North Church, a hundred years old, one of the oldest, largest, and most elegant of our churches, has always been packed to repletion. The singing has always been especially exhilarating, led by the founder of the meeting, accompanied by the grand organ. The unwonted sound of song rolling out into the street, arrested the crowd of teams, cars, coaches, and blocked up the sidewalk, while men listened to the unwonted sound. Eminent ministers and laymen, representing all Christian denominations, indicated the unity of the noonday meeting.

VI.

THE FOUNDER.

AND David said unto Saul, Who *am* I? and what *is* my life, *or* my father's family in Israel, that I should be son in law to the King? Although my house *be* not so with God; yet he hath made with me an everlasting covenant, ordered in all *things*, and sure: for *this is* all my salvation, and all *my* desire, although he make *it* not to grow. For since I spake, I cried out, I cried violence and spoil; because the word of the Lord was made a reproach unto me, and a derision, daily. Then I said, I will not make mention of him, nor speak any more in his name. But *his word* was in mine heart as a burning fire shut up in my bones, and I was weary with forbearing, and I could not *stay*. He raiseth up the poor out of the dust, *and* lifteth the needy out of the dunghill; that he may set *him* with princes, *even* with the princes of his people.

JEREMIAH CALVIN LANPHIER enjoys the honor of originating this daily meeting with its marked peculiarities. Tall, with a pleasant face and affectionate manner, he possesses indomitable energy and perseverance. His gifts eminently fitted him for the position he was called to fill. He is a good singer, gifted in prayer, and earnest and fluent in exhortation. He has great tact, and good, plain common-sense. He gave up his business as a merchant to enter the field as a missionary. His business experience served him in his new calling. He knew how difficult it was for a merchant to attend an evening devotional meeting. He knew how much the hour of leisure was the hour of noon. As a part of his missionary work with the Collegiate Church, the Fulton-street Meeting was established.

The 23d of September, 1857, was an eventful day. The missionary sat in a small upper room of the Consistory Building, waiting for an audience, but no audience came. Half-past twelve, a solitary step was heard on the stairs. Another and another were added, until six persons entered the room. These made up the meeting. The next meeting numbered twenty; the next numbered forty. On the 8th of October, the central Consistory-room was thrown open for daily service. From that hour, the meeting has known no interruption. The singing, which has been uniformly congregational, has been led by Mr. Lanphier, with scarcely the absence of a day during eighteen years.

It has demanded great executive ability to keep up the daily service and enforce the rules. Unreasonable people attempt unreasonable things. Men who have large notions of liberty try to break the rules; others try to do a little business, carry on a little trade, beg money, or do some secular business. All such efforts are immediately put down; parties must conform to the rules or be quiet.

The Fulton-street Meeting has become the great religious exchange of the city. Christians bring to it tidings from every part of Zion. Requests from every quarter of the globe bring before the meeting every variety of want and suffering peculiar to humanity. Many regard the meeting as the Pool of Healing.

VII.

MARVELS OF PRAYER.

ELIAS was a man subject to like passions as we are, and he prayed earnestly that it might not rain, and it rained not on the earth by the space of three years and six months. And he prayed again, and the heaven gave rain, and the earth brought forth her fruit. Then Peter arose and went with them. When he was come, they brought him into the upper chamber: and all the widows stood by him weeping, and showing the coats and garments which Dorcas made, while she was with them. But Peter put them all forth, and kneeled down, and prayed; and turning *him* to the body said, Tabitha, arise. And she opened her eyes: and when she saw Peter, she sat up. And he gave her *his* hand, and lifted her up; and when he had called the saints and widows, he presented her alive. And it was known throughout all Joppa; and many believed in the Lord.

MINISTRY OF TUBEROSES.

A LADY in deep mourning came into the meeting. She laid on the table a bunch of tuberoses. She was all unknown to those present, and took her seat among the worshipers. At the close of the service, Mr. Lanphier, who is passionately fond of flowers, took the bouquet in his hand, and started for home. He saw that he was followed by a stranger. The man attended his steps up Broadway, over to St. John's Park, and up the steps of the missionary's house, keeping his eye fixed upon the flowers, pointing to them occasionally, and evidently greatly excited. He could not speak a word of English; he gesticulated furiously, and manifested a desire to talk about the roses. Efforts were made to find some one who could interpret his words. The Irishman who attended the door was at fault; the cook, a foreigner, was brought from the kitchen in vain. A cobbler was at length summoned, who was able to explain the strange conduct of the excited German. The man had a dream, he said, while on his way to America. He thought he was standing on his father's grave; something told him that, on reaching America, if he saw a man with white flowers in his hand, to speak to him. That man would give him a Bible, and tell him about Christ and the way of salvation. When the German saw the missionary turning out of Fulton street, carrying a bunch of flowers, he thought he was the man referred to in his dream. He followed him, and his dream had a literal fulfillment. A German Bible was given him, and he was instructed in the way of life. He now rejoices in the Saviour. He is a devoted Christian, earnestly engaged in mission work, and especially desirous to elevate and save his countrymen.

VIII.

SERVICE OF PRAYER.

AND when the day of Pentecost was fully come, they were all with one accord in one place. And suddenly there came a sound from heaven as of a rushing mighty wind, and it filled all the house where they were sitting. And when he had thus spoken, he kneeled down and prayed with them all. And they all wept sore, and fell on Paul's neck, and kissed him, sorrowing most of all for the words which he spake, that they should see his face no more. And they accompanied him unto the ship. Now when Daniel knew that the writing was signed, he went into his house; and, his windows being open in his chamber toward Jerusalem, he kneeled upon his knees three times a day, and prayed, and gave thanks before his God, as he did aforetime. Then these men assembled, and found Daniel praying and making supplication before his God.

A RESCUED SOUL.

A GENTLEMAN of ability and position, long connected with the press, became a drunkard. He ran down to the lowest state of degradation; he lost position after position; he became a vagrant, wandering about the streets, without money, poorly clad, ill fed, and lodging at night in the lowest haunts of New-York. Recovering from a debauch, he one day walked down Broadway. He turned down Fulton street, on his way to the slums and dance-houses of Water street. He passed Fulton-street Church as the meeting was breaking up. He paused on the curbstone to let the crowd pass. He had heard of the business men's prayer-meetings, and knew this must be the place. A large number of well-dressed ladies and gentlemen came pouring out on to the street. Every one seemed cheerful and happy; hand-shaking, congratulations, and good wishes were exchanged. Surely, he said, if these people are Christians, religion must be a cheerful thing. I have flung away my inheritance, my manhood, my respectability, and perhaps my soul. What have I got to show for it? I am penniless, in disgrace, ragged, wretched, and homeless. Suddenly, he resolved to change his course of life. He hung around the church-door, wondering whether any one would help him get free from the curse of rum. He spoke to a man who was leaning against the door-post. In answer to his inquiry for help, the man advised him to go to Judge Dowling, and get sent up to the Island. Just then the missionary came out. His face was so kind and his manner so considerate and tender, that the poor fellow took courage to repeat his request for help. "Yes, I will help you," said the missionary; "I'll do more than that—I will take care of you. But, my friend, come up-stairs; first let me pray with you." Lodging, food, and clothes were provided. In one week, the poor outcast was a new man; the profane, drunken, blasphemous person, sleeping in gutters or mud-cellars, herding with the vilest, an outcast, and in disgrace, he stood erect, a reformed and saved man. A member of the Church, his time is devoted to rescuing him that has no helper. He needs no charity, his commanding talents giving him abundant support.

IX.

HUMILIATION OF OUR LORD.

FOR ye know the grace of our Lord Jesus Christ, that, though he was rich, yet for your sakes he became poor, that ye through his poverty might be rich. Let this mind be in you, which was also in Christ Jesus: who, being in the form of God, thought it not robbery to be equal with God: but made himself of no reputation, and took upon him the form of a servant, and was made in the likeness of men: And being found in fashion as a man, he humbled himself, and became obedient unto death, even the death of the cross. Wherefore God also hath highly exalted him, and given him a name which is above every name: That at the name of Jesus every knee should bow, of *things* in heaven, and *things* in earth, and *things* under the earth; and *that* every tongue should confess that Jesus Christ *is* Lord, to the glory of God the Father.

FOR HIS SAKE.

A NOBLEMAN came to his estate on the death of his father. He was recalled from his studies in a foreign land to enter upon his property. He was almost unknown to his tenants, many of whom lived far from the mansion. Clustering around the colliery on the estate was a little village of hamlets, occupied by the miners and their households. His lordship was out one day hunting. He got separated from his companions, lost his way, and became mired in the swamp. Wet from head to foot and covered with mud, he went to the door of a cottage, and was rudely repulsed. No one knew him, and no one who shut the door in his face imagined that he was lord of the manor. In the poorest cottage in the cluster dwelt a widow, aged and in penury. He knocked at her door, and received the response, "Come in, thou blessed of the Lord." She placed a chair by her rude hearthstone, brought down some coarse clothing, the property of her only boy lost at sea, and spread her table with the homely fare the cottage afforded. He wore away the dry clothing, and promised to send for his own. The next day, a coroneted carriage, with out-riders, stopped at her cabin-door. The team was well known in the neighborhood, and known to belong to the heir of the old master. The poor widow was filled with astonishment and terror, when she saw descending from the carriage her guest of the day before. It was the heir of the estate to whom she had proffered the coarse clothing of her lost son. The young lord thanked her for the kindness she had shown him, when his rank and position were unknown. He presented her with a comfortable cottage and an annuity for life. "But how was it," he said, "that you welcomed me to your fireside when every other cottage was closed against me?" "Well, I thought of my poor boy cast away at sea, and thought he might be needing a shelter. Then I thought of Him who for my sake had not where to lay his head, and for His sake I opened my door."

X.

RELIGIOUS CONSOLATION.

AND I heard a voice from heaven saying unto me, Write, Blessed *are* the dead which die in the Lord from henceforth: yea, saith the Spirit, that they may rest from their labors; and their works do follow them. But I would not have you to be ignorant, brethren, concerning them which are asleep, that ye sorrow not, even as others which have no hope. For if we believe that Jesus died and rose again, even so them also which sleep in Jesus will God bring with him. For this we say unto you by the word of the Lord, that we which are alive *and* remain unto the coming of the Lord shall not prevent them which are asleep. For the Lord himself shall descend from heaven with a shout, with the voice of the archangel, and with the trump of God: and the dead in Christ shall rise first. Then we which are alive *and* remain shall be caught up together with them in the clouds, to meet the Lord in the air: and so shall we ever be with the Lord. Wherefore comfort one another with these words.

A PASTOR'S STORY.

I HAVE had a very heavy affliction. I had a bright and happy home. Three little sons made our house cheerful and buoyant. First, God removed my youngest child. He was nervous, excitable, and noisy; he disturbed my studies. I am sensible I was not as gentle with him as I ought to have been. His racket, impetuosity, and loud voice drove me almost to distraction. Our house has been quiet enough since we laid him beneath the green sod. My second son soon followed his brother. A few months after, my only boy, like the Shunamite lad, came into the house, crying, "My head! my head!" and they carried him to his mother. I knew he would not live from the hour he was taken. I nursed him through all his long and painful sickness; I held his hand, closed his eyes when he died. A few hours before he passed away, he looked me in the face, and said, "Father, don't mourn for me; I am going home. I will give father's love to Charlie and Willie." Heaven has seemed more real to me from that hour. I believe in the mansions our Saviour has prepared, and know that I have treasures in that blessed abode.

I now believe in the ministry of children. I have a little trunk, open to no curious eyes. Once a week, my dear wife and myself make a pilgrimage, as to a sacred shrine. When the trunk is opened, what do we see? A broken top, a little whip, a few toys, and a pair of worn shoes. But crown jewels could not buy those memorials of happier days.

XI.

RELIGIOUS INTEGRITY.

AND now, behold, the king walketh before you: and I am old and grayheaded; and, behold, my sons *are* with you: and I have walked before you from my childhood unto this day. Behold, here I *am*: witness against me before the Lord, and before his anointed: whose ox have I taken? or whose ass have I taken? or whom have I defrauded? whom have I oppressed? or of whose hand have I received *any* bribe to blind mine eyes therewith? and I will restore it you. Then the presidents and princes sought to find occasion against Daniel concerning the kingdom; but they could find none occasion nor fault; forasmuch as he *was* faithful, neither was there any error or fault found in him. Then said these men, We shall not find any occasion against this Daniel, except we find *it* against him concerning the law of his God.

A GOVERNOR'S COLLAR.

THE chief magistrate of one of our States had some peculiarities of dress. He wore a huge black stock without a collar. Dainty people thought he did not dress well enough for a governor. Allusions were frequently made to this oddity. A party of gentlemen were dining with the governor when the matter of dress came up. One of the gentlemen said, "Governor, if it's a fair question, why do you never wear a collar to your shirt?" "I will tell you a story," was the reply. "I was a hatter when a young man, and worked at the kettle. Whether it was the steam or the business that constantly surrounded us, I do not know, but nearly every one of my associates was addicted to drinking. I signed the pledge when I was a boy, and it saved me from a thousand temptations. One of my associates was a young man to whom I was greatly attached. He was generous, genial, and affectionate. He was a good workman, manly, and frank; but he would have his sprees, and these more than once cost him his place. He had a young wife and a mother whom he supported, and to whom he was devotedly attached. I often spoke to him on the subject of drinking, for I wanted to save him. He turned on me one day, and said with a great deal of vehemence and feeling, 'I don't want you to preach to me. You have your faults as well as I. You don't drink; but you are as proud as a peacock. When your work is done, you go to your little room, shake out your shirt-frill, put on your cravat, curl your hair, draw on your gloves, and with your cane and your glossy hat, start out to be admired. If you will tear that ruffle from your bosom, your collar from your shirt, and never wear either again, I will sign the pledge, and keep it as long as you keep your promise.' I took my hand out of the steaming water, reached it across the kettle, and said, 'Sam, it's a bargain.' That young man is now in Congress. He occupies a position of importance in the West. Before I would break my vow, or risk the throwing of him back to his old habits, I would resign my office as governor of the State."

XII.

THE HOLY SCRIPTURES.

AND that from a child thou hast known the holy Scriptures, which are able to make thee wise unto salvation through faith which is in Christ Jesus. All Scripture *is* given by inspiration of God, and *is* profitable for doctrine, for reproof, for correction, for instruction in righteousness: that the man of God may be perfect, thoroughly furnished unto all good works. Search the Scriptures; for in them ye think ye have eternal life: and they are they which testify of me. And ye will not come to me, that ye might have life. And the brethren immediately sent away Paul and Silas by night unto Berea: who coming *thither* went into the synagogue of the Jews. These were more noble than those in Thessalonica, in that they received the word with all readiness of mind, and searched the Scriptures daily, whether those things were so.

CHILD'S OFFERING.

ONE of our mission-schools is located in the midst of poverty and crime. The attendance is large. The children are ragged, neglected, and suffering, and probably can not be matched in the city. The superintendent believes in every one doing something. He proposed a contribution for the missionary Sunday, for children more miserable and wretched than those in the school. "You may bring any thing you please, but bring something."

A motley offering was laid on the altar. Some of the donations were not only curious, but touching. Boys brought their marbles and tops. One lad brought a jack-knife that he must have found in an ash-barrel. A little girl brought her necklace. She had never known a bright thing nor heard a kind word till she came to school. Her small face was furrowed with suffering, and she looked upon her well-dressed and kindly-spoken teacher as if she were an angel.

On the second day of her attendance, she had evidently tried to mend her personal appearance. Out of variegated tissue-paper she had constructed a collar, and fastened it with a pin run through a bead. This collar, probably the most precious thing the child had ever owned, lay in the basket, an offering to missions.

Among the donors was a little girl scarcely four years old. Her face was unwashed, her hair uncombed, barefooted, with a thin dress pinned around the neck. She handed a basket to the superintendent.

"What have you here, Susie?"

"Our contribution, sir. But you mustn't let them get out."

"Is there any thing alive in the basket?"

"Yes, sir, two mice. I caught 'em. We have got lots of 'em at our house."

"Two mice! What do you suppose we can do with mice? we are overrun with them now."

The little girl stood her ground; her bosom heaved and tears came into her eyes. She then said,

"If the Saviour had been here, he'd a took 'em!"

"Took two mice! What do you mean?"

"A man said the other day that a poor woman brought two mice to Jesus, and he said it was more than any of 'em."

The poor little thing had made a mistake in the word, but she had the substance. The superintendent told the school that when the story of the poor widow in the Gospel should be told at the last great day, the blessed Saviour would not overlook the gift of the little mission-girl in New-York.

XIII.

OUR GOD A REFUGE.

HAST thou not known? hast thou not heard, *that* the everlasting God, the Lord, the Creator of the ends of the earth, fainteth not, neither is weary? *there is* no searching of his understanding. He giveth power to the faint; and to *them that have* no might he increaseth strength. Even the youths shall faint and be weary, and the young men shall utterly fall: but they that wait upon the Lord shall renew *their* strength; they shall mount up with wings as eagles; they shall run, and not be weary; *and* they shall walk, and not faint. Verily thou *art* a God that hidest thyself, O God of Israel, the Saviour. *But* Israel shall be saved in the Lord with an everlasting salvation: ye shall not be ashamed nor confounded world without end. I said not unto the seed of Jacob, Seek ye me in vain: I the Lord speak righteousness, I declare things that are right.

BURGLAR'S CONVERSION.

DR. BARNES, of Philadelphia, had his library in his church. He was one of the hardest of students. His custom was to begin his labors at four o'clock in the morning, summer and winter. His notes on the New Testament were mainly written before his brethren were awake. When he first removed to Philadelphia, the watchmen proposed to lock him up, supposing him to be a robber. One dark and rainy morning, the watchman forbid his entering in the church. He announced himself as the pastor, and that only deepened the suspicion of the guardian of the night. "City ministers," he said, "were sensible men, and were not in the habit of hanging around their churches before daylight."

Passing from his house to his study one morning, he had the impression that he was followed. He unlocked the gates, and entered his study with the uncomfortable impression that some one was dogging his steps. He had scarcely taken his seat, when he heard footsteps coming up the long passage. His first impression was to lock the door; his next to throw himself on his knees, and commit himself to God. Closer and closer the visitor drew near, and the pastor knew that he had already crossed the threshold. His prayer ceased not; it was continued, earnest, tender, importunate.

Dr. Barnes came to his feet, and stood face to face with a burglar, one of the most desperate of his class, and armed to the teeth. His eyes were moist, and his voice trembled. He approached the table, and laid upon it his weapons and the tools of his perilous trade.

"You have saved me to-night," he said, turning to the astonished pastor. "I have remembered my mother and my Saviour. I shall abandon this business, and, with God's help, become a Christian."

A Christian he did become. The sincerity of his conversion was proved by years of faithful service as a city missionary.

XIV.

DRUNKENNESS.

WINE *is* a mocker, strong drink *is* raging: and whosoever is deceived thereby is not wise. Awake, ye drunkards, and weep; and howl, all ye drinkers of wine, because of the new wine; for it is cut off from your mouth. Who hath woe? who hath sorrow? who hath contentions? who hath babbling? who hath wounds without cause? who hath redness of eyes? They that tarry long at the wine; they that go to seek mixed wine. Look not thou upon the wine when it is red, when it giveth his color in the cup, *when* it moveth itself aright. At the last it biteth like a serpent, and stingeth like an adder. Know ye not that the unrighteous shall not inherit the kingdom of God? Be not deceived: neither fornicators, nor idolaters, nor adulterers, nor effeminate, nor abusers of themselves with mankind, nor thieves, nor covetous, nor drunkards, nor revilers, nor extortioners, shall inherit the kingdom of God.

GRACE IN A GUTTER.

WALKING back and forth on the sidewalk in front of the Old Dutch Church, a dilapidated, forlorn-looking man could be seen, dressed in a check shirt, with striped pantaloons. He was a hard case, and bore the marks of one who had had a fierce struggle with intemperance and been conquered. He was attracted by the singing, and struggled up-stairs into the room where the daily meeting was in progress. He asked, "Can such a miserable-looking object as I am enter?" "Come in, and welcome," was the response. The meeting took such hold upon him that he resolved to quit drinking. He had no home, no money, no food. He lodged in some den in Water street, or slept on a truck in the market. It is the custom at Fulton street to feed the hungry, shoe the shoeless, and provide for the temporal wants of the suffering, as well as pray for their salvation. The kind care extended to him touched him, and he soon became anxious about his soul. At his request, prayers were offered for him. But the burden was heavy upon him, and he could not rest. One night, he drifted about the streets, little caring what became of him. Overcome with fatigue, he sat down upon the curbstone, and called upon God for help. Tears of penitence filled his eyes, and God, for Christ's sake, pardoned his sins. He had no one to speak to, no one to whom he could tell his joy. As the morning dawned, he went into one of the public parks, sat down upon the grass, and began to read the New Testament. "What book are you reading?" said a gentleman who drew near. "The New Testament; I got it at Fulton street." "Do you attend the Fulton-street Prayer-meeting?" "I do." He told the story of his shame and suffering, and how the Saviour had found and blessed him in the small hours of the morning. "Call on me at my store," said the man, "at ten o'clock to-day;" and he handed the poor fellow his card. He kept the appointment, and found waiting for him a decent suit of clothes, with work and fair wages. He ran to Fulton street to tell the kind missionary who had given him a helping hand, how gracious the Lord had been to him, in the salvation of his soul and in rescuing him from want. This man is now a devoted Bible-reader to the blind in the Almshouse—a blessing to himself and to others. He finds healthy, remunerative, and cheerful labor. In a nicely fitted-up room, three hundred inmates daily assemble, and this rescued man reads to the company the Word of God.

XV.

IMMORTAL LIFE.

THE Lord killeth, and maketh alive: he bringeth down to the grave, and bringeth up. For there is hope of a tree, if it be cut down, that it will sprout again, and that the tender branch thereof will not cease. Though the root thereof wax old in the earth, and the stock thereof die in the ground; *yet* through the scent of water it will bud, and bring forth boughs like a plant. But man dieth, and wasteth away: yea, man giveth up the ghost, and where *is* he? So when this corruptible shall have put on incorruption, and this mortal shall have put on immortality, then shall be brought to pass the saying that it is written, Death is swallowed up in victory. O death, where *is* thy sting? O grave, where *is* thy victory? The sting of death *is* sin; and the strength of sin *is* the law. But thanks *be* to God, which giveth us the victory through our Lord Jesus Christ.

THE LAST CALL.

A CLERK in a mercantile house felt an impulse that he could not resist, drawing him one day to a noon-day prayer-meeting.

The scripture read was Stephen's prayer as he fell beneath the blows of his enemies. The leader of the meeting, an old acquaintance, as he passed out, said to the young man,

"I hope you and I will be able to utter that prayer of the blessed martyr when we die."

It was the last visit of the young man to Fulton street. He was taken suddenly sick, and brought to the gates of death. He said to his mother,

"Do you know, I was never so much impressed with the reading of the Bible as I was the last time I was at Fulton street. I saw the whole scene of Stephen's martyrdom: the maddened throng as they rushed on him, gnashing their teeth. I saw his agonized face, and heard his death-cry, 'Lord Jesus, receive my spirit!' I resolved then that I would die a Christian. Do you believe, mother, that Jesus will save to the uttermost all who call upon him?"

"Yes, my son, I firmly believe it."

"Then I will trust him."

He threw his head back on the pillow, lifted his eyes to heaven, and said, "Lord Jesus, receive ——." He could say no more. His spirit passed away with that utterance. Nor did he go alone through the valley and shadow of death.

XVI.

THE HOLY SPIRIT.

NEVERTHELESS I tell you the truth; it is expedient for you that I go away: for if I go not away, the Comforter will not come unto you; but if I depart, I will send him unto you. But the Comforter, *which is* the Holy Ghost, whom the Father will send in my name, he shall teach you all things, and bring all things to your remembrance, whatsoever I have said unto you. Peace I leave with you, my peace I give unto you: not as the world giveth, give I unto you. Let not your heart be troubled, neither let it be afraid. For ye have not received the spirit of bondage again to fear; but ye have received the Spirit of adoption, whereby we cry, Abba, Father. The Spirit itself beareth witness with our spirit, that we are the children of God: and if children, then heirs; heirs of God, and joint heirs with Christ; if so be that we suffer with *him*, that we may be also glorified together.

REMARKABLE CONVERSION.

A MAN was marked for his wickedness and enmity to the Gospel. He seized the hour when people were going to church to drive through the streets with his fishing-tackle strung over his shoulders. Gaming was his delight, and his blasphemy was terrible. Going home from dissipation one Sunday night, he heard that an associate, with whom he had played cards the evening before, was dead. He died without hope, and in great terror; died, calling on God to have mercy upon his own soul and that of his friend. Alarm seized upon him. As his servant came in to kindle the morning fire, the man threw himself on his knees and cried for mercy. He then and there found the Saviour. He at once went to work leading his friends to religion. He pretended to be a preacher in his wild and wicked days, and now he commenced preaching in earnest. When he appeared in the streets and began to preach, people thought he was trying on his old tricks. One of his old cronies and boon companions stood at the foot of the pulpit. He could not tell whether his friend was acting or was in earnest. When the sermon closed, he went up to the preacher and said,

"Are you in earnest, or are you doing it for a wager? If you are only trying it on, you are acting splendidly."

"Oh! no, my poor friend, I am in dead earnest, and so is my God. He is willing to receive you, as he was to receive me. He has answered prayer for me, and he will answer prayer for you."

Crowded congregations follow this devoted servant of the Lord, and under his ministry, desperadoes and the perishing press into the kingdom of God.

XVII.

CHILDHOOD OF OUR LORD.

NOW when Jesus was born in Bethlehem of Judea in the days of Herod the King, behold, there came wise men from the east to Jerusalem, saying, Where is he that is born King of the Jews? for we have seen his star in the east, and are come to worship him. And when they were come into the house, they saw the young child with Mary his mother, and fell down, and worshiped him: and when they had opened their treasures, they presented unto him gifts; gold, and frankincense, and myrrh. And it came to pass, that after three days they found him in the temple, sitting in the midst of the doctors, both hearing them and asking them questions. And all that heard him were astonished at his understanding and answers. And he went down with them, and came to Nazareth, and was subject unto them: but his mother kept all these sayings in her heart. And Jesus increased in wisdom and stature, and in favor with God and man.

SAMMY AND HIS MATE.

THE teacher of one of our schools was a great martinet. He enforced his rules with exactness and impartiality; rarely a culprit escaped. One day, a little boy, Jimmy by name, was called up for punishment. He was a poor little fellow, half clothed and evidently half fed. His father was a drunkard, and his mother no better. He was a quiet, timid boy, and greatly loved by his mates. But he had broken the rules, and the master ordered him to take off his jacket, in order to be whipped. The jacket was not removed, and the order was repeated. Jimmy's only response was a beseeching look—not of defiance, but of fear. As Jimmy did not remove his jacket, the master proposed to do it for him. It was not hard to do; the spencer was without buttons, and held together, top and bottom, by pins. As the frail garment flew open, the reluctance of Jimmy was apparent; he wore no shirt. His scraggling, bony little body showed how hard a struggle he had with life. The school was hushed to silence; there was not a scholar in the room that did not pity the poor child; they said it was a shame that a shriveled, half-starved boy like Jimmy, whose father and mother were drunkards, should be whipped. There was a boy in school by the name of Sammy; he was a heavy-moulded, overgrown boy, well fed and well clothed. His father was a forehanded farmer, and kept a well-supplied table. As the master took up the rod, Sammy left his seat, walked down to the desk, and stood beside the culprit. "Don't whip Jimmy," he said; "he is such a poor little fellow."

"He has broken the rules, and I must."

"Well, then, whip me; I am better able to stand it than he is."

"I can take you, for you will be a substitute; but you must know what you are doing: if I whip you in Jimmy's stead, I shall do it in earnest; there will be no boys' play about it."

"Well, I don't care what you do, so long as you do not whip him."

The strokes were laid on his back, but Sammy never flinched. When the school closed, Sammy remained; the master said something to him about that Blessed One who was wounded for our transgressions, and by whose stripes we are healed. Jimmy went home with Sam that day, and he was well clothed and well fed all that winter.

XVIII.

THE NEW BIRTH.

WHICH were born, not of blood, nor of the will of the flesh, nor of the will of man, but of God. And the Word was made flesh, and dwelt among us (and we beheld his glory, the glory as of the only-begotten of the Father), full of grace and truth. Being born again, not of corruptible seed, but of incorruptible, by the word of God, which liveth and abideth forever. Whosoever believeth that Jesus is the Christ is born of God: and every one that loveth him that begat loveth him also that is begotten of him. Forasmuch as ye know that ye were not redeemed with corruptible things, *as* silver and gold, from your vain conversation *received* by tradition from your fathers; but with the precious blood of Christ, as of a lamb without blemish and without spot.

ASK MY WIFE.

THIS is a sacred place to me; I came into it a poor, miserable outcast. I was hanging round the curbstone when a volume of song fell on my ear. I said, "Who is so happy as to be singing at this time of day?" A kind hand lifted me from the gutter; a kind voice said, "Come in, come in; you need help, you need food." Prayer was offered for me; I think no one ever prayed for me before. My life has been a changed one from that hour; I am a sober man, with plenty of work and good wages. For years I squandered my wages in drink ; the money I spent in vile company now feeds and clothes my children. There is no home in the country happier than mine. The other day, I was sent by my employer down into Water street; I met some of my old companions. "Halloo!" they said, "Tom, they say you have got religion. What has religion done for you? We would like to know."

"Go and ask my wife; she will tell you," I replied. "For twelve years, I was a drunkard. I earned some money, but I squandered it. My home was cold and repulsive; there was no fire on the hearth and no bread in the closet; my children were shoeless and cried for bread, while I was carousing in the back rooms at the corner-groceries. One dram-shop was an especial favorite; night after night, in cold and in bitter weather, my wife would take her stand outside of the liquor-store, waiting often till after midnight to take me home, that I might not freeze. She knew I would curse her, perhaps beat her; yet she was kind, considerate, and faithful through it all. Go and ask her what religion has done for me; she will ask you to walk in and look at our pleasant home. The barrel wastes not, and the fire goes not out on the hearth. No hard-hearted landlord threatens to turn the family on to the sidewalk on a cold and stormy night because my rent is not paid; my little ones do not run and hide when they hear my step on the threshold. They shout the glad welcome, 'Father is coming! Father is coming!' All this, religion has done for me, and it will do it for you. Come, go with me to Fulton street, and it will save you as it has saved me."

XIX.

CONTROL OF THE TONGUE.

BEHOLD, we put bits in the horses' mouths, that they may obey us; and we turn about their whole body. Behold also the ships, which though *they be* so great, and *are* driven of fierce winds, yet are they turned about with a very small helm, whithersoever the governor listeth. Even so the tongue is a little member, and boasteth great things. Behold, how great a matter a little fire kindleth! And the tongue *is* a fire, a world of iniquity: so is the tongue among our members, that it defileth the whole body, and setteth on fire the course of nature; and it is set on fire of hell. If any man among you seem to be religious, and bridleth not his tongue, but deceiveth his own heart, this man's religion *is* vain. But above all things, my brethren, swear not, neither by heaven, neither by the earth, neither by any other oath: but let your yea be yea; and *your* nay, nay, lest ye fall into condemnation.

TWO-EDGED SWORD.

An eminent man was convicted of a crime. He had been a decided Christian. He was especially earnest in his work among the lowly. The cause that he knew not he searched out.

He made the orphan glad, and the widow's heart to leap for joy. In an evil hour, temptation overtook him and conquered him; he fell, wounding his own name and the honor of religion; he was borne from the courts to the prison. On his way, a woman met him whose path he had once crossed, and whom more than once he had exhorted to walk in that way that, though strait and narrow, is the way of pleasantness and the path of peace. As the carriage drove along, she exulted over his downfall, and shouted, "Where is now thy God?" The carriage halted, and the criminal, addressing his assailant, said, "I hope you will seek the Lord, and that God will pardon you as I have this day." He handed her a slip of paper, and added, "Make me one promise: that you will go home and read from the Bible the passages marked on that paper." "I will do so," was the reply, as the woman turned away. In the solitude of her chamber, she took down her neglected Bible, and, turning to the prophet Micah 7 : 8, she read:

"Rejoice not against me, O mine enemy: when I fall, I shall arise; when I sit in darkness, the Lord shall be a light unto me.

"I will bear the indignation of the Lord, because I have sinned against him, until he plead my cause, and execute judgment for me: he will bring me forth to the light, and I shall behold his righteousness.

"Then she that is mine enemy shall see it, and shame shall cover her which said unto me, Where is the Lord thy God? mine eyes shall behold her; now shall she be trodden down as the mire of the streets."

The woman was appalled; fear seized upon her; in the solitude of her room, she threw herself upon her knees, and cried to God for mercy. He to whom the cry of the outcast and sinful is never made in vain, heard her prayer, and granted her the peace and joy that belong to a pardoned soul.

XX.

PRIVATE DEVOTIONS.

AND it came to pass in those days, that he went out into a mountain to pray, and continued all night in prayer to God. But thou, when thou prayest, enter into thy closet, and when thou hast shut thy door, pray to thy Father which is in secret; and thy Father which seeth in secret shall reward thee openly. And at midnight Paul and Silas prayed, and sang praises unto God: and the prisoners heard them. And suddenly there was a great earthquake, so that the foundations of the prison were shaken: and immediately all the doors were opened, and every one's bands were loosed. Then was the secret revealed unto Daniel in a night vision. Then Daniel blessed the God of heaven. Daniel answered and said, Blessed be the name of God for ever and ever: for wisdom and might are his.

SOLDIER'S DYING REQUEST.

A POOR widow lived among the green hills of Vermont. She had an only son, on whom she lavished all the wealth of a mother's love. The war broke out, and she offered her son on the altar of her country. He was a Sabbath-school boy, fixed in his religious principles, and she knew he would do well. Perhaps he would be a captain, or come home with the shoulder-straps of a colonel on his shoulder. The first news she heard of her son paralyzed her. He had been tried for sleeping on his post, and sentenced to be shot, and the day of his execution was near. The poor woman was nearly distracted; she begged and borrowed a little money, and started for Washington. On her way, she learned the story of her son's disgrace. He was among the early volunteers, and knew all the hardships of that early struggle. Without food, or tent, or blanket, for six days and six nights he had been on duty. He was put on the picket-guard. Nature was too strong for him; he leaned on his gun a moment, and was found by the officer of the day asleep at his post. She knew little of official life in Washington, but she knew the President had a kind heart, and that pardoning power was in his hands. She made for the White House, and with a trembling hand rang the bell. The official who answered the door saw only a forlorn-looking woman in rusty black, and thought her a beggar. As the door was about to be closed, she pressed in and demanded to see the President. "You can't see him this morning." "I must; my poor boy is going to die. He is not guilty, and I must see Mr. Lincoln." During the altercation, the President providentially passed through the hall. He had a quick ear for sorrow, and came near to see what was the matter. "Come in," said Mr. Lincoln; "tell me your story." "But I must see the President." "I am the President." "I want to see Mr. Lincoln; I must see Mr. Lincoln." "I'm Mr. Lincoln." She gave him a sharp, quick look, and, falling on her knees before him, said, "You must save my poor boy, for he is not guilty." "Get up," said the President; "don't kneel to me, kneel to God." She told him her story, and he found it was a true one. He sent a special messenger to arrest the execution, and bring the boy to his mother. That boy died in the swamps of Chickahominy. His dying message through the chaplain who leaned over him was, "Tell mother that I died a Christian. Tell Mr. Lincoln how I loved him and prayed for him with my dying breath."

XXI.

IMMEDIATE ANSWERS.

IT shall come to pass, that before they call, I will answer; and while they are yet speaking, I will hear. The wolf and the lamb shall feed together, and the lion shall eat straw like the bullock: and dust *shall be* the serpent's meat. They shall not hurt nor destroy in all my holy mountain, saith the Lord. And while I was speaking, and praying, and confessing my sin and the sin of my people Israel, and presenting my supplication before the Lord my God for the holy mountain of my God; yea, while I *was* speaking in prayer, even the man Gabriel, whom I had seen in the vision at the beginning, being caused to fly swiftly, touched me about the time of the evening oblation. Now when all the people were baptized, it came to pass, that Jesus also being baptized, and praying, the heaven was opened, and the Holy Ghost descended in a bodily shape like a dove upon him, and a voice came from heaven, which said, Thou art my beloved Son; in thee I am well pleased.

CASES FROM REAL LIFE.

"I ADVANCED ten dollars to a poor family," said the missionary. "I knelt down and prayed, saying, 'Lord, if it please thee to send it back, let it come.' I could ill afford to part with the money, but I could not see suffering without relieving it. The next day, in the noon-day meeting, a stranger met me and said, 'There is ten dollars. You must have a great many calls for material aid.' As this was the exact amount I advanced, I took it as a direct answer to prayer."

"I WAS passing through the street one day, and found a number of boys making fun of prayer. They were a rough, hard set, and one of them attempted to pray. He broke down. I lifted my hat, took up the boy's prayer, and finished it. I prayed tenderly, and especially for the leader. I found tears in the leader's eyes when I closed. He said to me, 'I will stand up for Jesus.' That boy is now an honored pastor in the Christian Church."

"I HAVE been a very wicked man, with a rough life. My Sabbaths have been principally spent in cock-fighting, dog-fighting, and gambling. My company has been the vilest and most vicious, yet there has not been a day for ten years that I have not remembered my mother's prayers, which she offered for me at the side of my bed. They have followed me—not only reformed me, but made me a Christian."

"YOUR prayers and ours have been answered. Our boy has come back to us, prodigal as he is, and we rejoice in him who was lost and is found. Give glory to God!"

"I AM eighty years of age. I am seeking the Saviour, but have not been able to find him. I have no Christian friend to write for me. My right hand is nearly useless. Oh! pray for a mother of eighty, who must be lost unless Christ soon appear." One week after, thanksgivings for mercies received were read in the Fulton-street Meeting.

PRAYER was offered for a sick girl in Kansas, hopelessly ill. Within ten days an answer came announcing the healing. The relief treading so closely on the request produced a profound sensation among all the kinsfolk and the acquaintances of the healed.

XXII.

WENT ABOUT DOING GOOD.

HOW God anointed Jesus of Nazareth with the Holy Ghost and with power: who went about doing good, and healing all that were oppressed of the devil; for God was with him. And we are witnesses of all things which he did both in the land of the Jews, and in Jerusalem; whom they slew and hanged on a tree: Jesus answered them, Many good works have I showed you from my Father; for which of those works do you stone me? The Jews answered him, saying, For a good work we stone thee not; but for blasphemy. When Jesus understood *it*, he said unto them, Why trouble ye the woman? for she hath wrought a good work upon me. I know both how to be abased, and I know how to abound: everywhere and in all things I am instructed both to be full and to be hungry, both to abound and to suffer need. I can do all things through Christ which strengtheneth me.

SMALL UPPER CHAMBER.

IN the Fulton-street Church there is a little room occupied by the missionary. Much prayer is offered there, but other things are done besides praying. Like the pool of healing, Fulton street confers temporal blessings. Around it are crowds of impotent folk. The lame, the halt, and the blind gather daily for help. A woman with a sick child in her arms wants bread. A poor laborer out of work must secure his rent, or be thrown on to the street. A widow wants a little coal to keep her from freezing. A vagrant who has known better days must have shelter and food, or he will perish. In one attic there is sickness; in another, death. To relieve these wants, money, patience, and grace are needed. The drunkard must sign the temperance pledge, but before he signs it he must kneel down and join in prayer, for prayer and alms go together in this place. A colored wife appeals to the missionary to heal the family disturbance. The household are brought together in the little chamber in the old church. All kneel together while the missionary prays. All sign the pledge, for rum has caused the mischief. Prayer and praise now take the place of blasphemy around that hearthstone. A whole family sober and in the church in answer to prayer.

XXIII.

WINE AND MILK.

HO, every one that thirsteth, come ye to the waters, and he that hath no money; come ye, buy, and eat; yea, come, buy wine and milk without money and without price. Wherefore do ye spend money for *that which is* not bread? and your labor for *that which* satisfieth not? hearken diligently unto me, and eat ye *that which is* good, and let your soul delight itself in fatness. I will heal their backsliding, I will love them freely: for mine anger is turned away from him. I will be as the dew unto Israel: he shall grow as the lily, and cast forth his roots as Lebanon. His branches shall spread, and his beauty shall be as the olive-tree, and his smell as Lebanon. They that dwell under his shadow shall return; they shall revive *as* the corn, and grow as the vine: the scent thereof *shall be* as the wine of Lebanon. Come, eat of my bread, and drink of the wine *which* I have mingled. Forsake the foolish, and live; and go in the way of understanding.

"THIS OR THAT."

"THERE were nine children of us. My father died, and mother became a poor minister's widow. Oh! how she toiled to give us bread and keep the little household together! She always told us that our Heavenly Father was the widow's God, and the Father of the fatherless, and she should trust him. She carried all her wants and sorrows to the Lord. I don't know how we got along, but somehow we were always provided for, and never lacked for any good thing. All the children were early converted, and seven sons were consecrated to the work of the ministry."

"I DON'T want you to talk to me on religion, and I don't want to be a Christian."

This was said to me by a young woman who was visiting at my house. The next morning, she was entirely changed in her temper and spirit. She said to me,

"I resolved last night to give my heart to the Saviour, and I yielded to him all that I have to give."

She turned from me, and, being a resolute girl, I knew that further conversation then was useless.

Six months afterward, she came to my house, a cheerful and happy Christian. She said,

"Do you remember my refusal to talk with you on the subject of religion? Well, I meant what I said. A change came over me as I entered my chamber, and I could not account for it. About a week ago, I learned that, on that very day, my brother asked prayers for me in the Fulton-street meeting, and I believe my change was in answer to prayer."

"YOUR prayers are asked for the inmates of a State prison." So came a request to Fulton street. Soon after, a revival of religion broke out in that prison, and one hundred and sixty-five convicts were converted to the Lord.

XXIV.

HOPE AS AN ANCHOR.

WHICH *hope* we have as an anchor of the soul, both sure and steadfast, and which entereth into that within the vail; whither the forerunner is for us entered, *even* Jesus, made a high priest forever after the order of Melchisedec. In whom ye also *trusted*, after that ye heard the word of truth, the gospel of your salvation: in whom also, after that ye believed, ye were sealed with that Holy Spirit of promise, which is the earnest of our inheritance until the redemption of the purchased possession, unto the praise of his glory. In that day shall this song be sung in the land of Judah: We have a strong city; salvation will *God* appoint *for* walls and bulwarks. Open ye the gates, that the righteous nation which keepeth the truth may enter in. Thou wilt keep *him* in perfect peace, *whose* mind *is* stayed *on thee:* because he trusted in thee. Trust ye in the Lord forever: for in the Lord Jehovah *is* everlasting strength.

SALVATION BY TELEGRAPH.

A YOUNG man in Ohio, telegraph operator, was told that a friend of his, another operator on the road, had been converted. He said,

"That may be true. But these Christians tell so many stories of that kind, that I hardly know what to think."

He seated himself at his instrument. He was soon in communication with an office a hundred miles away.

"Was there a conversion in your office yesterday?"

"Yes."

"Who was it?"

"It was me;" adding, "Seek ye the Lord while he may be found."

"Will you pray for me that I may find the Saviour?"

"I will. Pray for yourself."

In ten days, both of these young men witnessed a good confession before the great congregation.

"MY mother's God is my God. Her prayers have been many. I was an only son, very, very wicked. She never gave me up. I have felt her influence over me when far from home, and have felt it all my life. Two days ago, I gave my heart to the Saviour. Praise the Lord!"

A YOUNG actor, who was passionately fond of singing, passing through Fulton street, was arrested by the music he heard in the old Dutch Church. He entered the house, and looked on with wonder to see three or four hundred people bowing in prayer at noonday. There was a fascination about the place. He improvised a tenor as he joined in the singing. The fact that he was not always in tune drew the attention of the leader to him. He revealed his history to the missionary; he joined in the prayers offered for his conversion, abandoned the stage, and became a devout Christian.

XXV.

LET THERE BE NO STRIFE.

AND Abram said unto Lot, Let there be no strife, I pray thee, between me and thee, and between my herdmen and thy herdmen ; for we *be* brethren. *Is* not the whole land before thee? separate thyself, I pray thee, from me: if *thou wilt take* the left hand, then I will go to the right; or if *thou depart* to the right hand, then I will go to the left. Behold, how good and how pleasant *it is* for brethren to dwell together in unity! *It is* like the precious ointment upon the head, that ran down upon the beard, *even* Aaron's beard: that went down to the skirts of his garments; as the dew of Hermon, *and as the dew* that descended upon the mountains of Zion: for there the Lord commanded the blessing, *even* life for evermore. He that passeth by, *and* meddleth with strife *belonging* not to him, *is like* one that taketh a dog by the ears. As a mad *man* who casteth firebrands, arrows, and death.

ON THE PACIFIC COAST.

"IN 1866, I was in California. The town in which I lived was a very wicked place, morality and religion being fearfully low. No minister of the Gospel or public means of grace had been known in the place for ten years. I sent a letter to Fulton-street meeting, asking you to pray for this town. Oh! how soon the answer came! Thanks be to God! we have the ministry of the Gospel among us, a church has been organized, and many added of such as shall be saved."

"I FELT my need of a Saviour. I had no one to help me or pray for me. I sent a request to Fulton street, but months passed before the Lord heard your prayers. A season of revival followed, and myself with many other young men have turned to the Lord."

"WITH little faith and much misgiving, I asked your prayers for a desperate case. One week after the request was read, the subject of our prayers, a bold, proud, resolute man, bowed his head in contrition and godly sorrow. So marked was the case, that it has impressed every one with the mighty power of God, who can turn the rebellious in a moment as the rivers of water are turned."

"I DWELL on the Pacific coast. I am a missionary among the sparse settlements of an interesting territory. I have sent many requests to your meeting. Some of the answers have been wonderful. One case has especial interest; it was that of a wife and mother for her whole family. Even while you were praying, the Lord hearkened and heard. And the measure of faith was filled in converting the whole household."

XXVI.

PRAYER AND ALMS.

HE saw in a vision evidently, about the ninth hour of the day, an angel of God coming in to him, and saying unto him, Cornelius. And when he looked on him, he was afraid, and said, What is it, Lord? And he said unto him, Thy prayers and thine alms are come up for a memorial before God. Let brotherly love continue. Be not forgetful to entertain strangers: for thereby some have entertained angels unawares. Remember them that are in bonds, as bound with them; *and* them which suffer adversity, as being yourselves also in e body. If I have seen any perish for want of clothing, or any poor without covering; if his loins have not blessed me, and *if* he were *not* warmed with the fleece of my sheep; if I have lifted up my hand against the fatherless, when I saw my help in the gate: *then* let mine arm fall from my shoulder-blade, and mine arm be broken from the bone.

REACHING THE MASSES.

Lord Shaftesbury presides over an association that has wonderful influence with the working classes. The hearts of men are touched through the power of temporal aid. Bread, coal, medicine, house-rent become means of grace. A wealthy clergyman felt impressed to leave his fashionable congregation one Sunday, and go out and preach to the neglected and infamous in and around the Seven Dials. He took with him two or three of his rich friends. He was well dressed, held in his hand a gold-headed cane, while over his arm hung a comfortable overcoat. He saw a group standing in a doorway, sullen and unhappy. To them the clergyman was an intruder, and the men didn't care to hide their displeasure. An empty box became a pulpit, and the voice of song soon drew a crowd. "May I hold your reverence's cane?" said one of the company. "I will take your coat," said a second; while a third proposed to hold the clergyman's "'at." These offers of assistance were graciously accepted. The service was brief and not very enthusiastic. At the close, the minister looked round for his property. The person with the gold-headed cane had gone for a walk; the man with the "'at" was not in sight; the coat fitted too well to be returned. The clergyman was indignant. "I came here at great personal inconvenience to do you good. One man has stolen my hat, another my cane, and the third has walked off with my overcoat. You are a set of ingrates. I wash my hands of you all. You may die in your sins if you will; I will have no more to do with you." A coarse, derisive laugh was the only response.

XXVII.

TRUE VINE.

I AM the true vine, and my Father is the husbandman. Every branch in me that beareth not fruit he taketh away: and every *branch* that beareth fruit, he purgeth it, that it may bring forth more fruit. I am the vine, ye *are* the branches. He that abideth in me, and I in him, the same bringeth forth much fruit; for without me ye can do nothing. If a man abide not in me, he is cast forth as a branch, and is withered; and men gather them, and cast *them* into the fire, and they are burned. The sceptre shall not depart from Judah, nor a lawgiver from between his feet, until Shiloh come; and unto him *shall* the gathering of the people *be*. Binding his foal unto the vine, and his ass's colt unto the choice vine; he washed his garments in wine, and his clothes in the blood of grapes: his eyes *shall be* red with wine, and his teeth white with milk.

DESPERADOES SUBDUED.

Another clergyman proposed to preach to the masses. Like a sensible man, he surveyed the ground before he commenced. His dress attracted no attention and excited no repugnance.

He went into the cottages of the London workmen and the London poor. He was surprised to see how much physical suffering there was among the lowly. He did not go empty-handed. He sent a little coal to one house, and wood to another; here he left medicine, and there food; he provided surgical aid for the children of the poor. Every form of suffering which fell under his eye he relieved. He sent out tickets for a tea. Fully five hundred responded to the call. Having won the confidence of the people by his kindness and humanity, he proposed to hold a Sunday service. "We will be glad to hear you preach," the people said, "for you have got some heart and know how to pity the poor." Fully four hundred persons met the preacher at the service. Workmen built a comfortable platform as a compliment to the minister. One thing caused disquietude: the stand was surrounded by a crowd of well-known desperadoes, who evidently were bent on mischief. The preacher was plucky and resolved to do his work. There was no disturbance. Even the bullies and thieves lifted their hats in token of respect as the preacher retired.

XXVIII

WATERS OF SALVATION.

FOR I will pour water upon him that is thirsty, and floods upon the dry ground: I will pour my Spirit upon thy seed, and my blessing upon thine offspring: and they shall spring up *as* among the grass, as willows by the watercourses. In the last day, that great *day* of the feast, Jesus stood and cried, saying, If any man thirst, let him come unto me, and drink. He that believeth on me, as the Scripture hath said, out of his belly shall flow rivers of living water. I Jesus have sent mine angel to testify unto you these things in the churches. I am the root and the offspring of David, *and* the bright and morning star. And the Spirit and the Bride say, Come. And let him that heareth say, Come. And let him that is athirst come. And whosoever will, let him take the water of life freely. But whosoever drinketh of the water that I shall give him shall never thirst; but the water that I shall give him shall be in him a well of water springing up into everlasting life.

WATER, WATER!

A COMPANY of officers were riding through a dry and dusty country; the wells were dry, the horses nearly famished, and the throats of the men parched with thirst. All at once, the horses gave a snort, lost their weary exhaustion, and started forward on a full trot. Soon a flowing river came in sight, with water enough to quench the thirst of the world. The horses plunged into the stream and soon satisfied their longings. Suddenly the surgeon cried out,

"Hush! I hear a moaning; there is sorrow and anguish in that cry."

"Nothing but the wind sighing through the trees," said a comrade.

The doctor was not to be deceived; he sprang from his horse and disappeared. A shout brought others to his assistance. Lying on the bank was a wounded man, dying with thirst. In full sight of the river, he could hear its gurgle and murmur as it rushed along in its fullness. He was nearly dead when the hand of the surgeon was laid upon him. The dying man looked in his face, and with a faint whisper said, "Water, water!" The doctor had no cup, but it is easy to improvise one when the life of a man trembles in the balance. A sharp blow on his soft hat made a vessel of capacity sufficient to bear the cooling water from the bed of the river to the lips of the sufferer. The best horse was placed at his disposal. Tender hands lifted him from his turfy bed and conveyed him to the hospital, where he was cared for as a brother.

He arose a new man. He knew what this meaneth: "He that drinketh of this water shall thirst again, but whoso drinketh of the water of life shall never thirst." There was abundance of water in that river, but unless some kind hand had borne the precious fluid to his lips, the sufferer would have died. From that hour he thirsted not, neither did he come thither to draw.

XXIX.

CHILDHOOD.

AND they brought young children to him, that he should touch them; and *his* disciples rebuked those that brought *them.* But when Jesus saw *it,* he was much displeased, and said unto them, Suffer the little children to come unto me, and forbid them not; for of such is the kingdom of God. Verily I say unto you, Whosoever shall not receive the kingdom of God as a little child, he shall not enter therein. And he took them up in his arms, put *his* hands upon them, and blessed them. Children, obey your parents in the Lord: for this is right. Honor thy father and mother; which is the first commandment with promise; that it may be well with thee, and thou mayest live long on the earth. And, ye fathers, provoke not your children to wrath: but bring them up in the nurture and admonition of the Lord. Children, obey *your* parents in all things: for this is well pleasing unto the Lord.

"*DEAR GOD.*"

CHRISTMAS season came with all its bright and precious memories. At one of our mission-houses at Five Points, a postman came in one morning with a letter. He asked,

"Does this belong here? I did not know where else to put it." The letter was addressed: "Dear God, New-York." It was a letter from a little girl residing in Albany. An answer was solicited, and the number of the street given. The letter, in the handwriting of a child, ran on this wise: "Dear God, I am a poor little girl. My mother is poor and sick; she takes in washing. I want a nice warm cloak to run errands in this winter. My little brother wants a pair of boots. Won't you please send the things, and I'll be a real nice little girl?" A messenger was sent, and the house easily found. The mother told this story: As Christmas approached, her little girl said she was going to write a letter to Santa Claus. She meant to ask him to send her a warm cloak and her brother a pair of boots. Her mother was a poor sick woman, who got a scanty living by washing when she was able. "I would not ask Santa Claus," the mother said, "for those things, but I would ask God." The children acted on this suggestion. They had a long consultation as to where God lived. They concluded he must live in New-York, and to that place the letter was directed. The brother and sister exhausted their combined purses to furnish a postage-stamp. Having mailed the letter, the little girl took her station at the window, and day by day watched the postman from the time he entered the street until he disappeared around the corner, until her heart nearly died within her and tears moistened her eyes. The missionary at Five Points was not idle. He enlisted the sympathies of several warm-hearted ladies. The cloak and boots were obtained with a general outfit for the family. One morning, an express-wagon drove up to the door and laid a box on the threshold. The little girl clapped her hands with glee and shouted, which brought her mother to the window. "They have come," she said, "the cloak and the boots have come!" And so it proved. With the box came a kind letter from the Superintendent, telling the little girl that God often answered prayer by putting it into the hearts of his children to relieve the wants of the distressed.

XXX.

DEVOTION AND BUSINESS.

AND over these three presidents; of whom Daniel *was* first: that the princes might give accounts unto them, and the king should have no damage. Then this Daniel was preferred above the presidents and princes, because an excellent spirit *was* in him; and the king thought to set him over the whole realm. And said unto the king, Let the king live forever: why should not my countenance be sad, when the city, the place of my fathers' sepulchres, *lieth* waste, and the gates thereof are consumed with fire? Then the king said unto me, For what dost thou make request? So I prayed to the God of heaven. And they prayed, and said, Thou, Lord, which knowest the hearts of all *men*, show whether of these two thou hast chosen, that he may take part of this ministry and apostleship, from which Judas by transgression fell, that he might go to his own place.

"YE DID IT UNTO ME."

A YOUNG man was very poor. Being a decided Christian, he always gave something to the cause of religion. He was distressed often that his gifts were so small. One day, he came home from his work quite out of sorts. His wife asked him why he was low-spirited. "The subscription for Foreign Missions has been taken up to-day in the factory. I could give so little, I was ashamed to subscribe. Oh! I wish I was rich, that I could give like other folks!" One morning, as he went out to his work, his wife said, "Get me a dozen button-moulds and a stick of twist, and I will see what I can do for you." An English silk button had fallen into her hands. While her husband slept, she took it to pieces, and thought she could imitate it. She sent her first specimen to a Christian merchant in New-York. "If any thing can be done with them," she said, "the money shall be my husband's contribution to missions." The merchant was delighted with the sample. He wrote back, "Make as many as you choose; I can sell a hundred dozen." Joy was diffused through the household, for the venture had been made a subject of prayer. Till the answer came, the husband was ignorant of what the wife had been doing. A new field was open to him; business increased and friends and neighbors were called in. Machinery took the place of the nimble fingers of the devoted wife. The indigent mechanic became a prosperous and wealthy manufacturer. His gigantic factory is known through all the land. His gifts, increasing with his riches, became large as the seas. Prayer was the corner-stone of his success. A desire to do something for the spread of the Gospel opened the avenues which led to wealth and distinction.

XXXI.

SIN AGAINST THE HOLY SPIRIT.

IF any man see his brother sin a sin *which is* not unto death, he shall ask, and he shall give him life for them that sin not unto death. There is a sin unto death: I do not say that he shall pray for it. Verily I say unto you, All sins shall be forgiven unto the sons of men, and blasphemies wherewith soever they shall blaspheme: but he that shall blaspheme against the Holy Ghost hath never forgiveness, but is in danger of eternal damnation: For if we sin willfully after that we have received the knowledge of the truth, there remaineth no more sacrifice for sins, but a certain fearful looking for of judgment and fiery indignation, which shall devour the adversaries. He that despised Moses' law died without mercy under two or three witnesses: of how much sorer punishment, suppose ye, shall he be thought worthy, who hath trodden under foot the Son of God, and hath counted the blood of the covenant, wherewith he was sanctified, an unholy thing, and hath done despite unto the Spirit of grace?

AS BY FIRE.

A YOUNG lady, moving in the upper fashionable circles, lived in New-York. She had every thing that heart could wish. Her parents were rich, liberal, and indulgent. She had a lady friend to whom she was ardently attached. Together, during the summer, they swung round the circle of gayety and fashionable pleasure. On her return to the city, she took to her bed, from which it was feared she would never rise. She became gloomy and desponding, and persisted in the idea that she had grieved the Holy Spirit and committed the unpardonable sin. She resisted all consolation and refused to listen to the promises of the Gospel. The gracious calls of the Saviour were not for her, she said. She must die, and die without hope of a better life. She begged to see her young friend, who hastened to her bedside. Her message was a brief but touching one: "My dear friend, I am going to die; my doctor gives me little hope, but I feel that I shall go alone through the dark valley and shadow of death. I have had many calls and gracious offers, but I have resisted them all. I have sinned against great light, have trodden under foot the covenant of love. But, my dear friend, I do not want you to perish. You have not sinned as I have. Go home and settle the great question to day; give your heart to the Lord before the sun goes down." Alarmed at what she saw and heard, the young lady fled to her chamber, threw herself on her knees, and made her peace with the Lord. She hurried back to tell her friend of the great acceptance. She did not leave the bedside until the gloom of despair was removed and the joy of the Lord took possession of the heart. The Holy Spirit seemed to bear healing on his wings. With the acceptance of the Saviour, she began to mend; and now both friends are walking hand in hand together in the new way of life and peace.

XXXII.

OUR FATHER IN HEAVEN.

AFTER this manner therefore pray ye: Our Father which art in heaven, Hallowed be thy name. Thy kingdom come. Thy will be done in earth, as *it is* in heaven. If ye then, being evil, know how to give good gifts unto your children, how much more shall your Father which is in heaven give good things to them that ask him? Blessed *be* God, even the Father of our Lord Jesus Christ, the Father of mercies, and the God of all comfort; Who comforteth us in all our tribulation, that we may be able to comfort them which are in any trouble, by the comfort wherewith we ourselves are comforted of God. For there are three that bear record in heaven, the Father, the Word, and the Holy Ghost: and these three are one. And there are three that bear witness in earth, the spirit, and the water, and the blood: and these three agree in one.

PRAYERS IN A CART.

A LABORING man fell and broke his leg. He maintained a large family when he was able to work. Now he was confined to his house, want and suffering came into the door. Some good people thought it would be a nice thing to visit the poor man and pray with him. Permission was obtained, and a time appointed for a service of praise and prayer. A pious deacon led the meeting. Prayer was offered that the man might be comforted in his affliction, resigned to the will of God, and find his calamity overruled for his eternal good. The services were interrupted by a loud knocking at the door, and a stalwart young man presented himself with a goad in his hand. He was known as a laborer on a neighboring farm. His employer was not very spiritually minded, but was very charitable, and was known as the Squire. The message was a brief one. The Squire could not attend the meeting; he had sent his prayers, and they were out in the cart; will somebody help me bring them in? The prayers consisted of a mixture of flour, potatoes, ham, and other necessaries to sustain and comfort the poor sufferer on his bed of pain. There was little talking after the lad departed, but a good deal of resolution. The meeting suddenly dissolved, but it bore much rich, ripe fruit. A load of dry wood was dropped at the door, and the table groaned with good things.

XXXIII.

RELIGIOUS PRINCIPLE.

THEN the presidents and princes sought to find occasion against Daniel concerning the kingdom; but they could find none occasion nor fault; forasmuch as he *was* faithful, neither was there any error nor fault found in him. Then said these men, We shall not find any occasion against this Daniel, except we find *it* against him concerning the law of his God. Then the king made Daniel a great man, and gave him many great gifts, and made him ruler over the whole province of Babylon, and chief of the governors over all the wise *men* of Babylon. And if thou wilt walk before me, as David thy father walked, in integrity of heart, and in uprightness, to do according to all that I have commanded thee, *and* wilt keep my statutes and my judgments; then I will establish the throne of thy kingdom upon Israel forever, as I promised to David thy father, saying, There shall not fail thee a man upon the throne of Israel.

BUTCHER'S CONVERSION.

A STOUT, burly fellow was seen, one day, standing at the door of the Fulton-street church. He did not seem to take any special interest in the meeting. The missionary, as he is wont to do, spoke to the stranger. He said to him, "I am glad to see you here; are you a Christian?" "No," said the man in a surly tone. "What are you here for?" "The singing brings me; I don't know why it should. Every day I find myself coming up these steps to hear you sing." "I hope you will be a Christian, and give your heart to God." "I don't; I want nothing to do with religion, but I like your singing." "What is your business?" "I am a butcher; and we butchers are a tough set." "Well, come up-stairs, I want to talk with you," and up the party went. On reaching the little room, the missionary threw himself on his knees. Over him stood the tall, burly butcher. "Kneel down," said the missionary, "I am going to pray with you." "No, you don't; I never knelt in my life; I shan't begin in this church." But the missionary prevailed, and the resolute sinner bowed in prayer. Fervent supplications were offered for his salvation. "It is the first time any body ever prayed for my soul," said the butcher. Two days after, the visitor sought the missionary. He shook like an aspen leaf; his eyes were red with weeping, but soon his tears were turned to praise. He had beauty for ashes, and the oil of joy for mourning. "Oh! I am so happy," he said, "I have found the Saviour, and he has pardoned my sins." "Another witness to the power of prayer," said a man who had himself been rescued from the lowest depths.

XXXIV.

COMPASSION OF CHRIST.

WHO can have compassion on the ignorant, and on them that are out of the way; for that he himself also is compassed with infirmity. And by reason hereof he ought, as for the people, so also for himself, to offer for sins. And all the city was gathered together at the door. And he healed many that were sick of divers diseases, and cast out many devils; and suffered not the devils to speak, because they knew him. But when he saw the multitudes, he was moved with compassion on them, because they fainted, and were scattered abroad, as sheep having no shepherd. Then saith he unto his disciples, The harvest truly *is* plenteous, but the laborers *are* few; pray ye therefore the Lord of the harvest, that he will send forth laborers into his harvest. Behold, I have graven thee upon the palms of *my* hands; thy walls *are* continually before me.

BURNING THE BIBLE.

A Christian lady selected a mission work all her own. With a few copies of the Bible, she passed from cottage to cottage, leaving a book here and there as opportunity offered. Standing in an open door, in one of the open wards of the city, was an unwashed laborer. The woman asked him if he would accept a copy of the Word of God. He replied, "No; and if you leave one in my house, I will fling it into the fire." Irresistibly impelled, the lady laid a copy on the table and departed. In a rage, the man seized it, and, in defiance of the expostulations of his wife, flung it on a bed of coals. Horror-stricken, the woman fled from the house; after a time, she returned, and picked up a leaf that had blown out of the flames. On it she read: "Heaven and earth shall pass away, but my word shall not pass away." The furious man tore the leaf from his wife's hand, and flung that into the flames, but not until he had read it.

That word was sharper than a two-edged sword. The man flung himself on his bed, but not to sleep. The leaden steps of night moved slowly. "I can't sleep," he said. "Neither can I," responded the wife. "Can you tell me where the kind lady lives who left the Bible?" The woman knew her well. Early in the morning, the high-handed sinner sought her house. He confessed the great wrong he had done, begged a Bible and an interest in her prayers. That book made him wise unto salvation; his own sins found him out, his daring wickedness convicted him, the terror of the Lord drove him to the cross.

XXXV.

READING AND UNDERSTANDING.

AND Ezra the priest brought the law before the congregation both of men and women, and all that could hear with understanding, upon the first day of the seventh month. And he read therein before the street that *was* before the water gate from the morning until midday, before the men and the women, and those that could understand; and the ears of all the people *were attentive* unto the book of the law. And Philip ran thither to *him*, and heard him read the prophet Esaias, and said, Understandest thou what thou readest? And he said, How can I, except some man should guide me? And he desired Philip that he would come up and sit with him. And it came to pass, that after three days they found him in the temple, sitting in the midst of the doctors, both hearing them, and asking them questions. And all that heard him were astonished at his understanding and answers.

PERSONAL CONSECRATION.

IN one of the Southern cities lived a young lady of large fortune. She was a decided Christian, and devoted her wealth to religious and benevolent uses. One of her rules was never to see a human being in waut or suffering without attempting to relieve. Riding in the country one day, she saw a young man lying on a bank dead drunk. His face was covered with flies, and the hot sun beat down upon him. She stopped her carriage, and looked on the prostrate form before her. The young man was well dressed; had a noble forehead; clusters of curly black hair hung over his brow, and he was evidently accustomed to good society. She dipped her handkerchief in a stream that ran near by, wiped the face of the inebriate, covered it with her handkerchief, entered the carriage, and drove back to town. She notified the police that the suffering man needed attention. A week afterward, a stranger called on the young lady and sought an interview. "I am ashamed to look you in the face," he said; "I am the young man you so kindly cared for the other day. The name on the handkerchief with which you covered my face revealed my benefactress. I have come to thank you for your considerate kindness. It may, perhaps, interest you to know that I have signed the pledge. With my hand on my mother's Bible, I have sworn, God being my helper, that I will never taste another drop of intoxicating liquor." That vow he never broke. Prominent in church and state, he attained to the dignity of United States Attorney-General. Eloquent in voice and brilliant with pen, he became one of the most eminent men of the nation.

XXXVI.

ENEMIES BEING JUDGES.

FOR their rock *is* not as our Rock, even our enemies themselves *being* judges. How should one chase a thousand, and two put ten thousand to flight, except their Rock had sold them, and the Lord had shut them up? When the Lord turned again the captivity of Zion, we were like them that dream. Then was our mouth filled with laughter, and our tongue with singing: then said they among the heathen, The Lord hath done great things for them. The Lord hath done great things for us; *whereof* we are glad. Many times did he deliver them; but they provoked *him* with their counsel, and were brought low for their iniquity. Nevertheless he regarded their affliction, when he heard their cry: and he remembered for them his covenant, and repented according to the multitude of his mercies.

HUT OUT WEST.

A LAWYER told the story of his conversion. Religion to him was an idle tale; professors were not sincere; men out of the Church were as good as men in it. Traveling in the West on horseback, in a dark and stormy time, night overtook him.

He was up to his saddle-girths in mud. He came to a place where two roads met; either was bad enough. The only person he met, in answer to the question which was the best road, said, "Neither. If you take the one, you will wish you had taken the other." He reined up in front of a miserable-looking hut, and sought shelter from the drenching rain. He entered the scantily furnished room, which served for kitchen, bedroom, and parlor. Permission to remain was reluctantly given. The horse was tied in the shed. The traveler seated himself by the fire. It was a rude shelter: the room was coarse and dark; the floor was composed of rough boards; a small loft served as a chamber. The rude walls of the hut were hung with pistols, bowie-knives, and shot-guns. The traveler felt sure that he was in a banditti's den. He wished he had braved the elements. The old man, a complete specimen of a prairie ruffian, came in armed to the teeth. His words were few and his welcome scant. Soon, the son came in, looking more like a bandit than his father. A long, low, earnest conversation was carried on between the members of the family. The young man knew that the consultation related to himself. Nothing less than robbery was expected; perhaps murder. Pale with terror, the lawyer resolved to flee and trust to the darkness of the night. The old man approached, and said, "Stranger, we are a rough, poor people, and live by hunting. We start early in the morning. Before we go to bed, we always read a little in the Bible, and have a word of prayer. Have you any objection?" "Oh! no. Do pray, do pray," said the young man. Tears came into his eyes, for he knew that those who prayed before they went to bed did not cut people's throats. As he lay on his rude couch, he said, "How is this? This seemed like a banditti's den, and the old man and his son like robbers. Yet when he said, 'Let us pray,' I felt as safe as if I was pressing the bosom of my mother. There must be something in religion after all. I will seek my mother's Saviour, and trust in my mother's God."

XXXVII.

PERSONAL WORK.

FOR we are laborers together with God: ye are God's husbandry, *ye are* God's building. According to the grace of God which is given unto me, as a wise masterbuilder, I have laid the foundation, and another buildeth thereon. But let every man take heed how he buildeth thereupon. For I will not dare to speak of any of those things which Christ hath not wrought by me, to make the Gentiles obedient, by word and deed, through mighty signs and wonders, by the power of the Spirit of God; so that from Jerusalem, and round about unto Illyricum, I have fully preached the gospel of Christ. Yea, so have I strived to preach the gospel, not where Christ was named, lest I should build upon another man's foundation: neither was there any among them that lacked: for as many as were possessors of lands or houses sold them, and brought the prices of the things that were sold, and laid *them* down at the apostles' feet: and distribution was made unto every man according as he had need.

A MISSIONARY DOG.

A WELL-KNOWN physician was riding through the streets. He heard the crying of a little dog, who was lying in the gutter, apparently in great pain. The kind doctor left his carriage, and lifted the dog up. He had been run over by a passing carriage, and his leg badly crushed. The doctor bore him to his office, tenderly set his limb, and cared for him from day to day. The dog became a great favorite in the family, and seemed very much attached to his kind friend the doctor. One day, the office-door being open, the dog darted out and disappeared. "That's the way," the doctor said, "it is with dogs and men. They get all they can out of you, and when you can do no more for them they disappear. There is no gratitude in the world." The dog and his relations to the family had nearly passed out of mind. One morning, the doctor was sitting in his office, when he heard a whining at the door. He opened it, and there stood the little dog whom the doctor had cured, bringing with him another little dog who had been run over. He had communicated his relief to a suffering friend, and, in the spirit of a true missionary, had brought the sufferer to a skillful physician whom he knew was ready to aid. Nor did his instincts mislead him. He came occasionally to see his companion, but no persuasion could induce him to make the doctor's house his home. That is the true missionary spirit. Get relief yourself. Then go out and tell the suffering, and bring them to the Great Physician.

XXXVIII.

LOVE TO THE SAVIOUR.

SO when they had dined, Jesus saith to Simon Peter, Simon, *son* of Jonas, lovest thou me more than these? He saith unto him, Yea, Lord; thou knowest that I love thee. He saith unto him, Feed my lambs. Grace *be* to you, and peace, from God our Father, and *from* the Lord Jesus Christ. Blessed *be* the God and Father of our Lord Jesus Christ, who hath blessed us with all spiritual blessings in heavenly *places* in Christ: according as he hath chosen us in him before the foundation of the world, that we should be holy and without blame before him in love: but ye, beloved, building up yourselves on your most holy faith, pray in the Holy Ghost, keep yourselves in the love of God, looking for the mercy of our Lord Jesus Christ unto eternal life.

BOBBY AT GREYFRIARS.

I SAW in the Old Greyfriars burying-ground an instance of animal affection that was very touching. A little shepherd's dog lay on the grave of his master, and had lain there, when I saw him, five years. A stranger died on the streets of Edinburgh.

He was buried in Greyfriars, a sort of Potter's Field, at the public charge. There was nothing about him to indicate who he was or where he belonged. While the burial services were being performed, a little dog was seen standing at the gate, watching the movements of the party. When the services closed, the little dog walked up to the grave and laid down upon it. He was found there the next morning by the sexton. He was taken to a baker's shop, and some crackers given to him for his breakfast. A kind butcher gave him his dinner. He returned immediately to the grave. One dark and stormy night, the sexton, out of compassion, shut him up in the vestry. He was found the next morning on the grave of his master, having carried away the entire window-sash to secure his freedom. For five years, as the hour of eight was chimed out daily, Bobby started for the baker's. At noon, he visited the butcher's. On Sundays, though the heavy chimes of Greyfriars rang, Bobby never stirred from the grave. Eight and twelve pealed out as usual from the old ivy-clad tower, but the dog never left the churchyard. He never mistook seven for eight, nor eleven for twelve. He knew when Sunday came; he never mistook Saturday for Sunday. He knew his kind friends, the butcher and the baker, closed their stores on the Lord's day. On Saturday, he laid apart a portion of his breakfast and a portion of his dinner for Sunday use. He dug a little cupboard under a neighboring tombstone, where he hid his food. Strangers visiting Edinburgh called for Bobby. The Lord Mayor gave him a gold collar with his name engraved on it. A fund was provided by the citizens lest the kindness of the butcher and baker should give out. The little dog has an annuity for life, and can never be in want.

If Christians should love their Saviour as this little dog loved his master, what a power the Church would be in the world!

XXXIX.

INFLUENCE OF EXAMPLE.

TAKE, my brethren, the prophets, who have spoken in the name of the Lord, for an example of suffering affliction, and of patience. There hath no temptation taken you but such as is common to man: but God *is* faithful, who will not suffer you to be tempted above that ye are able; but will with the temptation also make a way to escape, that ye may be able to bear *it.* Nevertheless, whereto we have already attained, let us walk by the same rule, let us mind the same thing. Brethren, be followers together of me, and mark them which walk so as ye have us for an ensample. We give thanks to God always for you all, making mention of you in our prayers; remembering without ceasing your work of faith, and labor of love, and patience of hope in our Lord Jesus Christ, in the sight of God and our Father.

BRAVE PASTOR.

THE Earl of Rochester was one of the wickedest men in England. He was a young man of commanding influence, but he threw it against purity and religion. He led the youth astray, and was foremost in every bold, bad thing. Riding in disguise one day over his estate, he overtook a preacher who was on his way to perform some religious service. The Earl entered into conversation with the preacher, and bantered him on his profession.

"What good do you priests do the kingdom? You cost a great deal of money, but I don't see as you do any thing in return."

The young man admitted that ministers were nearly powerless, and regretted that no more reforms or conversions attended their labors.

"How do you account for this absence of success?"

"Well," replied the preacher, "the realm is very wicked, and the noblemen throw their influence against morality and religion. What can a poor preacher do, when vice is clothed in scarlet and stalks openly over the land? Now, there is the Earl of Rochester, one of the most abandoned and licentious men in the kingdom. He has a thousandfold more influence than I have; and while he is the champion of vice and impiety, what do my reproofs or instruction avail?"

The Earl said but little, turned his horse and rode in another direction. The next day, the young clergyman received an invitation to visit the Earl of Rochester. He was both astonished and alarmed. He concluded that his free remarks the day before had been reported to the Earl. But his alarm heightened into terror when he saw, in the person of the Earl, the very gentleman to whom he had been so outspoken. Assuming a stern manner, he demanded,

"What do you think of the Earl of Rochester to-day?"

"Would to God, my lord, that I had occasion to change my opinion."

The nobleman thanked the young clergyman for his boldness, and dismissed him with a reward. His reform dated from that hour. On his death-bed, the Earl sent for his gay companions, and, pointing to the Bible, said,

"In that book will be found true philosophy. The only complaint that you or I can make against the Bible is that it rebukes a bad life."

XL.

STEADFASTNESS.

AND they continued steadfastly in the apostles' doctrine and fellowship, and in breaking of bread, and in prayers. Ye therefore, beloved, seeing ye know *these things* before, beware lest ye also, being led away with the error of the wicked, fall from your own steadfastness. But grow in grace, and *in* the knowledge of our Lord and Saviour Jesus Christ. To him *be* glory both now and forever. Amen. And have no root in themselves, and so endure but for a time: afterward, when affliction or persecution ariseth for the word's sake, immediately they are offended. Thou therefore endure hardness, as a good soldier of Jesus Christ. No man that warreth entangleth himself with the affairs of *this* life; that he may please him who hath chosen him to be a soldier. Beware lest any man spoil you through philosophy and vain deceit, after the tradition of men, after the rudiments of the world, and not after Christ.

THROUGH TICKET.

AN English preacher who has had remarkable success in reaching the London workmen, and bringing the lowly to the Saviour, is celebrated for his graphic figures and illustrations, taken from common life. Speaking to an immense crowd of British workmen, he said,

"I came here to-day in the cars. I am not a very well-dressed man, as you see, and I generally travel second-class. I went to the booking-office to get my ticket, when a friend met me, asked me where I was going, and if I had a ticket. I told him I was going to Manchester, and that I was on my way to buy my ticket. 'Just wait,' he said, 'and I'll get you one.' The ticket admitted me to a first-class car. We had several changes to make, but my friend said, 'That ticket is good clear through.' On approaching the gate, the guard said to me, Second-class?' 'No, first-class.' 'Let me see your ticket. All right, pass in.' I didn't look much like a first-class passenger. It wasn't my clothes, nor my looks, that gave me my seat, but my ticket; that carried me through. We came to our first change. The man at the iron gate repeated the question, 'Second class?' 'No.' 'Let me see your ticket.' And on I went. Change followed change, till at length I was landed in the station at Manchester. One ticket brought me clear through. Nobody asked me where I came from, how old I was, whether I was rich or whether I was poor. The authorities asked for my ticket; if that was all right, I was all right. I took the right ticket at the booking-office before I started, and needed no changes, no alterations, no additions. It landed me just where I would be. It is just so with religion. Get it at the start, get it genuine. Have it stamped with the blood of the Saviour, and it will carry you clear through to the pearly gates. No matter what may happen; no matter what there is in the future, you will be safe. Your ticket will pass as you enter the gates of death; and if the golden gates swing inward to your approach, it will be because your ticket is right."

XLI.

OPPORTUNITIES.

AS we have therefore opportunity, let us do good unto all *men*, especially unto them who are of the household of faith. And she said unto her mistress, Would God my lord *were* with the prophet that *is* in Samaria! for he would recover him of his leprosy. But a certain Samaritan, as he journeyed, came where he was; and when he saw him, he had compassion *on him*, and went to *him*, and bound up his wounds, pouring in oil and wine, and set him on his own beast, and brought him to an inn, and took care of him. And Elisha sent a messenger unto him, saying, Go and wash in Jordan seven times, and thy flesh shall come again to thee, and thou shalt be clean. And at midnight Paul and Silas prayed, and sang praises unto God: and the prisoners heard them. And he took them the same hour of the night, and washed *their* stripes; and was baptized, he and all his, straightway. And when he had brought them into his house, he set meat before them, and rejoiced, believing in God with all his house.

MY FATHER OWNS ALL.

An English missionary, who is very successful in his field of labor, has a rule never to let any one go from his presence until he has said something to him on the subject of personal religion. He is a man of consummate wisdom. His words are fitly spoken, and are like "apples of gold in baskets of silver." He is a living illustration of that scripture, "A word in due season, how good is it!" He found himself one day in a compartment with a well-to-do, conceited, and self-satisfied landholder. Passing an elegant mansion, with park and acres spreading out in beauty, the land-owner called the attention of his companion to the charming view. The missionary admired it, but said quietly, "Yes, my father owns that estate." "You don't look like a rich man's son," was the response. Soon a castle hove in sight. "My father owns that also," said the missionary, "and all the broad acres and cattle you see." "Why don't you dress better, if your father is so rich? You are evidently a man of little culture. Why didn't your father send you to Oxford? If your father had as much money as you say he has, he would have brought you up more tenderly." Still the missionary asserted that his father was rich and owned all the property through which the train had passed since it had left London. "And there are so many suffering, sorrowing people living on his property that he would rather I would spend my money in relieving the poor than to spend it on myself." The cars approached the fields of an evidently well-to-do farmer. The cattle were sleek and abundant. The hedges were radiant with beauty. The lawns were soft as velvet. The dwellings and out-buildings indicated thrift and wealth. "I suppose this farm belongs to your father," said the farmer. "Yes," was the reply. "Now, I know you lie, and you've been lying all the while. This is my farm. I own every foot of it. There's not a pound of debt on the whole place." "Notwithstanding," said the missionary, "my father owns it." "Your father!" exclaimed the excited man; "who is he?" "He made this world. The cattle on a thousand hills are his." "Surely, young man, you are right." He raised his hat, lifted his tearful eyes to heaven, and repeated, "The cattle on a thousand hills are his. All glory to his blessed name."

XLII.

BUSINESS VALUE OF RELIGION.

HAPPY *is* the man *that* findeth wisdom, and the man *that* getteth understanding: for the merchandise of it *is* better than the merchandise of silver, and the gain thereof than fine gold. Surely the isles shall wait for me, and the ships of Tarshish first, to bring thy sons from far, their silver and their gold with them, unto the name of the Lord thy God, and to the Holy One of Israel, because he hath glorified thee. And the sons of strangers shall build up thy walls, and their kings shall minister unto thee: for in my wrath I smote thee, but in my favor have I had mercy on thee. They that go down to the sea in ships, that do business in great waters; these see the works of the Lord, and his wonders in the deep. And he spake unto Ephron in the audience of the people of the land, saying, But if thou *will give it*, I pray thee, hear me: I will give the money for the field; take *it* of me, and I will bury my dead there.

FARRAGUT AT TEN.

I PREACHED one Sunday in the parlors at Long Branch. The war was over, and Admiral Farragut and his family were spending the summer at the Branch. Sitting on the portico of the hotel on Monday morning, he said to me, "Would you like to know how I was enabled to serve my country? It was all owing to a resolution I formed when I was ten years of age. My father was sent down to New-Orleans, with the little navy we then had, to look after the treason of Burr. I accompanied him as cabin-boy. I had some qualities that I thought made a man of me. I could swear like an old salt; could drink a stiff glass of grog as if I had doubled Cape Horn, and could smoke like a locomotive. I was great at cards and fond of gaming in every shape. At the close of the dinner, one day, my father turned every body out of the cabin, locked the door, and said to me, 'David, what do you mean to be?' 'I mean to follow the sea.' 'Follow the sea! Yes, be a poor, miserable, drunken sailor before the mast, kicked and cuffed about the world, and die in some fever hospital in a foreign clime.' 'No,' I said, 'I'll tread the quarter-deck and command, as you do.' 'No, David; no boy ever trod the quarter-deck with such principles as you have, and such habits as you exhibit. You'll have to change your whole course of life if you ever become a man.' My father left me and went on deck. I was stunned by the rebuke and overwhelmed with mortification. 'A poor, miserable, drunken sailor before the mast, kicked and cuffed about the world, and to die in some fever hospital! That's my fate, is it? I'll change my life, and change it at once. I will never utter another oath, I will never drink another drop of intoxicating liquors, I will never gamble.' And, as God is my witness, I have kept those three vows to this hour. Shortly after, I became a Christian. That act settled my temporal as it settled my eternal destiny.

XLIII.

CURSE OF RICHES.

GO to now, *ye* rich men, weep and howl for your miseries that shall come upon *you*. Your riches are corrupted, and your garments are moth-eaten. Your gold and silver is cankered; and the rust of them shall be a witness against you, and shall eat your flesh as it were fire. Ye have heaped treasure together for the last days. Labor not to be rich: cease from thine own wisdom. Wilt thou set thine eyes upon that which is not? for *riches* certainly make themselves wings; they fly away as an eagle toward heaven. He that oppresseth the poor to increase his *riches, and* he that giveth to the rich, *shall* surely *come* to want. A little that a righteous man hath *is* better than the riches of many wicked. But they that will be rich fall into temptation and a snare, and *into* many foolish and hurtful lusts, which drown men in destruction and perdition. For the love of money is the root of all evil: which while some coveted after, they have erred from the faith, and pierced themselves through with many sorrows.

LIFE A BURDEN.

IT was a hot, sultry day. I had been called to attend the funeral of a poor man's child, in a desolate and offensive region of the city. I stepped on the ferry-boat, heated, tired, exhausted. Just then a coach, with a driver in livery, came on. The impatient horses champed the bits and flung the foam right and left. I thought the establishment one of the most complete I had ever seen. The horses were superb. The harness, gold-mounted, and fitting like a glove, was imported from Paris. The coach, on its double springs, C and elliptic, with its satin lining, was as luxurious as money could buy. I felt the least bit envious. I said, How nice it would be to have plenty of money, a fine team of horses, with plenty of servants, and ride to this mission work, instead of tramping around in the heat and dust. How happy the owner of this fine turn-out must be! How much good he can do with his money. I said to the driver, "Whose team is that?" As he mentioned the name, I felt rebuked and confounded. I knew the name of the owner only too well. He began life poor. He set his mark high, and resolved to be rich. He trampled every thing down that stood in his way. He broke through every influence and every tender tie that held him back. He did hard things, mean things, severe things, but kept within the letter of the law. He prospered every way on the land and on the sea. Every thing he touched turned to gold. His name stood high among the merchant-princes. He had his city house and his country house. His summer retreat, on a rock peninsula, was the most elegant in the State. Like Solomon, "he gathered him silver and gold, horses, chariots, and servants. He withheld from his eye no joy, and from his heart no desire." His life was purely selfish. He lived for nobody, for no cause, and was bound up with no good thing outside of his family. God took his children from him when they were young, and he had no source of happiness but his wealth. He tired of life. Every thing cloyed, and existence became a burden. He was missed one morning from the breakfast-table. He was found in a little cove, with the surf of the ocean beating upon him.

XLIV.

ORIGINAL SABBATH.

AND on the seventh day God ended his work which he had made; and he rested on the seventh day from all his work which he had made. And God blessed the seventh day, and sanctified it: because that in it he had rested from all his work which God created and made. Remember the Sabbath-day to keep it holy. Six days shalt thou labor, and do all thy work: but the seventh day *is* the Sabbath of the Lord thy God: *in it* thou shalt not do any work, thou, nor thy son, nor thy daughter, thy man-servant, nor thy maid-servant, nor thy cattle, nor thy stranger that *is* within thy gates.

VALUE OF THE SABBATH.

THE Sabbath was made for man; for his temporal, intellectual, social, and religious welfare. Every Sabbath-breaker damages himself and damages his race. In countries where there is no Sabbath, or where it is devoted to sinful amusements and worldly recreations, the tone of society is low; crime abounds, and general demoralization marks the community. Hospitals, schools, colleges, are found only in countries where the Sabbath is observed as a divine institution. A stranger in Ireland can tell the moment he passes the line between the South and North of Ireland. On the one side of the line, the Sabbath is a holiday, and the Bible is kept from the masses ; on the other side, the Sabbath is holy unto the Lord, and the Bible is in every man's hand. Where this institution is honored, there is thrift, industry, and an absence of want and beggary. The cottages are comfortable, clean with whitewash, with abundance, the fruit of labor. The gardens are walled in, and every foot is cultivated. Even the women and children are happy at their employ, and bear some part in the general industry of the country.

On the southern side of the line, the streets are crowded with beggars ; indolence covers the people like a pall ; the dwellings are mean and poor, and general superstition broods over the people. Give the South of Ireland the Sabbath with its moral and social power, then they would have the Bible. With these would come general education ; the value of industry would be recognized ; the fertile island would bloom under the chemic touch of labor like the garden of the Lord; the unrest which now marks the people of the Emerald Isle would give way to cheerful industry, for the Sabbath is identified by the divine appointment with the best temporal interests of man. Homes do not create the Sabbath nor preserve it ; but the Sabbath creates homes. Public worship does not conserve the Sabbath, but the Sabbath perpetuates public service. Carry it anywhere, among the mountains of cruelty; give it to the pirate at Pitcairn's Island, the savage cannibals at the Sandwich Isles—everywhere it produces the same fruits. It gathers the solitary into families, creates homes, and makes the mother's heart sing for joy ; fills the air with the hum of labor, and whitens distant seas with the canvas of the merchant-men.

XLV.

DAY OF THE LORD.

IN those days saw I in Judah *some* treading winepresses on the Sabbath, and bringing in sheaves, and lading asses; as also wine, grapes, and figs, and all *manner of* burdens, which they brought into Jerusalem on the Sabbath-day: and I testified *against them* in the day wherein they sold victuals. Then I contended with the nobles of Judah, and said unto them, What evil thing *is* this that ye do, and profane the Sabbath-day? And it came to pass, that, when the gates of Jerusalem began to be dark before the Sabbath, I commanded that the gates should be shut, and charged that they should not be opened till after the Sabbath: and *some* of my servants set I at the gates, *that* there should no burden be brought in on the Sabbath-day.

THE SABBATH AND WOMEN.

A FEW hours' ride carries the traveler from the staid commercial capital of England to the gay city of France. Were London and Paris a thousand miles apart, and did oceans roll between them instead of a narrow channel, the two cities could not be more unlike. The country that lies between the two capitals is stranger still. Leaving Calais, the traveler is borne through the country known as Normandy. The train passes in sight of the home of William the Conqueror, which he left when he went forth to subdue England. The natural advantages of Normandy are very great: its soil is fertile, its clime is fair, and its choice and elegant fruits could supply abundantly the great cities of London and Paris. But Normandy has no Sabbath in the Christian sense. The curse that attends Sabbath violation strikes the eye everywhere. The men are indolent, dissolute, and worthless. What little work is done, is done by the women—a tall, brawny, rudely-dressed, rough set—proving that woman never comes to the front to do a man's work and take a man's place, till man is degraded. The women do what work is done in the fields; they not only plow, and sow, and hoe, and gather in the harvest, but they can often be seen fastened to the plow, yoked with and pulling beside the mule and the steer, tramping in the furrow, quite as degraded as the beast of burden.

At Rouen, the principal business is fishing. When the boat is ready for the sea, twenty or thirty women, rudely dressed, looking like the weird sisters of the blasted heath, attach themselves to a rope, and, like mules on a towpath, warp the vessel down the long pier, and secure it at the end; their husbands then leave their drinking bouts and gaming, and consent to go out and fish. On arriving at the pier with the cargo, the men desert the vessel, and go to their favorite haunts. The women put the rope over their shoulders, and tow the vessel up to the dock, take out the fish, sell the cargo, and again warp the vessel out, ready for the use of their lords and masters. As it is in Rouen, so is it in every country where the Sabbath is unknown. Delicacy, refinement, the charms of home, the elegancies of domestic life, are the fruits of the Sabbath, and the Sabbath is the Magna Charta of woman.

XLVI.

ACCEPTABLE SERVICE.

IF thou turn away thy foot from the Sabbath, *from* doing thy pleasure on my holy day; and call the Sabbath a delight, the holy of the Lord, honorable; and shalt honor him, not doing thine own ways, nor finding thine own pleasure, nor speaking *thine own* words: then shalt thou delight thyself in the Lord; and I will cause thee to ride upon the high places of the earth, and feed thee with the heritage of Jacob thy father: for the mouth of the Lord hath spoken *it.* Thou shalt be like a watered garden, and like a spring of water, whose waters fail not. And *they that shall be* of thee shall build the old waste places: thou shalt raise up the foundations of many generations; and thou shalt be called, The repairer of the breach, The restorer of paths to dwell in.

TEMPORAL BENEFITS.

THE powers of man are limited. Too much work, too much watching, too much anxiety, bring a bitter harvest. There is a point beyond which even a mother's love will not sustain her in weary watching in the care of sick children. The anxious merchant must hold up, and cool his throbbing brows, or ruin attends him. The student must limit his investigations, or brain-fever will fling him on a burning couch. Divine beneficence gave man the Sabbath ; divine authority could alone make selfish man close the ledger, and stop the flow of gain one day in seven. A grasping, avaricious, money-loving mortal could never have invented an institution that would lift the rod of the oppressor, bid the laboring man rest, and silence the hum of industry one day in seven. The man who works fifty-two Sundays in the year simply adds fifty-two days of toil to his allotted task, and toils for toil's sake. He will do less work in the year and accomplish less than if he had rested on the Lord's day, according to the commandment. Statistics show that Sabbath-working is unprofitable. Men whose business demands Sunday work occupy a low plane. Sunday newsboys are the lowest of their class. Merchants in New-York, who, during a period of twenty-five years, have kept their counting-houses open on Sunday, have invariably failed. No miracle is needed to explain this. God ordains a temporal rest one day in seven; man disobeys this law; he goes beyond his ability ; his brain becomes heated ; he can not pause for cool reflection ; his judgment becomes warped ; he makes rash ventures, and finally goes under. During forty years of service on the bench, Sir Matthew Hale, the great jurist of England, never touched secular work on Sundays; he felt the refreshing influence of the Sabbath on his entire work of the week. His health was invariably good, his intellect keen, his judgment sound, and his judicial decisions abide to this day. The slaves in the West-India Islands who were allowed the Sabbath, contrasted strongly in health and physical vigor with those who had no Sabbath, or who were compelled to work for themselves on the Lord's day. The influence of the Sabbath is seen on the barns, fences, cattle, women, and children. As Victor Immanuel moved on the Papal States and took possession, his pathway was marked by the track of cleanliness that he left behind him. The accumulated filth of half a century was removed.

XLVII.

REDEEMER IN ZION.

AND the Redeemer shall come to Zion, and unto them that turn from transgression in Jacob, saith the Lord. As for me, this *is* my covenant with them, saith the Lord; my Spirit that *is* upon thee, and my words which I have put in thy mouth, shall not depart out of thy mouth, nor out of the mouth of thy seed, nor out of the mouth of thy seed's seed, saith the Lord, from henceforth and forever. And the Gentiles shall come to thy light, and kings to the brightness of thy rising. Lift up thine eyes round about, and see: all they gather themselves together, they come to thee: thy sons shall come from far, and thy daughters shall be nursed at *thy* side.

DAY OF THE LORD.

THE Sabbath of the New Testament is indicated by the term, the Lord's Day. "I was in the spirit on the Lord's day," said John on the Isle of Patmos. The phrase is as well understood as is that of the Lord's Supper. Christ announces himself as Lord of the Sabbath, and as such, he could, if he chose, appoint the first day of the week for divine service instead of the seventh. We celebrate the birthday of Washington on the 22d of February; but the Father of his Country was not born on the 22d of February—he was born on the 11th day of that month; but, by common consent, to answer a great public benefit, eleven days were added to the calendar, and the 11th day of the month became the 22d. The change produced no confusion in the world; broke no contract; canceled no obligation; violated no compact; wronged no man out of money or time. The times were changed, but the spirit of public and private obligations was as faithfully kept on the new reckoning as on the old. So, whether the Sabbath be on the seventh day or on the first, it is of binding force, and the solemnities are the same.

But it is not certain that what we call the seventh day is any nearer the original Sabbath than was the first day of our reckoning. Men who sail in one direction to Pitcairn's Island, reach there on Saturday. Sailing in another direction, according to the reckoning, the Saturday on the one side becomes Sunday on the other. During their long captivity in Babylon, the Jews lost their language, their knowledge of the Bible, the sanctions of public worship, and probably the day of the Sabbath itself. Centuries before Christ died, it was a matter of prophecy that he should rise from the dead on the Lord's Day, or the day the Lord hath made. On that day, the stone which the builders refused was to become the headstone of the corner. This scripture our Lord quotes at the close of his ministry, and applies to himself. "Did ye never read in the Scriptures," he said, "the stone which the builders rejected, the same has become the head of the corner; this is the Lord's doings, and it is marvelous in our eyes." Marvelous indeed is it, that the day the Lord made as his own, placing it as a crown on the creation, should, in the march of ages, become the day on which our Lord was raised from the dead, and the day of Christian observance and worship throughout the world.

XLVIII.

SACRIFICES AND REJOICINGS.

ALSO that day they offered great sacrifices, and rejoiced: for God had made them rejoice with great joy: the wives also and the children rejoiced: so that the joy of Jerusalem was heard even afar off. And both the singers and the porters kept the ward of their God, and the ward of the purification, according to the commandment of David, *and* of Solomon his son. For in the days of David and Asaph of old *there were* chief of the singers, and songs of praise and thanksgiving unto God. And all Israel in the days of Zerubbabel, and in the days of Nehemiah, gave the portions of the singers and the porters, every day his portion: and they sanctified *holy things* unto the Levites; and the Levites sanctified *them* unto the children of Aaron.

THE HOLY LAND.

THE localities of sacred story are little known. With all the improvements, discoveries, and travels, the popular mind is feebly instructed in regard to the places where the great events of the Bible transpired. As we read the sacred history from Eden to the Flood, and from the Flood to the baptism of

John, the location of the scenes recorded seems far off, and in lands unknown to this generation. The interior of Africa is not more mythical. Should we study sacred history as we do profane; follow the march of God's people, as we do the march of armies; study their encampment, as we do that of great generals, we should find that sacred localities have been preserved with an accuracy as exact as sacred history itself.

The Saviour stood on the Mount of Olives, overlooking the doomed capital of his fathers, over whose extinction he wept. His eye swept over a circuit of fifty miles; his eye rested on the locality where nearly all the events took place from Eden to the regions round about Jordan, where John preached. The mountains and vales, the seas and towns, celebrated in story and song, can be seen. The priest who offers sacrifice on Calvary and Moriah—near where Abraham's altar stood—can be hailed. The mountain of corruption, where Solomon sacrificed to idols, and the Valley of Hinnom, where the people offered their children to Moloch, lie at the base of Olives. Carmel, bathing its feet in the blue Mediterranean, its ceaseless verdure a type of the gospel, rises in beauty before the eye. The hills of Nazareth, identified with the boyhood of the Saviour, backed by the mountains of Samaria, are plainly seen. Hermon, still wet with the dew of the morning; Tabor, where Deborah fought, and Moses and Elias talked with Christ; Sychar, the tent-house of Jacob, with the well where Joseph drank, and the seed of Jacob asked for water—are in sight.

Standing on the same spot where the Saviour wept over Jerusalem, the traveler can see the field on which Abraham pitched his tent, and Hebron, where his ashes lie; Sodom, with its sullen lake; Bethlehem, where Rachel died and Ruth gleaned; Bethel, where God appeared to Jacob; Nebo, from whose summit Moses saw the goodly land; and Kerjath Jerim, where the Ark rested; thus grouping the sites of miracles, victories, and judgments, from Moses to Eli, and from David to Herod.

CONSISTORY BUILDING OF THE NORTH CHURCH.

XLIX.

INFLUENCE OF THE HOLY SPIRIT.

FOR I will pour water upon him that is thirsty, and floods upon the dry ground: I will pour my Spirit upon thy seed, and my blessing upon thine offspring: and they shall spring up *as* among the grass, as willows by the watercourses. One shall say, I *am* the Lord's; and another shall call *himself* by the name of Jacob; and another shall subscribe *with* his hand unto the Lord, and surname *himself* by the name of Israel. And I will pray the Father, and he shall give you another Comforter, that he may abide with you forever; *even* the Spirit of truth; whom the world can not receive, because it seeth him not, neither knoweth him: but ye know him; for he dwelleth with you, and shall be in you. Howbeit when he, the Spirit of truth, is come, he will guide you into all truth: for he shall not speak of himself; but whatsoever he shall hear, *that* shall he speak: and he will show you things to come. He shall glorify me: for he shall receive of mine, and shall show *it* unto you.

ILLUSTRATIONS OF PRAYER.

I HAVE been in the employ of one of the railroad companies, and had duties to perform around Fulton and Ann streets. At the hour of noon, I heard singing every day that arrested my attention. One day, I followed the crowd up the stairs, and found myself in the famed Fulton-street meeting. I had scarcely crossed the threshold, when my heart seemed to melt within me. I felt that I was a sinner, as I had never felt it before. My sins stared me in my face, and seemed to be set in order before me.

My wife was a Christian, and after a few days, I told her my situation. "Kneel down," she said, "and let us pray together." "You must wait a few days," I replied. "No—no—no," she said. "Now is the time. We will make this chair the family altar. Let us here kneel, and ask God to pardon your sins. Consider, you are getting quite old, and have never yet given your heart to God." We knelt down, and as my wife poured out her whole soul in prayer, I found peace in believing. I have had occasion ever since that hour to bless God for the influences that drew me into the noon-day meeting.

I came to New-York, from a religious home, but I was not a Christian. I wanted to be under religious influences, and I took board in a Christian family. One of the boarders, a young man, was a skeptic. We sat up late at night to discuss religious topics. To make myself better fitted to defend my side of the argument, I commenced to study infidel books. I was drawn into the vortex, and exceeded my friend in deistical views. My morals kept pace with my new opinions. I sank lower and lower in vice; my companions were disreputable, and my dissipations shattered my health. One morning, I was standing on the corner of William street and Fulton. Without any thought as to what I was doing, I drifted with the crowd into the Fulton-street meeting. A shudder came over me. I could not repress my tears. At the conclusion, a stranger took me by the hand, and said he was glad to see me in the meeting. In a few days, I was a changed man. My feet were taken out of the pit and placed on a rock. I looked back into the abyss from which I had been taken. The Saviour is my friend and my portion.

L.

QUENCH NOT THE SPIRIT.

QUENCH not the Spirit. Despise not prophesyings. To give knowledge of salvation unto his people by the remission of their sins, through the tender mercy of our God; whereby the dayspring from on high hath visited us, to give light to them that sit in darkness and *in* the shadow of death, to guide our feet into the way of peace. And the child grew, and waxed strong in spirit, and was in the deserts till the day of his showing unto Israel. And thou, child, shalt be called the prophet of the Highest: for thou shalt go before the face of the Lord to prepare his ways: thou hast put all things in subjection under his feet. For in that he put all in subjection under him, he left nothing *that is* not put under him. But now we see not yet all things put under him. But we see Jesus, who was made a little lower than the angels for the suffering of death, crowned with glory and honor; that he by the grace of God should taste death for every man.

A STRANGER'S STORY.

I CAME to this country from the old world. I sought in vain for a situation. Before I left home, I signed the temperance pledge, which was as sacred to me as my consecration to the Lord. My little money soon ran out. Piece by piece my clothing went to the pawnbroker's. My spirits were broken, and my faith in God's helping me nearly ceased. A British captain, who had known me in the old country, said he could get me a place. It was a very important position, and the proprietor wanted a young man who could be depended upon. My temperance principles would recommend me. I was exuberant with joy, and promised to accompany my friend the next morning. O the bitterness of my disappointment! Every thing was what the captain had stated. The pay was liberal, a good commission was offered me in addition, and the proprietor of the place was evidently pleased. The man kept a sailor boarding-house, with a dance-room and liquor-saloon in the basement. My business was to see that the sailors were well plied with liquor, until they were placed on board ship; to secure their half-pay papers, and to hold on to the luggage till all debts were paid. Bad as the place was, and distasteful as was the business, the temptation was very strong.

Not knowing which way to turn nor what to do, with starvation staring me in the face, I sauntered into the Fulton-street Daily Meeting. My case was made the subject of prayer. I left the room, resolved to starve rather than engage in the business to which I was invited. My way was dark and hedged up. But before the week closed, work was thrown in my way. A business opened to me, attractive and remunerative. I came into the meeting to return thanks to the Lord.

LI.

HE BORE OUR SICKNESSES.

WHEN the even was come, they brought unto him many that were possessed with devils: and he cast out the spirits with *his* word, and healed all that were sick: that it might be fulfilled which was spoken by Esaias the prophet, saying, Himself took our infirmities, and bare *our* sicknesses. And Jesus went about all the cities and villages, teaching in their synagogues, and preaching the gospel of the kingdom, and healing every sickness and every disease among the people. We then that are strong ought to bear the infirmities of the weak, and not to please ourselves. Let every one of us please *his* neighbor for *his* good to edification. For even Christ pleased not himself; but, as it is written, The reproaches of them that reproached thee fell on me.

REMARKABLE CURE.

AN humble, devoted missionary in Kansas had a little girl twelve years of age. For years she had suffered with chronic rheumatism. It settled in her leg, and defied the skill of physicians. The leg was shrunken, stiff at the knee, and shorter by two inches than the other. The hip-joint was drawn down from its socket, and the medical opinion was that the child was a cripple for life. Unable to obtain the help of man, the child turned its thoughts to the Saviour. One day, she said to her mother, "Mother, the Bible says, 'The prayer of faith shall save the sick.' Do you believe the Saviour could cure me if I had faith enough? Does Jesus mean what he says, mother, 'Whatsoever ye ask in faith, believing, ye shall receive'?" The mother could only answer, "Yes." "Then, mother, I have got the faith; haven't you?" The mother was troubled and distressed. She attempted to reason with the child, and show her that her sickness was perhaps a cross, which she ought to be willing to bear. But the answer of the little girl steadily was, "I have faith, and now, mother, if you have, there will be two of us, and then I can be cured." Sitting one day with her mother, in the absence of her father, the little sufferer said, "Now, mother, I want you to pray now to Jesus to cure me." Overcome by the importunity of the little girl, the mother knelt down to pray. How long she remained in that posture she does not know. Whether she was in a stupor, or in a swoon, or in a vision, she could not tell. She was aroused by her little girl, who shouted, "Mother, dear mother, wake up! Jesus has cured me! Oh! I am well, I am all well!" as she went skipping about the room, literally healed. All the mother can say is, that her child has been whole from that hour. The limb, no longer distorted and shrunken, is full, round, and perfect like the other. To all questions, the little girl cries out, in the fullness of her loving heart, "The Saviour has cured me!"

LII.

RELIGIOUS AFFECTION.

AND Ruth said, Entreat me not to leave thee, *or* to return from following after thee: for whither thou goest, I will go; and where thou lodgest, I will lodge: thy people *shall be* my people, and thy God my God: where thou diest, will I die, and there will I be buried: the Lord do so to me, and more also, *if aught* but death part thee and me. The Lord recompense thy work, and a full reward be given thee of the Lord God of Israel, under whose wings thou art come to trust. Beloved, let us love one another: for love is of God; and every one that loveth is born of God, and knoweth God. He that loveth not, knoweth not God; for God is love. In this was manifested the love of God toward us, because that God sent his only begotten Son into the world, that we might live through him. Herein is love, not that we loved God, but that he loved us, and sent his Son *to be* the propitiation for our sins.

"DID YOU EAT MY GRAPES, JOHNNY?"

WHEN I was a child, my mother-in-law was very sick. We were very poor, and as the fever burned her up she longed for fruits and cooling drink. A kind neighbor sent in some grapes, and oh! how delicious they were, and how my mother enjoyed them! I was set by her bedside to watch her while she slept. The grapes looked so luscious and tempting that I put one into my mouth, and then another. Before I knew what I was doing, I had eaten up every grape that was on the plate. Soon after, my mother opened her eyes, and looked wistfully toward the table. She then turned to me and said, "Johnny, did you eat up my grapes?" I said, "No, mother, I didn't touch 'em." Oh! how that lie burned in my throat! The next day, my mother died. Boy as I was, I would have given the world to have had her forgive me before she was carried to the tomb. Thirty years passed away after I had eaten my mother's grapes. I left California for New-York. The steamer was wrecked. It was thought at one time that every body on board would perish. At night, as the vessel was thumping herself on the rocks, the waves dashing around us, the water up to my middle, I got into an upper berth for a little sleep. As I lay there, I heard my mother's voice as distinctly as I heard it thirty years before, when I was a little boy. It said to me, "Johnny, did you eat my grapes?" I was stricken with terror. I prayed as I never prayed before. The Lord heard my prayer, and in the very jaws of death he pardoned my sins, and gave me the assurance that even that great wrong against my poor mother was pardoned.

LIII.

GRACE OF GOD

WHO hath saved us, and called *us* with a holy calling, not according to our works, but according to his own purpose and grace, which was given us in Christ Jesus before the world began; but is now made manifest by the appearing of our Saviour Jesus Christ, who hath abolished death, and hath brought life and immortality to light through the gospel: For the grace of God that bringeth salvation hath appeared to all men, teaching us that, denying ungodliness and worldly lusts, we should live soberly, righteously, and godly, in this present world; looking for that blessed hope, and the glorious appearing of the great God and our Saviour Jesus Christ; who gave himself for us, that he might redeem us from all iniquity, and purify unto himself a peculiar people, zealous of good works. These things speak, and exhort, and rebuke with all authority. Let no man despise thee.

BELOVED PHYSICIAN.

THERE was a poor man, blind from his birth. He had never seen the sun, the flowers, nor the face of kindred. He found a martyr woman, who was willing to walk with him through life. Children were born to him. He knew their tones, and could call them by name, though he had never seen their faces. He was brought one day into the presence of a celebrated physician. After an examination, he said to the blind man, "If you could endure an operation, I think I could give you sight; but at your time of life, it would be hazardous." "Oh!" said the sufferer, "I will submit to any thing, I will endure any thing, if I can only see." He submitted to the operation, and it was successful. Day by day, a little light was admitted, till at length the bandages were removed, till he who had been blind from his birth was permitted to look on the beauties of nature. What a ravishing sight opened before him! It seemed that he would never tire looking on the face of his faithful wife. As his children came before him, one by one, he made them speak, that he might know that he was not deceived. He looked on the flowers, and was glad; on the sun, and he was astonished; but he turned away from all, saying, "Bring me the kind doctor who has opened this great and glorious world to me; I love him better than all the rest." Such is the love of a pardoned sinner for his Saviour. "We love him because he first loved us." Ye are not your own. Ye are bought with the precious blood of Christ. Ye are not redeemed by corruptible things, such as silver and gold.

LIV.

DILIGENCE.

AND besides this, giving all diligence, add to your faith virtue; and to virtue, knowledge; and to knowledge, temperance; and to temperance, patience; and to patience, godliness; and to godliness, brotherly kindness; and to brotherly kindness, charity. For if these things be in you, and abound, they make *you that ye shall* neither *be* barren nor unfruitful in the knowledge of our Lord Jesus Christ. Beloved, when I gave all diligence to write unto you of the common salvation, it was needful for me to write unto you, and exhort *you* that ye should earnestly contend for the faith which was once delivered unto the saints. And thou shalt teach them diligently unto thy children, and shalt talk of them when thou sittest in thine house, and when thou walkest by the way, and when thou liest down, and when thou risest up. And thou shalt bind them for a sign upon thine hand, and they shall be as frontlets between thine eyes. I went by the field of the slothful, and by the vineyard of the man void of understanding.

THIRSTING FOR SALVATION.

A WEALTHY merchant had an only son to whom he was tenderly attached. He spared no expense with his education; he sent him to foreign lands, and at home denied him no gratification. To the sorrow of his father, he became despondent, and a deep melancholy settled upon him. Physicians were called in, who prescribed amusements, entertainments, recreation, and pastimes. All this did no good; young associates surrounded him; he was taken to the theatre, to balls, parties, and soirées. Nothing relieved him; like the woman in the gospel, he seemed no better, but rather worse. The physician thought a sea-voyage might do him good. A yacht was fitted out to scud along the coast. On the land and on the water, the settled melancholy weighed him down. The yacht ran into a harbor on Cape Cod; the young man stepped ashore, listless, indifferent, careless about where he was or where he was going. The shades of evening fell upon him. He saw a light in the distance, and walked on toward it. As he approached the building, he heard the voice of song. The house was a carpenter's shop, fitted up for worship with a rude altar and ruder benches. It was a season of revival, and a few earnest Christians had assembled for prayer and praise. Exhortation followed prayer, and praise followed exhortation. As one after another spoke of the love of the Saviour and the joy of religion, the despondent individual arose. "This that you've been talking about is what I want. Will your Saviour accept me? Are there any blessings left for one as wretched as I am?" Christians gave the poor seeker a hearty welcome; led him to the altar and prayed with him. That night, he found peace in believing. With an elastic step, he went on board his yacht, and turned its prow homeward. He entered his home, and informed his astonished household what great things the Lord had done for him, and what great peace he had imparted. He entered a theological seminary, fitted himself for the ministry, and went out to tell a dying world what peace and joy there were in religion.

LV.

SAVING FAITH.

BUT without faith *it is* impossible to please *him:* for he that cometh to God must believe that he is, and *that* he is a rewarder of them that diligently seek him. And truly, if they had been mindful of that *country* from whence they came out, they might have had opportunity to have returned. But now they desire a better *country*, that is, a heavenly: wherefore God is not ashamed to be called their God: for he hath prepared for them a city. Therefore being justified by faith, we have peace with God through our Lord Jesus Christ: by whom also we have access by faith into this grace wherein we stand, and rejoice in hope of the glory of God. And these all, having obtained a good report through faith, received not the promise: God having provided some better thing for us, that they without us should not be made perfect.

FOUND AFTER MANY DAYS.

A COACH-LOAD of passengers was driven over Hackensack bridge. Said one of the passengers, "This is a very interesting place to me. Sixteen years ago, I rode over this bridge as we are riding to-day. We had got nearly across, when the bridge broke down. Providentially, none of the passengers were hurt or drowned. It was pitch-dark, and we were all groping our way to the shore. All at once, one of the women set up a loud wailing, crying out, 'Oh! my child, my child is gone!' The little one had slipped from her arms, and the current had carried it down-stream. I started in pursuit; I could see nothing distinctly; I thought I saw a little glimmering of white in the distance. I pursued, and found the little girl fastened to a bush by its clothes. It had been buoyed up and floated down, and was caught in the branches of a small tree. All unhurt, I bore the little thing to its mother's arms, who overwhelmed me with thanks. All at once, the company were astonished by an outcry from a woman sitting on the back-seat of the coach. 'O sir!' said she, 'I am that little girl that you saved; my mother has prayed for you every night since I was rescued. Oh! how she longed to see you before she died! She charged me, if I ever heard of you or knew where you were, to tell you how precious your memory was to her.'" This was indeed fruit after many days.

LVI.

RELATION OF MASTERS.

MASTERS, give unto *your* servants that which is just and equal; knowing that ye also have a Master in heaven. Servants, obey in all things *your* masters according to the flesh; not with eyeservice, as menpleasers; but in singleness of heart, fearing God. No servant can serve two masters: for either he will hate the one, and love the other; or else he will hold to the one and despise the other. Ye can not serve God and Mammon. Ye call me Master and Lord: and ye say well; for *so* I am. If I then, *your* Lord and Master, have washed your feet; ye also ought to wash one another's feet. For I have given you an example, that ye should do as I have done to you. Verily, verily, I say unto you, The servant is not greater than his lord; neither he that is sent greater than he that sent him. *Exhort* servants to be obedient unto their own masters, *and* to please *them* well in all things; not answering again; not purloining, but showing all good fidelity; that they may adorn the doctrine of God our Saviour in all things.

"I'LL MAKE A MAN OF YOU."

Two merchants were talking together in relation to their clerks. One of them, not a Christian, said, "I am going to dismiss my clerk." "What's the matter with him?" "Well, he's smart, prompt, and, for aught that I know, reliable, yet I'm afraid of him. He was sick the other day, and I called upon him. His room was handsomely furnished and adorned with books and pictures. He lives in too good a style for the money I pay him." The other man was a Christian and a Sunday-school superintendent. He said, "Let me give you a little bit of my own experience. You know I do a snug banking business. At the time I refer to, I had but one clerk, and I had to trust him fully. He was an energetic, driving young fellow, and, on the whole, I was satisfied with him. Yet there were some things that were not right. I missed small sums of money from time to time. I disliked to charge the loss on my clerk, and yet I felt satisfied that he was the pilferer. At the close of a day's business, I called him into my private room, and after closing the door, I told him that I wanted to talk with him on an important personal matter. It was so important that I thought it but proper, before we entered upon it, that we should kneel down and ask God's blessing upon the interview. I then took down my private memorandum-book, and showed him how I did my business, and how impossible it was for a penny to be abstracted from my funds without my knowing it. I then showed him the sums that I had missed for ten days. They were little paltry sums, but the exactness with which I marked the deficiency overwhelmed him with confusion and astonishment. He flung himself on the floor, crying out, 'I am ruined, I am ruined! Don't disgrace me; don't tell my mother. Let me go, and I will pay it all up if I work my fingers up to my joints.' I said to him, 'Get up. Take a seat. I shan't disgrace you, and I shan't dismiss you. I mean to keep you and make a man of you. There are two paths before you: one leads to honor, one leads to ruin. You must decide to-day which you will accept.' The young man took his resolution. He is now a banker, of position and wealth, in the city of New-York." The forbearance, consideration, and Christian charity of his employer, by the grace of God, saved him.

LVII.

TOWARD THEM THAT ARE WITHOUT.

AND that ye study to be quiet, and to do your own business, and to work with your own hands, as we commanded you; that ye may walk honestly toward them that are without, and *that* ye may have lack of nothing. Take heed unto thyself, and unto the doctrine; continue in them: for in doing this thou shalt both save thyself, and them that hear thee. But now I have written unto you not to keep company, if any man that is called a brother be a fornicator, or covetous, or an idolater, or a railer, or a drunkard, or an extortioner; with such a one no not to eat. For what have I to do to judge them also that are without? do not ye judge them that are within? But them that are without God judgeth. Therefore put away from among yourselves that wicked person. But sanctify the Lord God in your hearts: and *be* ready always to *give* an answer to every man that asketh you a reason of the hope that is in you, with meekness and fear.

"SIR, I AM A CHRISTIAN."

There was a gay company at Long Branch, and pleasure held high revel in the saloons and drawing-rooms of the hotels. Among the company was a young lady, who attracted a great deal of attention. She was rich, beautiful, and fascinating. In a very quiet and undemonstrative way, she was a Christian, and spent time and money in doing good in her Master's name. It was proposed to have a masked ball, and a well-known member of Congress was detailed to invite the young lady to become one of the managers. She was found in the parlors, and the subject opened. The young lady not only declined the position of manager, but also declined to attend the ball. The persuasive politician plied all his arts to induce his fair friend to change her purpose. He praised her beauty and talent; reminded her of her great popularity, and the keen disappointment that would be felt at her absence. She simply replied, "It will be impossible for me to gratify my friends." "Would you be kind enough to give me your reason for refusal?" said the gentleman. "Certainly, sir; I am a Christian, and I can't attend without violating what I consider my religious obligations." The gentleman, evidently astonished, said, "I have heard before of religious principle, but I never saw it exemplified till now. From this hour, I shall have a higher respect for Christian character."

LVIII.

IN NO WISE CAST OUT.

AND Jesus said unto them, I am the bread of life: he that cometh to me shall never hunger; and he that believeth on me shall never thirst. But I said unto you, That ye also have seen me, and believe not. All that the Father giveth me shall come to me; and him that cometh to me I will in no wise cast out. Wherefore in all things it behooved him to be made like unto *his* brethren, that he might be a merciful and faithful high priest in things *pertaining* to God, to make reconciliation for the sins of the people. Seeing then that we have a great high priest, that is passed into the heavens, Jesus the Son of God, let us hold fast *our* profession. For we have not a high priest which can not be touched with the feeling of our infirmities; but was in all points tempted like as *we are, yet* without sin. Let us therefore come boldly unto the throne of grace, that we may obtain mercy, and find grace to help in time of need.

SAVE TO THE UTTERMOST.

I CAME home one night late, very tired, and had gone to bed to seek needed rest. The friend with whom I boarded awoke me out of my first refreshing sleep, and informed me that a little girl wanted to see me. I turned impatiently over in my bed, and said, 'I am very tired; tell her to come in the morning, and I will see her.' My friend soon returned, and said, 'I think you had better get up. The girl is a poor little suffering thing. She is thinly clad, is without bonnet or shoes. She has seated herself on the door-step, and says she must see you, and will wait till you get up.' I dressed myself, and opening the outside door, I saw one of the most forlorn-looking little girls I ever beheld. Want, sorrow, suffering, neglect seemed to struggle for the mastery. She looked up to my face, and said, 'Be you the man that preached last night, and said that Christ could save to the uttermost?' 'Yes.' 'Well, I was there, and I want you to come right down to my house, and try to save my poor father.' 'What's the matter with your father?' 'He's a very good father when he don't drink. He's out of work, and he drinks awfully. He's almost killed my poor mother; but if Jesus can save to the uttermost, he can save him. And I want you to come right to our house now.' I took my hat and followed my little guide, who trotted on before, halting as she turned the corners to see that I was coming. Oh! what a miserable den her home was! A low, dark, underground room, the floor all slush and mud—not a chair, table, or bed to be seen. A bitter cold night, and not a spark of fire on the hob; and the room not only cold, but dark. In the corner, on a little dirty straw, lay a woman. Her head was bound up, and she was moaning, as if in agony. As we darkened the door-way, a feeble voice said, 'O my child, my child! why have you brought a stranger into his horrible place?' Her story was a sad one, but soon told. Her husband, out of work, maddened with drink, and made desperate, had stabbed her because she did not provide him with a supper that was not in the house. He was then up-stairs, and she was expecting every moment that he would come down and complete the bloody work he had

(CONTINUED ON PAGE 118.)

LIX.

PUT ON THE NEW MAN.

LIE not one to another, seeing that ye have put off the old man with his deeds; and have put on the new *man*, which is renewed in knowledge after the image of him that created him: for our gospel came not unto you in word only, but also in power, and in the Holy Ghost, and in much assurance; as ye know what manner of men we were among you for your sake. But after that the kindness and love of God our Saviour toward man appeared, not by works of righteousness which we have done, but according to his mercy he saved us, by the washing of regeneration, and renewing of the Holy Ghost; which he shed on us abundantly through Jesus Christ our Saviour; that being justified by his grace, we should be made heirs according to the hope of eternal life.

begun. While the conversation was going on, the fiend made his appearance. A fiend he looked. He brandished the knife, still wet with the blood of his wife.

The missionary, like the man among the tombs, had himself belonged to the desperate classes. He was converted at the mouth of a coal-pit. He knew the disease and the remedy; knew how to handle a man on the borders of delirium tremens.

Subdued by the tender tones, the madman calmed down and took a seat on a box. But the talk was interrupted by the little girl, who approached the missionary, and said,

"Don't talk to father; it won't do any good. If talking would have saved him, he would have been saved long ago. Mother has talked to him so much, and so good. You must ask Jesus, who saves to the uttermost, to save my poor father."

Rebuked by the faith of the little girl, the missionary and the miserable sinner knelt down together. He prayed as he never prayed before; he entreated and interceded in tones so tender and fervent that it melted the desperate man, who cried for mercy. And mercy came. He bowed in penitence before the Lord, and lay down to sleep that night on his pallet of straw a pardoned soul.

Relief came to that dwelling. The wife was lifted from her dirty couch, and her home was made comfortable. On Sunday, the reformed man took the hand of his little girl, and entered the infant-class, to learn something about the Saviour who "saves to the uttermost." He entered upon a new life; his reform was thorough. He found good employment, for, when sober, he was an excellent workman; and, next to his Saviour, he blesses God for the faith of his little girl who believed in a Saviour who was able to save to the uttermost all that come unto God by him.

LX.

UNSELFISHNESS.

WE then that are strong ought to bear the infirmities of the weak, and not to please ourselves. Let every one of us please *his* neighbor for *his* good to edification. For even Christ pleased not himself; but, as it is written, The reproaches of them that reproached thee fell on me. Neither was there any among them that lacked: for as many as were possessors of lands or houses sold them, and brought the prices of the things that were sold. Charge them that are rich in this world, that they be not high-minded, nor trust in uncertain riches, but in the living God, who giveth us richly all things to enjoy; that they do good, that they be rich in good works, ready to distribute, willing to communicate; laying up in store for themselves a good foundation against the time to come, that they may lay hold on eternal life. For it is easier for a camel to go through a needle's eye, than for a rich man to enter into the kingdom of God.

LESSON APPLIED.

A SPELLING-BEE is an institution well known in some parts of our country. Once or twice a season, the whole school come together to spell. It is a trial of skill between the scholars. The time selected is usually a moonlight evening, when the sleighing is good. Parents and children, friends and neighbors, old and young, crowd the school-room. Words are given out, and all spell who choose. The exercise narrows down usually to two or three. Then the excitement is general.

The school came together in one of the districts to spell. The prize was an elegantly-bound Bible that lay on the master's desk. The girls said it was no use to try, for one of two scholars would be sure to win. The two girls referred to were the brightest children in the school. One was a rich man's daughter, and her name was Susie. The other was the child of a poor widow, who went out washing. Her mother was very, very poor. But her little girl Lizzie was so sweet-tempered, so gentle, so thankful for any thing done for her, that she won the hearts of all the school. There wasn't a scholar that didn't hope that Lizzie would win. So she did.

The meeting broke up. Susie was put into the sleigh, tucked up with buffaloes, and rode home between her father and mother. Not a word was spoken for some time.

"Susie, couldn't you have spelt that word?"

"Yes, ma."

"Well, why didn't you do it?"

"Lizzie, you know, is a poor little girl, and she hasn't many presents. She wanted the Bible dreadfully, and she tried so hard for it, that I thought I'd let her have it."

"What made you do that, Susie?"

"You know my Sunday-school lesson, mother? That said, 'In honor, preferring one another.' So I thought I'd try it. I'm glad I did."

A few days afterward was Susie's birthday. As she awoke in the morning, she found an elegant Bible on her table, with the golden text on the fly-leaf, "In honor, preferring one another."

LXI.

PRESENT HELP IN TROUBLE.

O THE hope of Israel, the Saviour thereof in time of trouble, why shouldest thou be as a stranger in the land, and as a wayfaring man *that* turneth aside to tarry for a night? Why shouldest thou be as a man astonished, as a mighty man *that* can not save? yet thou, O Lord, *art* in the midst of us, and we are called by thy name; leave us not. I will lift up mine eyes unto the hills, from whence cometh my help. My help *cometh* from the Lord, which made heaven and earth. He will not suffer thy foot to be moved: he that keepeth thee will not slumber. Behold, he that keepeth Israel shall neither slumber nor sleep. The Lord knoweth how to deliver the godly out of temptation, and to reserve the unjust unto the day of judgment to be punished. They that trust in the Lord *shall be* as Mount Zion, *which* can not be removed, *but* abideth forever.

THE WIDOW'S GOD.

A LABORING man agreed to pay in installments for the little house and garden where he lived. He spent his leisure in planting trees and cultivating his garden. One hundred pounds was the price of the property. He was to pay ten pounds a year, with interest. Year after year, he met his obligation, and when he died, there were but ten pounds due on the cottage. By hard toil and much saving, the poor widow scraped together ten pounds, and was rejoicing in the prospect of a comfortable shelter for herself and child during the rest of her life. The man who owned the mortgage had died, as well as her husband; but great was her astonishment and grief, when she visited the attorney to pay off the remaining encumbrance on the cottage, to find a bill presented for one hundred pounds, instead of ten.

"You must pay the money, or produce the receipts, or I shall sell your property under the hammer."

The poor widow searched her cottage from top to bottom, and emptied drawers and closets to find receipts; but all in vain. The prospect of being turned out of her little house stared her in the face. Her little boy said to her,

"Mother, don't you think Jesus would help us in our trouble if we should pray to him?"

"He is our only help in this our time of distress. Let us kneel down and pray."

The little boy offered a sweet prayer to the Saviour, begging him to interpose to keep his poor mother from being turned out of her home. As he arose from his knees, the lad saw a large fire-fly coming in at the window. Boy-like, he started for it. He chased the fly round and round the room, till at length the brilliant little creature made a dive under a chest of drawers. The little boy tried to reach him, but could not.

"O mother!" he said, "just pull the drawers out a little bit, and I'll catch him!"

As the drawers moved, something fell on the floor. It was her husband's lost receipt-book. The attorney was so astonished when she produced it, and heard the story, that he refused to receive the remaining ten pounds, but gave her a receipt in full.

That night, as the widow sat with her little son by the cosy fire, she told him how easy it was for the Saviour to answer prayer by little things. The fire-fly, conducting Freddy to the lost receipt-book, was as good as if an angel had been sent from heaven.

LXII.

RELATION OF SERVANTS.

SERVANTS, be obedient to them that are *your* masters according to the flesh, with fear and trembling, in singleness of your heart, as unto Christ; let every man abide in the same calling wherein he was called. Art thou called *being* a servant? care not for it: but if thou mayest be made free, use *it* rather. For he that is called in the Lord *being* a servant, is the Lord's freeman: likewise also he that is called, *being* free, is Christ's servant. Ye are bought with a price; be not ye the servants of men. For *the kingdom of heaven is* as a man traveling into a far country, *who* called his own servants, and delivered unto them his goods. And unto one he gave five talents, to another two, and to another one; to every man according to his several ability; and straightway took his journey.

UNDER THE DOOR-MAT.

MR. SPURGEON says that one of the most satisfactory experiences that he ever heard in his church was from a poor servant-girl, who was very ignorant about every thing but the fact that she loved the Saviour. She hardly knew the difference between one denomination and another. As to doctrines, she knew nothing, except that she was a sinner, and that Christ came into the world to save such.

"Why do you think you are a Christian?" said the pastor.

"Because, sir, because I now always sweeps under the door-mat!"

Her mistress gave her strict orders every morning to remove the door-mat and sweep under it. This duty she often neglected. But after she became a Christian, she was faithful in little things.

A POOR German girl renounced her faith in Romanism, and became a Christian. Great efforts were made to turn her back to the faith of her fathers. Learned priests talked to her about councils, sinners, and the fathers. This perplexed but did not shake her. "I know but little about the fathers or the grandfathers," she said; "for they are dead: but I know the word of the Lord, and that liveth and abideth forever."

A MERCHANT, himself not a Christian, returned from Europe. His attention was drawn toward one of the clerks who seemed greatly changed. He spoke of the change to one of his partners. "I don't understand," he said, "what has come over George. He don't seem like the same person he did before I went away. He was always smart, but now he seems to be, somehow, tender, respectful, genial. I think I should love him if I had much to do with him." "I suppose you know what has happened to him, since you've been gone?" "I don't know what you refer to." "Why, George has become a Christian, and is quite an active Sunday-school worker." The merchant gave a long, loud whistle, saying, "Oh! that's it, is it?' as he turned away.

LXIII.

BIRDS OF THE AIR.

BEHOLD the fowls of the air: for they sow not, neither do they reap, nor gather into barns; yet your heavenly Father feedeth them. Are ye not much better than they? For every kind of beasts, and of birds, and of serpents, and of things in the sea, is tamed, and hath been tamed of mankind: yea, the sparrow hath found a house, and the swallow a nest for herself, where she may lay her young, *even* thine altars, O Lord of hosts, my King, and my God. *Gavest thou* the goodly wings unto the peacocks? or wings and feathers unto the ostrich? which leaveth her eggs in the earth, and warmeth them in the dust, and forgetteth that the foot may crush them, or that the wild beast may break them. She is hardened against her young ones, as though *they were* not hers: her labor is in vain without fear; because God hath deprived her of wisdom, neither hath he imparted to her understanding.

THE BIRDS OF VENICE.

VENICE is the City of the Sea. Its streets are canals, its omnibuses and street-cars are boats. In the centre of the city is a square. Here the great cathedral of St. Mark stands, beneath which it was said St. Mark was buried. Every day at twelve o'clock, as the great bell of the cathedral booms out the hour of noon, strangers gather to see the pigeons flock into the square. Scarcely a bird is seen during the morning. But with the first stroke of the hour of noon, they begin to gather. They come in pairs, in dozens, and by fifties. Before the hour of noon is fully rung out, crowds of pigeons hover round a particular portion of the plaza. These pigeons never mistake the hour. They never come at ten or eleven, but always at twelve. They come but once a day, but never on Sundays. The story of this daily gathering of pigeons in Venice is very interesting. A hundred years ago nearly, a lady lived in Venice. She was very rich, but she was a widow, and childless. She was very methodical, and walked every day at noon in the grand square of St. Mark's. One bitter, cold morning, she was taking her promenade, with her servant behind her. She saw a few birds that seemed to be cold and hungry. She thought she would feed them. She sent her servant and bought a handful of grain, which she flung to the birds and passed on. The next day, as she entered the square, she was surprised at the flock of birds that surrounded her. Her servant suggested that these were the birds she fed the day before, with their relations. She repeated the kindness of the preceding day. Day by day she fed the birds, and the flock increased to an astonishing size. Every day at noon, except Sundays, she continued to feed the pigeons till she died. She left a handsome sum in her will, by which the pigeons were to be fed every day at the hour of noon, through all time. How these birds of the air know twelve o'clock from eleven; how they know Saturday from Sunday; how they communicate the knowledge of this provision from generation to generation, is a mystery that few are wise enough to solve. They seem to have faith and trust in a large measure, and, like the birds to whom our Saviour alludes, they may teach us lessons of confidence and faith.

LXIV.

BUYING AND SELLING.

AS the nail sticketh fast between the joinings of the stone, so sin sticketh between the buyer and the seller. *It is* naught, *it is* naught, saith the buyer: but when he is gone his way, then he boasteth. I counsel thee to buy of me gold tried in the fire, that thou mayest be rich; and white raiment, that thou mayest be clothed, and *that* the shame of thy nakedness do not appear; and anoint thine eyes with eye-salve, that thou mayest see. Happy *is* the man *that* findeth wisdom, and the man *that* getteth understanding: for the merchandise of it *is* better than the merchandise of silver, and the gain thereof than fine gold. She *is* more precious than rubies: and all the things thou canst desire are not to be compared unto her. Length of days *is* in her right hand: *and* in her left hand riches and honor. Her ways *are* ways of pleasantness, and all her paths *are* peace.

MARKET VALUE OF WORSHIP.

A YOUNG man came to the city to set up business in a small way. He reached New-York on Saturday afternoon, a stranger, in a strange city. At the hour of worship, he went down to the Wall-street church. An elder in that church was one of the wealthiest and most honored merchants in the city. He took it upon himself to seat strangers. He saw a rustic-looking boy evidently not at home in the city, and went up and spoke to him kindly. The lad told his story; said that it was his first Sunday in New-York; that he hoped to get into business. But he said he meant to be true to his Sabbaths and to his religion. The merchant was delighted with the frankness of the boy and his principles, and invited him to take a seat in his pew whenever he came to church. The next morning, he took a letter that he brought with him, and went into the Swamp, to see if he could get a little leather on credit, to begin with. The leather merchent eyed the boy, and said, "Didn't I see you in Robert Lennox's pew in church yesterday?" "I don't know," said the lad. "I went to church yesterday, and a kind gentleman asked me to sit in his pew. I don't know who it was." "Don't know who he was! That man is Robert Lennox, and I'll trust any body with leather that Robert Lennox invites to sit in his pew." That boy's success was guaranteed from that hour.

LXV.

RELATION OF PARENTS.

CHILDREN, obey *your* parents in all things: for this is well-pleasing unto the Lord. Fathers, provoke not your children *to anger*, lest they be discouraged. Furthermore, we have had fathers of our flesh which corrected *us*, and we gave *them* reverence: shall we not much rather be in subjection unto the Father of spirits, and live? For they verily for a few days chastened *us* after their own pleasure; but he for *our* profit, that *we* might be partakers of his holiness. I write unto you, fathers, because ye have known him *that is* from the beginning. I write unto you, young men, because ye have overcome the wicked one. I write unto you, little children, because ye have known the Father. This know also, that in the last days perilous times shall come. For men shall be lovers of their own selves, covetous, boasters, proud, blasphemers, disobedient to parents, unthankful, unholy, without natural affection, trucebreakers, false accusers, incontinent, fierce, despisers of those that are good.

MOTHER'S EXPERIENCE.

A LADY had the training of four boys; she was a decided Christian, but her husband was not. He was not only not a lover of the Lord, but a man fond of arguing against the Bible and against experimental religion. His choicest invective and sarcasm were reserved for prayer. He took every opportunity to express his sentiments at the table, on the Lord's day, by the way, and when he rose up and when he laid down. His infidel talk had no effect upon his boys; they were regular in their attendance at church, belonged to the Sunday-school, and early professed religion. Her neighbors and friends were curious to know how she guarded her boys, and preserved them from the evil principles of their father. In answer to some inquiry, the lady said, "I have never argued on the subject of religion or the Bible with my husband. I never reply to his taunts, or seem moved by his untimely jests. I have never prejudiced my children against their father, or cautioned them against imbibing his sentiments. I have relied solely on the Word of the Lord and prayer. When my husband has said his bitterest things against the Bible, I have taken my children alone to my chamber, and said to them, as I took down the Bible, 'This is the Word of God,' and I have read to them a few precious passages from its sacred pages. Morning and evening, I have knelt with them at the throne of grace. I have put the Word of God over against infidelity, and prayer over against impiety. I have left these to do their work, and what the result is you can see."

LXVI.

KINDNESS.

BE kindly affectioned one to another with brotherly love; in honor preferring one another: distributing to the necessity of saints; given to hospitality. Dearly beloved, avenge not yourselves, but *rather* give place unto wrath: for it is written, Vengeance *is* mine; I will repay, saith the Lord. Therefore if thine enemy hunger, feed him; if he thirst, give him drink: for in so doing thou shalt heap coals of fire on his head. Be not overcome of evil, but overcome evil with good. For the love of Christ constraineth us; because we thus judge, that if one died for all, then were all dead: and *that* he died for all, that they which live should not henceforth live unto themselves, but unto him which died for them, and rose again. If I have withheld the poor from *their* desire, or have caused the eyes of the widow to fail; or have eaten my morsel myself alone, and the fatherless hath not eaten thereof.

HARD-HEARTED MERCHANT.

RELIGION enjoins forbearance, generosity; a willingness to share our success with others. The man who eats his morsel alone is not a pious man, nor can he be a happy man. The servant who, having been forgiven a heavy debt, went out and took his fellow by the throat, who owed him a small debt, was denounced as an ingrate by his lord. These principles of forbearance and brotherly regard are elements of success. A merchant in New-York was distinguished for his severity; he was hard and exacting in all his dealings; if a debtor was unable to pay, or a tradesman failed and came to him to make terms of settlement, and asked the merchant, "How much will you take on your debt?" the answer was, "One hundred cents on the dollar, sir; I can wait." Over his counting-house were the ominous words, printed in large letters, "No compromise." Shrewd men said that he would see trouble before he died; that a man so ungenerous, so hard-hearted, and so severe, would have the bitter cup commended to his own lips. And so it happened; he went down suddenly, and went down with a crash. He did not recover, as many do, but passed away out of sight. "With what measure ye mete, it shall be measured to you again."

LXVII.

PURE RELIGION.

IF any man among you seem to be religious, and bridleth not his tongue, but deceiveth his own heart, this man's religion *is* vain. Pure religion and undefiled before God and the Father is this, To visit the fatherless and widows in their affliction, *and* to keep himself unspotted from the world. Jesus said unto him, If thou canst believe, all things *are* possible to him that believeth. And straightway the father of the child cried out, and said with tears, Lord, I believe; help thou mine unbelief. When Jesus saw that the people came running together, he rebuked the foul spirit, saying unto him, *Thou* dumb and deaf spirit, I charge thee, come out of him, and enter no more into him. The Lord *is* merciful and gracious, slow to anger, and plenteous in mercy. He will not always chide: neither will he keep *his anger* forever.

UNSAFE FOUNDATION.

A CROWDED congregation assembled in a church one Sunday evening. The house had been used for public worship for thirteen years. All at once the floor gave way. Fortunately, there was no cellar under the house, and after being thoroughly frightened, the congregation escaped without damage. On examination, it was found that the house had never been safe; an unfaithful builder had put an imperfect stone under an important column, and the reason the floor had not fallen before was, that the exact pressure needed to make it fall had never been brought to bear upon it. That house was like some persons: they appear sound, and seem true and earnest Christians, but when the pressure comes, they give way.

A builder, in Boston, ran up a block of granite stores. "You may fill them with pig-lead," he said, "and they will stand." The lofts were not really filled with dry goods before the whole concern gave way, carrying beams, rafters, and goods into the cellar. The foundations were insecure, and no exterior strength availed. This truth our Lord has put in a different form: "Some fell upon stony places, where they had not much earth: and forthwith they sprung up, because they had no deepness of earth: and when the sun was up, they were scorched; and because they had no root, they withered away."

LXVIII.

INTEMPERANCE.

BE not among winebibbers; among riotous eaters of flesh: for the drunkard and the glutton shall come to poverty: and drowsiness shall clothe *a man* with rags. And as he reasoned of righteousness, temperance, and judgment to come, Felix trembled, and answered, Go thy way for this time; when I have a convenient season, I will call for thee. And they that are Christ's have crucified the flesh with the affections and lusts. If we live in the Spirit, let us also walk in the Spirit. Let us not be desirous of vain-glory, provoking one another, envying one another. And that, knowing the time, that now *it is* high time to awake out of sleep, for now *is* our salvation nearer than when we believed. The night is far spent, the day is at hand: let us therefore cast off the works of darkness, and let us put on the armor of light. Let us walk honestly, as in the day, not in rioting and drunkenness, not in chambering and wantonness, not in strife and envying: but put ye on the Lord Jesus Christ, and make not provision for the flesh, to *fulfill* the lusts *thereof*.

DRUNKARD'S DOOM.

At a service in one of our neighboring cities, a man present seemed to be greatly affected. He was well known in the town as a dissolute, drunken, indolent, profane fellow, whose house was destitute of all comforts, whose children grew up in ignorance and sin, and who had never been known to attend church or keep the Sabbath. As the meeting was closing, he arose and asked if he might sign the temperance pledge.

There was no pledge present, but one was extemporized for him. He signed the pledge, and seemed relieved. "What brought you here?" said the pastor. "I was afraid of the drunkard's doom." "What do you know about the drunkard's doom? Has any one been talking to you?" "No." "Have you been to church?" "Not once in twenty years! I was not always what you see me. I had a happy childhood and a bright future before I wandered off into the dark ways of sin and folly. One of the lessons of my childhood was the text, 'No drunkard shall inherit the kingdom of God.' It has followed me more than you would have supposed. I have heard it in the night watches, and above the revel of a drunken bout. It seemed to burn on the walls of dissipation in letters of light. I have resolved to fling off this thraldom and escape the doom. Will you give me a helping hand?" Needed assistance was given, the man was placed on his feet, and he is now a good citizen and a consistent Christian. When the Saviour entered his dwelling, he brought with him, as he always does, a train of temporal, as well as spiritual blessings.

LXIX.

REPENTANCE.

SEEK ye the Lord while he may be found, call ye upon him while he is near: let the wicked forsake his way, and the unrighteous man his thoughts: and let him return unto the Lord, and he will have mercy upon him; and to our God, for he will abundantly pardon. And the times of this ignorance God winked at; but now commandeth all men everywhere to repent: because he hath appointed a day, in the which he will judge the world in righteousness by *that* man whom he hath ordained; *whereof* he hath given assurance unto all *men*, in that he hath raised him from the dead. Suppose ye that these Galileans were sinners above all the Galileans, because they suffered such things? I tell you, Nay: but, except ye repent, ye shall all likewise perish. Or those eighteen, upon whom the tower in Siloam fell, and slew them, think ye that they were sinners above all men that dwelt in Jerusalem? I tell you, Nay: but, except ye repent, ye shall all likewise perish.

PRAYER AND THE PLEDGE.

A YOUNG lawyer of great promise was addicted to his cups. All attempts to reform him proved in vain. He signed the pledge, over and over again, and broke it. In one of his seasons of sobriety, he got married. But he relapsed, and dragged his young wife down to dishonor and want. He kept descending, lower and lower, till he was literally taken out of the gutter and borne to his wretched home. One evening, he was persuaded to go to a prayer-meeting. His unwonted presence created a great deal of interest, and he was remembered in several very fervent prayers. A change seemed to come over him. He trembled from head to foot. He rose slowly, went to the altar, and kneeling down, grasped the rail, while his sobs and cries rent all hearts. He arose a ransomed man. The chains and thraldom of the cup he flung from him. He lifted his hand to heaven, and said, "Brethren, I am a free man. The Son hath set me free." And so it proved. He entered at once into a large practice. He is now one of the most successful and eminent lawyers in the State. The prayer of faith saved him. "This kind goeth out only by fasting and prayer."

LXX.

GLORY OF THE GOSPEL.

O ZION, that bringest good tidings, get thee up into the high mountain; O Jerusalem, that bringest good tidings, lift up thy voice with strength; lift *it* up, be not afraid; say unto the cities of Judah, Behold your God! And it shall come to pass in the last days, *that* the mountain of the Lord's house shall be established in the top of the mountains, and shall be exalted above the hills; and all nations shall flow unto it. And many people shall go and say, Come ye, and let us go up to the mountain of the Lord, to the house of the God of Jacob; and he will teach us of his ways, and we will walk in his paths: for out of Zion shall go forth the law, and the word of the Lord from Jerusalem. And he shall judge among the nations, and shall rebuke many people: and they shall beat their swords into ploughshares, and their spears into pruninghooks: nation shall not lift up sword against nation, neither shall they learn war any more.

MAIDEN OF ISRAEL.

"I AM a man on whom the hand of the Lord has been laid very heavily. My wife, one of the most beautiful and lovely of her sex, was removed suddenly, and myself and only child, a daughter, 'would not be comforted, because she was not.' Consumption laid its fatal hand on my darling child. One morning, as I held her fragile hand in mine, I said to her, 'O my child! is there any thing I can do for you? Is there any request that I can meet?' She looked me calmly and steadily in the face, and said, 'O my dear father! there is one request I have to offer.' 'Name it, my child, and it shall be granted, if it takes every thing I possess.' 'Then, O my dear father! promise me that you will not speak any more against Jesus of Nazareth. I don't know much about him; the book that speaks of him is a sealed book in this house; but I think he has visited me in my sickness, and has shown mercy to me, a poor sinner. I shall trust him as I go "through the dark valley and the shadow of death." I want you to love him, and join me in that better land.' I was overwhelmed with sadness. I could deny my dear child nothing, and I said, 'My child, I never will reproach the name of Jesus again, seeing you love him. I will read the book that speaks of him, and see if I can accept him as the Messiah.' A sweet smile of joy and submission covered her face, and she passed away to join the angels. And now, sir, I have come to ask you something about that wondrous Personage for whom millions will die to-day." He was a wise counselor who had the instruction of that erring one. The Jew and the Christian knelt together at that mercy-seat over which the Son of God presides. Before the interview closed, the Holy Spirit did its work. The Jew breathed his first prayer to the Father of Spirits, through Christ the Son. In his affliction, he knew the words of Christ to be true, "I will not leave you comfortless." A pardoned sinner, like the publican, he went down from that house justified.

LXXI.

DEATH OF CHILDREN.

IN Rama was there a voice heard, lamentation, and weeping, and great mourning, Rachel weeping *for* her children, and would not be comforted, because they are not. And when the child was grown, it fell on a day, that he went out to his father to the reapers. And he said unto his father, My head, my head! And he said to a lad, Carry him to his mother. And when he had taken him, and brought him to his mother, he sat on her knees till noon, and *then* died. And she went up, and laid him on the bed of the man of God, and shut *the door* upon him, and went out. So she went and came unto the man of God to Mount Carmel. And it came to pass, when the man of God saw her afar off, that he said to Gehazi his servant, Behold, *yonder is* that Shunammite: run now, I pray thee, to meet her, and say unto her, *Is it* well with thee? *is it* well with thy husband? *is it* well with the child? And she answered, *It is* well. And it came to pass on the seventh day, that the child died. And the servants of David feared to tell him that the child was dead: for they said, Behold, while the child was yet alive, we spake unto him, and he would not hearken unto our voice: how will he then vex himself, if we tell him that the child is dead?

LITTLE CHILD SHALL LEAD THEM.

A CLERGYMAN was settled over a large and influential church. He was a man of commanding talents, but was distinguished for his intellectual strength, rather than for his susceptibility. He was not sympathetic or tender. He had no magnetism, yet his grip on the intellect was strong. He hardly knew what sickness was. Death had never come into his family. Though he was kind, and meant to console the sick and afflicted, he lacked the gush and heart that only experience can give. He seemed out of place at a sick-bed, and at a funeral he appeared awkward, embarrassed, and almost indifferent. The Lord had a discipline in store for him. He put him in the furnace of affliction, and tried him "as by fire." He loved his youngest child, a bright, beautiful boy, as he had never loved any thing else. He would turn aside from his books for his prattle, and the study-door, barred against all visitors at certain hours of the day, was always opened at the tap of the child. A scourge came into his household. Every member but the pastor was sick. The mother was helpless, and assistance was sought in vain. The darling boy sickened at the last, sickened with a noisome disease. The father was his nurse. He attended him night and day, and, like David, he prayed God earnestly that the child might be spared. He would have borne the disease, taken the pain, and even died for his darling boy. But no human aid could avail. The little boy died in convulsions, and died in the arms of his father.

The pastor came out of that furnace a changed man. He had seen affliction, and it melted him. He was tender, considerate, and tearful. He was especially a comforter at funerals. The death of a child unmanned him. He was a constant visitor to the homes of the lowly, and took a special interest in sick and poor children. Like his exalted Master, he seemed to be "made perfect through suffering."

LXXII.

GOOD HOPE IN DEATH.

BLESSED *be* the God and Father of our Lord Jesus Christ, which according to his abundant mercy hath begotten us again unto a lively hope by the resurrection of Jesus Christ from the dead. To an inheritance incorruptible, and undefiled, and that fadeth not away, reserved in heaven for you. Which *hope* we have as an anchor of the soul, both sure and steadfast, and which entereth into that within the vail; whither the forerunner is for us entered, *even* Jesus, made a high priest forever after the order of Melchisedec. Behold, what manner of love the Father hath bestowed upon us, that we should be called the sons of God: therefore the world knoweth us not, because it knew him not. Beloved, now are we the sons of God, and it doth not yet appear what we shall be: but we know that, when he shall appear, we shall be like him; for we shall see him as he is. And every man that hath this hope in him purifieth himself, even as he is pure.

ELEVENTH HOUR.

One of the bravest heroes of the Revolutionary War professed to be an infidel. He wrote a book against the Christian religion. His wife was a Christian, and he had an only daughter, who was as dear to him as the apple of his eye. His wife died, and a year after, the daughter was brought to the gates of death. She was a delicate, frail, ethereal person, and the father, gruff, strong, and robust; yet the two blended like the oak and the ivy—the ivy gathering strength from the gnarled and knotty limbs, and the rugged oak receiving grace and beauty from the vine. One day, as the father sat by the bedside, holding the frail hand of his daughter in his, the daughter said, "Father, I'm going to die. The doctor was here today, and I asked him to tell me plainly what my condition was. It is a great thing, I said, to exchange worlds, and if I must die, I wanted time to prepare for my great change. He said to me, 'My child, human skill will not avail you. A few more suns will rise and set, and then they will carry you out and place you beside your mother.' It is a solemn thing to die, father, and I want to ask you one question. You and mother did not agree on the subject of religion. Mother used to talk to me about the Saviour that died for sinners. Every night when she put me to bed, she knelt down and prayed that dear Saviour to bless you and me. Before she died, she told me she was going home to her Saviour, and bade me trust him and join her in that bright mansion he had promised those who love him. And now I am going to take the leap in the dark all alone; and tell me, father, shall I take your faith, or shall I trust my mother's Saviour?" There was an honest heart beneath that rough exterior. He spoke through his tears, saying, "My child, cling to your mother's Saviour, and I'll try to join you in that better land."

LXXIII.

ACCIDENTAL SALVATION.

AND *Jesus* entered and passed through Jericho. And, behold, *there was* a man named Zaccheus, which was the chief among the publicans, and he was rich. And when Jesus came to the place, he looked up, and saw him, and said unto him, Zaccheus, make haste, and come down; for to-day I must abide at thy house. And he made haste, and came down, and received him joyfully. And they came to Jericho: and as he went out of Jericho with his disciples and a great number of people, blind Bartimeus, the son of Timeus, sat by the highway side begging. And when he heard that it was Jesus of Nazareth, he began to cry out, and say, Jesus, *thou* Son of David, have mercy on me. Then the Spirit said unto Philip, Go near, and join thyself to this chariot. And Philip ran thither to *him*, and heard him read the prophet Esaias, and said, Understandest thou what thou readest?

JUDGE'S CONVERSION.

DURING the revival in Kansas, the work spread in every direction. Laboring men left their business, merchants closed their stores, litigation ended, and the courts adjourned, and artisans, merchants, lawyers, and judges were found in the house of prayer. Among the large congregation were numbers who were not serious, but who attended out of curiosity, attracted by a great crowd and vigorous singing. At one of the services, the crowd filled the aisles. Seated in a chair was a well-known judge. A call was made on all who felt a wish for personal religion to rise. The judge kept his seat. Just then, some one touched him on the shoulder and said, "Won't you get up? We want to clear the aisle." He did not wish to appear to be standing for prayer, so he declined. The press was so great, however, that he found his seat slipping from under him. He arose to readjust his seat, when it slipped away from him and he was left standing. As his tall form towered up, he was observed on all sides. He was immediately prayed for. A warm-hearted friend took him by the hand, and talked to him about salvation. A lady friend of the family made her way through the crowd to tell him how often she had prayed for him, and how it rejoiced her heart to see him take so decided a stand. The astonished judge found himself committed to the subject of religion without intending it. "Why not now!" something seemed to say to him. He obeyed the impulse, and that night decided the great question of his personal acceptance of the Saviour. He did not go to the house of prayer that night for conversion. He did not rise to be prayed for. Like Zaccheus, he was in the way as the Saviour passed. Like Bartimeus, he uttered the successful cry as the throng passed.

LXXIV.

PRAISE TO OUR GOD.

THE Lord *is* my light and my salvation; whom shall I fear? the Lord *is* the strength of my life; of whom shall I be afraid? Though a host should encamp against me, my heart shall not fear: though war should rise against me, in this *will* I *be* confident. The Lord *is* my strength and song, and he is become my salvation: he *is* my God, and I will prepare him a habitation; my father's God, and I will exalt him. Thou stretchedst out thy right hand, the earth swallowed them. Thou in thy mercy hast led forth the people *which* thou hast redeemed: thou hast guided *them* in thy strength unto thy holy habitation. Who *is* like unto thee, O Lord, among the gods? who *is* like thee, glorious in holiness, fearful *in* praises, doing wonders?

CONVERSION OF AN ACTRESS.

A STAR actress was drawing crowds in the city. One evening, while on her way to the play-house, she heard the voice of song. She was a fine singer, and fond of music. A full chorus went up from a small tenement, which she paused to hear. She entered the hall-way, and through a door that stood ajar, she saw a crowd of colored people at worship. The company was singing the well-known hymn:

> "Depth of mercy, can there be
> Mercy still reserved for me?"

The singing melted the actress to tears. She turned back, and failed that night to keep her engagement. Under deep conviction, she notified the manager that she must terminate her contract. He insisted that she must keep it; at least she must appear once upon the boards and make an explanation. She consented to do this. Crowds came to listen to their favorite singer. As she came upon the stage, she was greeted with thunders of applause. She sang, however, what was not on the programme; and mid the hushed stillness of the house, she sang the well-known hymn of Wesley, that had so moved her own soul:

> "Depth of mercy, can there be—"

Overwhelmed with emotion, she was carried out, leaving the audience dissolved in tears. She never appeared on the boards again.

LXXV.

TURNING THE CAPTIVITY.

AND the Lord turned the captivity of Job, when he prayed for his friends: also the Lord gave Job twice as much as he had before. When the Lord turned again the captivity of Zion, we were like them that dream. Then was our mouth filled with laughter, and our tongue with singing: then said they among the heathen, The Lord hath done great things for them. The Lord hath done great things for us; *whereof* we are glad. Turn again our captivity, O Lord, as the streams in the south. Therefore I make a decree, That every people, nation, and language, which speak any thing amiss against the God of Shadrach, Meshach, and Abednego, shall be cut in pieces, and their houses shall be made a dunghill; because there is no other God that can deliver after this sort. Then the king promoted Shadrach, Meshach, and Abednego, in the province of Babylon. The Lord knoweth how to deliver the godly out of temptation, and to reserve the unjust unto the day of judgment to be punished.

FROM THE LOWEST DEPTHS.

GOING into the school-room one Sunday morning, a man was found curled up in a corner, dead drunk. Awaking him from his stupor, the superintendent said, "This is no place for you. The children are gathering, and you must leave." The man staggered toward the door. "I ought not to have dismissed the poor fellow so rudely," he said, "and I should have asked him to come at a more proper time." The next morning, he saw the man enter the noon-day prayer-meeting. He was not then sober, but was suffering from his previous debauch. He found him to be a well-educated young Scotchman. He had been connected with the press, but drunkenness had ruined him, and he seemed a perfect wreck. On his knees he signed the pledge. Before the week was out, he fell, and seemed worse than before. In his deep distress, he turned again to Fulton street. Again the pledge was presented to him on his knees, and while fervent prayer was being offered for his deliverance, as the man said, "the love for liquor departed." Soon after, he became a Christian, and united with the Fulton-street Church. One of the benevolent societies gave him employment. He exhibited a great taste for the cultivation of flowers; he built a rude hothouse with his own hands. His taste and success were so manifest, that the directors decided to build him a fine greenhouse. The flowers raised are distributed among the poor, and become ministers to the homes of the lowly, the wretched, and suffering. Those flowers are as much means of grace as are tracts and songs of praise. He is a consistent member of the Church, and an earnest worker in the mission field. Rare plants, choice flowers, and elegant bouquets adorn the altar at Fulton street from time to time—a floral tribute of gratitude, from a rescued soul, to the Fulton-street meeting.

LXXVI.

KINGDOM OF GOD.

FOR the kingdom of God is not meat and drink; but righteousness, and peace, and joy in the Holy Ghost. For he that in these things serveth Christ *is* acceptable to God, and approved of men. Let us therefore follow after the things which make for peace, and things wherewith one may edify another. Know ye not that the unrighteous shall not inherit the kingdom of God? Be not deceived: neither fornicators, nor idolaters, nor adulterers, nor effeminate, nor abusers of themselves with mankind, nor thieves, nor covetous, nor drunkards, nor revilers, nor extortioners, shall inherit the kingdom of God. And such were some of you: but ye are washed, but ye are sanctified, but ye are justified in the name of the Lord Jesus, and by the Spirit of our God. Wherefore we receiving a kingdom which can not be moved, let us have grace, whereby we may serve God acceptably with reverence and godly fear: for our God *is* a consuming fire.

BETTER CHOICE.

A YOUNG man, in good business, was addicted to intemperance. He felt a strange drawing toward the Fulton-street meeting. He came in contact with the missionary, who urged him to sign the pledge. "You must do it on your knees, give your heart to Christ, and he will take away the love of the intoxicating cup." Kneeling in the place of prayer, though all alone with his friend, all at once a change came over him. "My appetite for drink is gone," he said; "I never felt in my life as I do now." "I think you are a converted man," was the reply; "praise the Lord!" So it proved. He united with a Christian church, and became an earnest worker. His business interfered with the mission work, and he resolved to throw up his position, and go out and labor among the lowly. He made a full and entire consecration of himself to the service of God. He is one of the noblest workers in the city, and for over five years he has worked in the mission field; during all that time, he has given clear evidence of a complete consecration to Christ.

LXXVII.

NOT BY MIGHT.

THEN he answered and spake unto me, saying, This *is* the word of the Lord unto Zerubbabel, saying, Not by might, nor by power, but by my Spirit, saith the Lord of hosts. Who *art* thou, O great mountain? before Zerubbabel *thou shalt become* a plain: and he shall bring forth the headstone *thereof with* shoutings, *crying*, Grace, grace unto it. And there shall come forth a rod out of the stem of Jesse, and a Branch shall grow out of his roots: and the Spirit of the Lord shall rest upon him, the spirit of wisdom and understanding, the spirit of counsel and might, the spirit of knowledge and of the fear of the Lord; and shall make him of quick understanding in the fear of the Lord: and he shall not judge after the sight of his eyes, neither reprove after the hearing of his ears: but with righteousness shall he judge the poor, and reprove with equity for the meek of the earth, and he shall smite the earth with the rod of his mouth, and with the breath of his lips shall he slay the wicked. Finally, my brethren, be strong in the Lord, and in the power of his might. Put on the whole armor of God, that ye may be able to stand against the wiles of the devil.

A CATHOLIC SAVED.

In one of the lower wards of the city resided a man who was an earnest Catholic, and very bitter. Being out of work, his wife, who was more bitter toward Protestants than himself, went into the country to live with her friends. Having nothing to do, he read the papers from time to time, to see if he could not find some employment. He saw a notice of the Fulton-street meeting. One day, he drifted toward the church, and stood opposite the entrance. He was astonished to see a multitude of men passing in through the gate and entering the house. Soon he heard the heavy volume of song rolling out. This so interested him that he approached the door and looked in. He remained during the service, feeling that he had never seen the like before. As his time hung on his hands, he spent much of it in the Fulton-street meeting. The singing impressed him; the prayers impressed him; and, in spite of himself, the hour of noon found him crowding in with the worshipers in the old temple. He was soon under deep conviction, and became hopefully converted. He immediately found employment. One of our large institutions put him at its head, where for ten years he has remained, with distinguished fidelity and success. His work among the children has never been exceeded. Scores have been converted through his instrumentality, and hundreds reformed and saved. When his wife came in from the country, she embraced her husband's Saviour, united with the same church, and for years has been matron of the same institution.

LXXVIII.

COME UNTO ME.

COME unto me, all *ye* that labor and are heavy laden, and I will give you rest. Take my yoke upon you, and learn of me: for I am meek and lowly in heart; and ye shall find rest unto your souls. For my yoke *is* easy, and my burden is light. And when she had so said, she went her way, and called Mary her sister secretly, saying, The Master is come, and calleth for thee. Jesus answered and said unto her, If thou knewest the gift of God, and who it is that saith to thee, Give me to drink; thou wouldest have asked of him, and he would have given thee living water. That if thou shalt confess with thy mouth the Lord Jesus, and shalt believe in thine heart that God hath raised him from the dead, thou shalt be saved. For with the heart man believeth unto righteousness; and with the mouth confession is made unto salvation.

A HOLLANDER'S PRAYER.

A FAMILY of Hollanders were reduced to suffering and want. The father was a 'longshoreman. As hundreds of others have done, this family sought temporal relief from the kind-hearted missionary of the church. The father was prostrated by sickness, and had no prospect of ever again earning his bread. Prayers were offered for this poor family—prayers that were often accompanied with alms. Salvation came to that house, and the poor sufferer found the blessed Lord making for him his bed in all his sickness. The great burden of the family was connected with a son. He had enlisted in the war, but nothing had been heard from him since the time he left home. The case was especially made the subject of prayer at the noonday meeting. A letter was written and sent to the West at a venture. It passed from pillar to post for several months. At last it reached a hand that could throw light on the subject. The boy was dead, but a pension was secured, which has been regularly paid to the family, keeping the poor sufferer above want, and leaving him firm in the conviction that his lost boy was found through the agency of the noonday meeting.

LXXIX.

NOT OF BLOOD.

BUT as many as received him, to them gave he power to become the sons of God, *even* to them that believe on his name: which were born, not of blood, nor of the will of the flesh, nor of the will of man, but of God. And the Word was made flesh, and dwelt among us (and we beheld his glory, the glory as of the only begotten of the Father), full of grace and truth. And they sung a new song, saying, Thou art worthy to take the book, and to open the seals thereof: for thou wast slain, and hast redeemed us to God by thy blood out of every kindred, and tongue, and people, and nation; and hast made us unto our God kings and priests: and we shall reign on the earth. Let us draw near with a true heart in full assurance of faith, having our hearts sprinkled from an evil conscience, and our bodies washed with pure water. Let us hold fast the profession of *our* faith without wavering; for he *is* faithful that promised.

SEEKING LIGHT.

A BUSINESS man, doing a successful trade, had three partners. One of them proved to be unfaithful, committed marked frauds, and finally ran away with the capital of the concern. Anxious to retrieve his misfortunes and do business, he purposed to carry on the store alone. He wanted five thousand dollars capital; he made it the subject of earnest, importunate prayer. An entire stranger came to see him the next day; told him that he had watched his business career; he knew what his losses had been. He had five thousand dollars capital which he would put into his hands to trade with. The merchant considered this a direct answer to prayer, and accepted the loan. The business prospered, and the loaned money was returned from the profits of the trade. Then came a disaster which swept every thing away. The merchant had for years been deeply interested in mission work among the lowly. He had a kind, cheery, genial face that won the confidence of children. He was a fine singer, and organized a band, whose mission it was to sing to the sick poor, conduct a service of praise in the habitations of the neglected, make joyful neighborhood meetings, and to do mission work generally. The little company went from place to place—now at Blackwell's Island—where desperate men were confined. This company sang praises unto God, and the prisoners heard them. For many years, the merchant felt that he ought to devote himself and his gifts wholly to mission work; he read in his reverses a loud call to duty. In other days, God had signally answered his prayer. He had furnished him with means in a marvelous way to continue his business. His kind friend who had trusted him had lost nothing. But, beside returning the loan, nothing had been gained. Perhaps, God had hedged up his way, to turn his attention to better things. He had purposed to renew his business, and had taken a store; but it was empty. On the bare floor, with no auditor but God, he flung himself, and prayed to be directed in the right way. Sixteen years of continuous, successful service in that field puts the stamp of reality on this case.

LXXX.

FATHER OF LIGHTS.

EVERY good gift and every perfect gift is from above, and cometh down from the Father of lights, with whom is no variableness, neither shadow of turning. *That* was the true Light, which lighteth every man that cometh into the world. He was in the world, and the world was made by him, and the world knew him not. He came unto his own, and his own received him not. Arise, shine; for thy light is come, and the glory of the Lord is risen upon thee. For, behold, the darkness shall cover the earth, and gross darkness the people: but the Lord shall arise upon thee, and his glory shall be seen upon thee. And the Gentiles shall come to thy light, and kings to the brightness of thy rising. Lift up thine eyes round about, and see: all they gather themselves together, they come to thee: thy sons shall come from far, and thy daughters shall be nursed at *thy* side.

OUR DAILY BREAD.

One morning, among the requests sent into the Fulton-street meeting was one from a poor woman asking for bread, coal, and help. She was starving in a Christian city. She could get no work and could get no help, and unless relief came from the charitable, she would starve. The missionary started out to inquire into the case. The request, written evidently with great difficulty, named the place of residence.

A poor woman was left with three children. She could not support them, and they were placed in a public asylum. She was greatly distressed; was without home or friends. She knew not how, but she was drawn into the Fulton-street meeting. She listened with astonishment at the requests. One person was in temporal want, another needed bread; one could not pay rent, another was embarrassed in business; one was sick, would God heal him? another had a disobedient son, would God subdue him? Then came answers to prayer, joyful thanksgivings for food, rent, and healing. "Does God answer the prayers of these people, I wonder—would he hear my prayer—would he help me take care of my three little children, keep them from want, and bring them up to be good? I'll try him." And she did. The next morning, the poor suppliant heard her request read out, and it sounded strangely in her ears. In that petition, she could not help joining, praying as she never before prayed. A new light dawned upon her. How strange the sensation! "Perhaps it is salvation," she said. Almost instantly, God seemed to bless her in her temporal affairs. The children were taken out of the asylum, for the mother had a cheerful hearthstone of her own. One daughter is married to a wealthy merchant; a son is soon to graduate and enter the ministry. This grateful woman believes that her temporal interests were settled when, in the pew at the old Fulton-street church, she cast her burdens upon the Lord and her soul upon the Saviour.

LXXXI.

BROTHERLY LOVE.

LET brotherly love continue. Be not forgetful to entertain strangers: for thereby some have entertained angels unawares. Remember them that are in bonds, as bound with them; *and* them which suffer adversity, as being yourselves also in the body. But speaking the truth in love, may grow up into him in all things, which is the head, *even* Christ: from whom the whole body fitly joined together and compacted by that which every joint supplieth, according to the effectual working in the measure of every part, maketh increase of the body unto the edifying of itself in love. And Abram said unto Lot, Let there be no strife, I pray thee, between me and thee, and between my herdmen and thy herdmen; for we *be* brethren. *Is* not the whole land before thee? separate thyself, I pray thee, from me: if *thou wilt take* the left hand, then I will go to the right; or if *thou depart* to the right hand, then I will go to the left. Use hospitality one to another without grudging. As every man hath received the gift, *even so* minister the same one to another, as good stewards of the manifold grace of God. If any man speak, *let him speak* as the oracles of God; if any man minister, *let him do it* as of the ability which God giveth him; that God in all things may be glorified through Jesus Christ: to whom be praise and dominion for ever and ever. Amen.

TO THEE SHALL ALL FLESH COME.

A YOUNG gunsmith came down to Fulton street for advice. He married a rich man's daughter; but his father-in-law was rich and ugly. He made his life so wretched that he resolved not to live at home. "I can't help you," said the missionary, "but the Lord can. Let us seek light from above." The young man disappeared from sight. After a few months, he appeared again at Fulton street. His domestic troubles were worse than ever. Life was a burden, and he resolved to destroy himself. "Don't do that; don't shoot yourself. You had better look to Christ. He will help you." He arose from his knees a new man. From that moment, his business began to amend. The father-in-law died, leaving all his property and business to his son-in-law and his wife. The young man is now in very prosperous business, has a happy home, and he and his wife are devoted members of the church of Christ. The force of prayer kept him from self-murder, and made him what he is—a devoted child of God.

MEN suffering from intemperance, men and women wretched in domestic life, men out of business, men in embarrassments, men suffering under any and all the ills that flesh is heir to, bring their wants to the Fulton-street meeting day after day, and prayers are offered for all who are in affliction or in trouble of body or mind. Some very strange cases are presented, and answers to prayer are often very marvelous.

LXXXII.

WILL GOD DWELL WITH MEN?

BUT will God in very deed dwell with men on the earth? Behold, heaven and the heaven of heavens can not contain thee; how much less this house which I have built! One shall say, I *am* the Lord's; and another shall call *himself* by the name of Jacob; and another shall subscribe *with* his hand unto the Lord, and surname *himself* by the name of Israel. Thus saith the Lord the King of Israel, and his Redeemer the Lord of hosts; I *am* the first, and I *am* the last; and besides me *there is* no God. Till we all come in the unity of the faith, and of the knowledge of the Son of God, unto a perfect man, unto the measure of the stature of the fullness of Christ: that we *henceforth* be no more children, tossed to and fro, and carried about with every wind of doctrine, by the sleight of men, *and* cunning craftiness, whereby they lie in wait to deceive.

GRACE, FREE GRACE.

ONE day, as the missionary entered the church, he found a young man sitting in the gallery. His clothes were soiled and poor, and he seemed every way offensive and dilapidated. "This is no place for me," he said, starting up, as he saw the people coming in to service. "Yes, it is, just the place for you. Come in here," drawing him into his private room. Prayer was offered, both kneeling before any thing was said. The young man was Scotch, of good family, and fitted to adorn respectable society. He had been a wayward youth. Like the prodigal, he was an outcast, wretched, degraded, and in want. His first feeling after he rose from his knees was that of hope. "Somebody cares for me. One man, at least, sees something in me worth saving. With God's help, I'll reform." "You must be a Christian," said the missionary, "before you can do any thing. Give your heart to Christ, and all will be well with you yet." And so it proved; kind friends wrote to his family. Inquiries were made through the British Consul to see if all was right. A good home was provided for the young man, and his expenses paid till he could hear from his family. A joyful letter came welcoming the prodigal home. The news was so good! Not only a reformed man, but a Christian! The fatted calf would indeed be killed, and the best robe provided for his wear. Sufficient funds were sent on to meet his necessities and pay his expenses to his father's roof.

A young man from the old country brought his troubles; they were family troubles. He was under the influence of drink when he called. There was evidently something in him. He was taken up-stairs and examined. Drunk as he was, he was prayed with, and after prayer induced to sign the pledge. He had a fine home in the old country and rich relatives; but the love of strong drink had made him an outcast. He had just come out of the hospital, and but for the shelter it afforded him, he would have died of exhaustion and want. He was taken care of and relieved temporarily. Strong drink is raging, and carried him again captive. It took two years to get the drink out of him. Then he bowed to the Saviour, and with that consecration the love of sin departed. Soon after his conversion, he heard from his friends. He went home a redeemed man, resolved to devote his time and means to the cause of the Redeemer.

LXXXIII.

HO, EVERY ONE THAT THIRSTETH.

HO, every one that thirsteth, come ye to the waters, and he that hath no money; come ye, buy, and eat; yea, come, buy wine and milk without money and without price. Wherefore do ye spend money for *that which is* not bread? and your labor for *that which* satisfieth not? hearken diligently unto me, and eat ye *that which is* good, and let your soul delight itself in fatness. In the last day, that great *day* of the feast, Jesus stood and cried, saying, If any man thirst, let him come unto me, and drink. He that believeth on me, as the scripture hath said, out of his belly shall flow rivers of living water. And the Spirit and the Bride say, Come. And let him that heareth say, Come. And let him that is athirst come. And whosoever will, let him take the water of life freely.

VICTORY.

IT is an almost daily occurrence for young men enthralled with drink to visit the Fulton-street meeting for relief—for help, temporal as well as spiritual. A young man sitting in a pew during the hour of service made himself very offensive to persons in the neighborhood. His conduct drew the attention of the missionary toward him. He was taken up-stairs into the little room, where prayer was wont to be made. He belonged to a wealthy and excellent family at the East. He had a wife and two beautiful children; but he was so dissolute and drunken that his family could do nothing with him. His wife went home to her father's, and even his mother cast him off. He came to New-York only to sink into deeper degradation. Out of money, out of work, ragged and forlorn, he stumbled into the Fulton-street meeting. He heard that men as hungry as he had been fed; men as ragged had been clothed; men as houseless had been sheltered; men sunk as low as himself had been rescued. A pledge, preceded by prayer, was offered to him. The future looked brighter. After a few weeks, he fell, and was as wretched and degraded and drunken as ever. The untiring missionary did not give him up, but took hold of him a second time. He was made the subject of earnest and continuous prayer. Grace completed the work. His mother sent for him to come home. He gathered his children about him and blessed the name of the Lord. He points to his happy home as a proof that the Lord will hear and answer prayer. A belief in God's ability to help in temporal troubles; to give wisdom to the blinded, help to the perplexed, medicine and healing to the sick; to soothe the ills of life; to remove anger and heal dissension, are among the objects of faith in this meeting. Elias's God is ours, ever the same.

LXXXIV.

JOY OF PUBLIC WORSHIP.

MY soul longeth, yea, even fainteth for the courts of the Lord: my heart and my flesh crieth out for the living God. Blessed *is* the man whose strength *is* in thee; in whose heart *are* the ways *of them.* For a day in thy courts *is* better than a thousand. I had rather be a door-keeper in the house of my God, than to dwell in the tents of wickedness. As the hart panteth after the water-brooks, so panteth my soul after thee, O God. My soul thirsteth for God, for the living God: when shall I come and appear before God? Walk about Zion, and go round about her: tell the towers thereof. Mark ye well her bulwarks, consider her palaces; that ye may tell *it* to the generation following. For this God *is* our God for ever and ever: he will be our guide *even* unto death.

KEEP THE SABBATH HOLY.

A YOUNG man held the position of confidential clerk in a large banking-house; he was a decided Christian, but not a demonstrative one; his religion was one of principle, rather than enthusiasm. One Saturday, the president came to the young man, and handing him a bundle of papers, told him they must be copied and ready for use Monday morning. "I will have to work all Sunday," was the reply, "to finish that job."

"That may be," said the president, "but my work must be done when I want it, and my employees must meet my wishes." "But I am a Sunday-school superintendent," said the clerk, "and I would not have my scholars know that I worked on Sunday for your salary." "Well, you must choose between complying with my wishes and losing your place." "With such an alternative, I should not hesitate a moment," was the reply. The president was not prepared for such a stout resistance, and was a little touched. "You'd better consider well what you're doing," he said; "I can put you in the fore-front of financiers; if I discharge you, you'll be ruined." "'I have been young, now am I old: yet I have never seen the righteous forsaken, nor his children begging bread,' that was my father's text," said the young man. Of course there could be but one issue. The clerk took his discharge. Sunday was a gloomy one in his house; his associates said he was a fool to be so nice. On Monday, the banker was visited by some gentlemen; they were about to start a bank, they said; they wanted a cashier, a man prompt, capable, reliable. "I know just the man you want." "Where is he now?" "He is not in any employment. He has been discharged." "We don't want any cast-off man," was the reply; "if the man is what you say, he would not be unemployed, for such men are rare." "The fact is," said the president, "I discharged him because he wouldn't work Sundays; even then I admired his principles, and I'll be his bondsman to any amount." Over the mantel of this cashier's dining-room can be found, in a handsome frame, the golden text, "I have been young, but now am I old: but I have not seen the righteous forsaken, nor his seed begging bread."

LXXXV.

GOD BLESS THE LADS.

THE Angel which redeemed me from all evil, bless the lads; and let my name be named on them, and the name of my fathers Abraham and Isaac; and let them grow into the multitude in the midst of the earth. When Jesus then lifted up *his* eyes, and saw a great company come unto him, he saith unto Philip, Whence shall we buy bread, that these may eat? And this he said to prove him: for he himself knew what he would do. Philip answered him, Two hundred pennyworth of bread is not sufficient for them, that every one of them may take a little. One of his disciples, Andrew, Simon Peter's brother, saith unto him, There is a lad here, which hath five barley loaves, and two small fishes: but what are they among so many? And Jesus said, Make the men sit down. Now there was much grass in the place.

MOTHER'S BIBLE.

THE Scotia left the Mersey for New-York; she had been out but a few days when a terrific gale came on, which lasted with fury for twenty-four hours. When the storm lulled, Captain Judkins said to his chief officer, "Go aloft and look out for wrecks; all vessels are not as staunch as the Scotia!"

The mate ran up the shrouds, but before he reached the main-truck, he shouted, "A wreck, a wreck!" "Where away?" "Off the port bow," was the response. The boats were immediately lowered, and as the sea was running mountain high, it was a perilous thing to go to the relief. The captain could have ordered a boat's crew to that service, but he chose a different plan. "I want twenty volunteers to man these boats." Forty brave tars sprang forward and offered their services. The boats were lowered into the stormy sea, and were soon out of sight. They were gone so long that it was feared they were swamped. A joyful shout soon relieved the anxiety. A half dozen dripping, exhausted men were lifted on the deck, and among them a lad about twelve years of age; the boy had lost every thing, and he wore a pea-jacket loaned him by one of the crew. "Who are you, my boy?" said Captain Judkins. 'I 'am a little Scotch boy; my father and mother are both dead, and I have no friends, no home. I am going to America to find my uncle who lives in Illinois." "What is this?" said the captain, as he pulled open the pea-jacket and brought to light a rope across his breast. "It's a piece of cord, sir." "But what is this tied under your arm?" "It's my mother's Bible; she told me never to lose it." "That's all you've saved?" "Yes, sir." "Couldn't you have saved something else?" "Not and save that." "Didn't you expect to be lost?" "Yes, sir; but I meant, if I went down, to take my mother's Bible down with me." "All right," says the captain; "I'll take care of you." The Scotia reached the port in safety. The captain took the lad by the hand and visited a well-known Christian merchant, to whom he told the boy's story. "I'll take the lad," said the merchant; "I want no other recommendation; a boy that holds on to his mother's Bible in such perils will give a good account of himself."

LXXXVI.

SOW BESIDE ALL WATERS.

IN the morning sow thy seed, and in the evening withhold not thine hand: for thou knowest not whether shall prosper, either this or that, or whether they both *shall be* alike good. Blessed *are* ye that sow beside all waters, that send forth *thither* the feet of the ox and the ass. They that sow in tears shall reap in joy. He that goeth forth and weepeth, bearing precious seed, shall doubtless come again with rejoicing, bringing his sheaves *with him.*

COAL-SCUTTLE.

A CHRISTIAN gentleman is an ardent friend to missions; he believes in seeking opportunity, in embracing opportunity, and in making opportunity. One day, at his boarding-house, in the absence of the servant, he went down to the coal-bin for a scuttle of coal. He met the cook, a colored Catholic, who was busy at the coal-bin. This servant had recently come from the South, and seemed to be a sober, honest, hard-working girl. He put one or two questions to her in relation to her religious experience, questions which seemed to interest her very much. On going up-stairs, the cook spoke to her mistress. "The gentleman that occupies the parlor spoke to me to-day about religion. I never heard a man talk so; if he speaks truly, I don't think I'm a Christian." A short time afterward, the lady of the house spoke to the merchant, and said, "My colored cook seems to be in great concern about her soul; your conversation with her the other morning seemed to present religion to her in a new light." Repeated conversations were had. The servant, really an intelligent person, sought the way of the Lord earnestly. As the gentleman who had been instrumental in calling her attention to personal religion was warmly interested in the Fulton-street meeting, this case was presented, and warmly responded to. In a short time, the seeker found rest in the Saviour, united with the North Church, and for a long time has been an earnest and consistent member.

A PERTINENT QUESTION.

THE same gentleman referred to in the preceding section sat down to the table one evening for tea. A person unknown to him was sitting at the table, and apparently acquainted with no one. In a kindly way the merchant said, "Are you a stranger?" "I am," was the reply. The conversation took a general turn, and the question and the stranger both passed out of the merchant's mind. Some months afterward, to the joy of the merchant, the stranger appeared before the consistory of the North Church to be examined for admission. He referred to the first night that he met the merchant at the tea-table. "I was a careless, indifferent, worldly man then, engrossed in the affairs of life; I was a drinking man; your question, 'Are you a stranger?' struck me oddly. I said mentally, 'A stranger, yes; I am a stranger in the city; I am a stranger to sobriety; I am a stranger to God.' The impression followed me day after day, and never left me till I found peace in believing. Then I ceased to be a 'stranger,' and became a fellow-citizen of the saints and of the household of God." This man is now one of the most successful superintendents of Sunday-schools in the city.

LXXXVII.

HEALING LEAVES.

THE harvest is past, the summer is ended, and we are not saved. For the hurt of the daughter of my people am I hurt; I am black; astonishment hath taken hold on me. *Is there* no balm in Gilead? *is there* no physician there? why then is not the health of the daughter of my people recovered? And he cried unto the Lord; and the Lord showed him a tree, *which* when he had cast into the waters, the waters were made sweet: there he made for them a statute and an ordinance, and there he proved them, and said, If thou wilt diligently hearken to the voice of the Lord thy God, and wilt do that which is right in his sight, and wilt give ear to his commandments, and keep all his statutes, I will put none of these diseases upon thee, which I have brought upon the Egyptians: for I *am* the Lord that healeth thee. Praise ye the Lord: for *it is* good to sing praises unto our God; for *it is* pleasant; *and* praise is comely. The Lord doth build up Jerusalem: he gathereth together the outcasts of Israel. He healeth the broken in heart, and bindeth up their wounds.

FRENCH TRACT.

ALL instrumentalities are used in the mission work at Fulton street. Bread, clothes, coal, money, are means of grace. Medicine, surgical aid, and employment, prayer, power of sacred song, personal toil, cheerful reproof, and words of encouragement, Bibles, tracts, and religious books are ready for all the nationalities on earth. The name of the church is embossed on every book, tract, and paper distributed. Through this instrumentality, hundreds are guided to the noon-day service, and to personal salvation. A well-educated Catholic woman, brought up in a convent, received one day a French tract. She was interested to have a book on religion in her own language. Being greatly embarrassed in worldly matters, and not knowing which way to turn, she read on her tract, "North Reformed Dutch Church, corner Fulton and William streets, Union Prayer-meeting from 12 till 1 o'clock. Stop 5, 10, or 15 minutes, or the hour." Curiosity led her down to the meeting. "Why not join my request with the others?" she said. "I am poor, I am in trouble; I don't know which way to turn; these seem like good, honest people, and I don't think a little prayer will hurt any body." So she laid her simple supplication on the altar. It was soon buried up from human eyes, and driven away from human thoughts. But He who notes the sparrow when it falls, and numbers the hairs of our head, was not inattentive to the cry of the lowly. She was soon heard to rejoice in God, and joy in the God of her salvation. Instantly her temporal affairs began to mend. A wealthy Christian was in search of a housekeeper. Accidentally, as the world would say, this gentleman became acquainted with the history of the woman, and the desire of her heart was answered by being introduced into a genial and remunerative labor.

LXXXVIII.

YOUR FATHER KNOWETH THEM.

WHEREFORE, if God so clothe the grass of the field, which to-day is, and to-morrow is cast into the oven, *shall he* not much more *clothe* you, O ye of little faith? Therefore take no thought, saying, What shall we eat? or, What shall we drink? or, Wherewithal shall we be clothed? Take therefore no thought for the morrow: for the morrow shall take thought for the things of itself. Sufficient unto the day *is* the evil thereof. If ye then be not able to do that thing which is least, why take ye thought for the rest? Consider the lilies how they grow: they toil not, they spin not; and yet I say unto you, that Solomon in all his glory was not arrayed like one of these. If then God so clothe the grass, which is to-day in the field, and to-morrow is cast into the oven; how much more *will he clothe* you, O ye of little faith? And seek not ye what ye shall eat, or what ye shall drink, neither be ye of doubtful mind.

THE TRUNK-KEY.

In front of the old North Church, an old man had a stand, selling dried fruits. He was a Catholic, and all his family were brought up in that faith. His path in life was rough, and he had great difficulty in keeping the wolf from his door. His wife was a drinking woman, and her three little children were children of neglect and sorrow. The singing at the hour of noon arrested his attention. He found himself day by day drawn up to the door, listening, not only to the songs, but to the prayers. He became interested in the meeting, and persuaded his wife also to attend. A change came over them both. As an inquirer, the wife came to see a minister. Her breath was so foul with ale and vile liquors, that she had to be turned away. "You must get this demon out of you," the missionary said, "and this can only be done by your becoming a Christian." Both the husband and wife eventually became members of the church. The family disappeared, as hundreds of others disappear who are relieved and saved. After a time, the man appeared in his accustomed haunts. He was sober and devout. He was prompt at the noonday meeting, and regular at the church services. He sickened and sent for the missionary. He found him very near the grave; he could just speak. Drawing out from his bosom a trunk-key, he said, "Take care of that, take care of that." He laid his head down on his pillow, and passed away. The key unlocked his trunk under the bed; in it was found a sum of money sufficient to make his family comfortable. This money he earned after he became a Christian. What was before squandered in drink and dissipation was carefully treasured up, that his family might not be in want when he was removed. "Godliness is profitable unto all things, having the promise of the life that now is, and of that which is to come."

LXXXIX.

MERCY FOR THOUSANDS.

I THE Lord thy God *am* a jealous God, visiting the iniquity of the fathers upon the children unto the third and fourth *generation* of them that hate me; and showing mercy unto thousands of them that love me, and keep my commandments. Who redeemeth thy life from destruction; who crowneth thee with loving-kindness and tender mercies; who satisfieth thy mouth with good *things; so that* thy youth is renewed like the eagle's. For as the heaven is high above the earth, *so* great is his mercy toward them that fear him. As far as the east is from the west, *so* far has he removed our transgressions from us. Like as a father pitieth *his* children, *so* the Lord pitieth them that fear him. For he knoweth our frame; he remembereth that we *are* dust. Let Israel hope in the Lord: for with the Lord *there is* mercy, and with him *is* plenteous redemption. And he shall redeem Israel from all his iniquities.

PERSEVERANCE.

A GENTLEMAN, whose field of labor brings him into connection with the lowly and unfortunate, one day passed a man who was standing on the curbstone. Supposing him to be a clergyman, he gave him a sharp look, and passed on. Six months afterward, the stranger was seen on the streets very drunk. One year after, the parties met. It had gone hard with the stranger; he was drunk; his clothes were dirty and tattered; he was suffering for food. The missionary relieved him, and promised to call and see him. "You will never call," said the disconsolate man, "you will never come." One Sunday, he found him in the little den he called his home, lying on the bed, cold and hungry. He was still drunk, and though he could find no money for food, he could find money enough to buy drink. The parties visited a saloon and got supper. Both attended an evening service. The man was then taken to the boarding-house of the missionary, where he was attacked with delirium tremens, and roared for brandy. He was shut up in a room for four weeks, and lived at the missionary's expense. He then fell, and was again rescued; fell again. The missionary never tired; though poor himself, and needing many necessaries of life, he shared his pittance with the visitor; and for a whole year, the missionary furnished the money for his board and clothing in the hope that this outlay would make him manly enough to support himself. Nearly a whole year, he kept sober. But one Sunday night, he came to the missionary's house beastly drunk. For ten years, this style of life continued—now drunk, now sober; now down, then up again. Several positions were opened to him, some of them of great promise; he lost them by drunkenness. His case was presented, over and over again, in the meeting, but no power seemed to avail. One night, he knocked at the door of his friend. "I am in trouble," he said; "I feel that I am a sinner, and I don't know that there is salvation for me." He there gave himself to God, and stood before the congregation, and made the consecration. With that act, the love of sin departed. This was fifteen years ago. He is an honored and useful member of the church. His business has prospered, and he is rich, considerate, and liberal.

XC.

IF SINNERS ENTICE THEE.

MY son, if sinners entice thee, consent thou not. If they say, Come with us, let us lay wait for blood, let us lurk privily for the innocent without cause: cast in thy lot among us; let us all have one purse: my son, walk not thou in the way with them; refrain thy foot from their path. An ungodly man diggeth up evil: and in his lips *there is* as a burning fire. A froward man soweth strife: and a whisperer separateth chief friends. Blessed *is* the man that endureth temptation: for when he is tried, he shall receive the crown of life, which the Lord hath promised to them that love him. And I, brethren, when I came to you, came not with excellency of speech or of wisdom, declaring unto you the testimony of God. For I determined not to know any thing among you, save Jesus Christ, and him crucified. And I was with you in weakness, and in fear, and in much trembling. And my speech and my preaching *was* not with enticing words of man's wisdom, but in demonstration of the Spirit and of power.

SAILOR'S STORY.

At one of the meetings, a young man in sailor's garb said he would like to relate an incident. He said he had just returned from a long voyage. He had been careful of his wages. The day he was paid off, a company of shipmates got round him, and took him by violence into a drinking-saloon. He had refused to drink during his voyage; he had often been tempted in foreign ports, but had maintained his integrity. A combination had been formed to force him to drink, and now they threatened, if he did not voluntarily, they would hold him by violence, and pour the liquor down his throat. He said,

"Boys, will you hear me before you compel me to drink?"

They said that was only fair.

"I was an only son," he said. "My father was a poor sailor. He was an excellent man when sober, but he ruined every thing with drink. He would come home from a long voyage, and in a few days be penniless; and not only penniless, but almost a furious maniac. He died in one of his maddened fits, and he was buried at public expense. My mother remained at the grave after the friends had departed. She knelt on the new-made grave, and made me kneel beside her; and there I took a vow that, while I lived, I would not taste a drop of intoxicating drinks. My poor old mother lives, and I support her. I inherit the love of strong drink. If I should break my pledge, I should follow my father's practices, and find a drunkard's grave. Boys, you don't want me to do that, do you?"

"No, no!" they said; "Jim, you may go. I wish we were as free as you are."

"I came into this meeting this morning from that trial to give God thanks for my deliverance."

XCI.

ENSAMPLE.

NOW we command you, brethren, in the name of our Lord Jesus Christ, that ye withdraw yourselves from every brother that walketh disorderly, and not after the tradition which he received of us. For yourselves know how ye ought to follow us: for we behaved not ourselves disorderly among you; neither did we eat any man's bread for naught; but wrought with labor and travail night and day, that we might not be chargeable to any of you: not because we have not power, but to make ourselves an ensample unto you to follow us. Brethren, be followers together of me, and mark them which walk, so as ye have us for an ensample. (For many walk, of whom I have told you often, and now tell you even weeping, *that they are* the enemies of the cross of Christ: whose end *is* destruction, whose God *is their* belly, and *whose* glory *is* in their shame, who mind earthly things.) For our conversation is in heaven; from whence also we look for the Saviour, the Lord Jesus Christ.

THE NEWSBOY.

A WIDOW was left with a little household. She found it difficult to give her children bread. Her son said he wouldn't be a burden to his mother, and would go out and seek his fortune, for he couldn't be worse off than now. His education was scant, his clothes coarse and poor. The morning he left his home, his mother took him into her room, and commended him to God. He started on foot for a city a hundred miles away.

It was a sad parting. The widow threw her arms around the neck of her son, blessed him, and bade him be a good boy. He had but little money, and when he reached his destination, foot-sore and weary, he was nearly penniless.

"I'll not disgrace my mother," he said. "I will earn my own living, and earn something for her beside."

With a few coppers, he purchased the next morning some papers, and began the work of a newsboy. He soon obtained a place in a printing-office. He joined the Sunday-school, because he thought it would please his mother. He became a favorite in the printing-office, employed his leisure hours in study, attended an evening-school, and improved his hours of leisure in fitting himself for life.

His attendance at Sunday-school and diligence at his business attracted the attention of his friends. A place was found him to learn the trade of dentistry. He early united with the Church, and through all his early life was faithful to his duties in trade and religion.

It was an accidental thing that led him into the Sunday-school. While a newsboy, he was met one Sunday by a kind Christian gentleman, who entered into conversation with him, and invited him to go to the Sunday-school. He is now one of the leading dentists in a large city, and one of the most devoted friends of mission work and Sunday-schools.

XCII.

SALVATION OF OUR GOD.

TAKE heed unto thyself, and unto the doctrine; continue in them: for in doing this, thou shalt both save thyself, and them that hear thee. Who hath saved us, and called *us* with a holy calling, not according to our works, but according to his own purpose and grace, which was given us in Christ Jesus before the world began; but is now made manifest by the appearing of our Saviour Jesus Christ, who hath abolished death, and hath brought life and immortality to light through the Gospel. But let us, who are of the day, be sober, putting on the breastplate of faith and love; and for a helmet, the hope of salvation. For God hath not appointed us to wrath, but to obtain salvation by our Lord Jesus Christ, who died for us, that, whether we wake or sleep, we should live together with him. Wherefore comfort yourselves together, and edify one another, even as also ye do.

SAVED FROM SUICIDE.

A young man, living in a genteel position, became addicted to drink. He was so brutal that his wife and child were taken from him, and he became a houseless vagrant. He was in great distress, did not know that he had a friend in the world, and the little money that he earned he spent in drink. He became distressed on account of his sins, but sought relief at a bar. Even the rough bartender was touched with his sufferings, and said to him,

"You don't want rum, you want a minister. You had better go and find some minister of religion, and tell him how you feel."

Instead of doing this, he proposed to commit suicide, and went down to the dock. A policeman had his eye upon him, and he turned away. He found himself near the Fulton-street meeting. The singing attracted his attention, and he went into church. He came in contact with some kind friends in the meeting, who were interested in his condition. But the appetite mastered him. The money given him to buy lodging and bread went for rum. One day, he was made the subject of special prayer. The appetite left him. He became a decided Christian, and united with the Old North Church. He had no more trouble about business after he became a Christian. He had friends enough ready to help him when he was willing to help himself. He joined his wife and children, and is now an honored, respected Christian man.

XCIII.

VICTORY THAT OVERCOMETH.

BUT thanks *be* to God, which giveth us the victory, through our Lord Jesus Christ. Therefore, my beloved brethren, be ye steadfast, unmovable, always abounding in the work of the Lord, forasmuch as ye know that your labor is not in vain in the Lord. Then sang Moses and the children of Israel this song unto the Lord, and spake, saying, I will sing unto the Lord, for he hath triumphed gloriously; the horse and his rider hath he thrown into the sea. The Lord *is* my strength and song, and he is become my salvation: he *is* my God, and I will prepare him an habitation; my father's God, and I will exalt him. For whatsoever is born of God, overcometh the world: and this is the victory that overcometh the world, *even* our faith. Who is he that overcometh the world, but he that believeth that Jesus is the Son of God?

HOW GOD ANSWERS.

A MOTHER had two sons. They were separated from home, and lived many hundred miles apart. She sought out her pastor, and said, "Won't you pray for my two sons? They are careless and indifferent about personal religion; but I think, if you would pray for them, they might be saved?" He thought he would send the request on to the Fulton-street meeting. He marked the day that he mailed the request in his memorandum. Time flew by. One day, the mother came to her pastor in great joy, showing a letter from each of her sons, informing her that they had set up a family altar, and had resolved to lead a religious life. The date of the letter was the same as that on which the request was sent to New-York. Both letters were dated the same day. Neither brother knew the feelings of the other, and, when the letters were sent to the mother, neither brother knew that their cases had been remembered at the Fulton-street meeting. Both sons are now devoted Christians, and bless the name of the Lord who answers prayer.

During the years of this meeting, instances quite as marvelous as this mark its career. Often a revival, a conversion, the return of a prodigal, the reform of bad men, follow fervent and united prayer put up.

XCIV.

GOD A STRONG TOWER.

THE Lord liveth; and blessed *be* my rock; and exalted be the God of the rock of my salvation. *He is* the tower of salvation for his king: and showeth mercy to his anointed, unto David, and to his seed for evermore. For who *is* God, save the Lord? and who *is* a rock, save our God? God *is* my strength *and* power; and he maketh my way perfect. *As for* God, his way *is* perfect; the word of the Lord *is* tried: he *is* a buckler to all them that trust in him. From the end of the earth will I cry unto thee, when my heart is overwhelmed: lead me to the rock *that* is higher than I. For thou hast been a shelter for me, *and* a strong tower from the enemy. The name of the Lord *is* a strong tower: the righteous runneth into it, and is safe. I will love thee, O Lord, my strength. The Lord *is* my rock, and my fortress, and my deliverer; my God, my strength, in whom I will trust; my buckler, and the horn of my salvation, *and* my high tower.

THANKSGIVINGS.

A VERY godly mother had a very ungodly son. His chief delight was to tantalize his mother, and make himself appear more wicked, if possible, than he really was. Maddened one day at some reproof she gave him, he left the room, and, with curses, said he never would come back. The poor mother lifted her eyes to heaven, and said, "God bless my poor son, and save him!" He became a sailor, a drunkard, a gambler. He went round the world; everywhere dissolute and abandoned. The vessel put in in distress, and the sailor went ashore. He strolled into a religious meeting, where there was an especial religious interest. He was so drunk that he could not walk straight, but staggered up to the altar. He was not repulsed, but welcomed with kind words. Religion sobered him. He found peace at the cross. He is now a preacher of the gospel of the grace of God.

AT a meeting for prayer, a young man arose to render thanks to God for his great mercy. "I have been an infidel for fourteen years," he said. "I had the prayers of a pious mother, but I spurned them. I have not seen her for fifteen years. I suppose she has given me up as lost. I don't know where to find her, but I would like to tell her what the Lord has done for me in answer to her earnest supplications." "O my son, my son!" a voice cried out. "And they gave the lad to his mother." Had she received her son from the dead, she would not have been more astounded.

ONE day, a request for prayer came from the Ohio Penitentiary. A Christian man conducted a Bible-class every Sunday. There was so much interest among the prisoners, that the leader felt impelled to send a request to the noonday meeting, that the Ohio State prison might be remembered. Almost immediately, a revival of religion broke out in that institution, and within the year a hundred and sixty-five prisoners were hopefully converted.

XCV.

LOOKING TO JESUS.

LOOKING unto Jesus the author and finisher of *our* faith; who for the joy that was set before him endured the cross, despising the shame, and is set down at the right hand of the throne of God. For consider him that endureth such contradiction of sinners against himself, lest ye be wearied and faint in your minds. The next day John seeth Jesus coming unto him, and saith, Behold the Lamb of God, which taketh away the sin of the world! He was oppressed, and he was afflicted, yet he opened not his mouth: he is brought as a lamb to the slaughter, and as a sheep before her shearers is dumb, so he openeth not his mouth. Yet it pleased the Lord to bruise him; he hath put *him* to grief: when thou shalt make his soul an offering for sin, he shall see *his* seed, he shall prolong *his* days, and the pleasure of the Lord shall prosper in his hand.

ANSWER OF PRAYER.

MEN ask, Does God hear and answer prayer now, as he did in the olden time? Will the God of Elias, who shut up the heaven three years and six months, and then gave rain in answer to prayer, hear our petitions? Can men be cured in this nineteenth century, as was Naaman, the Assyrian. Can prayer stop the mouths of lions, quench the violence of fire, and turn the edge of the sword? Will Christ heal if we pray to him, as he healed the paralytic who was let down through the tiling? Is there healing in his touch, as when the woman laid her fingers on the hem of his garment? George Müller, of Bristol, after an experience of thirty years, says that he has often asked favors for himself and been denied. But he never asked needed things for his orphan children without receiving them. Fulton street bears precious testimony that God is a faithful God through all generations. Hopeless men have been reformed; brutal men have sat at the feet of Jesus; deadly diseases have been exorcised, and more than once the prayer of faith has healed the sick.

XCVI.

PRESENCE OF CHRIST.

THE same came therefore to Philip, which was of Bethsaida of Galilee, and desired him, saying, Sir, we would see Jesus. Philip cometh and telleth Andrew: and again Andrew and Philip tell Jesus. And again he entered into Capernaum after *some* days; and it was noised that he was in the house. And straightway many were gathered together, insomuch that there was no room to receive *them*, no, not so much as about the door: and he preached the word unto them. And it came to pass, as he sat at meat with them, he took bread, and blessed *it*, and brake, and gave to them. And their eyes were opened, and they knew him; and he vanished out of their sight. Jesus saith unto him, I am the way, the truth, and the life: no man cometh unto the Father, but by me. If ye had known me, ye should have known my Father also: and from henceforth ye know him, and have seen him. Philip saith unto him, Lord, show us the Father, and it sufficeth us.

NO OTHER REFUGE.

A MAN lost his place, and sought for work in vain. He tramped round the city, and went from store to store seeking employment without success. Reduced in money, disheartened, and in want, he stood on the string-piece of one of the docks. The temptation was to throw himself into the river. He partly resolved to do it. "What is life good for?" he said. "It is full of toil and suffering. I am of no use to any body, and never shall be, and the sooner I am out of the way the better." He had been an occasional attendant at Fulton street. While he was meditating suicide, a strain of music that he had heard at the noonday meeting came into his mind. Something suggested, "You had better go and talk with the missionary." As he crossed the threshold of the old church, his ear caught the words:

"Other refuge have I none,
Hangs my helpless soul on thee."

He accepted the invitation to cast himself on the Lord. He bowed in prayer, and the burden of his prayer was that God would give him deliverance. As he turned away from the church, a man whom he had not seen for a long time came up and said, "Would you like a job?" "I should above all things," was the answer. "I have just opened a lumber-yard up-town, and I want somebody to take care of it. I know you are both capable and honest. So come along." The poor despondent sufferer was almost transformed with joy. Before night, he was installed in his new position, one every way suited to his ability and taste. There are a great many grateful hearts in the noonday meeting, but none more grateful than the man who meditated suicide on the string-piece of the dock.

Interior View of Chapel of Fulton Street Daily Prayer-Meeting.

XCVII.

INTERCESSION.

AND he saw that *there was* no man, and wondered that *there was* no intercessor: therefore his arm brought salvation unto him; and his righteousness, it sustained him. Likewise the Spirit also helpeth our infirmities: for we know not what we should pray for as we ought: but the Spirit itself maketh intercession for us with groanings which cannot be uttered. And he that searcheth the hearts knoweth what *is* the mind of the Spirit, because he maketh intercession for the saints according to *the will of* God. He that spared not his own Son, but delivered him up for us all, how shall he not with him also freely give us all things? Who shall lay any thing to the charge of God's elect? *It is* God that justifieth. Who *is* he that condemneth? *It is* Christ that died, yea rather, that is risen again, who is even at the right hand of God, who also maketh intercession for us.

A BURDENED SOUL.

"OH! how glad I should be if my three sons were converted! I will send their case to the Fulton-street meeting." So said a father. He wrote the request, watered them with tears, and consecrated them with prayers. The date of the request he carefully preserved. The sons were far away from home and in separate localities. Only a short time elapsed before the father received the joyful intelligence in three letters from his three sons, each announcing the glad tidings of their conversion, and giving a detailed account of the manner in which they had been led to the Saviour. A comparison of dates showed that the request and the conversions trod hard upon each other. "Were there not ten cleansed?" said our Lord. None came to give glory to God, save one. How marvelous, how exhilarating would a complete record be of the conversions and all the saved these seventeen years!

XCVIII.

GOSPEL TRIUMPHANT.

THE voice of him that crieth in the wilderness, Prepare ye the way of the Lord, make straight in the desert a highway for our God. Every valley shall be exalted, and every mountain and hill shall be made low: and the crooked shall be made straight, and the rough places plain: and the glory of the Lord shall be revealed, and all flesh shall see *it* together: for the mouth of the Lord hath spoken *it*. Thus saith the Lord, The labor of Egypt, and merchandise of Ethiopia and of the Sabeans, men of stature, shall come over unto thee, and they shall be thine: they shall come after thee; in chains they shall come over, and they shall fall down unto thee, they shall make supplication unto thee, *saying*, Surely God *is* in thee; and *there is* none else, *there is* no God. Then thou shalt see, and flow together, and thine heart shall be enlarged; because the abundance of the sea shall be converted unto thee, the forces of the Gentiles shall come unto thee.

BEFORE THOU CALLEST.

A VISITOR from the West was in the prayer-meeting. Struck with the character of the requests, she offered one for the conversion of her husband. She heard nothing about his religious state till she returned home. Three weeks had elapsed since she offered the request. The husband met his wife cordially at the depot, and on his way home said, "There has been a great change come over me since you went away. I think God has had mercy on my soul; and I have set up a family altar." The time in which the altar was erected was the evening of the very day that prayers were offered for this man in Fulton-street.

A WILD, wayward boy drifted into the noonday meeting. Almost immediately he was impressed. A friend sent up a request for prayer. He became a Christian that day, and is now one of the most earnest workers in the city.

ONE man came into the meeting with a request that prayers might be offered for the salvation of his only child. Immediately, all unknown to the father, a note of thanksgiving was read from the daughter.

XCIX.

BUILD THE WASTE PLACES.

THOU shalt arise, *and* have mercy upon Zion: for the time to favor her, yea, the set time, is come. For thy servants take pleasure in her stones, and favor the dust thereof. And they shall build the old wastes, they shall raise up the former desolations, and they shall repair the waste cities, the desolations of many generations. And strangers shall stand and feed your flocks, and the sons of the alien *shall be* your ploughmen and your vinedressers. They that trust in the Lord *shall be* as Mount Zion, *which* cannot be removed, *but* abideth forever. *As* the mountains *are* round about Jerusalem, so the Lord *is* round about his people from henceforth even forever. Surely the isles shall wait for me, and the ships of Tarshish first, to bring thy sons from far, their silver and their gold with them, unto the name of the Lord thy God, and to the Holy One of Israel, because he hath glorified thee.

THE BETTER CHOICE.

A YOUNG man in business had heard of the Fulton-street meeting. He said he would like to see how business men looked praying at noon, instead of doing their work. A young friend called on him, saying, "I am going to the Fulton-street prayer-meeting; won't you come along?" The young man hesitated. He had agreed to attend the theatre that night, and he thought a prayer-meeting at noon would not join well with a seat in the theatre in the evening. He hesitated but a moment, and then said, "I will go." The meeting was one of unusual power. The singing entranced him. His eyes were filled with tears. He felt his need of the Saviour, and found the Saviour he needed. He was not in the theatre that evening, but in the place of prayer, relating what great things the Lord had done for his soul. It is no uncommon thing for men who come to scoff, to remain to pray.

C.

HOLY SABBATH.

BLESSED *is* the man *that* doeth this, and the son of man *that* layeth hold on it; that keepeth the sabbath from polluting it, and keepeth his hand from doing any evil. If thou turn away thy foot from the sabbath, *from* doing thy pleasure on my holy day; and call the sabbath a delight, the holy of the Lord, honorable; and shalt honor him, not doing thine own ways, nor finding thine own pleasure, nor speaking *thine own* words: then shalt thou delight thyself in the Lord; and I will cause thee to ride upon the high places of the earth, and feed thee with the heritage of Jacob thy father: for the mouth of the Lord hath spoken *it.* There remaineth therefore a rest to the people of God. For he that is entered into his rest, he also hath ceased from his own works, as God *did* from his. Let us labor therefore to enter into that rest, lest any man fall after the same example of unbelief.

WONDROUS CHANGE.

IN one of the lager-beer saloons of the city was a young girl of surpassing beauty. Her graceful movements, delicate complexion, and courtly manners attracted general attention. A Fifth-avenue belle could not have been more winning. Her parents were coarse and repulsive, and from her birth she had been brought up in the vile atmosphere of a low drinking-place; yet she was as delicate, sensitive, and lady-like, as though all her surroundings had been the most refined. One day, she came down to the meeting, and begged to be taken from the saloon. She was placed in a mission-school, and developed surprising musical ability. A Christian friend placed within her reach facilities for musical culture. She early became a Christian. She has been for some years the leading soprano at a leading church, at a fine salary, and supports her father and mother, whom she has induced to abandon their trade. Cultivated, beautiful, and refined, she is soon to be married to a young man connected with one of the wealthiest families in the city. Her friends are all acquainted with her story, and honor her all the more for the tribulations through which she has passed. Religion has done great things for her and her family.

It was a miserable dwelling in a rear tenement-house, around which crowded the vile, the sorrowful, and the drunken. Here, a little girl was found having in charge five little children. The mother was dead, and the father had deserted his family. The elder sister, nothing but a child herself, was doing her best to silence the cries of the children for food. The room, nearly bare, was without fire, comfort, or bread. She asked God to help her in her distress, she said. The relief that came, she believed to be in answer to prayer. What else should she do but give herself to the Lord, who had redeemed her in her time of trouble? She never withdrew her watchful care over her sisters and brother. She was instrumental in leading them all into the church where she found safety and repose. The entire family are not only Christians, but are in positions where they will be useful members of society.

CI.

PRECIOUS PROMISES.

THE sun shall be no more thy light by day; neither for brightness shall the moon give light unto thee: but the Lord shall be unto thee an everlasting light, and thy God thy glory. Thy sun shall no more go down; neither shall thy moon withdraw itself: for the Lord shall be thine everlasting light, and the days of thy mourning shall be ended. Thy people also *shall be* all righteous: they shall inherit the land forever, the branch of my planting, the work of my hands, that I may be glorified. Wherein ye greatly rejoice, though now for a season, if need be, ye are in heaviness through manifold temptations: that the trial of your faith, being much more precious than of gold that perisheth, though it be tried with fire, might be found unto praise and honor and glory at the appearing of Jesus Christ. Whom having not seen, ye love; in whom, though now ye see *him* not, yet believing, ye rejoice with joy unspeakable and full of glory.

OMNIPOTENT GRACE.

A SCOTCH woman kept a very noted saloon near the Tombs, in New-York. She had been well brought up, but had fallen from her position, although she never abandoned herself to any thing worse than keeping a drinking-place for men and women. Her husband was blind, but she managed to keep her family together, and secure a good living. But she was far from being happy. Like so many others, she was found one day in the Fulton-street meeting. She never could tell what special influences drew her there. One of her own countrymen led the meeting. That impressed her. Prayers were offered for a person in disreputable business. That came home to her bosom. She was agitated, distressed, and vexed, and more vexed to think she was agitated. Again and again she was seen in the meeting, till at length she was under the deepest conviction for sin. She sold out her business, and turned her attention to other pursuits. She was prospered, and her prosperity seemed to date from the hour when she abandoned her disreputable business, and resolved to devote herself to God. Her whole family now are in circumstances of affluence.

A POOR mechanic became discouraged because nothing seemed to prosper with him. He thought it would not hurt his children to go to Sunday-school. He became a new man, not only in grace, but in the affairs of daily life. In the Sunday-school, his daughters developed extraordinary musical talent. The son, a bright lad, early joined the church, and through the assistance of friends, began to prepare for the ministry. The daughters are fine concert-singers and music-teachers, besides having a profitable place in a choir. The son will graduate in a few months, a preacher of the gospel. One of the daughters will soon be the mistress of a brown-stone mansion. A rich Christian young man is soon to lead her to the altar. This case, with hundreds of others, are within the reach of any who are disposed to inquire into the reality of such relief. "In her right hand are length of days; in her left hand riches and honor."

CII.

ACQUAINTANCE WITH GOD.

ACQUAINT now thyself with him, and be at peace: thereby good shall come unto thee. Unto thee lift I up mine eyes, O thou that dwellest in the heavens. Behold, as the eyes of servants *look* unto the hand of their masters, *and* as the eyes of a maiden unto the hand of her mistress; so our eyes *wait* upon the Lord our God, until that he have mercy upon us. And thou, Solomon my son, know thou the God of thy father, and serve him with a perfect heart and with a willing mind: for the Lord searcheth all hearts, and understandeth all the imaginations of the thoughts: if thou seek him, he will be found of thee; but if thou forsake him, he will cast thee off forever. And they shall teach no more every man his neighbor, and every man his brother, saying, Know the Lord: for they shall all know me, from the least of them unto the greatest of them, saith the Lord: for I will forgive their iniquity, and I will remember their sin no more.

POLICEMAN'S TROUBLE.

A MEMBER of the police found it difficult to provide for his family. He came into the Sunday-school of the Old North Church, and asked assistance for his children. The wardrobe of this church is inexhaustible. It has bread for the hungry, shoes for the shoeless, medicine for the sick, and relief for the deserving. The necessities of this suppliant were met, and the relief touched his own heart. He became a Christian. With his consecration to Christ, his temporal troubles seemed to end. He is now in excellent business, and all his children are in good positions. Had he taken to the bottle, or to dissipated companions to drown his sorrows, it is easy to foresee what his end would have been.

One of the touching sights at the meeting is the attendance of the city guardians. On their beat they find time often to hear a touching prayer, join a verse, and then away to their tramp. Off duty these men come in and remain there all the session—the singing attracts them.

CIII.

BEHAVIOR IN GOD'S HOUSE.

BUT if I tarry long, that thou mayest know how thou oughtest to behave thyself in the house of God, which is the church of the living God, the pillar and ground of the truth. Keep thy foot when thou goest to the house of God, and be more ready to hear, than to give the sacrifice of fools: for they consider not that they do evil. Be not rash with thy mouth, and let not thine heart be hasty to utter *any* thing before God: for God *is* in heaven, and thou upon earth: therefore let thy words be few. And Jacob awaked out of his sleep, and he said, Surely the Lord is in this place; and I knew *it* not. And he was afraid, and said, How dreadful *is* this place! this *is* none other but the house of God, and this *is* the gate of heaven. And Jacob rose up early in the morning, and took the stone that he had put *for* his pillows, and set it up *for* a pillar, and poured oil upon the top of it. And he called the name of that place Beth-el: but the name of that city *was called* Luz at the first.

DIRECT ANSWER.

A MAN of God gave to the meeting this incident in his own life. For sixteen years he has been at work among the lowly, the sick, and the sorrowing. He is well known wherever there is wretchedness, sickness, or suffering. The debased keepers of drinking-saloons, when they can get no more out of a poor creature, send him to this friend, knowing that he will turn no one away. Debased outcasts ask him for a little bread, and for money for a night's lodging. He received a letter asking him to call at one of the most wretched tenements in the city. He went. The poor sufferer lay on his bed. He wanted five dollars to carry him into the country. Said the visitor, "I am nearly as poor as you are. I have just five dollars, that I was going to spend on my family, but I will give it to you, and I think the Lord will return it to me." "I gave it to the poor man," said the relator, "and when I went to my closet, I said, 'O Lord! if it is thy will, return me the money needful to meet my necessities to-night.' I came from my closet to this meeting. The first man I met—and he sits before me now—said, 'You must see a great deal of suffering in your rounds, and must have a great many calls upon you for aid. I can't do much for you, but here is a little to help you on your way.' He gave me a five-dollar bill. It was the exact sum I gave the poor sufferer; it was the exact sum I needed and asked for. I accepted it as a direct answer to prayer."

CIV.

SERVICE OF SONG.

AND these *are they* whom David set over the service of song in the house of the Lord, after that the ark had rest. All these *were* under the hands of their father for song *in* the house of the Lord, with cymbals, psalteries, and harps, for the service of the house of God, according to the king's order to Asaph, Jeduthun, and Heman. So the number of them, with their brethren that were instructed in the songs of the Lord, *even* all that were cunning, was two hundred fourscore and eight. For in the days of David and Asaph of old *there were* chief of the singers, and songs of praise and thanksgiving unto God. And all Israel in the days of Zerubbabel, and in the days of Nehemiah, gave the portions of the singers and the porters, every day his portion: and they sanctified *holy things* unto the Levites ; and the Levites sanctified *them* unto the children of Aaron.

HARD TO REFORM.

I HAVE done a little work in the desolate and wretched region of Five Points, as well as in other parts of the city. I was walking through Worth street one day. I heard some one call my name. Not supposing that I was referred to, I walked on. My name was pronounced still sharper, and I turned to see who was calling me. A man stood on the edge of a cellar. He was a forlorn-looking creature, wretched in dress and look, his features indicating that sin, a hard master, had paid him fully his wages. I said, "Did you call me?" "Yes, sir." "Do you know me?" "Yes, I do." "Where did you ever see me?" "At Blackwell's Island." "When?" "A month ago. You spoke there. I had a month to serve on the Island when you were there. I thought I would try and mend my ways, and when I came out, get an honest living. Every body knew me, every body was afraid of me, nobody would trust me. I got a place as porter in a store. I think my employer liked me. One day, a man came in who had a bundle of tracts under his arm. He said to my employer, 'Do you know who that fellow is out there?' 'I think he's a pretty nice sort of a fellow.' 'Well, you'd better look out for him, he's been up on the Island. I've seen him there.' My employer asked me if that was so, and I told him it was. I saw he was turned against me. I knew my fate was sealed. My resolutions were distrusted, and my prayer unheeded. I was soon adrift, through no fault of mine. I haven't gone back to my old ways yet, but I'm afraid I shall starve. Look down here, and see where I sleep in this foul den, because it's cheap. It is hard, sir, to reform, very hard."

CV.

TRUST IN THE LORD.

IN that day shall this song be sung in the land of Judah; We have a strong city; salvation will *God* appoint *for* walls and bulwarks. Trust ye in the Lord for ever: for in the Lord Jehovah *is* everlasting strength. They that trust in the Lord *shall be* as Mount Zion, *which* can not be removed, *but* abideth forever. *As* the mountains *are* round about Jerusalem, so the Lord *is* round about his people from henceforth even forever. Blessed *be* the Lord my strength, which teacheth my hands to war, *and* my fingers to fight: my goodness, and my fortress; my high tower, and my deliverer; my shield, and *he* in whom I trust; who subdueth my people under me. Behold, God *is* my salvation; I will trust, and not be afraid: for the Lord Jehovah *is* my strength and *my* song; he also is become my salvation. Therefore with joy shall ye draw water out of the wells of salvation. And in that day shall ye say, Praise the Lord, call upon his name, declare his doings among the people, make mention that his name is exalted.

QUICK AND POWERFUL.

Among the benevolent organizations at work among us is a company of gentlemen united for the service of song. They visit charitable institutions, prisons, hospitals, and even lunatic asylums, to entertain their inmates. They were present at the meeting on Blackwell's Island, referred to in the incident above. It was a bright Sunday morning, and full six hundred prisoners were marched into the prison chapel for service. All nationalities were gathered—all classes, conditions, and colors. The desperadoes of the city came in, with ball and chain around them, heavily handcuffed, for they were not to be trusted, even in the sanctuary. The speaker was a well-known clergyman, eminent for tact, a workman and no botch, who knew how to divide the word of truth. He could "offer butter in a lordly dish," and speak to prisoners tenderly, without offense. The theme was the prodigal son. It was treated like a narrative. The boy was traced from the time he left his father's home, through all his career downward, till he had squandered all his living, and, in disgrace, found himself keeping swine. The effect of the address was simply marvelous. Men, giants in crime, wept, and women, notorious for their hardihood, sobbed audibly under the tender appeal, while the singing melted the entire assembly. The sword of the Spirit did its work, and many came out of that prison-house into the liberty wherewith Christ maketh free.

CVI.

PRAISE TO THE LORD.

AND he leaping up stood, and walked, and entered with them into the temple, walking, and leaping, and praising God. And all the people saw him walking and praising God: and they knew that it was he which sat for alms at the beautiful gate of the temple: and they were filled with wonder and amazement at that which had happened unto him. And David and all Israel played before God with all *their* might, and with singing, and with harps, and with psalteries, and with timbrels, and with cymbals, and with trumpets. Thou shalt fear the Lord thy God; him shalt thou serve, and to him shalt thou cleave, and swear by his name. He *is* thy praise, and he *is* thy God, that hath done for thee these great and terrible things, which thine eyes have seen.

"DRUNKARDS CLAIM ME."

A GENTLEMAN was invited to make a temperance address in a church not far from the city. He was quartered in the family of a lawyer, who had never signed the pledge, and it was his boast that he had never drank a drop of intoxicating liquors in his life. He said it would be an absurdity for him to solemnly agree that he would not do what he never had done, and what he had no disposition to do. He thought the pledge a good thing for drunkards, and wished the cause success. Some months afterward, the same speaker went to the same place to lecture, and was entertained by the same host. But he found him now at the head of the temperance movement, and president of the society. "But how is this?" the lecturer said; "you must have signed the pledge, and if you have done that, you have changed your views somewhat since I was here." "Well, the fact is," said the lawyer, "I had to unite with my temperance friends to keep me out of bad company. All the drunkards in town claimed me. They didn't care about my not drinking, they said, as long as I kept out of those fanatical organizations. The drinking men and the rum-selling men made me their head, voted for me, lifted their hats to me, ran after me, and pointed to me, to show how good a man could be and not be a fanatic. To get out of their company, I have had to sign the pledge, and I wish I had taken it sooner."

CVII.

CHARITY.

AND now abideth faith, hope, charity, these three; but the greatest of these *is* charity. Charity suffereth long, *and* is kind; charity envieth not; charity vaunteth not itself, is not puffed up. Charity never faileth: but whether *there be* prophecies, they shall fail; whether *there be* tongues, they shall cease; whether *there be* knowledge, it shall vanish away. I therefore, the prisoner of the Lord, beseech you that ye walk worthy of the vocation wherewith ye are called, with all lowliness and meekness, with longsuffering, forbearing one another in love; endeavoring to keep the unity of the Spirit in the bond of peace. Put on therefore, as the elect of God, holy and beloved, bowe's of mercies, kindness, humbleness of mind, meekness, longsuffering.

"MAN, DO YOU LOVE GOD?"

My youngest child is a very devout little fellow. He seems to have an intuitive regard for sacred times and sacred themes. He has a Bible of his own for family worship, though he can not read a word. No service can be omitted that is usual, without its being noticed by our little monitor. One morning, I was in a hurry for my breakfast, and I did not wait for the family, nor indeed did I wait for the usual blessing. My little son dropped his knife and looked up with perfect astonishment, and cried out, "Bless God, papa, bless God." He sleeps in an adjoining room, and his custom is, as soon as it is light, to jump out of his crib, come into my room, and get into my bed. One evening, a clerical friend called to spend the night with me. He was not in good health, and I gave up my room to him because it was warm. My little boy was not notified of this new arrangement. In the morning, he came trotting into my room as usual, went round to the back side, and as he stepped into bed, he saw a strange face covered with black hair resting on the pillow. He was wonderfully frightened, and was equally afraid to go back or to remain. He breathed hard, under great excitement. Laying his hand on the face of the stranger, he said, "Man, do you love God?" "I hope I do," says my friend. "Then I guess I'll lay down and take a nap." He was soon asleep, feeling, in his childish confidence, that a man who loved God wouldn't hurt a little boy.

CVIII.

LARGENESS OF HEART.

AND God gave Solomon wisdom and understanding exceeding much, and largeness of heart, even as the sand that *is* on the sea-shore. There is that scattereth, and yet increaseth; and *there is* that withholdeth more than is meet, but *it tendeth* to poverty. The liberal soul shall be made fat: and he that watereth shall be watered also himself. He that withholdeth corn, the people shall curse him: but blessing *shall be* upon the head of him that selleth *it.* Every man according as he purposeth in his heart, *so let him give;* not grudgingly, or of necessity: for God loveth a cheerful giver. And God *is* able to make all grace abound toward you; that ye, always having all sufficiency in all *things*, may abound to every good work: (as it is written, He hath dispersed abroad; he hath given to the poor: his righteousness remaineth forever.)

RELIGION HELPS MEN.

A JANITOR had a good position, and earned a comfortable living. He took to drink, lost his position, and came to want. His wife found her way into the Fulton-street meeting. She persuaded her husband to go with her the other day. He exhibited so much interest that he was brought in contact with the missionary. "You must kneel down, and let me pray with you. We bring every body to God who comes here. We have no help ourselves." The astonished man bent his knee for the first time in many years. He arose a new man. As he said, the love of drink had departed. He obtained a place in a carpet-store, and became a first-class salesman. He has never had any desire for the intoxicating cup since. He owns a pleasant place in the country. His children are well brought up, and are in good situations.

"SING till the love of sin departs." Men not only sign the pledge here; that is a great thing. But all pledges are made with prayer. Sobriety not only follows, but the *love* of drinking is removed.

CIX.

GLORY TO OUR GOD.

GIVE unto the Lord, ye kindreds of the people, give unto the Lord glory and strength. Give unto the Lord the glory *due* unto his name: bring an offering, and come before him: worship the Lord in the beauty of holiness. Glory to God in the highest, and on earth peace, good-will toward men. But let him that glorieth glory in this, that he understandeth and knoweth me, that I *am* the Lord which exercise lovingkindness, judgment, and righteousness, in the earth: for in these *things* I delight, saith the Lord. His name shall endure forever: his name shall be continued as long as the sun: and *men* shall be blessed in him: all nations shall call him blessed. Blessed *be* the Lord God, the God of Israel, who only doeth wondrous things. And blessed *be* his glorious name forever: and let the whole earth be filled *with* his glory. Amen, and Amen. The prayers of David the son of Jesse are ended.

A RESCUED SOUL.

A WELL-KNOWN clergyman, in visiting one of our public institutions, noticed a young girl scrubbing the floor. She seemed to have more than ordinary intelligence, and he entered into conversation with her. She was a Catholic, she said, but wanted to reform, and would be glad to go into some good, pious Protestant family. He took her to his own home. She signed the pledge, joined in the family devotions, went to the Protestant church, and soon was converted. She remained in the family two years, and then went into the mission work, and is now at the head of one of the most important institutions of the city.

CX.

SUMMER ENDED.

THE harvest is past, the summer is ended, and we are not saved. For the hurt of the daughter of my people am I hurt; I am black; astonishment hath taken hold on me. *Is there* no balm in Gilead? *is there* no physician there? why then is not the health of the daughter of my people recovered? Incline your ear, and come unto me: hear, and your soul shall live; and I will make an everlasting covenant with you, *even* the sure mercies of David. Behold, I have given him *for* a witness to the people, a leader and commander to the people. Seek ye the Lord while he may be found, call ye upon him while he is near. Let the wicked forsake his way, and the unrighteous man his thoughts: and let him return unto the Lord, and he will have mercy upon him; and to our God, for he will abundantly pardon.

GO NOT WITH THEM.

A MAN started from the East with his family for Chicago. In New-York, he got drunk, and lost his boy. He kept on his journey. The lad was taken care of by one of our mission establishments, and was brought into the noonday meeting. He was soon converted. He obtained an honorable position in the city, but never could hear from his mother. One day, he came into the meeting, resolved to ask prayers that God would direct him in his search after his parents. He had not heard from them for years, and he did not know whether they were dead or alive. The mother was in the meeting that day, and made herself known, to the joy of her son and to the astonishment of all present.

A MAN, who has had great business success, was put out to a trade. At the end of a week the lad came home. "I can't stay there, father. I have to go out every day and buy rum for the men. I break my pledge, and I can not do it."

CXI.

SPEAKING THE TRUTH.

BUT speaking the truth in love, may grow up into him in all things, which is the head, *even* Christ: wherefore, laying aside all malice, and all guile, and hypocrisies, and envies, and all evil speakings. And withal they learn *to be* idle, wandering about from house to house; and not only idle, but tattlers also and busybodies, speaking things which they ought not. In all things showing thyself a pattern of good works: in doctrine *showing* uncorruptness, gravity, sincerity, sound speech, that can not be condemned; that he that is of the contrary part may be ashamed, having no evil thing to say of you. Let all bitterness, and wrath, and anger, and clamor, and evil speaking, be put away from you, with all malice: and be ye kind one to another, tender-hearted, forgiving one another, even as God for Christ's sake hath forgiven you.

WIDOW'S PRAYER.

THE widow of an Episcopal minister is a Bible-reader in this city. Her only child, a son, left his home eighteen years ago. The father regarded him as dead. The mother never gave him up. She was left alone in the world on the death of her husband, but believed firmly that her boy was living. Impressed with this idea, she came down to Fulton-street meeting, and earnestly entreated the prayers of God's people for news of her boy. Her prayer was, "O Lord! if my boy is alive, let me know it." Two weeks from the day the request was read, a letter came from London from her long-lost son. She sought the house of the Lord to give thanks for his great mercies.

A SALOON-KEEPER became very sick, and anxious about his soul. The singing attracted him, and he had been accustomed to attend the noonday meeting. He wanted to see somebody connected with that service. He was visited. On his sick-bed, he professed faith in the Saviour, and the communion was administered to him. He died. His whole family came into the church, and are now prospered.

CXII.

HONESTLY.

LET us walk honestly, as in the day; not in rioting and drunkenness, not in chambering and wantonness, not in strife and envying. But put ye on the Lord Jesus Christ, and make not provision for the flesh, to *fulfill* the lusts *thereof*. And that ye study to be quiet, and to do your own business, and to work with your own hands, as we commanded you; that ye may walk honestly toward them that are without, and *that* ye may have lack of nothing. Be careful for nothing; but in every thing by prayer and supplication with thanksgiving let your requests be made known unto God. And the peace of God, which passeth all understanding, shall keep your hearts and minds through Christ Jesus. Finally, brethren, whatsoever things are true, whatsoever things *are* honest, whatsoever things *are* just, whatsoever things *are* pure, whatsoever things *are* lovely, whatsoever things *are* of good report; if *there be* any virtue, and if *there be* any praise, think on these things.

DIRECT ANSWERS.

"SEND us a pastor, O Lord!" was the earnest cry from a destitute church, two years without a minister. On the Sabbath following, an entire stranger came into the church. He was invited to preach a part of the day. With the invocation, the church felt that the right man had come. This impression deepened as the services progressed. He was called. Months have justified the first impression. Among the letters on file in Fulton-street is one from this church, giving thanks to God for answers to prayer.

A WHOLE family, father, mother, and three sons, came to the private rooms of the meeting, to have a request drawn up in behalf of the eldest son, who was intemperate. The father was a drinking man, though not a drunkard. "Let us all kneel down," said the missionary, "and ask God to help us." It was a weeping time. The whole family took the pledge, and in a few weeks all united with the church of Christ.

A YOUNG man became interested in religion. He did not know what to do nor where to go. He had heard of the daily prayer-meeting, and urged his mother to go with him to the Fulton-street church. He heard the requests read, and said to his mother, "That is what I want." He went home, and by the aid of his mother, wrote a request for himself. It was presented, and earnestly responded to. This was ten years ago. A short time since, a young man came into the meeting to return thanks to God for his great mercy. He was the same young man who had before sought salvation on the threshold of the old North Church. "I am a pastor over a beloved flock to-day, brethren," he said, "in answer to your prayers."

CXIII.

PEACE LIKE A RIVER.

OH! that thou hadst hearkened to my commandments! then had thy peace been as a river, and thy righteousness as the waves of the sea: thy seed also had been as the sand, and the offspring of thy bowels like the gravel thereof; his name should not have been cut off nor destroyed from before me. And the work of righteousness shall be peace; and the effect of righteousness, quietness and assurance forever. And my people shall dwell in a peaceable habitation, and in sure dwellings, and in quiet resting places; when it shall hail, coming down on the forest; and the city shall be low in a low place. And there shall be no more curse: but the throne of God and of the Lamb shall be in it; and his servants shall serve him: and they shall see his face; and his name *shall be* in their foreheads. And there shall be no night there; and they need no candle, neither light of the sun; for the Lord God giveth them light: and they shall reign forever and ever.

MOTHER KNEW GOD.

"Mother knew God," said a young man in the prayer-meeting. "Five years ago, I landed in New-York. Mother and I knew nobody, but mother knew God. I got into bad company; staid out late; but mother's door was always ajar when I came home. When she thought I was asleep, she came into my room, knelt down by my bedside, and prayed audibly that the Lord would preserve me, and keep me from bad company. I had been in America but a little while when I came down to this meeting. The requests affected me strangely. I wondered if I could be saved if the meeting would pray for me. I tremblingly presented a request to the meeting, and found that the Lord was indeed a hearer and answerer of prayer."

When James Harper got into the wagon to go to New-York to learn a trade, his mother, a godly woman, prayed with him, and said, "James, you have got blood in you. Don't disgrace it."

CXIV.

NOT AS OUR WAYS.

FOR my thoughts *are* not your thoughts, neither *are* your ways my ways, saith the Lord. For *as* the heavens are higher than the earth, so are my ways higher than your ways, and my thoughts than your thoughts. For thus saith the high and lofty One that inhabiteth eternity, whose name *is* Holy; I dwell in the high and holy *place*, with him also *that is* of a contrite and humble spirit, to revive the spirit of the humble, and to revive the heart of the contrite ones. For I will not contend forever, neither will I be always wroth: for the spirit should fail before me, and the souls *which* I have made. The eternal God *is thy* refuge, and underneath *are* the everlasting arms: and he shall thrust out the enemy from before thee; and shall say, Destroy *them*. Happy *art* thou, O Israel: who *is* like unto thee, O people saved by the Lord, the shield of thy help, and who *is* the sword of thy excellency! and thine enemies shall be found liars unto thee; and thou shalt tread upon their high places.

SEWING-GIRL'S CONSCIENCE.

IN that part of the city where the lowly dwell resided a young sewing-girl. Her home was a very scanty one, and her living precarious. In the hallway stood a gay and dashing girl, fashionably dressed, who had in her arms a bundle. "Can you do some work for me? do it right away? do it nicely? If you can, I will pay you well for it." The gay creature, without seeming to notice the surprise of the sewing-girl, undid her bundle. She displayed the rich and costly material that was to be manufactured into a fashionable attire. The material was not only costly but gaudy. "I am an actress," she said; "I am disappointed in some work that must be done; I want to wear it on the stage; I must have it at once, and I will pay you handsomely for it." "I don't think I can do it," said the sewing-girl; "I am afraid, if I make this dress, that I shall partake of the sin of acting." "You want work, don't you? You have been praying for it, for I heard you; and now it has come, hasn't it?" "I am afraid it is a temptation of the devil," said the poor girl. "I will ask God what I shall do about it." She locked her door, and knelt down before the astonished actress, and asked her heavenly Father whether she should starve, or make the dress for the actress. The visitor was overwhelmed. In agony she came and knelt down beside the girl, crying out in agony, "Don't pray any more about the dress; pray for me. Pray that I may forsake a sinful life and become a Christian." The pair arose from their knees. "You shan't do this work for me; I shall pay you the same as if you did it. Nobody shall make it. I will abandon the stage; I will never appear on the boards again." The wants of the poor sewing-girl were over. A location was provided, attractive and genteel, with plenty of work. Three years after, a letter was received from the actress. "I loved the stage," she said; "I loved my profession; I expected to make my mark and to realize a fortune. Since the night you prayed for me, I have never entered a theatre. I have now a happy home, and am a member of a Christian church, and bless God for the night that I brought my dress for the stage for you to make."

CXV.

CHRISTIAN SYMPATHY.

AND it came to pass, when they were come to Beth-lehem, that all the city was moved about them, and they said, *Is* this Naomi? And she said unto them, Call me not Naomi, call me Mara: for the Almighty hath dealt very bitterly with me. I went out full, and the Lord hath brought me home again empty: why *then* call ye me Naomi, seeing the Lord hath testified against me, and the Almighty hath afflicted me? Now when he came nigh to the gate of the city, behold, there was a dead man carried out, the only son of his mother, and she was a widow: and much people of the city was with her. And when the Lord saw her, he had compassion on her, and said unto her, Weep not. But I have all, and abound: I am full, having received of Epaphroditus the things *which were sent* from you, an odor of a sweet smell, a sacrifice acceptable, well pleasing to God. But my God shall supply all your need according to his riches in glory by Christ Jesus. Now unto God and our Father *be* glory for ever and ever. Amen.

PRAYER-MEETING ON THE ALPS.

I WAS crossing the Alps with a large party. An avalanche, the night before, piled the snow sixteen or seventeen feet on the railroad-track. The passengers were packed into sleighs. A halt was called in a miserable cavern. The night was dark and cold, and the whole party rushed into the gloomy room of the cavern for shelter. The drivers, thirty or forty in number, a desperate-looking set of fellows, were not far removed from brigands. A single candle lighted the blackened room. Around the long, low, dirty table, the ill-clad and dark-browed drivers sat. A few embers glowed on the hearth, and over them hung a large pot with offensive-looking broth, which was ladled out to the men. Robbery was no uncommon thing in that desolate place. There was no house or cottage of relief for miles. The company crowded the room; but had the desperate fellows set upon us, both robbery and murder could have been inflicted with impunity. As it was, blackmail was levied on the entire company. Scarcely a word was spoken. Every one was impressed with the peril of our position. A hand took hold of mine; it was a stranger's voice: "I wish we were in Fulton-street Prayer-meeting," was the utterance. The face I could not see, and do not know to this day who the friend was that spoke. It turned all thoughts heavenward. Deliverance came; no one was harmed. Desperate men were kept back, and we crossed the Alps in safety.

CXVI.

TIMES OF REFRESHING.

REPENT ye therefore, and be converted, that your sins may be blotted out, when the times of refreshing shall come from the presence of the Lord; for the Lord your God *is* God of gods, and Lord of lords, a great God, a mighty, and a terrible, which regardeth not persons, nor taketh reward: he doth execute the judgment of the fatherless and widow, and loveth the stranger, in giving him food and raiment. O Lord, I have heard thy speech, *and* was afraid: O Lord, revive thy work in the midst of the years, in the midst of the years make known; in wrath remember mercy. Do good in thy good pleasure unto Zion: build thou the walls of Jerusalem. Then shalt thou be pleased with the sacrifices of righteousness, with burnt offering and whole burnt offering: then shall they offer bullocks upon thine altar.

GREAT DELIVERANCE.

A MERCHANT in a neighboring city stood very high in social life. He was an earnest, devoted Christian, and bore a distinguished part in Sunday-school and mission work. Financial reverses overtook him. He yielded to the intoxicating cup, and fell from his high position. Full of shame and mortification at his disgrace, he signed the pledge, and resolved once more to be a man. Though he stood pledged to abstain, the love of intoxicating drinks was very strong, so strong that it overpowered him the second time. The ruin of the man seemed complete. His family became alienated and left him. He seemed to have no friends. Poverty came upon him like an armed man, and he was literally an outcast. He came to New-York, in the hope of picking up some work, but was disappointed. He resolved to put an end to his life, and purchased laudanum with that intent. Something held him back, and he started for Fulton street, where, in sunnier days, he had enjoyed the presence of the Lord. He took a back seat. Among the requests was one for a poor, unfortunate drunkard, who was struggling with his appetite. He was impressed to send a request for himself. Perhaps here might be found the help that he had sought for in vain elsewhere. He went home, wrote a request asking the meeting to pray for one who was "an outcast from his house, from his church, and from his friends, by reason of strong drink." This was sent to the room by a little boy. He was present when the request was read. In the meeting was one who related his experience. A man said he had fallen six times, and had been taken up each time by a Christian brother, and it was not until he had committed himself wholly to the Saviour that he found his appetite for drink conquered. The desperate man took courage. He went to his room, locked the door, fell on his knees, and told the Saviour all. Before he arose, he felt that he was fully pardoned. He arose with the love of strong drink taken wholly from him—from him, as he believes, in answer to earnest prayer. Months have passed, and the desire for strong drink has not returned. He has been readmitted to the church of God, and a happy home and good business awaits him.

CXVII.

FOOTSTEPS ON THE MOUNTAINS.

HOW beautiful upon the mountains are the feet of him that bringeth good tidings, that publisheth peace; that bringeth good tidings of good, that publisheth salvation; that saith unto Zion, Thy God reigneth! Then took he him up in his arms, and blessed God, and said, Lord, now lettest thou thy servant depart in peace, according to thy word: for mine eyes have seen thy salvation, which thou hast prepared before the face of all people; a light to lighten the Gentiles, and the glory of thy people Israel. I will open rivers in high places, and fountains in the midst of the valleys: I will make the wilderness a pool of water, and the dry land springs of water. I will plant in the wilderness the cedar, the chittah tree, and the myrtle, and the oil tree; I will set in the desert the fir tree, *and* the pine, and the box tree together.

INFLUENCE OF THE PRAYER-MEETING.

I CAME to this meeting five years ago. My field of labor is in the far West. The short, crisp, earnest prayers taught me how to pray. I had often sent requests here for prayer, but the influence of the meeting itself upon me was the most remarkable thing about it. I went home to pray for the outpouring of the Holy Spirit upon my people. The answer came in a copious revival.

MY first visit to this meeting was eight years ago. I came because my mother begged me to attend. She had read of the meeting in the papers, and somehow felt that my salvation was connected with that visit. In the old consistory-room I sat down with the company. I listened to the requests; one of them I knew meant me. I left the place reconciled to God. I am now a young preacher of the Gospel, but I feel that I was born here.

A CONVERTED Israelite came into the meeting, one day, with a specially burdened heart. Valuable papers of his were in the hands of a lawyer who refused to give them up. He could not prosecute a claim he had against the government without them. "I will carry the case to God," he said. Alone in a pew he kneeled down, and seemed oblivious to every thing in the room. He went directly from the meeting to the office of the lawyer. He demanded his papers. Without a word, the lawyer went to his safe, took out the package and handed it to him. "I got down on my knees and told my Messiah, Jesus Christ the Lord, all about it. I knew he heard and answered my prayer before I left the meeting."

CXVIII.

THE SEA IS HIS.

THE sea *is* his, and he made it: and his hands formed the dry *land*. For *in* six days the Lord made heaven and earth, the sea, and all that in them *is*, and rested the seventh day: wherefore the Lord blessed the Sabbath day, and hallowed it. They that go down to the sea in ships, that do business in great waters; these see the works of the Lord, and his wonders in the deep. For he commandeth, and raiseth the stormy wind, which lifteth up the waves thereof. O Lord, how manifold are thy works! in wisdom hast thou made them all: the earth is full of thy riches. *So is* this great and wide sea, wherein *are* things creeping innumerable, both small and great beasts. Fear ye not me? saith the Lord: will ye not tremble at my presence, which have placed the sand *for* the bound of the sea by a perpetual decree, that it can not pass it: and though the waves thereof toss themselves, yet can they not prevail; though they roar, yet can they not pass over it?

WHOLE CREW FOR JESUS.

I AM a sea-captain. I attend this meeting when I am in port. I want my vessel to be a place of prayer. I found myself on the lea-shore going on to the breakers, but the Good Pilot came to my rescue. I want my men to be as happy in the Lord as I am. I treat my sailors so that I am not ashamed on the Lord's day to be their minister, to read to them the word of God, and talk about the blessed Saviour. I say to them, "Shipmates, I was a bad fellow, drifting on the lea-shore. I had not a minute to lose; I resolved to 'bout ship at once and claw off shore. I want you to sign the articles, and sail with my Captain, and he will bring you safely into port." I cast anchor the other day in this harbor. I had sixteen men aboard, and they were all for Jesus. We have a nightly prayer-meeting, sometimes in the forecastle, sometimes in the cabin. We sing the songs of Zion, and a happier crew never sailed into the port of New-York.

"I WAS converted on board of a ship, down in a gun-room," said a stout-built sailor. "I took the Pilot on board while the old ship rolled in the tempest and storm. When the Lord appeared to me on the sea, I said, 'Howl, ye winds! blow, ye tempests! roar, ye billows! The Master has come, and my soul is safe.'"

CXIX.

CONSECRATION.

FOR when for the time ye ought to be teachers, ye have need that one teach you again which *be* the first principles of the oracles of God; and are become such as have need of milk, and not of strong meat. Not purloining, but showing all good fidelity; that they may adorn the doctrine of God our Saviour in all things. For the grace of God that bringeth salvation hath appeared to all men, teaching us that, denying ungodliness and worldly lusts, we should live soberly, righteously, and godly, in this present world. By a new and living way, which he hath consecrated for us, through the vail, that is to say, his flesh; and *having* a high priest over the house of God; let us draw near with a true heart in full assurance of faith, having our hearts sprinkled from an evil conscience, and our bodies washed with pure water.

PRAYER AND TRADE.

A NEIGHBOR of mine was struggling with intemperance. It alienated him from his family. His wife had an independent fortune, but would do nothing for him. Again and again he signed the pledge, and was put into positions of trust and fell. Once more he was put on his feet. Nobody would help him. "You have broken all your promises, and we have no confidence in you," was the general reply. His wife refused to assist him. "We must pray over this matter," said the pastor. A meeting was held, and earnest prayer offered. As the meeting was breaking up, the pastor said, "Go down and see your wife to-morrow; I think she will help you." "Will you allow me to build a house on that vacant lot of yours?" he said to his wife. "Yes." But nobody would trust him for lumber, and no builder would undertake the job. He went back to his wife and said, "I can do nothing; nobody will help me, and if you do not come to my rescue I must go under." She instantly wrote, "I will be responsible for any contracts made with my husband." He went out, resolved in God's strength to be a man. He looked upon the readiness of his wife to help him as a direct answer to prayer. From that hour he became a devoted Christian and an ornament to the church.

I HAVE a man in my employ who is a very smart, energetic workman, faithful in all his duties, but a despiser of religion. I became interested in him and anxious about him. That anxiety I one day addressed to him. "You need not trouble yourself about me," he said; "I do not wish to be a Christian; if such men," naming two or three, "are Christians, I am content to remain irreligious." "Suppose these men are not Christians, are only pretenders? Suppose they die and go to hell, will it better your condition that you go in such company?" "I don't think it would, but I never thought of that before."

CXX.

CUP OF COLD WATER.

AND whoever shall give to drink unto one of these little ones a cup of cold *water* only in the name of a disciple, verily I say unto you, he shall in no wise lose his reward. And he looked up, and saw the rich men casting their gifts into the treasury. And he saw also a certain poor widow casting in thither two mites. And he said, Of a truth I say unto you, that this poor widow hath cast in more than they all: for all these have of their abundance cast in unto the offerings of God: but she of her penury hath cast in all the living that she had. And they, continuing daily with one accord in the temple, and breaking bread from house to house, did eat their meat with gladness and singleness of heart, praising God, and having favor with all the people. And the Lord added to the church daily such as should be saved.

DONE WHAT SHE COULD.

ONE day, a lady came into the meeting, evidently a lady in affluent circumstances. She approached the missionary, and handed him a valuable diamond, saying, "I wish you to dispose of that, and apply the proceeds to relieving the sick and suffering this winter. Her history soon became known. She was connected with one of the first families in the State. Her husband had a high position in the army, and inherited large wealth. The husband and wife took an elegant country-seat, and adorned it in the highest style of art and taste. Carriages, servants, plate, and all the appliances of an affluent life were secured.

The season was unusually gay. Parties, balls, soirées were enjoyed. As the spring advanced, a protracted meeting was opened in a little unpretentious church, and continued for a week. A good deal of interest was created, and among the attendants was the fashionable lady referred to. She was intensely interested in the services. As she entered the gay saloons, the words of the preacher rang in her ears, "This night shall thy soul be required of thee; then whose shall those things be that thou hast provided?" She told her husband that she could no longer spend her time frivolously and vainly in swinging round the circle of fashion. Cards and wine, dancing and frivolity, were no longer her delight.

She was soon converted, and her diamond was her first offering to the cause of religion. Soon a dark cloud came over her. Her husband was accused of crime; his fair name was disgraced. She believed her husband to be innocent, and that God would make his innocence to appear in his own good time. She clung to him, and clung to her Saviour. His innocency was brought to light, and he was honorably acquitted. Struck with the steadfast devotion and piety of his wife, the husband was led to the Saviour; and now, hand in hand, they walk together in the ordinances of the Lord, consecrating their talent and wealth to the services of Christ's kingdom.

CXXI.

DIVINITY OF OUR LORD.

AND from Jesus Christ, *who is* the faithful witness, *and* the first-begotten of the dead, and the prince of the kings of the earth. Unto him that loved us, and washed us from our sins in his own blood, and hath made us kings and priests unto God and his Father; to him *be* glory and dominion for ever and ever. Amen. I am Alpha and Omega, the beginning and the ending, saith the Lord, which is, and which was, and which is to come, the Almighty. *I am* he that liveth, and was dead; and, behold, I am alive for evermore, Amen; and have the keys of hell and of death. Moreover, brethren, I would not that ye should be ignorant, how that all our fathers were under the cloud, and all passed through the sea; and were all baptized unto Moses in the cloud and in the sea; and did all eat the same spiritual meat; and did all drink the same spiritual drink; for they drank of that spiritual Rock that followed them: and that Rock was Christ. Who, being the brightness of *his* glory and the express image of his person, and upholding all things by the word of his power, when he had by himself purged our sins, sat down on the right hand of the Majesty on high; being made so much better than the angels, as he hath by inheritance obtained a more excellent name than they.

GRACE AND TOBACCO.

I WAS a great smoker; I smoked for forty years. Again and again, I resolved to give up tobacco; but the habit was too strong for me. I was an active Christian, and delighted to lead sinners to the Saviour. In seasons of religious fervor, I was always at the altar, talking to those who were seeking salvation.

One day, I heard a young lady speak of a brother. "He came and spoke to me," she said, "as I knelt at the altar. His breath made me sick, it was so foul with tobacco." The words came to me with wondrous power. Perhaps people talk just so about me.

I went to the Northport camp-meeting. I said to my wife, "I am going to quit smoking." "You can't do it. You have tried over and over again, for years." "Well, I am going down to the grove. I mean to fall down on my knees and pray God for grace to help me. I shan't come back until I have conquered." I need not tell you how long I prayed. When I came back, I handed my old pipe, that had been my companion for years, to my wife. "Put that on the mantle," I said; "I am boss now." I not only broke off smoking, but the love of tobacco departed; not the least hankering remained. Smokers and smoking are alike indifferent to me. I can walk among them as the holy three walked amid the flames. It is now four years since I had the fight in the grove, and conquered through prayer. To God be all the glory!

CXXII.

OUR HEAVENLY HOME.

AND I saw no temple therein: for the Lord God Almighty and the Lamb are the temple of it. And the city had no need of the sun, neither of the moon, to shine in it: for the glory of God did lighten it, and the Lamb *is* the light thereof. And the nations of them which are saved shall walk in the light of it: and the kings of the earth do bring their glory and honor into it. And there shall be no night there; and they need no candles, neither light of the sun; for the Lord God giveth them light, and they shall reign for ever and ever. And I heard a voice from heaven, as the voice of many waters, and as the voice of a great thunder: and I heard the voice of harpers harping with their harps: and they sung as it were a new song before the throne, and before the four beasts, and the elders: and no man could learn that song but the hundred *and* forty *and* four thousand, which were redeemed from the earth. And God shall wipe away all tears from their eyes; and there shall be no more death, neither sorrow, nor crying, neither shall there be any more pain: for the former things are passed away.

PRODIGAL'S RETURN.

I BELONG to a family from which a brother strayed away fifteen years ago. We thought he might be in California, but could hear nothing from him. We advertised largely, and sent letters in every direction. One day, a member of our family was in Fulton-street meeting. Requests were read for the sorrowing, the afflicted, the unconverted, the erring and the lost. The thought was suggested, why not send in a request for our absent brother? With much trembling and fear, the request was written. The next day, I was seated amidst the crowd of worshipers in this famed meeting. I had been a professor of religion many years; but I never before was so affected by a song of praise. The Scripture read went to my heart. It seemed fitted to my case; I melted under the prayer.

I trembled from head to foot when the leader held up a bundle of papers, and began to read the requests. Oh! how my heart throbbed when the leader said, "Will some one pray for this afflicted family, and restore the lost brother to its fond embrace?" I turned from the sanctuary, saying, in the fullness of my heart, "How dreadful is this place! It is none other than the house of God and the gate of heaven."

In a short time, and in a very extraordinary manner, we heard from our lost brother. Better than all, he was a new man in Christ Jesus. We are now a family happily united, as we believe, in answer to prayer. I now come to return thanksgiving to the Lord for his great mercy to our household.

CXXIII.

THE GREAT APOSTASY.

FOR the mystery of iniquity doth already work: only he who now letteth *will let*, until he be taken out of the way. And then shall that Wicked be revealed, whom the Lord shall consume with the spirit of his mouth, and shall destroy with the brightness of his coming. And the woman was arrayed in purple and scarlet color, and decked with gold and precious stones and pearls, having a golden cup in her hand full of abominations and filthiness of her fornication: and upon her forehead *was* a name written, MYSTERY, BABYLON THE GREAT, THE MOTHER OF HARLOTS AND ABOMINATIONS OF THE EARTH. Ever learning, and never able to come to the knowledge of the truth. Now as Jannes and Jambres withstood Moses, so do these also resist the truth: men of corrupt minds, reprobrate concerning the faith. But they shall proceed no further: for their folly shall be manifest unto all *men*, as theirs also was.

ARROW AT VENTURE.

A STRANGER in New-York, drifting about to look at the great city, I turned from Broadway down Fulton street, and thought I would take a look at the ferries. At the corner of Fulton and William streets, every thing was blocked ; a car stretched over the crossing, and carts, vans, omnibuses, and coaches, and heavily laden teams, were jammed together. Men were shouting and swearing, and confusion reigned everywhere. I stopped to look, and wondered if the street could ever be cleared. All at once, an unusual sound struck my ear. Above the roar and din, the shouting and blasphemy, came forth the swelling voice of song. I said, "What does this mean? This must be Fulton street, and this the famed Fulton-street Meeting that I have heard of on the prairies." I had often read accounts of this daily service, of prayers offered and answers received, and thought, if I was ever in New-York, I would gratify my curiosity, and see the inside of Fulton-street Church. At least four hundred persons were bowing before the Lord. The song of praise came up like the sound of many waters. The prayers were short, direct, fervent, and tender. I never was so impressed. I covered my heart with my hand, for I felt I was wounded. My sorrow was not of long continuance; the new song was on my lip, and I went home to consecrate myself to the service of Christ. It is five years since curiosity turned my feet toward this ancient sanctuary. I have never been in New-York since till the present time. I came to the church this morning to thank the Lord publicly for the great mercy I received in this place, when, as a stranger to God, I came in to worship among you.

CXXIV.

PEOPLE OUTSIDE.

BLESSED *are* they that do his commandments, that they may have right to the tree of life, and may enter in through the gates into the city. For without *are* dogs, and sorcerers, and whoremongers, and murderers, and idolaters, and whosoever loveth and maketh a lie. He that is unjust, let him be unjust still: and he which is filthy, let him be filthy still: and he that is righteous, let him be righteous still: and he that is holy, let him be holy still. Know ye not that the unrighteous shall not inherit the kingdom of God? Be not deceived: neither fornicators, nor idolaters, nor adulterers, nor effeminate, nor abusers of themselves with mankind, nor thieves, nor covetous, nor drunkards, nor revilers, nor extortioners, shall inherit the kingdom of God. And such were some of you: but ye are washed, but ye are sanctified, but ye are justified in the name of the Lord Jesus, and by the Spirit of our God. But the fearful, and unbelieving, and the abominable, and murderers, and whoremongers, and sorcerers, and idolaters, and all liars, shall have their part in the lake which burneth with fire and brimstone: which is the second death.

PRAY TO YOUR GOD; I'LL PRAY TO MINE.

Our pastor conducts a weekly Bible-class. It is a congregational class, open to all who choose to attend. One of my neighbors is an infidel, a tonguey, conceited person, and very much prone to give utterance to his notions. He told his chums that he was going to the Bible-class; he proposed to challenge the Dominie to an argument, and he would find out what sort of mettle there was in him. One evening, a large number of persons were present who were not accustomed to attend a Bible-class or prayer-meeting. It was evident that my infidel neighbor was going to discuss religion, as he called it. After the meeting was opened, he arose and said, "I believe you allow any one to ask you questions on the subject of religion?" He was answered in the affirmative. "Well, I am not satisfied with the Bible, nor religion, nor your preaching; and I would like to ask you some questions." "Any honest doubts deserve thoughtful consideration, and I am willing to help any of my friends in coming to the truth. At the start, let us kneel down and ask God to guide us. I will lead, and when I have prayed, you follow." "No, no," said the infidel, "I did not come to pray; I came to discuss religion." "You have come to our church, and you will submit yourself to our rules. We never talk religion here without first asking God's blessing; so kneel down." The pastor offered an earnest, touching, and affectionate prayer. At the close, he said to his antagonist, "Now you pray." "I can not pray, I can not pray; I have no God to pray to; no Saviour to call upon. Let me go, let me go!" and he rushed out of the house under great excitement. The stillness of death settled on the congregation. His comrades were overawed, and not one of them moved. A revival broke out; among the earliest fruits was the infidel who came to scoff but remained to pray. The most desperate cases in the town were the subjects of divine grace.

CXXV.

REDEEMED SHALL WALK THERE.

AND a highway shall be there, and a way, and it shall be called The way of holiness; the unclean shall not pass over it; but it *shall be* for those: the wayfaring men, though fools, shall not err *therein.* No lion shall be there, nor *any* ravenous beast shall go up thereon, it shall not be found there; but the redeemed shall walk *there.* And I heard a great voice out of heaven saying, Behold, the tabernacle of God *is* with men, and he will dwell with them, and they shall be his people, and God himself shall be with them, *and be* their God. And God shall wipe away all tears from their eyes; and there shall be no more death, neither sorrow, nor crying, neither shall there be any more pain: for the former things are passed away. And he that sat upon the throne said, Behold, I make all things new. And a voice came out of the throne, saying, Praise our God, all ye his servants, and ye that fear him, both small and great.

"*I DON'T WANT RELIGION.*"

I HAVE a man in my employ who is a smart, energetic workman; he is very skillful and very faithful. He was a despiser of religion. He spent his Sabbaths in wandering about the fields, as he called it, worshiping nature. I became deeply interested in him, and anxious about his spiritual condition. A favorable opportunity occurred, and I had a long and affectionate conversation with him on matters pertaining to his soul. He was very frank, but very bitter. He said, "You need not trouble yourself about me; I don't wish to be a Christian." He named several professors whom he thought were none the better for their profession. "If such men are Christians, I am content to remain as I am." I replied, "Suppose these men you name are only pretenders; suppose they are, what our Lord described that class to be, wolves in sheep's clothing; suppose they die in their sins, and are among the lost, as they will be if their religion is a pretense—for hypocrites as well as the wicked are to be banished from the presence of the Lord;—how will all that benefit you? Will it save your soul? Will it be any answer at the bar of God, that somebody who professed the name of Christ was not a true disciple? Will the hypocrisy, or wickedness, even, of a church-member write your name in the Lamb's book of life, blot out your sins, or give you an inheritance among those for whom the Saviour died?" "I never saw it in that light, exactly," said the man, in a subdued tone. "But why should there be so much hypocrisy in the world, if religion is true?" "Simply because it is true. Men don't sham the bad. You don't reject a twenty-dollar gold piece because there is false coin in the land, because there are counterfeit greenbacks. There is a way to test truth as there is to test currency. If religion is not a good thing, bad men would not call themselves by its name." That conversation induced the man to turn his attention to the things that belonged to his peace. Turning from the quicksands and morasses of unbelief, he placed his feet upon the Rock, and sang the new song of the Redeemer.

CXXVI.

MAJESTY OF GOD.

GOD came from Teman, and the Holy One from Mount Paran. Selah. His glory covered the heavens, and the earth was full of his praise. And *his* brightness was as the light, he had horns *coming* out of his hand: and there *was* the hiding of his power. Before him went the pestilence, and burning coals went forth at his feet. He stood, and measured the earth: he beheld, and drove asunder the nations; and the everlasting mountains were scattered, the perpetual hills did bow: his ways *are* everlasting. The great day of the Lord *is* near, *it is* near, and hasteth greatly, *even* the voice of the day of the Lord: the mighty man shall cry there bitterly. That day *is* a day of wrath, a day of trouble and distress, a day of wasteness and desolation, a day of darkness and gloominess, a day of clouds and thick darkness. A day of the trumpet and alarm against the fenced cities, and against the high towers. And I will bring distress upon men, that they shall walk like blind men, because they have sinned against the Lord: and their blood shall be poured out as dust, and their flesh as the dung.

MISSION OF A LEAFLET.

A Christian merchant is a volunteer tract distributer. His beat is in a wretched, poor, and wicked neighborhood. Corner-groceries, low dram-shops, and vile resorts are plenty; but churches and chapels can not be found. Distributing tracts is not the only business that this Christian man finds to do in this neglected and sinful location. Many a sick child has been visited by a skillful surgeon, and paid for out of the purse of the philanthropist. Many a feeble woman has had a good dish of broth; pails of coal have warmed a dreary chamber; and more than one mechanic during his sickness has had a roof over his head, for our friend paid his rent. Among the traders in the neighborhood was a man of more than usual intelligence. But he was a gruff, rough, uncomfortable fellow, hardened and avaricious. He bore a great hatred to the Christian merchant. He was interfering with his business, and breaking up his trade. One day, the Christian merchant, passing the door of the trader, offered him a tract. He took it, and said, "This will do for shaving-paper; I'll accept it." He was perfectly at leisure, and his eye glanced over the attractive title. The impulse was on him two or three times to destroy this little leaflet, and then he thought he wouldn't. His little daughter had been to the Mission School. She had learned to sing; more than once the father had listened at the door while his little one was singing "Come to Jesus, come to Jesus just now." He took the paper up-stairs in his room, and laid it beside his dressing-glass, ready for use the next morning. But he never used it. All night long the little tract disturbed him. Once he got up in the night, lit his gas, and read a page or two. When the morning dawned, the memory of childhood and home came over him. There were words in that leaflet that his mother had spoken to him when he was a boy with a bright future before him. From that hour he was a changed man. His groggery was closed, a coal and wood-yard opened, and he became a minister of mercy to the outcast and the suffering.

CXXVII.

PROPHECIES ABOUT JESUS.

FOR we have not followed cunningly devised fables, when we made known unto you the power and coming of our Lord Jesus Christ, but were eyewitnesses of his majesty. We have also a more sure word of prophecy; whereunto ye do well that ye take heed, as unto a light that shineth in a dark place, until the day dawn, and the daystar arise in your hearts: for the prophecy came not in old time by the will of man: but holy men of God spake *as they were* moved by the Holy Ghost. I will raise them up a Prophet from among their brethren, like unto thee, and will put my words in his mouth; and he shall speak unto them all that I shall command him. But thou, Beth-lehem Ephratah, *though* thou be little among the thousands of Judah, *yet* out of thee shall he come forth unto me *that is* to be ruler in Israel; whose goings forth *have been* from of old, from everlasting. And when he had gathered all the chief priests and scribes of the people together, he demanded of them where Christ should be born. And they said unto him, In Bethlehem of Judea: for thus it is written by the prophet, and thou Bethlehem, *in* the land of Juda, art not the least among the princes of Juda: for out of thee shall come a Governor, that shall rule my people Israel.

ON THE WESTERN SLOPE.

My father was a clergyman. For over forty years, he stood at the head of his profession. He was a leading professor in one of our prominent theological seminaries. As a teacher, a preacher, and a professor, he had few that rivaled him. In stormy times, he was set for the defense of the Gospel. He had a ready, trenchant pen, and was one of the great controversialists of his time. To a very advanced age, he held his foremost position. A short time before he died, he asked me to come and sit by the side of his bed. He took my hand and said, "My son, the Lord has been very gracious to me in preserving my life to this hour. I shall soon sleep with my fathers. I have been a great controversialist in my day. I have stoutly defended my theological opinions against all attacks, and in so doing have maintained a good conscience toward God. I have reached the summit, and am passing down the western slope, and, as I near the river, I find that all my theology is summed up in this: 'This is a faithful saying, and worthy of all acceptation—that Jesus Christ came into the world to save sinners, of which I am chief.'" Still fervently attached to the church of his choice, and the religious home of his childhood, he rejoiced that his own church did not contain all the faithful, and did not hold all the truth. He often quoted with great pleasure the words of our Lord: "Other sheep I have, that are not of this fold." During the few years that remained to him, he heard with profound delight of revivals in other churches—large contributions to the cause of Christ—building up of waste places, and the triumphs of the truth every where, saying, "One Lord, whether theirs or ours."

CXXVIII.

REJECTED SACRIFICES.

THE sacrifice of the wicked *is* an abomination to the Lord: but the prayer of the upright *is* his delight. The way of the wicked *is* an abomination unto the Lord: but he loveth him that followeth after righteousness. To what purpose *is* the multitude of your sacrifices unto me? saith the Lord: I am full of the burnt offerings of rams, and the fat of fed beasts; and I delight not in the blood of bullocks, or of lambs, or of he goats. When ye come to appear before me, who hath required this at your hand, to tread my courts? By faith Abel offered unto God a more excellent sacrifice than Cain, by which he obtained witness that he was righteous, God testifying of his gifts: and by it he being dead yet speaketh. I hate, I despise your feast days, and I will not smell in your solemn assemblies. Though ye offer me burnt offerings and your meat offerings, I will not accept *them;* neither will I regard the peace offerings of your fat beasts. Take thou away from me the noise of thy songs; for I will not hear the melody of thy viols. But let judgment run down as waters, and righteousness as a mighty stream.

THAT I MAY RECEIVE MY SIGHT.

An invalid was confined to his bed, and had been for thirteen years, with spine-disease. He could neither sit nor walk. The disease settled in his eyes. For four years, his eyes had been bandaged; he had to be kept in a dark room without fire or light; even the light of a candle distressed him. Those who served him were obliged to grope their way around his room, for every crack and crevice had to be closed. Every morning a relative read to him a chapter in the Bible, sitting in an outer room. Occasionally a hymn was sung. During his long confinement and sickness, he uttered no complaint, but rejoiced always in the mercies of the Lord. He felt a great desire to send a request written by his own hand to the Fulton-street meeting. An ingenious friend provided for him an apparatus by which he could write in the dark. He lay upon his back, unable to move, his room in darkness, and so cold that his friends could remain but a moment by his bedside. In this position he wrote a letter that was read in Fulton-street meeting. In the letter was not one note of complaint; no repining at his long years of confinement and suffering; no wondering why God should deprive him of the blessings of warmth and light and friendly attentions while on the bed of sickness. He did not ask God to restore him to health, or give him that help which human aid could not afford. He requested that special supplication should be made that the Lord would be pleased to continue his mercies in the future, as he had in the past, that he might be able to do and suffer according to his holy will in this life, and enjoy life everlasting in the world to come.

CXXIX.

HOW TO COME BEFORE GOD.

WHEREWITH shall I come before the Lord, *and* bow myself before the high God? shall I come before him with burnt offerings, with calves of a year old? will the Lord be pleased with thousands of rams, *or* with ten thousands of rivers of oil? shall I give my firstborn *for* my transgression, the fruit of my body *for* the sin of my soul? He hath showed thee, O man, what *is* good; and what doth the Lord require of thee, but to do justly, and to love mercy, and to walk humbly with thy God? And if ye offer the blind for sacrifice, *is it* not evil? and if ye offer the lame and sick, *is it* not evil? offer it now unto thy governor; will he be pleased with thee, or accept thy person? saith the Lord of hosts. And now, I pray you, beseech God that he will be gracious unto us: this hath been by your means: will he regard your persons? saith the Lord of hosts. Who *is there* even among you that would shut the doors *for nought?* neither do ye kindle *fire* on mine altar for nought. I have no pleasure in you, saith the Lord of hosts, neither will I accept an offering at your hand.

OPEN DOOR.

A POOR Scotchwoman had an only child, a daughter. She went regularly to her daily tasks, leaving her child to take care of the house. She was trained to industry, kept the cottage clean and tidy, and prepared the evening meal for the mother on her return. One dark and stormy night, as the mother came in sight of the cottage, she saw no cheerful light shining through the windows. An unusual darkness rested on the hut. A sense of danger came upon the poor woman as she passed over the stile into her enclosure. As she lifted the latch, she saw no cheerful fire, no table set, no provisions for her comfort. She called for her child, but no response came. Days and nights went by, and she heard nothing from the absent one. Months rolled into years, and five years passed without any knowledge of the prodigal. One night, the mother heard a step on the floor. She thought she recognized it. She pronounced a name that she had not spoken for five years. A sob was the response, and, in an instant, the daughter's arms were round the mother's neck. "I found the door unfastened," the girl said, "and you are so careful to keep it locked." "Yes, my child; that door has not been fastened since you left home. I thought you would come back; I thought the Good Shepherd would find the stray lamb upon the moutains, and bring it home on his shoulder. I meant you should have a warm welcome when you came home. So the Good Shepherd does who gives his life for the sheep."

CXXX.

WORLD WITHOUT GOD.

THAT at that time we were without Christ, being aliens from the commonwealth of Israel, and strangers from the covenants of promise, having no hope, and without God in the world: but now, in Christ Jesus, ye who sometime were far off are made nigh by the blood of Christ. For he is our peace, who hath made both one, and hath broken down the middle wall of partition *between us;* and whatsoever mine eyes desired I kept not from them, I withheld not my heart from any joy; for my heart rejoiced in all my labor: and this was my portion of all my labor. In the day of prosperity be joyful, but in the day of adversity consider: God also hath set the one over against the other, to the end that man should find nothing after him. Rejoice, O young man, in thy youth; and let thy heart cheer thee in the days of thy youth, and walk in the ways of thine heart, and in the sight of thine eyes: but know thou, that for all these *things* God will bring thee into judgment. Therefore remove sorrow from thy heart, and put away evil from thy flesh: for childhood and youth *are* vanity.

EASTERN FABLE.

THERE went a man from home, and to his neighbors twain
He gave, to keep for him, two sacks of golden grain.
Deep in the cellar one the precious charge concealed,
And forth the other went and strewed it in his field.
The man returns at last; asks of the first his sack.
"Here, take it; 'tis the same; thou hast it safely back."
Unharmed it showed without; but when he would explore
His sack's recess, corn there finds he now no more.
One half of what was there proves rotten and decayed;
Upon the other half have worm and mildew preyed.
The putrid heap to kindred air he doth return.
Then of the other asks, "Where is thy sack of corn?"
Who answering, "Come with me, and see how it is sped;"
And took and showed him fields with waving harvests spread.
Then cheerfully the man laughed out, and cried, "This one
Had insight to make up for the other that had none.
The letter he observed, but thou the precept's sense;
And thus to thee and me shall profit come from hence.
In harvest thou shalt fill two sacks of corn for me,
The residue of right remains in full for thee."

CXXXI.

VANITY OF VANITIES.

VANITY of vanities, saith the Preacher; all *is* vanity. The Preacher sought to find out acceptable words: and *that which was* written *was* upright, *even* words of truth. Let us hear the conclusion of the whole matter: fear God, and keep his commandments: for this *is* the whole *duty* of man. For God shall bring every work into judgment, with every secret thing, whether *it be* good, or whether *it be* evil. All the rivers run into the sea; yet the sea *is* not full: unto the place from whence the rivers come, thither they return again. All things *are* full of labor; man can not utter *it:* the eye is not satisfied with seeing, nor the ear filled with hearing. There is an evil which I have seen under the sun, and it *is* common among men. A man to whom God hath given riches, wealth, and honor, so that he wanteth nothing for his soul of all that he desireth, yet God giveth him not power to eat thereof, but a stranger eateth it: this *is* vanity, and it *is* an evil disease.

A HEROIC DAUGHTER.

A MAN who was in the main a kind father and a good provider, was a bitter hater of the Gospel. His only daughter became interested in a revival that was in progress in her Sunday-school. Giving her heart to her Saviour, she desired to make a profession of faith in his name. She asked her father's permission to unite with the church. To her astonishment, he flew into a passion, and not only refused to give her permission, but threatened to disown her if she took a step in that direction. Taking counsel of her friends, she resolved to go forward in the way of duty and leave the consequences to God. Coming home from her first communion, she found her father in a terrible rage. He refused to receive her into the house, bade her begone and never again darken his doors. With a heavy heart, she hurried from the home of her childhood, taking with her nothing but the clothes she wore. Her father was true to his dreadful promise. He passed her in the street without speaking. She came into the house, at times, by stealth, to throw her arms on her mother's neck and weep. A kind friend gave her shelter, and she earned her bread by daily toil. So passed five years of her life. Sickness at last did for that proud man what natural affection could not do. He was thrown on his bed, the victim of a loathsome disease. His daughter came to him like a ministering angel, and tended him when others deserted him. She uttered no complaint, but cheerfully met all the duties of her position. He was not only restored to health, but he found that Balm of Gilead which the Great Physician alone can apply. There was no more estrangement or alienation in that household. The family sat happy at the feet of the Saviour.

CXXXII.

SINFULNESS OF SIN.

WHAT then? shall we sin, because we are not under the law, but under grace? God forbid. Know ye not, that to whom ye yield yourselves servants to obey, his servants ye are to whom ye obey; whether of sin unto death, or of obedience unto righteousness? But God be thanked, that ye were the servants of sin, but ye have obeyed from the heart that form of doctrine which was delivered you. Let not sin therefore reign in your mortal body, that ye should obey it in the lust thereof. Neither yield ye your members *as* instruments of unrighteousness unto sin: but yield yourselves unto God, as those that are alive from the dead, and your members *as* instruments of righteousness unto God. And Cain talked with Abel his brother: and it came to pass, when they were in the field, that Cain rose up against Abel his brother, and slew him. For as by one man's disobedience many were made sinners, so by the obedience of one shall many be made righteous. Moreover the law entered, that the offense might abound. But where sin abounded, grace did much more abound: that as sin hath reigned unto death, even so might grace reign through righteousness unto eternal life by Jesus Christ our Lord.

GLASS OF WINE DID IT.

THE panic carried down a large house. A friend said, "The times carried you under." "No!" was the reply, "a glass of wine did it. We had in our house a young man of great promise, in whom we put great confidence. He had been with us several years. He was smart, intelligent, and honest. Much was due us in the West and South, and we sent him out to make collections. He was very successful. Saturday found him at New-Orleans, with drafts and money to a large amount. The funds in his possession with what we had on hand would tide us over the panic, and make us easy. Our clerk was not a Christian, though we believed him to be perfectly moral. So Sunday found him without any special desire to attend church. He was not connected with any Sunday-school, or he would have sought proper company on that day. Sitting in the reading-room in the forenoon, a couple of well-dressed strangers opened a conversation with him. They were from New-York. They were on a collecting tour. Strange enough, they knew his house very well, and were in the same business. 'Come, let us go and take a glass of wine together.' Our clerk was not a pledged man, or it would have been enough to have said, 'I don't drink.' He had some scruples about going into a bar-room on Sunday and taking a drink. It was not exactly the thing. But his friends were importunate. It was no use, he thought, to be very set; a glass of wine wouldn't hurt any one. So he yielded. I presume he was drugged; but no one knows. All he would say was that from the time he took the glass of wine until Monday afternoon he was unconscious. He was in his room on his bed. His watch was gone, his jewelry gone, his money and drafts were gone. He was beggared and ruined. The crisis came upon us; we failed, losing our all through that glass of wine."

CXXXIII.

ANGELS UNAWARES.

BE not forgetful to entertain strangers: for thereby some have entertained angels unawares. Remember them that are in bonds, as bound with them; *and* them which suffer adversity, as being yourselves also in the body. *Let your* conversation *be* without covetousness; *and be* content with such things as ye have: for he hath said, I will never leave thee, or forsake thee. So that we may boldly say, The Lord *is* my helper, and I will not fear what man shall do unto me. Remember them which have the rule over you, who have spoken unto you the word of God: whose faith follow, considering the end of *their* conversation. Jesus Christ the same yesterday, and to-day, and forever. Go to now, ye that say, To-day or to-morrow we will go into such a city, and continue there a year, and buy and sell, and get gain: whereas ye know not what *shall be* on the morrow. For what *is* your life? It is even a vapor, that appeareth for a little time, and then vanisheth away. For that ye *ought* to say, If the Lord will, we shall live, and do this, or that. But now ye rejoice in your boastings: all such rejoicing is evil. Therefore to him that knoweth to do good, and doeth *it* not, to him it is sin.

BURGLAR'S TENDERNESS.

A COMPANY of desperate burglars entered what they supposed to be an unoccupied dwelling. They went through the house. Having completely riddled it, they set fire to the building, the better to cover up their work. As they were leaving the burning building, the cry of a child attracted the attention of the desperadoes. It seemed that a family were in charge of the building, and occupied the upper portion. Against the protest of his associates, one of the burglars went back through the smoke and flame, and bore a child to a place of safety. The police, attracted by the flames, arrested the incendiary on the threshold, and took him and the child to the station-house. His companions made their escape. One of them visited the burglar in his cell. "Jim, if you had minded what we said to you, and let that brat alone, you would not have been cooped up here in this cell with the prospect of five years in the State prison. "I would do it again," said Jim.

CXXXIV.

OLD AGE.

AND Pharaoh said unto Jacob, How old *art* thou? And Jacob said unto Pharaoh, The days of the years of my pilgrimage *are* a hundred and thirty years: few and evil have the days of the years of my life been, and have not attained unto the days of the years of the life of my fathers in the days of their pilgrimage. In the six hundredth year of Noah's life, in the second month, the seventeenth day of the month, the same day were all the fountains of the great deep broken up, and the windows of heaven were opened. And when Abram was ninety years old and nine, the Lord appeared to Abram, and said unto him, I *am* the Almighty God; walk before me, and be thou perfect. And I will make my covenant between me and thee, and will multiply thee exceedingly. And Sarah was a hundred and seven and twenty years old: *these were* the years of the life of Sarah. And Sarah died in Kirjath-arba; the same *is* Hebron in the land of Canaan: and Abraham came to mourn for Sarah, and to weep for her.

FARMER AND HIS OX.

I HAVE a neighbor who is a farmer. He is a forehanded man, and prides himself on his farm and his cattle. He is a very passionate man, and a hater of all good things. He not only made no contributions to religion and benevolence, but he took great delight in ridiculing all serious things and serious professions. His conversion was a singular one, brought about by the agency of his ox. The farmer seldom went to church, but a celebrated preacher being in the neighborhood, he was induced to hear him preach. The text arrested his attention: "The ox knoweth his owner, and the ass his master's crib: but Israel doth not know, my people do not consider." The theme of the discourse was ingratitude and forgetfulness. The farmer turned from the meeting displeased. Nothing pleased him. The prayer, the sermon, the singing were bitterly reviled. The text seemed to be especially offensive. He flew into a passion whenever it was alluded to. One morning, he seemed to be unusually ill-tempered. He undertook to plough his field. One of the oxen threw his foot over the chain. He flew at him, maddened and furious, and commenced beating him in a cruel manner. As he passed in front of the ox, the patient creature lifted up his eyes to his brutal master, and licked his sleeve with his tongue as he passed. The man was touched with the forgiveness of the poor brute. The text came into his mind, "The ox knoweth his owner, and the ass his master's crib: but my people do not consider." He unyoked his cattle, and turned them into the field, and went home to meditate. From that hour he was a changed man. He soon became a professing Christian. The ox that was so brutally beaten became his favorite. Over the stall was the motto, "The ox knoweth his owner."

CXXXV.

COVENANT-KEEPING GOD.

AND God said, This *is* the token of the covenant which I make between me and you, and every living creature that *is* with you, for perpetual generations: I do set my bow in the cloud, and it shall be for a token of a covenant between me and the earth. And it shall come to pass, when I bring a cloud over the earth, that the bow shall be seen in the cloud. Behold, the days come, saith the Lord, that I will make a new covenant with the house of Israel, and with the house of Judah: not according to the covenant that I made with their fathers, in the day *that* I took them by the hand to bring them out of the land of Egypt; which my covenant they brake, although I was a husband unto them, said the Lord: But this *shall be* the covenant that I will make with the house of Israel; After those days, saith the Lord, I will put my law in their inward parts, and write it in their hearts; and will be their God, and they shall by my people. And they shall teach no more every man his neighbor, and every man his brother, saying, Know the Lord: for they shall all know me, from the least of them unto the greatest of them, saith the Lord: for I will forgive their iniquity, and I will remember their sin no more.

NOTE PAID BY PRAYER.

It is a question in some minds how far the providence of God touches the minute affairs of life, and whether in temporal things God answers prayer. Facts are better than arguments. I heard to-day a request made that was put up by a man who was greatly distressed in worldly matters. He had obligations to meet that affected his character. His prayer was that God would raise up some friend to help him. I wish to relate an incident that came under my own observation. A friend of mine was induced to indorse a promissory note for a heavy amount. When the note matured, it was evident that the drawer did not intend to pay it. The indorser had no money, and he exhausted all efforts to obtain assistance. He was in great distress. The first and second days of grace went by. The morning of the third dawned. Weighed down with sorrow, heavy of heart, and grieved that his good name was to be injured, he bowed his head on the table like one about to give up in despair. A voice said to him, "Enter into thy closet, and shut the door; pray to thy Father which is in secret, and thy Father which seeth in secret shall reward thee openly." He arose, went up-stairs and knelt down to pray. A voice seemed to say, "Shut thy door." He arose and shut the door. With closed eyes he bowed again in prayer. A portrait of a friend seemed to float before him. Audibly he shouted, "Thank God!" He came into the presence of his family with a radiant face, saying, "I have found a friend who will loan me the money." That friend was a clergyman of large landed property. He went directly to his house and told him his story. He said, "What a silly fellow you are; why did you not come to me before?" He wrote a check. The indorser walked eight miles to reach the bank; and after he had taken the note up he had just five minutes before the closing of the bank on the last day of grace. A favorable change in his business enabled him to refund the money which his generous friend had loaned him in the hour of his great calamity.

CXXXVI.

SACRIFICES OF GOD.

THE sacrifices of God *are* a broken spirit: a broken and a contrite heart, O God, thou wilt not despise. Offer unto God thanksgiving; and pay thy vows unto the Most High: and call upon me in the day of trouble: I will deliver thee. But Christ being come a high priest of good things to come, by a greater and more perfect tabernacle, not made with hands, that is to say, not of this building. For if the blood of bulls and of goats, and the ashes of a heifer sprinkling the unclean, sanctifieth to the purifying of the flesh; how much more shall the blood of Christ, who through the eternal Spirit offered himself without spot to God, purge your conscience from dead works to serve the living God? And for this cause he is the mediator of the new testament, that by means of death, for the redemption of the transgressions *that were* under the first testament, they which are called might receive the promise of eternal inheritance.

WILL YOU TAKE BAIL?

AMONG the earnest missionaries who labor among the masses in England was a man of unusual eloquence; a rough, unpolished diamond, but a diamond of the first water. He had been a prize-fighter, and a leader of a rough gang who spent their nights in revelry and drunkenness. His conversion created a great sensation among the roughs and bullies who had looked up to him as a leader. He was a fine singer; he had an impassioned but untutored eloquence, and he drew crowds after him wherever he addressed the public. He could break up a den of gamblers on a muster-field, and the booths and drinking-dens on the race-course were emptied when he took his stand. He carried with him a rude sort of pulpit, or extemporized one from the seat of his wagon. He attracted the crowd by his exquisite singing. Holding up the Bible he would shout, "Here's the great prize! here you'll find the race in which all may win!" The turf-men, not liking the disturbance, found he was preaching in the bounds of a parish, and without a license. The parish priest, who was also a magistrate, ordered the preacher to desist. He refused, and was taken to jail. At once he improvised a prayer-meeting. He produced nearly as much excitement as Paul and Silas produced in the prison at Philippi. The jailer ordered him to be quiet. He refused. He said, "You've arrested me according to law, but you can go no further; I can sing and pray under the English flag as long as I like." "How long do you intend to keep up this disturbance?" said the officer. "Till my breath gives out," was the reply. The jailer offered to dismiss him. "It is right for me to be here, or it is not," was the reply; "you must let me out as publicly as you put me in, or you will report that I broke jail and ran away." During the evening, a company of friends called at the prison, and asked if the missionary was there. "We have a crazy fellow here," said the officer. "Will you take bail?" said the gentleman. "Bail! bail! We've been trying to get rid of him these two hours, and we've had no peace since we locked him up." And the missionary departed with flying colors, and was the next morning producing consternation among the gamblers and boxers on the race-course.

CXXXVII.

MUTUAL DEPENDENCE.

BEHOLD, I have created the smith that bloweth the coals in the fire, and that bringeth forth an instrument for his work; and I have created the waster to destroy. But if thy brother be grieved with *thy* meat, now walkest thou not charitably. Destroy not him with thy meat, for whom Christ died. They helped every one his neighbor; and *every one* said to his brother, Be of good courage. So the carpenter encouraged the goldsmith, *and* he that smootheth *with* the hammer him that smote the anvil, saying, It *is* ready for the soldering: and he fastened it with nails, *that* it should not be moved. Withhold not good from them to whom it is due, when it is in the power of thine hand to do *it*. Say not unto thy neighbor, Go, and come again, and to-morrow I will give; when thou hast it by thee. Devise not evil against thy neighbor, seeing he dwelleth securely by thee.

YOU INSULTED MY MASTER.

A POOR, debased, drunken, miserable man was a sort of leader among the roughs. When sober, he was a fellow of great pluck and undaunted courage. He was rescued by some Christian philanthropists, and not only sobered, but brought to

Christ. The announcement that a former leader was to speak in the theatre produced a profound impression, and was sufficient to crowd the house from pit to dome. The house was not only filled, but the vestibule and the stage. Desperadoes, bullies, prize-fighters, and criminals of every grade came in crowds. The desperate men of the community were huddled upon the stage and jostled the speaker as he came in. He was no coward, and conducted the opening exercises as if he was a veteran preacher. While relating his experience, one of the most desperate of the neighborhood walked up to him, and, interrupting the discourse, said, "Dick, do you know me?" "Yes, I know you very well; we've worked together in the mines." "They say, Dick, that you've got religion; that you're another man. I'm going to try you. There, take that," and he spat in his face, an insult that can not be exceeded among Englishmen. The speaker took out his handkerchief with great deliberation, wiped the offensive matter from his face, and said, "Jim, when you and I worked together, did you think I was a coward?" "No, you were plucky enough." "Don't you know that if you had done this before I was converted, it would have cost you your life." "I suppose it would," said the coward, trembling from head to foot. "But, Jim, you do not do this to me; you did it to my Saviour. He was wounded, insulted, and spit upon for me, and the least I can do is to bear these reproaches for Him." The ruffian slunk out of sight, and the preacher finished his discourse. At midnight, the convert was called from his bed to pray with his assailant. "O Dick, will you forgive me?" "I've nothing to forgive. Kneel down, and I'll ask the Saviour to forgive you." He did. He was pardoned on his knees. A more humble, earnest, Christian worker than the ruffian Jim, can not be found.

CXXXVIII.

ADOPTION.

AND because ye are sons, God hath sent forth the Spirit of his Son into your hearts, crying, Abba, Father. Wherefore thou art no more a servant, but a son; and if a son, then an heir of God through Christ. And I heard a great voice out of heaven saying, Behold, the tabernacle of God *is* with men, and he will dwell with them, and they shall be his people, and God himself shall be with them, *and be* their God. And God shall wipe away all tears from their eyes; and there shall be no more death, neither sorrow, nor crying, neither shall there be any more pain: for the former things are passed away. For the Lord hath called thee as a woman forsaken and grieved in spirit, and a wife of youth, when thou wast refused, saith thy God. For a small moment have I forsaken thee; but with great mercies will I gather thee. In a little wrath I hid my face from thee for a moment; but with everlasting kindness will I have mercy on thee, saith the Lord thy Redeemer.

CONVERT IN INDIA.

THE United Presbyterian Church has a fine female school in Egypt. Over seven hundred peasant girls were gathered in this seminary for an education. One of them was a girl of remarkable sweetness of character, an humble, devoted Christian, having been converted when a mere child. She lived some miles away from school, with her mother, who was very poor. She wore the poorest costume allotted to the poorest Egyptian girls. She walked the whole distance between her home and the school, morning and evening. Barefooted, and in the simple costume of her country, she came through rain and sunshine, and ate her frugal lunch off a plantain leaf. One day the school was visited by an Indian prince. He was heir to one of the thrones of India. He transferred his possessions to the British Government, and received in exchange a large landed estate and a royal income. He was recognized as a sovereign, preceded the English nobility in the presence, and his court dress, stiff with embroidery and jewels, outshone those of the proudest peers of the realm. He could have allied himself with some of the proudest houses of England. But he turned from the titled ladies of Britain to seek a wife from among the students at the American Seminary of Egypt. She rejected the glittering offer without a moment's hesitation. The wealth of the universe would not tempt her to enter any sphere where she could not give her time and talents to that Saviour who left His throne for her. The prince renewed his offer. He promised that she should have the control of his entire fortune, and dispose of it for benevolence as she saw fit. He gave her a year to make up her mind, and started on his travels round the globe. He came back, was married, and took his bride to London, where the queen received her as a daughter. Her palace home, near London, in gorgeousness and elegance is only exceeded by the state residence of the queen. She is the same simple-hearted, devoted Christian, living in regal splendor, that she was when eating her dinner in Egypt on a plantain leaf.

CXXXIX.

SEVERITY OF GOD.

NAY but, O man, who art thou that repliest against God? Shall the thing formed say to him that formed *it*, Why hast thou made me thus? Hath not the potter power over the clay, of the same lump to make one vessel unto honor, and another unto dishonor? And even as they did not like to retain God in *their* knowledge, God gave them over to a reprobate mind, to do those things which are not convenient. For we know him that hath said, Vengeance *belongeth* unto me, I will recompense, saith the Lord. And again, The Lord shall judge his people. *It is* a fearful thing to fall into the hands of the living God. He that despised Moses' law died without mercy under two or three witnesses: of how much sorer punishment, suppose ye, shall he be thought worthy, who hath trodden under foot the Son of God, and hath counted the blood of the covenant, wherewith he was sanctified, an unholy thing, and hath done despite unto the Spirit of grace?

PRINCESS AND FLOWERS.

THE English working classes are extravagantly fond of pictures. The Christian gentlemen of that country have formed an association, the aim of which is to furnish handsome engravings, at a low cost, to drive out impure and demoralizing pictures. One of the finest and largest engravings of this class, which is very popular—which hangs in the halls of the great and the cottages of the lowly—represents an incident in the life of the Princess of Wales. She came to England, a fragile girl from the North, and found the Court sullen and the Queen in retirement. She resolved to bind herself up with the lowly. She visited the hospitals, took the charge of institutions for the relief of the poor and suffering, and originated that sweetest of all London charities—the hospital for sick children.

One day she visited the wards where the sick and wounded soldiers lay. She had in her hand a magnificent bouquet, the gift of Queen Victoria. As she passed along from cot to cot a flower fell to the floor. A soldier pointed to it, and the steward lifted it, and the sick man feebly clutched it and pressed it to his bosom. The Princess, turning at that moment, saw the act, and read it at a glance. She turned back to the head of the ward, and went down distributing the flowers right and left—a rose here and bud there, till every soldier had something. As the Princess left, the poor fellows tried to cheer her. The flowers were carefully preserved, and many a soldier said to the steward, "When I die put this flower in my coffin, for it's the brightest thing that I ever had." That condescension cost the Princess but a trifle, yet never in her life did she confer such genuine happiness. It was a cup of cold water in the name of a disciple. The simple act has been commemorated in the engraving which carries the Princess' name, and acts in every hamlet in the kingdom from Land's-end to John o' Groat's, and has reared a monument to her kindness that will endure when the bronze shall corrode and the marble perish by the touch of time.

CXL.

FORBEARANCE OF GOD.

HE that spared not his own Son, but delivered him up for us all, how shall he not with him also freely give us all things? Who shall lay anything to the charge of God's elect? *It is* God that justifieth. Who *is* he that condemneth? *It is* Christ that died, yea rather, that is risen again, who is even at the right hand of God, who also maketh intercession for us. O the depth of the riches both of the wisdom and knowledge of God! how unsearchable *are* his judgments, and his ways past finding out! For who hath known the mind of the Lord? or who hath been his counselor? or who hath first given to him, and it shall be recompensed unto him again? For of him, and through him, and to him, *are* all things, to whom *be* glory for ever. Amen. But now the righteousness of God without the law is manifested, being witnessed by the law and the prophets; even the righteousness of God, *which is* by faith of Jesus Christ unto all and upon all them that believe; for there is no difference: for all have sinned and come short of the glory of God.

SINGING GRACE.

THE poorest, the lowest, the most wretched and depraved of the English populace have a sense of the externals of religion that is very remarkable. Speak to a crowd from the slums of London, and, as you read the Scriptures, nearly every one will take out a Testament to follow. However poor, wretched, or debased these people may be, they will hold on to their little Testaments, and will part with every thing they possess before they will give that up. Gather a company of street girls for a tea on a cold and gusty night—from five to six hundred in number, as is often the case—and they will sing with great sweetness, though often nearly choked with their tears, the songs of salvation. Ask all who have been to Sunday-school to hold up their hands, and nineteen out of every twenty will do so. The very beggar on the curbstone, as he eats his crust, will reverently lift his hat and say, "The Lord make us thankful." At charity schools, tea-meetings, night-meetings, and other gatherings of the lowly, grace is sung. The audience come to their feet and sing:

> "Be present at our table, Lord;
> Be here as everywhere adored:
> Thy bounties bless, and grant that we
> May dwell in Paradise with Thee."

At the close of the meal the audience come to their feet and return thanks in song. At the Lord Mayor's receptions grace is sung. The lines are centuries old, and have been sung at all festivals of the Lord Mayors of London for centuries—as far back nearly as the time of William Rufus. In the absence of clergymen, not only the master of the house says or sings grace, but the wife and sons and daughters; and even little children ask a blessing on the food. On state occasions Her Majesty the Queen has a chaplain; but in the privacy of her own family, the Queen asks a blessing, or leads in the song which has been sung over the food of sovereigns for centuries, "In every thing give thanks."

CXLI.

OBEDIENCE TO RULERS.

PUT them in mind to be subject to principalities and powers, to obey magistrates, to be ready to every good work. I exhort, therefore, that, first of all, supplications, prayers, intercessions, *and* giving of thanks, be made for all men; for kings, and *for* all that are in authority; that we may lead a quiet and peaceable life in all godliness and honesty. Submit yourselves to every ordinance of man for the Lord's sake: whether it be to the king, as supreme; or unto governors, as unto them that are sent by him for the punishment of evil doers, and for the praise of them that do well. For rulers are not a terror to good works, but to the evil. Wilt thou then not be afraid of the power? Do that which is good, and thou shalt have praise of the same: for he is the minister of God to thee for good. But if thou do that which is evil, be afraid; for he beareth not the sword in vain: for he is the minister of God, a revenger to *execute* wrath upon him that doeth evil.

STORY-TELLING PREACHERS.

SOME men sneer at what they call story-telling preachers. The sarcasm would apply to Him who spake as never man spake. His discourses were full of metaphors, illustrations, and stories. Whether his stories were taken from real life; whether He pointed to the field already white to the harvest; or to the sower who went forth to sow; or to the fisher in the Sea of Galilee gathering his net to the shore full of every kind; or to the birds of the air flying overhead; or whether the incident was taken from real life—those two boys, one of whom said, "I go, sir," and went not; or a man literally fell among thieves on his way from Jerusalem to Jericho; or a beggar, by the name of Lazarus, laid at the gate of a well-known rich man—whether these be facts, or creations, or suppositions to illustrate some great truth; any way that we choose to consider it, the sneer of being a story-telling preacher will apply to our Lord. Ministers, who are the most celebrated for illustration, are the most celebrated for attracting the crowd and holding the masses. Whitfield, when a lad, was employed in a public-house. His business was to draw porter for the guests. He carried out to thirsty men on horseback, and to travelers who sat in their carriages by the wayside. He was a wild, dissolute boy, with a surpassing eloquence, even while young, that attracted and amused the patrons of the tavern who passed their evenings around the tap. The worship of the Established Church had no attractions for him. He was a Sabbath-breaker, profane, with hardly the fear of God or man before his eyes. In the town was a rude dissenting chapel. The congregation was made up of the poor, ignorant, and neglected. The preacher was as ignorant as his flock—an ignorant, painstaking cobbler. He loved the Saviour, had a rude, magnetic eloquence, and by his simple stories and illustrations drew a crowd who would not enter the fashionable places of worship. One Sunday night, George said to his companions, "Come, let us go down and hear old Cole tell his stories." And the illiterate, story-telling preacher gave to the world that preacher of surpassing eloquence, George Whitfield.

CXLII.

CHRISTIAN FIDELITY.

NOT purloining, but showing all good fidelity; that they may adorn the doctrine of God our Saviour in all things. For the grace of God that bringeth salvation hath appeared to all men, teaching us that, denying ungodliness and worldly lusts, we should live soberly, righteously, and godly, in this present world; let your loins be girded about, and *your* lights burning; and ye yourselves like unto men that wait for their lord, when he will return from the wedding; that, when he cometh and knocketh, they may open unto him immediately. Blessed *are* those servants, whom the Lord when he cometh shall find watching: verily I say unto you, that he shall gird himself, and make them to sit down to meat, and will come forth and serve them.

MINISTRY OF WINDOW-GARDENS.

Lord Shaftesbury is a believer in the ministry of the beautiful. He has done more than any leading Englishman to carry cheer and joy and beauty into the homes of the working poor. The English poor are very poor. A British working man will labor more intensely, fare harder, live poorer, without complaining, than any workingman on the face of the globe. The love of pictures and the love of flowers seem to be innate in a British workman. Crowded together in narrow and often dark and repulsive tenements, the London poor have little opportunity to cultivate or enjoy the love of flowers. To encourage the cultivation of flowers, Lord Shaftesbury introduced in London what are known as window-gardens. A society was formed to provide artistically shaped boxes that would fit into the front windows of each tenement. These gardens were given to every sober, industrious workman who would promise to cultivate flowers. The choicest seeds were also furnished, with slips of rare and costly plants. There are at least a thousand window-gardens in the lowest portion of London. A rivalry sprang up between the workmen that was both surprising and beneficent. Men were won from the ale-house and base companions to the cultivation of flowers. The slatternly woman became tidy in her gear, swept her hearthstone to make it conform to the new beauty, cleaned her children, and made her room presentable. A floral exhibition was gotten up at which none but working people were allowed to contribute. The show was remarkable, filling one of the largest halls of London, and attracting the nobility and royalty itself. No money can estimate the reformatory and social effect of these window-gardens. The religious uses of flowers our Lord did not pass by: "Consider the lilies of the field, how they grow; they toil not, neither do they spin: and yet I say unto you, That even Solomon in all his glory was not arrayed like one of these. Wherefore, if God so clothe the grass of the field, which to-day is, and to-morrow is cast into the oven, *shall he* not much more *clothe* you, O ye of little faith?"

CXLIII.

TESTIMONY FOR JESUS.

AND they which were sent were of the Pharisees. And they asked him, and said unto him, Why baptizest thou then, if thou be not that Christ, nor Elias, neither that prophet? For he received from God the Father honor and glory, when there came such a voice to him from the excellent glory, This is my beloved Son, in whom I am well pleased. And this voice which came from heaven we heard, when we were with him in the holy mount. And he shall send Jesus Christ, which before was preached unto you: whom the heaven must receive until the times of restitution of all things, which God hath spoken by the mouth of all his holy prophets since the world began. For Moses truly said unto the fathers, A Prophet shall the Lord your God raise up unto you of your brethren, like unto me; him shall ye hear in all things whatsoever he shall say unto you.

"OH! THAT'S IT!"

THERE was a large mercantile house in the city; a great number of clerks were employed. One member of the firm was a Christian, the other was not. The latter was sharp, energetic, worldly; a believer in business and business men.

This worldly member of the house went abroad. He came home to find the business of the house prosperous, with the balance-sheet showing large profit. Every thing was well done, orderly, systematic, efficient. The old hands were in their old places. Book-keeper, cashier, salesmen were the same. But through the whole house an entirely different atmosphere prevailed. The junior partner seemed himself out of place. His jokes and jibes and occasional oaths met with no response. He walked round his store like a stranger amid strange people. One day he said he desired to have a confidential conversation with his partner. The parties entered the private counting-room and closed the door. "Things have entirely changed since I've been gone." "Not for the worse, I hope," was the response; "we've never done a better business." "I've nothing to complain of; still there seems to have been an entire revolution among our clerks. There is Charles, the cashier: I should not have known him. He was always smart, but he seems to have lost that pertness, sauciness, that hot and hasty temper that would have led to his dismissal long ago if he hadn't been so able. There is John, the book-keeper: he's mellow, polite, and accommodating. Our two salesmen, I can't talk and joke with them. Indeed, the whole establishment is out of joint." "Don't you know what's happened?" "No, I don't." "Why, these young men that you've been talking about have made a profession of religion since you have been away, and I'm glad you see the difference in their lives." The junior partner thrust his hands down into his pockets, gave a long, low whistle, and said, "Oh! that's it, is it?" and walked away, to meditate on the change that religion works in character.

CXLIV.

FAMILY GOVERNMENT.

IF a man have a stubborn and rebellious son, which will not obey the voice of his father, or the voice of his mother, and *that*, when they have chastened him, will not hearken unto them: then shall his father and his mother lay hold on him, and bring him out unto the elders of his city, and unto the gate of his place; and they shall say unto the elders of his city, This our son *is* stubborn and rebellious, he will not obey our voice; *he is* a glutton, and a drunkard. And all the men of his city shall stone him with stones, that he die: so shalt thou put evil away from among you; and all Israel shall hear, and fear. For I know him, that he will command his children and his household after him, and they shall keep the way of the Lord, to do justice and judgment; that the Lord may bring upon Abraham that which he hath spoken of him. The rod and reproof give wisdom: but a child left *to himself* bringeth his mother to shame. Correct thy son, and he shall give thee rest; yea, he shall give delight unto thy soul. And, ye fathers, provoke not your children to wrath: but bring them up in the nurture and admonition of the Lord.

ROOM TO SWING A CAT.

Religion will not give a man brains if he have none, but will help him to use what he has very thoroughly. Godliness is profitable to the life that now is as well as that which is to come. A young man who was in the Sunday-school work, and who early made a profession of religion, is the room-clerk at one of our large hotels. He has a very large salary, and he earns his pay by his geniality, courtesy, and inexhaustible good nature. His hotel, one of the most popular in the city, is often very crowded. The assignment of rooms is a difficult task. Scores of travelers come in together, and men all clamor for the best rooms and the first attention. Our friend always proves himself equal to the emergency. He will crowd more people in the house than any other employee. He will send women and men to the sky-parlor, and tuck people away into nooks and corners and uncomfortable positions, and make them feel more comfortable than others would in rooms below offered in a gruff or surly manner.

One morning, the clerk came down to the office; he had been off duty during the night. He found a Western guest of some consequence pacing the marble floor, evidently out of sorts. Somebody had used him badly, and he didn't care to conceal it. He addressed the impatient gentleman with a "good morning," and received a surly answer—"Good morning!" "When did you come in last night? I hope they gave you a good room." "They did not; they sent me up to the sky, and gave me a room in which I could not swing a cat." "Oh! well," said the clerk, "the official did not know that you brought your cat with you. You shall have a room after breakfast large enough to swing four cats in, if you want to." The irate gentleman joined in the hearty laugh of the crowd, enjoyed a substantial breakfast, and illustrated in his own person the meaning of this scripture, "A soft answer turneth away wrath."

CXLV.

SOUND DOCTRINE.

AS I besought thee to abide still at Ephesus, when I went into Macedonia, that thou mightest charge some that they teach no other doctrine, neither give heed to fables and endless genealogies, which minister questions, rather than godly edifying which is in faith: *so do.* For I am the least of the apostles, that am not meet to be called an apostle, because I persecuted the church of God. But by the grace of God I am what I am: and his grace which *was bestowed* upon me was not in vain; but I labored more abundantly than they all: yet not I, but the grace of God which was with me. Therefore whether *it were* I or they, so we preach, and so ye believed. That we *henceforth* be no more children, tossed to and fro, and carried about with every wind of doctrine, by the sleight of men, *and* cunning craftiness, whereby they lie in wait to deceive; but speaking the truth in love, may grow up into him in all things, which is the head, *even* Christ.

THIS I KNOW, I NOW SEE.

A POOR peasant in France, like Bartimeus, was born blind. He had never seen the light of the sun, the beautiful bow of promise, nor the flowers of the field. He found a martyr-woman, who was willing to share with him life's burdens and joys. Children were born to him, and though he never saw their faces, he knew their voices, their steps, and even the touch of their hands. He had great talent in the care of horses. He was a favorite groom, skillful in medicine, and there seemed to be healing in his touch. One day, a well-known surgeon from Paris drove up to the tavern, threw the reins to the blind hostler, with special charge to have his foaming steeds well cared for. Having satisfied his bodily wants, quite late in the evening the surgeon went to the stable, and found the faithful groom still at work on the horses. The attention pleased him, and he resolved to fling the hostler a franc when he drove up the team in the morning. The pitiful look of the blind man struck the surgeon. He was one of the first oculists of the gay capital. During the whole evening, the blind man seemed to thrust himself into the presence of the surgeon. He hovered over the pillow after the doctor had retired to rest. He could not sleep. Fresh and gay with good grooming and rest, the well-appointed team came to the door. "Step out into the sunshine," said the doctor to the groom. "You're forty; earlier I could have relieved you. Your sight is perfect behind these excrescences. I can perform an operation, and the chances are even, that you can see, or die under my hand. Come to Paris. I will pay your expenses, and the experiment shall cost you nothing." Weeks passed; and he saw men as trees walking. Soon the full light dawned on him. How brilliant the sun appeared! how beautiful the rose! He looked on his wife, and called his children by name, that they might speak. He turned from them all, saying, "Let me look on my kind friend, the surgeon, who has opened all this beautiful world to me. He is better than wife or children or the beauties of nature." He felt toward his deliverer as the poor blind beggar felt toward the blessed Saviour, who answered his fervent prayer, "Jesus, thou Son of David, have mercy on me," who, when he received his sight, followed Jesus, glorifying God.

CXLVI.

THE YOUNG WARNED.

REJOICE, O young man, in thy youth; and let thy heart cheer thee in the days of thy youth, and walk in the ways of thine heart, and in the sight of thine eyes: but know thou, that for all these *things* God will bring thee into judgment. Therefore remove sorrow from thy heart, and put away evil from thy flesh: for childhood and youth *are* vanity. My son, keep my words, and lay up my commandments with thee. Keep my commandments, and live; and my law as the apple of thine eye. Bind them upon thy fingers, write them upon the table of thine heart. Say unto wisdom, Thou *art* my sister; and call understanding *thy* kinswoman: hear, ye children, the instruction of a father, and attend to know understanding. For I give you good doctrine, forsake ye not my law. For I was my father's son, tender and only *beloved* in the sight of my mother. He taught me also, and said unto me, Let thine heart retain my words: keep my commandments, and live. Get wisdom, get understanding: forget *it* not; neither decline from the words of my mouth.

PIRATES AT PITCAIRN'S ISLAND.

Send the Bible anywhere, in any part of the world, in the islands of the sea, among the savage cannibals, in the mountains of cruelty, or the valleys of slaughter; and if the Bible has any effect, social and domestic institutions of a peculiar type will spring from it. A ship known as the Bounty sailed from England. The crew mutinied, and the pirates disappeared from the face of men. After sixty years, the mystery was solved. A British ship touched at Pitcairn's Island. In the midst of idolatry and cannibalism, a most remarkable colony was discovered. A peaceful, industrious, sober, Christian commonwealth, modeled on the best type of English social life —the schools, education, the Christian Sabbath, with the marriage institution, and all the home-life of an English household of the better type. This commonwealth had seen no Christian or English society for over half a century, yet these people were the descendants of the crew of the Bounty. In the chest of one of the pirates was a Bible, which some careful mother, devoted wife, or loving sister had placed away with the sailor's truck. The mutineers landed on the island amid great peril. The poor fellow who owned the Bible resolved not to part with it. He took the Bible in his teeth, and threw himself into the sea, and was thrown up high on land. Wetted through, soiled and stained by the brine, the precious book was brought on shore. It became the corner-stone of the commonwealth. It transformed a reckless, daring, and desperate people into a model society, founded a church with its ordinances, in the midst of heathendom, away from all Christian association, sympathy, counsel. It created a model church and state, with more of the virtues and less of the vices than any commonwealth on the face of the globe. Proving that now, as 1800 years ago, the Bible is "profitable for doctrine, reproof, correction, instruction in righteousness, thoroughly furnishing the man of God unto all good works."

CXLVII.

PLEASURE IN HER DUST.

THOU shalt arise, *and* have mercy upon Zion: for the time to favor her, yea, the set time, is come. For thy servants take pleasure in her stones, and favor the dust thereof. When the Lord shall build up Zion, he shall appear in his glory. He will regard the prayer of the destitute, and not despise their prayer. Then I told them of the hand of my God which was good upon me; as also the king's words that he had spoken unto me. And they said, Let us rise up and build. So they strengthened their hands for *this* good *work.* Let them shout for joy, and be glad, that favor my righteous cause: yea, let them say continually, Let the Lord be magnified, which hath pleasure in the prosperity of his servant. And my tongue shall speak of thy righteousness *and* of thy praise all the day long. Do good in thy good pleasure unto Zion: build thou the walls of Jerusalem. Then shalt thou be pleased with the sacrifices of righteousness, with burnt offering and whole burnt offering: then shall they offer bullocks upon thine altar.

CUVIER, THE NATURALIST.

THAT eminent naturalist, Cuvier, could build up an animal from a single bone of the body, though the creature was unknown to him, and he was ignorant of its habits, knew nothing of its home, its food, or the clime in which it dwelt; yet he could not only build up the entire animal, but indicate the class to which it belonged, its home, habits, and food: and this on the principle of comparative anatomy. So character can be judged: the company one keeps, the favorite authors and poets, private pursuits, small utterances and little deeds indicate character. "I must dismiss my clerk," said a well-known merchant; "he dresses too well, he has too fine a library, too many pictures and works of art; on the salary I give him, he can not afford to live in that style. He may be honest, but I do not choose to trust him." The merchant who saw the cashier of the bank in which his money was deposited in a lager-beer saloon on Sunday, withdrew his account from the bank on Monday. In less than six weeks, the cashier was a defaulter. A director of one of our large moneyed institutions was jostled by some men on the platform of a street-car on Sunday night. The men were mellow and merry; their conduct called close attention to them. Among them, the director discovered the janitor of his own building. From three o'clock on Saturday afternoon till nine Monday morning, the building, with all its treasures, was in charge of the janitor. Spending Sunday among the upper saloons of gay New-York was not considered the best way to honor the trust committed to him. The men were marvelously astonished when they found themselves discharged in a lump; they complained of the harsh and ungenerous treatment they received. Young men drink, gamble, and live fast on sly occasions, and wonder that the thing is known. But what they do and don't do, where they go and do not go, the company they keep and avoid, reveal what they are.

CXLVIII.

GLORIOUS LIBERTY.

FOR the creature was made subject to vanity, not willingly, but by reason of him who hath subjected *the same* in hope; because the creature itself also shall be delivered from the bondage of corruption into the glorious liberty of the children of God. Stand fast therefore in the liberty wherewith Christ hath made us free, and be not entangled again with the yoke of bondage. For in Jesus Christ neither circumcision availeth any thing, nor uncircumcision; but faith which worketh by love. Let no man therefore judge you in meat, or in drink, or in respect of a holy-day, or of the new moon, or of the Sabbath *days:* which are a shadow of things to come; but the body *is* of Christ. Let no man beguile you of your reward in a voluntary humility and worshiping of angels, intruding into those things which he hath not seen, vainly puffed up by his fleshly mind, and not holding the Head, from which all the body by joints and bands having nourishment ministered, and knit together, increaseth with the increase of God.

MARKET VALUE OF YOUNG MEN.

MOSES F. ODELL was one of the most eminent Sunday-school men of the times. For many years, he was superintendent of one of the largest schools in Brooklyn. His heart was in his work, and no business engagements and no honors, political or social, could divert him from his toil. He had great magnetic power, and his grasp on young men was wonderful. Great numbers were gathered into his Bible-classes and his school. A pupil who presented to a business firm a letter of recommendation from Mr. Odell was almost sure to get a position. Merchants and business men often sent to the superintendent for a first-class Sunday-school young man. One day, a German importer accosted Mr. Odell. The man was one of the most noted liquor-dealers in the city. "I want you," he said, "to send me a first-rate clerk; one that you can recommend. He must be prompt, smart, and reliable. In short, he must be a first-class Sunday-school boy." "Why do you want a clerk out of my Sunday-school? You're not a Christian; you don't attend church; your children are not in the Sunday-school." "Oh! that's all very well," was the reply. "I can take care of myself, but I won't have any body in my store that I can't trust. I know these Sunday-school boys, and they'll do to tie to: they won't drink my liquor nor rob my till." "Wisdom is the principal thing; therefore get wisdom: and with all thy getting get understanding. Exalt her, and she shall promote thee: she shall bring thee to honor, when thou dost embrace her. She shall give to thine head an ornament of grace: a crown of glory shall she deliver to thee. Hear, O my son, and receive my sayings; and the years of thy life shall be many."

CXLIX.

GLORIOUS HIGH PRIEST.

SEEING then that we have a great high priest, that is passed into the heavens, Jesus the Son of God, let us hold fast *our* profession. For we have not a high priest which cannot be touched with the feeling of our infirmities; but was in all points tempted like *as we are, yet* without sin. Let us therefore come boldly unto the throne of grace, that we may obtain mercy, and find grace to help in time of need. Thou art fairer than the children of men: grace is poured into thy lips: therefore God hath blessed thee forever. Thy throne, O God, *is* forever and ever: the sceptre of thy kingdom *is* a right sceptre. Thou lovest righteousness, and hatest wickedness: therefore God, thy God, hath anointed thee with the oil of gladness above thy fellows. But now hath he obtained a more excellent ministry, by how much also he is the mediator of a better covenant, which was established upon better promises. For if that first *covenant* had been faultless, then should no place have been sought for the second. For finding fault with them, he saith, Behold, the days come, saith the Lord, when I will make a new covenant with the house of Israel and with the house of Judah.

WINNING A SOUL.

A YOUNG man came from the interior of the State, to begin business in New-York. He brought with him a letter introducing him to a leather house in the Swamp. He reached New-York on Saturday night. True to his principles and education, he proposed to keep holy-time in the house of the Lord. He was coarsely clad in home-spun, his boots were heavy, and his hat not in the reigning fashion. He drifted on toward the Wall-street church. He was dismayed as he saw the beauty and fashion of the city sweeping into the portals of the sanctuary. As he was turning from the doors, a voice arrested him: "Have you a seat, young man?" "No, sir." "Do you belong to the city?" "No, sir." "Where is your home?" "In the country." "How long have you been in the city?" "I came in last night." "What are you going to do here?" "I hope to go into business to-morrow." "This is right; you have begun well, young man! Never forsake the God of your fathers. Come, I'll give you a seat in my pew!" The next morning, the young man presented his letter at the Swamp. "What do you want, young man?" said the sharp Scotch merchant. "I want to get credit on some leather, upper and sole." "Have you references?" "I think I can get references. My father has friends here." "Young man, didn't I see you yesterday in Mr. Lennox's pew?" "I don't know, sir. I was at church; and a kind gentleman asked me to sit in his pew." "Yes, young man, that was Robert Lennox. I'll trust any one that Mr. Lennox invites into his pew; you needn't trouble yourself about references; when these goods are gone, come and get more." That young man became one of the most eminent merchants of New-York. To the day of his death, he attributed his success to that first fortunate Sabbath he spent in the city.

CL.

REWARD OF LABOR.

AND God saith, Behold, I have given you every herb bearing seed, which *is* upon the face of all the earth, and every tree, in the which *is* the fruit of a tree yielding seed; to you it shall be for meat. And out of the ground the Lord God formed every beast of the field, and every fowl of the air; and brought *them* unto Adam to see what he would call them: and whatsoever Adam called every living creature, that *was* the name thereof. Moreover the profit of the earth is for all: the king *himself* is served by the field. The sleep of a laboring man *is* sweet, whether he eat little or much: but the abundance of the rich will not suffer him to sleep. What profit hath a man of all his labor which he taketh under the sun? *One* generation passeth away, and *another* generation cometh: but the earth abideth forever. The sun also ariseth, and the sun goeth down, and hasteth to his place where he arose. The wind goeth toward the south, and turneth about unto the north it whirleth about continually, and the wind returneth again according to his circuits. All the rivers run into the sea; yet the sea *is* not full: unto the place from whence the rivers come, thither they return again. All things *are* full of labor; man cannot utter *it:* the eye is not satisfied with seeing, nor the ear filled with hearing.

GENERAL JACKSON AT CHURCH.

From his earliest life, General Jackson was a great respecter of religion, and an earnest friend of ministers. He did not make a profession of religion till long after his public life had closed, and just before his death. But the minister was not more regular at the morning service than was General Jackson while in Washington. To the White House, preachers of the Gospel were especially welcome. Whoever else were kept waiting in the anteroom, these were admitted at once, unless some special audience was being held. When the usual formula was uttered at the close of an interview, "I hope the Lord will bless you," the President would reverently bow his head, and respond, "I thank you for the benediction." The President's pew was in the Four-and-a-Half-street Church. It was located on the left-hand side of the preacher, front pew. The General was never late. As he entered, it was his custom to stop on the threshold and bow reverently to the pulpit, pass up preceded by the sexton, and, after being seated, engage in private prayer. As a hearer, he was very considerate and attentive; he never withdrew his eye from the preacher, and when any thing pleased him he nodded an approval. At the close of the service, it was the custom of the President to rise, bow reverently to the preacher as a token of respect, which was always returned, and then pass quietly down the aisle to the door. He held an informal court in the vestibule, saluted the crowd that gathered around his carriage, and, lifting his hat, gave a formal bow to the people, which no one knew better than he how to make.

CLI.

MERRY HEART.

A MERRY heart doeth good *like* a medicine: but a broken spirit drieth the bones. And when Boaz had eaten and drunk, and his heart was merry, he went to lie down at the end of the heap of corn: and she came softly, and uncovered his feet, and laid her down. A merry heart maketh a cheerful countenance: but by sorrow of the heart the spirit is broken. The heart of him that hath understanding seeketh knowledge: but the mouth of fools feedeth on foolishness. All the days of the afflicted *are* evil: but he that is of a merry heart *hath* a continual feast. I said in mine heart, Go to now, I will prove thee with mirth; therefore enjoy pleasure: and, behold, this also *is* vanity. I said of laughter, *It is* mad: and of mirth, What doeth it? I sought in mine heart to give myself unto wine, yet acquainting mine heart with wisdom; and to lay hold on folly, till I might see what *was* that good for the sons of men, which they should do under the heaven all the days of their life.

DECIDED CHRISTIAN.

MRS. PRESIDENT POLK, a decided Christian and Presbyterian, succeeded the volatile and flippant Mrs. Tyler in the White House. Mrs. Tyler made the White House very gay with parties, soirées, and balls. With all her fashionable frivolity, she was very unpopular in the city, and the staid and orderly society of Washington was greatly outraged by her flippancy. Even the terrible accident that sent the Secretary of State and members of the Cabinet to a premature burial could not induce Mrs. Tyler to omit her dancing-parties at the White House. A new order of things reigned in the executive mansion when Mrs. Polk crossed the threshold. She was one of the most elegant ladies of her day. Handsome, intelligent, popular, with strong common-sense, she changed the society of Washington in an hour. She banished dancing from the White House, and introduced social reforms long needed. The usual inauguration ball was to come off on the fourth of March. On the morning of the third of March, a deputation of Christian ladies waited on Mrs. Polk. They congratulated her on banishing dancing from the executive mansion. They desired her to move one step further, and throw her decided influence in favor of a reform much desired. The inauguration ball was to come off the next night; would Mrs. Polk remain away? She was a member of the Presbyterian Church, and that church denounced dancing as a sin. Her high example in refusing to attend the ball would be felt throughout the land. Her influence would be as widely felt if she graced the occasion with her presence. Such an opportunity would never occur again in her lifetime. To all this, Mrs. Polk replied, "In banishing dancing from the White House, I did not propose to touch the question whether dancing was or was not a proper social or family pastime. I did not think any entertainment should be allowed in the executive mansion that could justly give offence to any portion of the American people. The inauguration ball is a different matter. It is given in honor of my husband as President of the United States. He is not a professing Christian, and desires my attendance. I shall yield to his wishes. No American lady can plead my example until she is placed in the same circumstances. She will then probably feel it her duty, as I feel it mine, to conform to the customs of inauguration since the days of Washington."

CLII.

FRUITS OF RIGHTEOUSNESS.

UNTIL the Spirit be poured upon us from on high, and the wilderness be a fruitful field, and the fruitful field be counted for a forest. Then judgment shall dwell in the wilderness, and righteousness remain in the fruitful field. And the work of righteousness shall be peace; and the effect of righteousness, quietness and assurance forever. The fruit of the righteous *is* a tree of life; and he that winneth souls *is* wise. For where envying and strife *is*, there *is* confusion and every evil work. But the wisdom that is from above is first pure, then peaceable, gentle, *and* easy to be entreated, full of mercy and good fruits, without partiality, and without hypocrisy. And the fruit of righteousness is sown in peace of them that make peace.

"WE WANT TO LOVE THE LORD."

THE afternoon service in one of our mission-schools closed. Nearly five hundred children assembled for prayer and praise. The session had been one of unusual interest. Many of the poor fathers and mothers followed their children to school, and joined in the worship of the hour. Nearly all the children had gone home. Two little girls, evidently sisters, remained.

They were poorly clad, and sorrow and suffering had marked their faces with deep lines. Beside their scanty clothing, their pinched and sunken features showed they were familiar with want. It was a cold day, but their feet were bare and stockingless. "Well, my little girls, what do you want?" said the superintendent. Not a word in response. A quivering lip and moistened eyes alone answered. "Tell me what you wish," said the superintendent; "perhaps I can help you." The eldest spake, "Sister and me want to love Jesus, but we don't know how." They did not go home alone that night. The mission wardrobe furnished them good, stout clothing, and their feet were made warm by stockings and shoes. But what a home! A frightful abode for a human being. A shelter to which a humane man would not invite his dog; a home whose inhabitants were reeking with blasphemy and sin. A narrow, dark, offensive staircase led to a loft. No fire, no window; no food, no comfort. A drunken man and woman lay on a bundle of rags in a corner, the father and mother of the two little girls who were seeking the Lord in the mission-house. Yet the Saviour walked amid these outcasts. He bore the two neglected children in his arms as the shepherd carries the wee lamb in his bosom. The little girls found the Saviour they sought. They rescued both the father and the mother. The man now earns a good living; the woman is a member of the church. There are few happier homes in lower New-York than this. Grace works great temporal changes. When Jesus enters a family, he brings joy and comfort and relief as well as salvation.

CLIII.

HUSBANDS AND WIVES.

HUSBANDS, love your wives, even as Christ also loved the church, and gave himself for it; that he might sanctify and cleanse it with the washing of water by the word. And said, For this cause shall a man leave father and mother, and shall cleave to his wife: and they twain shall be one flesh? Wherefore they are no more twain, but one flesh. What therefore God hath joined together, let not man put asunder. And the woman which hath a husband that believeth not, and if he be pleased to dwell with her, let her not leave him. For the unbelieving husband is sanctified by the wife, and the unbelieving wife is sanctified by the husband: else were your children unclean; but now are they holy. Wives, submit yourselves unto your own husbands, as it is fit in the Lord. Husbands, love *your* wives, and be not bitter against them. Therefore as the church is subject unto Christ, so *let* the wives *be* to their own husbands in every thing. Husbands, love your wives, even as Christ also loved the church, and gave himself for it.

THE ABNEY HOUSE.

Dr. Watts, being in feeble health, was invited by that eminent Christian merchant of London, Mr. Thomas Abney, to pass a night at his elegant country-seat at Stoke Newington. He extended his visit through thirty-six years. In the groves that surrounded the mansion, Dr. Watts wrote some of his sublimest hymns. From the elegant surroundings of the place, he gathered some of his choicest imageries—"Sweet fields beyond the swelling flood" being among them. The house has been removed. The groves have been cut down. A cemetery occupies the place of the paths where, amid groves, flowers, and verdure, Dr. Watts walked and composed. One thing remains sacred to the memory of the great poet. In one end of the garden is a tufted bank guarded by a high iron fence. From the centre springs a tall, majestic growth of centuries. Under this tree, Watts often sat and wrote. One day, he was meditating on the redemption of Christ. On the bark of the then young tree, he drew with his penknife a cross. Cutting it into the trunk, sitting down, he there wrote the touching lyric called "Meditations in the Grove," two stanzas of which read :

I'll carve my passions on the bark,
And every wounded tree
Shall drop, and there some mystic mark
That Jesus died for me.

"The swains shall wonder when they read,
Inscribed on all the grove,
That Heaven itself came down
To win a mortal's love."

The Christian visitor, as he stands beneath the outspread arms of that majestic oak, can not fail to reverently lift his hat in honor of the sentiment and of the Christian poet who, though dead, yet speaketh.

CLIV.

ALL IN AUTHORITY.

AND over these three presidents; of whom Daniel *was* first: that the princes might give accounts unto them, and the king should have no damage. Then this Daniel was preferred above the presidents and princes, because an excellent spirit *was* in him; and the king thought to set him over the whole realm. And, behold, a man of Ethiopia, a eunuch of great authority under Candace queen of the Ethiopians, who had the charge of all her treasure, and had come to Jerusalem for to worship. Obey them that have the the rule over you, and submit yourselves: for they watch for your souls, as they that must give account, that they may do it with joy, and not with grief: for that *is* unprofitable for you. Let every soul be subject unto the higher powers. For there is no power but of God: the powers that be are ordained of God. Whosoever therefore resisteth the power, resisteth the ordinance of God: and they that resist shall receive to themselves damnation.

HEALING THE PRINCE OF WALES.

Albert, Prince of Wales, was sick unto death. The nations awaited the telegram announcing his decease. The sickness of the Prince excited an unusual degree of interest in the Fulton-street meeting. It was felt that his life was in some measure connected with amity and good feeling between America and England. His death would affect the cause of the Protestant religion. More than all, there was a deep sympathy for his mother. One day, when his death was momentarily expected, the whole session was given up to prayer for the recovery of the Prince. The telegraph bore this expression of sympathy over the land and over the seas. Prince Albert began immediately to mend. The Queen was so touched by the sympathy of American Christians, that she sent an autograph letter to the meeting, which was read amid fervent ejaculations for the health and happiness of her majesty.

It was no vaingloryíng that led to the offering this request. The surging cry to God that went up like a wail of sorrow from a nation that God would spare the young man to the British people, that the succession might not be changed, found a response in the American heart. England is still our mother. She gave the laws and the institutions that made us what we are—our free press, trial by jury, and our laws; and the ashes of our fathers repose beneath her monuments.

CLV.

O LORD OUR GOVERNOR!

THINE, O Lord, *is* the greatness, and the power, and the glory, and the victory, and the majesty: for all *that is* in the heaven and in the earth *is thine;* thine *is* the kingdom, O Lord, and thou art exalted as head above all. Both riches and honor *come* of thee, and thou reignest over all; and in thine hand *is* power and might; and in thine hand *it is* to make great, and to give strength unto all. Now therefore, our God, we thank thee, and praise thy glorious name. And said, I beseech thee, O Lord God of heaven, the great and terrible God, that keepeth covenant and mercy for them that love him and observe his commandments: let thine ear now be attentive, and thine eyes open, that thou mayest hear the prayer of thy servant, which I pray before thee now, day and night, for the children of Israel thy servants, and confess the sins of the children of Israel, which we have sinned against thee: both I and my father's house have sinned.

OLD FURGERSON THE MISER.

It is the custom of the Christian men of Edinburgh to maintain street-services in that city, especially on the afternoon of the Lord's day. A retired street is selected ; a band of Christian women and men who can sing gather by appointment, and the services are opened by song. Usually a crowd gathers, for street-preaching is much more popular in Great Britain than America. The blinds and windows are often thrown open, and whole families come to the front to listen to the music and be moved by the stirring exhortations. In one of the streets where divine service was held dwelt an old man, called by the populace Old Furgerson the Miser. His blinds where closed from Christmas to Christmas. No light, no fire, no cheer marked his dwelling. He lived in apparent abject want. He went out thinly clad, and his living was of the meanest kind. The speaker's stand was erected in front of Old Furgerson's house. Here the singing commenced with unwonted earnestness and force. Now the sacred songs of England are very ancient; they are handed down from sire to son ; they are sung to the same words, the same measure, and the same time, from generation to generation, from the time of the Covenanters. There was no response from the miser's house. The speakers of the crowd passed away. The company pitched their table a block off. The services were interrupted by a street Arab, who came shouting round the corner, "Misters, Old Furgerson the Miser wants you to come back and sing some more!" The table was put in its old place, and the services renewed. The miser's house gave no sign. Not a window moved or a blind stirred. No thanks, no response, and the disappointed company turned away. A week after, Old Furgerson was found dead in his chair, in the act of signing a check for fifty pounds. A will was found, leaving over half a million pounds to preach the Gospel to the neglected and destitute of the Scottish capital. Fruit after many days.

CLVI.

JESUS OUR KING.

BEHOLD, a king shall reign in righteousness, and princes shall rule in judgment. Give the king thy judgments, O God, and thy righteousness unto the king's son. He shall have dominion also from sea to sea, and from the river unto the ends of the earth. The kings of Tarshish and of the isles shall bring presents: the kings of Sheba and Seba shall offer gifts. Yea, all kings shall fall down before him: all nations shall serve him. Rejoice greatly, O daughter of Zion; shout, O daughter of Jerusalem: behold, thy King cometh unto thee: he *is* just, and having salvation; lowly, and riding upon an ass, and upon a colt the foal of an ass. Yea, all kings shall fall down before him: all nations shall serve him. For he shall deliver the needy when he crieth; the poor also, and *him* that hath no helper. He shall spare the poor and needy, and shall save the souls of the needy.

DYING REQUEST.

ETHAN ALLEN was a professed infidel. He wrote a book against the divinity of our blessed Lord. His wife was a Christian, earnest, cheerful, and devoted. She died early, leaving an only daughter behind who became the idol of her father. She was a fragile, sensitive child, and entwined herself about the rugged nature of her sire as the vine entwines itself around the knotty and gnarled limbs of the oak. Consumption marked this fair girl for its own ; and she wasted away day by day, till even the grasshopper became a burden. One day her father came in her room and sat down by the bedside. He took her wan, ethereal hand in his. Looking her father squarely in the face, she said, "My dear father, I'm going to die." "Oh! no, my child! oh! no. The spring is coming, and with the birds and the breezes and the bloom, your frail cheek will blush with health." "No ; the doctor was here today. I felt I was nearing the grave, and I asked him to tell me plainly what I had to expect. I told him that it was a great thing to exchange worlds; that I did not wish to be deceived about myself, and if I was going to die I had some preparations I wanted to make. He told me my disease was beyond the reach of human skill; that a few more suns would rise and set, and then I would be borne to my burial. You will bury me, father, by the side of my mother, for that was her dying request. But, father, you and mother did not agree on religion. Mother often spoke to me of the blessed Saviour who died for us all. She used to pray for both you and me, that that Saviour might be our friend, and that we might all see him as our Saviour, when he sits on his throne in his glory. I don't feel that I can go alone through the dark valley of the shadow of death. Now tell me, father, whom shall I follow, you or mother? Shall I reject Christ, as you have taught me, or shall I accept him, as he was my mother's friend in the hour of her great sorrow?" There was an honest heart beneath that rough exterior. Though tears nearly choked his utterance, the old soldier said, "My child, cling to your mother's Saviour ; she is right. I'll try to follow you to that blessed abode." A serene smile overspread the face of that dying girl, and who can doubt that there is an unbroken family in heaven?

CLVII.

BLESSINGS OF OBEDIENCE.

WASH ye, make you clean; put away the evil of your doings from before mine eyes; cease to do evil; learn to do well; seek judgment, relieve the oppressed, judge the fatherless, plead for the widow. If ye be willing and obedient, ye shall eat the good of the land: but if ye refuse and rebel, ye shall be devoured with the sword: for the mouth of the Lord hath spoken *it.* And Samuel said, Hath the Lord *as great* delight in burnt offerings and sacrifices, as in obeying the voice of the Lord? Behold, to obey *is* better than sacrifice, *and* to hearken than the fat of rams. For rebellion *is as* the sin of witchcraft, and stubbornness *is as* iniquity and idolatry. Because thou hast rejected the word of the Lord, he hath also rejected thee from *being* king. Then shall he give the rain of thy seed, that thou shalt sow the ground withal; and bread of the increase of the earth, and it shall be fat and plenteous: in that day shall thy cattle feed in large pastures.

CONSECRATING ONE'S SUBSTANCE.

THERE was a young mechanic in Massachusetts who consecrated to the Lord, when he gave himself to him, a portion of his time and of his earnings. His wages were not large; but he gave cheerfully out of his penury to every good cause. One day, he came home from his work quite cast down. He was not accustomed to be melancholy or gloomy in his own home. His wife knew that something troubled him, and affectionately sought for the cause. "Well," he answered, "I am downhearted because I'm so poor. The subscription for the cause of missions was taken up in the factory to-day, and nearly every one subscribed something. I was ashamed to put my name down because I could give so little. I don't want money simply to be rich, but I want money to do good with." The next morning, when he came home from his work, his wife said to him, "Husband, if you will get me some button-moulds and a stick of twist, I'll see what I can do for the cause of missions." Nearly all the buttons were imported at that time, and were quite expensive. This earnest Christian woman had taken an English button to pieces, examined its structure, and proposed to make a few dozen to promote foreign missions. The work was well and artistically done, the little package consigned and the story told to a Christian merchant in New-York. Soon an answer came back: "Make as many dozen as you choose; if they amount to hundreds, all the better: I'll sell all you make." A new branch of business sprang at once into existence. The mechanic and his wife found their hands full; machinery came to the rescue; factories sprang up, employing hundreds of hands. The poor mechanic who desired to do something for the foreign missions became a millionaire. He poured out his wealth like the sea. Colleges, schools, seminaries were built, placing the highest departments of education within the reach of the humblest. He has never denied his Master, but to-day admits that all his prosperity grew out of his earnest desire, when in penury, to honor the Lord with his increase, and to consecrate his substance to the cause of religion.

CLVIII.

JESUS OUR ADVOCATE.

MY little children, these things write I unto you, that ye sin not. And if any man sin, we have an advocate with the Father, Jesus Christ the righteous: and he is the propitiation for our sins: and not for ours only, but also for *the sins of* the whole world. Whom God hath set forth *to be* a propitiation through faith in his blood, to declare his righteousness for the remission of sins that are past, through the forbearance of God; for in that he himself hath suffered being tempted, he is able to succor them that are tempted. But we see Jesus, who was made a little lower than the angels for the suffering of death, crowned with glory and honor; that he by the grace of God should taste death for every man. For it became him, for whom *are* all things, and by whom *are* all things, in bringing many sons unto glory, to make the captain of their salvation perfect through sufferings.

POWER OF A BAD EXAMPLE.

One of the most influential banks of the city has an annual custom that would be more honored in the breach than in the observance. On the annual election, there is a liberal treat furnished: a table is spread, loaded with wines and liquors of a great variety. Here the president and dignitaries of the bank, the stockholders, the clerks and other employees, meet for a grand carouse. A huge punch-bowl occupies the position of honor; dignity is lost. Sedate old men go toddling home, and young men are often heard shouting, " We won't go home till morning." The habits formed under such influences are often as lasting as life, and are as baneful as poison. Eminent financiers, directly or indirectly connected with this institution, have passed under a cloud. How much this custom of annual drinking has had to do with the matter, who can tell? Situations lost; honor soiled; temptations triumphant. Bad company; secret rooms; dark chambers of sin; fast and extravagant living; defalcation, embezzlement, and fraud; flight, disgrace, and infamy. These are some of its fruits. " My son, if sinners entice thee, consent thou not. Consent thou not if saints entice!"

"Though prophets urge, we drink no wine."

CLIX.

JESUS OUR LORD.

BUT to us *there is but* one God, the Father, of whom *are* all things, and we in him; and one Lord Jesus Christ, by whom *are* all things, and we by him. O Lord our God, *other* lords besides thee have had dominion over us; *but* by thee only will we make mention of thy name. The word which *God* sent unto the children of Israel, preaching peace by Jesus Christ: (he is Lord of all:) how God anointed Jesus of Nazareth with the Holy Ghost and with power: who went about doing good, and healing all that were oppressed of the devil; for God was with him. I give thee charge in the sight of God, who quickeneth all things, and *before* Christ Jesus, who before Pontius Pilate witnessed a good confession; that thou keep *this* commandment without spot, unrebukable, until the appearing of our Lord Jesus Christ: which in his times he shall show, *who is* the blessed and only Potentate, the King of kings, and Lord of lords; who only hath immortality, dwelling in the light which no man can approach unto; whom no man hath seen, nor can see: to whom *be* honor and power everlasting. Amen.

PURPOSED IN HIS HEART.

Grace can do much for a man. When Whitfield could not life in a house with a person whom he admitted was a Christian, he said, "Grace can live where I can not." Daniel was a young man in Babylon: a slave, away from his religion and worship, and in the midst of idolatry. He was marked by the perilous blandishments of the court. He was young, handsome, intellectual. He was selected to grace the court and train of the monarch. The heating, debasing viands of the king's table were ordered, he was commanded to drink the king's wine. Daniel saw the drift of all this, and "purposed in his heart" not to do it. His pluck, with the help of the Lord, carried him through all his difficulties. Even without this direct interposition and help from God, pluck and principle may do much. The characters of eminent men have been distinguished for principle and persistency. "I can't drink a little wine," said Dr. Johnson; "I can drink a great deal, I can drink none; I therefore abstain." To show how absolutely the will is over matter, Loyola, the founder of the Jesuits, stood in a pool of ice up to his chin for an hour, in the presence of a debauchee, who pleaded the iron grip of his habits as a plea for his excesses. Wilberforce's conversion followed a resolution made at a faro-table, that he would handle cards no more. Sheridan owed his success as a parliamentary debater to the resolution formed on the night of his first speech and first disgrace in Parliament. His failure was complete and demoralizing. His best friends said he was a failure, and must seek some new field to display his talents, if he had any. "It is in me, and it shall come out," was the terse reply. The world knows by heart the rest of the story.

CLX.

THE LORD OUR RIGHTEOUSNESS.

BEHOLD, the days come, saith the Lord, that I will raise unto David a righteous Branch, and a king shall reign and prosper, and shall execute judgment and justice in the earth. In his days Judah shall be saved, and Israel shall dwell safely: and this *is* the name whereby he shall be called, THE LORD OUR RIGHTEOUSNESS. But now, in Christ Jesus, ye who sometime were far off are made nigh by the blood of Christ. For he is our peace, who hath made both one, and hath broken down the middle wall of partition *between us* and to know the love of Christ, which passeth knowledge, that ye might be filled with all the fullness of God. Now unto him that is able to do exceeding abundantly above all that we ask or think, according to the power that worketh in us. Unto him *be* glory in the church by Christ Jesus throughout all ages, world without end. Amen.

CUNARDER AND A NAIL.

The Bible makes much of little things—the little foxes destroy the vines. Life is full of examples showing that great excellences can be neutralized by small effects. A speck in the eye; a bit of dust in a watch; a screw loose in a machine, are illustrations. A little helm turns about the big ships; the small bit controls the horse and the equipage; the tongue, a little member, is more than an entire match for the whole man. Religion, taste, talent, position, good intentions, are often neutralized by small and insignificant things. A Cunarder left the Mersey Sound for New-York. It was a well-appointed vessel, staunchly built, well officered, with an imposing list of passengers and a valuable cargo. One bright and sunny morning, the ship, according to the reckoning, was two hundred miles from Nantucket Shoals, shoals on which no vessel ever struck her keel and escaped. All at once, the man on the look-out shouted, "Land ho!" The engines were reversed, and the ship brought up within twice her length of the dangerous coast. Two hundred miles away from the shoals according to reckoning, the ship was actually within two hundred yards of the treacherous shelves. Now for the cause. On leaving the Mersey, a stove was put up to warm the pilot-house. The steward drove an insignificant nail too near the compass. It did not act promptly; it did not act powerfully; it did not act directly. At once, it went to its insidious work. Imperceptibly, but really, operating on the needle, till, during the voyage, it produced the difference of two hundred miles in the course of the vessel. That insignificant nail was more than a match for compass and pilot, for captain and crew, for the skill of the officers and the strength of the vessel, and absolutely held freight and tonnage, and wealth and beauty in its own feeble grasp. But for the honest look-out and the timely alarm, the craft would have gone down carrying all with it, perhaps leaving no one to tell the story of its end.

CLXI.

FINISHER OF OUR FAITH.

LOOKING unto Jesus the author and finisher of *our* faith; who for the joy that was set before him endured the cross, despising the shame, and is set down at the right hand of the throne of God. Insomuch that we desired Titus, that as he had begun, so he would also finish in you the same grace also. Therefore, as ye abound in every *thing*, *in* faith, and utterance, and knowledge, and *in* all diligence, and *in* your love to us, *see* that ye abound in this grace also. After this, Jesus knowing that all things were now accomplished, that the Scripture might be fulfilled, saith, I thirst. Now there was set a vessel full of vinegar: and they filled a sponge with vinegar, and put *it* upon hyssop, and put *it* to his mouth. When Jesus therefore had received the vinegar, he said, It is finished: and he bowed his head, and gave up the ghost.

THE FATAL CHOICE.

In one of the New-England villages, there was a marked religious interest. The whole town was stirred. The bell calling to prayer stirred every family, and, like a general alarm, called out the whole household. The Sabbath had been a day of very marked solemnity. A special meeting for prayer was to be held in the evening, to which young men were specially invited. Two young men sat in a room which they occupied jointly. The bell for evening service commenced tolling. The elder said, "Come, it's time to go to church." The younger hesitated, and seemed confused. At length he said, "I will be glad to go with you, but I have an engagement to-night; I can't break it; I wish I could. You must not ask me where." All expostulation was in vain. The elder turned from his companion with a sorrowing heart. He had some religious conviction, and this seemed to be deepened as he entered the house of worship. He bowed before the altar that night, gave himself to the Lord, and, with a joyous spirit, sought his chamber, resolved, if he could, to lead his associate to Christ. His companion came not. The long hours changed into the short ones; midnight merged itself into the twilight. Yet he did not come. Filled with vague apprehension, the young man listened for the rumors in the morning. His companion was in prison, under a serious charge. His appointment on Sunday night was with a company of roistering young men, who proposed to hold a secret meeting and ward off the influence of the revival. In his case it was successfully done. Liquor was introduced, and the revels ran high. Bad blood was engendered. Words were followed by blows. A heavy stroke felled one to the floor. An arrest took place; a trial, and a conviction. On a succeeding Sunday, one of those young men professed faith in Christ, while the other trod the stone pavement of a felon's cell. So near the kingdom, and to miss it after all! Life is like a brook on a mountain: a small pebble can turn it east or west. A single act can turn the stream to be a river of life or a river of death.

CLXII.

JESUS IN HIS CHURCH.

AND I say also unto thee, That thou art Peter, and upon this rock I will build my church; and the gates of hell shall not prevail against it. And I will give unto thee the keys of the kingdom of heaven: and whatsoever thou shalt bind on earth shall be bound in heaven; and whatsoever thou shalt loose on earth shall be loosed in heaven. Unto the church of God which is at Corinth, to them that are sanctified in Christ Jesus, called *to be* saints, with all that in every place call upon the name of Jesus Christ our Lord, both theirs and ours: Grace *be* unto you, and peace, from God our Father, and *from* the Lord Jesus Christ. And he is the head of the body, the church: who is the beginning, the firstborn from the dead; that in all *things* he might have the pre-eminence. But if I tarry long, that thou mayest know how thou oughtest to behave thyself in the house of God, which is the church of the living God, the pillar and ground of the truth. And without controversy great is the mystery of godliness: God was manifest in the flesh, justified in the Spirit, see of angels, preached unto the Gentiles, believed on in the world, received up into glory.

CHANNING'S FATHER.

Dr. Channing, the popular Unitarian preacher, was the son of a Congregational elder. His home was in Newport, and the renowned Dr. Hopkins was his pastor. His father was an elder in the church. One night, Dr. Hopkins preached a very impressive and forcible sermon on future judgment. He showed that even on the ground of reason there ought to be a future retribution, and if revelation was true, all men must stand before the bar of God and give an account of the deeds done in the body. The truths he enforced with great effect on the conscience of his hearers. Young Channing, a lad about ten, was very greatly impressed. He thought that if that doctrine was true, it was quite time for him to be attending to the subject of his own salvation. At the close of the service, he took his father by the hand, and walked home by his side. He supposed his father believed all he heard, and was as much impressed as himself. He was in hopes that his father would speak to him on the subject of the evening sermon, but he said nothing. On reaching home, he took off his boots, called for his paper, and sat down to read. "I made up my mind," said Channing, "that my father did not believe one word that he had heard. He was not alarmed, why should I be? and I dismissed the whole subject from my thoughts." That night was the turning-point in young Channing's life.

CLXIII.

BUY AND EAT.

HO, every one that thirsteth, come ye to the waters, and he that hath no money; come ye, buy and eat; yea, come, buy wine and milk without money and without price. The sceptre shall not depart from Judah, nor a lawgiver from between his feet, until Shiloh come; and unto him *shall* the gathering of the people *be*. Binding his foal unto the vine, and his ass's colt unto the choice vine; he washed his garments in wine, and his clothes in the blood of grapes: his eyes *shall be* red with wine, and his teeth white with milk. Wisdom hath builded her house, she hath hewn out her seven pillars: she hath killed her beasts; she hath mingled her wine; she hath also furnished her table. She hath sent forth her maidens: she crieth upon the highest places of the city, Whoso *is* simple, let him turn in hither: *as for* him that wanteth understanding, she saith to him, Come, eat of my bread, and drink of the wine *which* I have mingled. Forsake the foolish, and live; and go in the way of understanding

HOW A BOY BUILT A CHURCH.

In the interior of the State stands a very fine Presbyterian church. It is large, convenient, and elegant. A little boy had a great deal to do with building it. The church worshiped in an old-fashioned, inconvenient house, and for years a struggling effort had been made to build a new place of worship. At length the land was purchased, and here matters rested. As the pastor could do nothing with the old folks, he tried to stir up the children. He told them the story of a lot of Sunday-school children, who went around selling bricks for a new church, and he asked his children if they would not like to have a brick and a new place in the sanctuary. One Monday morning, a loud ring was heard at the door of the parsonage. The pastor went to the door, and found a little boy, with a wheelbarrow full of bricks, standing on the sidewalk. "I have brought you," the little fellow said, "a lot of bricks for the new church." "All right," was the reply; "I'll get my hat, and show you where to dump them." A portion of the fence was removed, and the bricks tumbled out on the new site. Two or three wealthy men held the matter in their own hands. To them the pastor wrote in substance: "Brethren, the new church will be built. The first load of bricks is on the ground. If you are to take a hand in this work, you must stir yourselves betimes." Alarmed lest some other parties should lead in the matter, a meeting was at once called, funds were subscribed, a liberal amount pledged, and from that hour the work went bravely on to its completion. "A little child shall lead them."

CLXIV.

MERCIFUL AND GRACIOUS.

AND the Lord descended in the cloud, and stood with him there, and proclaimed the name of the Lord. And the Lord passed by before him, and proclaimed, The Lord, the Lord God, merciful and gracious, longsuffering, and abundant in goodness and truth, keeping mercy for thousands, forgiving iniquity and transgression and sin, and that will by no means clear *the guilty;* visiting the iniquity of the fathers upon the children, and upon the children's children, unto the third and to the fourth *generation.* The Lord *is* merciful and gracious, slow to anger, and plenteous in mercy. He will not always chide: neither will he keep *his anger* for ever. He hath not dealt with us after our sins ; nor rewarded us according to our iniquities. Now, therefore, our God, the great, the mighty, and the terrible God, who keepest covenant and mercy, let not all the trouble seem little before thee, that hath come upon us, on our kings, on our princes, and on our priests, and on our prophets, and on our fathers, and on all thy people, since the time of the kings of Assyria unto this day. For verily he took not on *him the nature of* angels : but he took on *him* the seed of Abraham.

WHOLE FAMILY SAVED.

ONE day, at Fulton street, the interest was very marked. Several distinguished answers to prayer were reported. The tone of the meeting was high and buoyant. Among those present was an earnest Christian merchant. His church prayer-meeting occurred that evening. Fatigued with the duties of the day, the merchant wished to go home and rest, but he was strongly impressed to visit a family composed of a man, his wife, and daughter. He yielded to the pressure, and, though late, and doubtful how he might be received, he was warmly welcomed. A short conversation revealed the fact that the wife was anxious, the husband indifferent, the daughter gay and thoughtless.

The conversation was direct and thorough. After prayer by the visitor, the wife was so impressed that she cried aloud for the salvation of her husband. This moved the daughter. She fell on her knees, praying for herself. This brought the man down. He joined the group. It was evident that God was in the place. At the next church meeting, the whole family came together to relate how gracious the Lord had been toward them. As an entire family, they entered the kingdom together, and are now rejoicing in the hope of the glory of God.

CLXV.

NOT CLEAR THE GUILTY.

THE Lord *is* longsuffering, and of great mercy, forgiving iniquity and transgression, and by no means clearing *the guilty*, visiting the iniquity of the fathers upon the children unto the third and fourth *generation.* The soul that sinneth, it shall die. The son shall not bear the iniquity of the father, neither shall the father bear the iniquity of the son ; the righteousness of the righteous shall be upon him, and the wickedness of the wicked shall be upon him. But if the wicked will turn from all his sins that he hath committed, and keep all my statutes, and do that which is lawful and right, he shall surely live, he shall not die. But when the righteous turneth away from his righteousness, and committeth iniquity, *and* doeth according to all the abominations that the wicked *man* doeth, shall he live? All his righteousness that he hath done shall not be mentioned: in his trespass that he hath trespassed, and in his sin that he hath sinned, in them shall he die.

LION OF THE TRIBE OF JUDAH.

JUDAH, as one of the tribes of Israel, bore on her banner the figure of a lion. When the tribes marched, the banner of

Judah led. When they encamped, the signal floated on the breeze, directing all wanderers and stragglers to his own encampment. Our Lord sprang out of Judah. He was the Shiloh, predicted by Jacob on his dying bed, unto whom all Israel should be gathered. He is called in the Revelation, "The Lion of the tribe of Judah," and his banner is to float supreme over the land and over the sea, from sea to sea, and from the rivers to the ends of the earth. Many years ago, the ancient city of Perth and surrounding cities of Scotland were infested by a bold and daring pirate. His signal was a blood-red flag, with a death's-head and cross-bones. He was a buccaneer of terrible cruelty, and when the pirate approached any city and ran up his blood-red flag, he filled the merchantmen and traders with the utmost alarm. William Wallace, the hero of Scotland, resolved to free the waters of this desperado, or perish in the attempt. He filled a merchant-vessel with armed men, hid them between decks, and sailed out of the harbor like a merchantman on a cruise. The pirate saw the vessel, and gave chase. All attempts to escape were futile, and Wallace struck his flag to the pirate. The boarders were met by a stout and unexpected resistance. The pirate was captured and hung at the yard-arm; the ship burned; the crew, in chains, were put below the hatches. The blood-red flag was hoisted to the head truck, and the merchantman sailed for the fair city of Perth. The citizens saw the terrible foe approaching. They were filled with alarm. The bells were rung backwards, as a peculiar sort of ringing was called. In the midst of the terror, the old flag of Scotland was run up above the bloody flag of the pirate. The joy of the city was excessive, and the conqueror was hailed as the saviour of his country. "So the Lion of the tribe of Judah will triumph over all his foes. So will he tread his enemies under his feet. King of kings, and Lord of lords, his banner everywhere shall proclaim, Peace on earth, and salvation to men."

CLXVI.

HARD TO BE UNDERSTOOD.

AND account *that* the longsuffering of our Lord *is* salvation; even as our beloved brother Paul also according to the wisdom given unto him hath written unto you; as also in all *his* epistles, speaking in them of these things; in which are some things hard to be understood, which they that are unlearned and unstable wrest, as *they do* also the other Scriptures, unto their own destruction. Then he said unto them, O fools, and slow of heart to believe all that the prophets have spoken: ought not Christ to have suffered these things, and to enter into his glory? And beginning at Moses and all the prophets, he expounded unto them in all the Scriptures the things concerning himself. And it came to pass, that after three days they found him in the temple, sitting in the midst of the doctors, both hearing them, and asking them questions. And all that heard him were astonished at his understanding and answers. And when they saw him, they were amazed: and his mother said unto him, Son, why hast thou thus dealt with us? behold, thy father and I have sought thee sorrowing. And he said unto them, How is it that ye sought me? wist ye not that I must be about my Father's business?

MOTHER'S BURNT HAND.

A MOTHER was bearing her little girl to bed. The right hand of the parent was burnt to a crisp; it was a black, unsightly deformity. The child had seen it a hundred times, but never before had it attracted attention. "Mamma," said the little one, "how did you burn your hand so?" She laid it softly on the pillow and whispered, "It was for you, my child; it was for your sake;" she then told her the story. "It was when you were littler than you are now. I had put you away cosily to bed. Soon after, I heard your screams; I fled to your bedside and found it on fire. I tore the burning fragments from your body. I saved your life and your beauty. But I lost my hand, and that was the price I paid." And then she talked to her about that blessed One who left his home in the skies for sinful men; who exchanged the worship of angels for the blasphemy of earth; who exchanged the worship of the holy for the derision of men. How, being rich for us, he became poor. Being in the form of God, he took on him the form of a servant. Owning all things, he was a homeless, houseless wanderer. He bore our sicknesses, carried our griefs, and took our burdens. Beaten with stripes, bruised and afflicted, he bears the marks of his wounds, and ever will. "If we ever get to heaven, my child, and see the blessed form of the Lamb slain for sinners, we shall see the wounds on his hands and side, and shall ask, 'What are these wounds?' as you asked me why my hand was burned. The Bible tells us all this, and the answer the Saviour will return: 'I was wounded for many and bruised for the iniquity of the world.'"

CLXVII.

AS A LITTLE CHILD.

AND Jesus called a little child unto him, and set him in the midst of them. And said, Verily I say unto you, Except ye be converted, and become as little children, ye shall not enter into the kingdom of heaven. Whosoever therefore shall humble himself as this little child, the same is greatest in the kingdom of heaven. And whoso shall receive one such little child in my name receiveth me. And they brought young children to him, that he should touch them; and *his* disciples rebuked those that brought *them* But when Jesus saw *it*, he was much displeased, and said unto them, Suffer the little children to come unto me, and forbid them not; for of such is the kingdom of God. Verily I say unto you, Whosoever shall not receive the kingdom of God as a little child, he shall not enter therein. And he took them up in his arms, put *his* hands upon them and blessed them. And the multitudes that went before, and that followed, cried, saying, Hosanna to the Son of David: blessed *is* he that cometh in the name of the Lord; Hosanna in the highest.

CHILD AND FAMILY ALTAR.

A DEEP religious interest prevailed in one of our churches. A large number were brought to a knowledge of the truth. The Sunday-school was generally affected, and many of the very youngest of the scholars gave their hearts to the Lord. Among them was a little girl, seven years old, very young in appearance. The authorities of the church had great doubts whether so young a child could turn to the Lord with full understanding of heart. When those were invited to appear before the church authorities who wished to make a profession of religion, this little girl appeared among them. She told an artless story with great simplicity, but much diffidence. The elders did not know about it. She was young and timid, and the tone of her experience much below that of many of her associates. Her case went over for a time. She neither abandoned her hope nor relaxed her labor, though disappointed. Her first work was at home. Her father, a timid man, had never had strength enough to speak in meeting, though a member of the church for years. She persuaded him to set up a family altar, and have morning and evening devotions. She took her brothers and sisters, one by one, and led them into the kingdom of the Lord. She began with her schoolmates, and persuaded them to make the better choice while they were young. Before the next communion came round, she was the most successful missionary of them all. There was no division in regard to bringing her into the church; and the little lamb was taken in out of the cold, and made secure in the fold of the Good Shepherd.

CLXVIII.

LOVELY AND PLEASANT.

SAUL and Jonathan *were* lovely and pleasant in their lives, and in their death they were not divided: they were swifter than eagles, they were stronger than lions. Ye daughters of Israel, weep over Saul, who clothed you in scarlet, with *other* delights; who put on ornaments of gold upon your apparel. Behold, how good and how pleasant *it is* for brethren to dwell together in unity! *It is* like the precious ointment upon the head, that ran down upon the beard, *even* Aaron's beard: that went down to the skirts of his garments; as the dew of Hermon, *and as the dew* that descended upon the mountains of Zion: for there the Lord commanded the blessing, *even* life for evermore. If *there be* therefore any consolation in Christ, if any comfort of love, if any fellowship of the Spirit, if any bowels and mercies, fulfill ye my joy, that ye be likeminded, having the same love, *being* of one accord, of one mind.

DR. GUTHERIE'S STORY.

I WAS at one time a banker. I was detained one night til midnight at the bank. I lived in a cottage a mile from town. I started for home. The night was dark, and I carried with me the bank keys. Soon I found I was followed. I quickened my pace; so did my pursuer. I crossed the road from side to side; so did my companion. I started on the run; the quickened gait of the man after me showed how vain was the attempt on my part to escape. I had no weapon but a small knife. I drew this, and turned on my pursuer. With a loud voice, my pursuer said, "Then it was you, Master Gutherie? I was sure it was your figure on the wall and on the sky. I did my best to make up with you; and it's no good your traveling alone at this time of night, and all that siller about ye." Instead of a highwayman, who was after my life, I found a poor, honest peddler, himself afraid of robbery, trying to keep up with me for company and protection. I never knew a better illustration of the passage, "fear hath torment." "Whosoever shall confess that Jesus is the Son of God, God dwelleth in him, and he in God. And we have known and believed the love that God hath to us. God is love; and he that dwelleth in love dwelleth in God, and God in him."

CLXIX.

RESTORED THE MONEY.

AND when he had restored the eleven hundred *shekels* of silver to his mother, his mother said, I had wholly dedicated the silver unto the Lord from my hand for my son, to make a graven image and a molten image: now therefore I will restore it unto thee. Yet he restored the money unto his mother; and his mother took two hundred *shekels* of silver, and gave them to the founder, who made thereof a graven image and a molten image: and they were in the house of Micah. Then Judas, which had betrayed him, when he saw that he was condemned, repented himself, and brought again the thirty pieces of silver to the chief priests and elders, saying, I have sinned in that I have betrayed the innocent blood. And they said, What *is that* to us? see thou *to that.* And he cast down the pieces of silver in the temple, and departed, and went and hanged himself. And Zaccheus stood, and said unto the Lord, Behold, Lord, the half of my goods I give to the poor; and if I have taken any thing from any man by false accusation, I restore *him* fourfold.

BOLDNESS AND SAFETY.

A MERCHANT of London was detained at his store till a late hour. The old city is a lonely place at night. Merchandise holds possession of the dwellings where once the citizens kept. A half million of people pour into the city in the morning, and leave at night for their homes in the suburbs. The merchant found he was followed. He attempted to outrun the footpad, but in vain. He attempted a piece of strategy. In a narrow lane, the merchant turned suddenly on his pursuer, and said, "Are you prepared to die?" The man proved to be no footpad, but a porter detained late, and in search of company. He thought the merchant was a highwayman. At once he fell on his knees, and proffered what little money he had, begging only that his life might be saved. "Acquaint now thyself with God and be at peace."

ONE of the cities of Carthage had rebelled against the king, and it was known by proclamation that the monarch had resolved to wipe out the city by fire and sword. On the approach of the king, the noblemen of the city were sent out barefooted, and with ropes about their necks, in token of submission. The king took the proffered keys, and said, "Live, O my children! for I love you still." So speaks the Lord our King, through Christ our Lord.

CLXX.

LENT TO THE LORD.

AND she said, O my lord, *as* thy soul liveth, my lord, I *am* the woman that stood by thee here, praying unto the Lord. For this child I prayed ; and the Lord hath given me my petition which I asked of him: therefore also I have lent him to the Lord; as long as he liveth he shall be lent to the Lord. And he worshiped the Lord there. Thine, O Lord, *is* the greatness, and the power, and the glory, and the victory, and the majesty: for all *that is* in the heaven and in the earth *is thine;* thine *is* the kingdom, O Lord, and thou art exalted as head above all. Both riches and honor *come* of thee, and thou reignest over all; and in thine hand *is* power and might; and in thine hand *it is* to make great, and to give strength unto all. Now therefore, our God, we thank thee, and praise thy glorious name. But who *am* I, and what *is* my people, that we should be able to offer so willingly after this sort? for all things *come* of thee, and of thine own have we given thee.

DEATH ON THE SEA.

A LETTER came to this city a short time since from Paris. It was full of sad intelligence. One of the items was this: "All of Mrs. Spofford's children were lost in the wrecked steamer Ville du Havre. Annie, aged eleven years; Maggie, nine; Bessie, five; and the youngest twenty months. Annie and Maggie united with the church last winter." An affecting history is connected with this family. Mr. Spofford resided in Chicago. His family were burnt out in the great fire. The mother seized the children and barely escaped with their lives. The family camped out for safety, and endured great suffering and privation. When it was decided that Mrs. Spofford and her children should go to Europe, the family were accompanied by Mr. Spofford. The two little girls early made a profession of religion. The family communed with the Madison Square Presbyterian Church the Sunday before leaving. The little children escaped the fire of the West only to be swallowed up in the waves of the Atlantic. When the steamer was struck, the mother and her four little children reached the deck—a babe in her arms, the others holding on to her dress. Little Bessie, five years old, asked a French clergyman to pray with her. As the prayer closed, she said, "Now I am all right." Annie followed the clergyman in prayer. Turning to her mother, she said, "Don't be frightened, God will take care of us. If he wants us to live, we will live. We can trust him. Then you know, mamma, 'the sea is his, and he made it.'" As these words were said, the vessel sank, carrying every body down. The mother was rescued, but all the children were carried down, to sleep among the coral until the sea shall give up its dead.

CLXXI.

LAMENTATION AND WOE.

BUT thou, son of man, hear what I say unto thee; Be not thou rebellious like that rebellious house: open thy mouth, and eat that I give thee. And when I looked, behold, a hand *was* sent unto me; and, lo, a roll of a book *was* therein; and he spread it before me; and it *was* written within and without: and *there was* written therein lamentations, and mourning, and woe. I also will laugh at your calamity, I will mock when your fear cometh; when your fear cometh as desolation, and your destruction cometh as a whirlwind; when distress and anguish cometh upon you. Then shall they call upon me, but I will not answer; they shall seek me early, but they shall not find me.

SAVED FROM THE FLAMES.

I WAS employed in a large manufacturing establishment. I was a godless young man. My employer was a devoted Christian. He asked me one day if I had a Bible. I said, "Yes, sir." "Do you read it?" "Yes, on Sundays." "I would advise you to read it every day." As I went home, I saw my Bible on the table. I took it up and began to read. I did read my Bible daily from that hour. Six years after my employer asked me the question, our manufactory burnt down. The loss was $300,000. Nothing was saved. Among the ruins was found a Bible, all black and charred: but each page as distinct as if it had never seen the fire. Plain was the text, "Seeing then that all these things shall be dissolved, what manner of persons ought we to be in all holy conversation and godliness." That text decided me to be a Christian.

A LITTLE boy reached New-York a few days since, and was entertained at a police-station. He was on his way home to New-England. He had come from Milwaukee. He walked most of the way. He begged from town to town. He had been badly treated, and wanted to get back to Massachusetts. Without money and without friends, he brought all the way the Bible his mother gave him, and would not let it be out of his sight one minute. That boy will succeed.

CLXXII.

BLOOD AT THINE HAND.

WHEN I say unto the wicked, O wicked *man*, thou shalt surely die; if thou dost not speak to warn the wicked from his way, that wicked *man* shall die in his iniquity; but his blood will I require at thine hand. Nevertheless, if thou warn the wicked of his way to turn from it; if he do not turn from his way, he shall die in his iniquity; but thou hast delivered thy soul. But if the watchman see the sword come, and blow not the trumpet, and the people be not warned; if the sword come, and take *any* person from among them, he is taken away in his iniquity; but his blood will I require at the watchman's hand. If when he seeth the sword come upon the land, he blow the trumpet, and warn the people; then whosoever heareth the sound of the trumpet, and taketh not warning; if the sword come, and take him away, his blood shall be upon his own head. And the tree of the field shall yield her fruit, and the earth shall yield her increase, and they shall be safe in their land, and shall know that I *am* the Lord, when I have broken the bands of their yoke, and delivered them out of the hand of those that served themselves of them.

ABIDETH FOREVER.

I TOOK a servant from an emigrant ship. She was green, untutored, could not speak a word of English, and was beside a bigoted Catholic. Her great desire was to learn to read and write. I took great pains with her, but was nearly worn out by her stupidity. I made a school-book of the Gospels, and was well repaid for my time and trouble. As a domestic, she was a prize such as a housekeeper seldom draws. Her kindness and patience to the children were above all praise. Soon she manifested an interest in the matter of religion. She took the children to Sunday-school, heard some of the hymns, and learned them with her work. Occasionally, she went with the children to church. I let her alone, and made no attempt to proselyte. The monthly Sunday-school concert had special attractions for Maria, and she never failed to attend. Her next step was to visit our prayer-meeting. Before I was aware of her purpose, she had visited our pastor, and he pronounced her a child of God. Maria asked both my consent and my advice about joining the church. The elders approved her religious experience, and the day was appointed for her baptism. Then came opposition from her friends. She was invited to visit some of them. She met a room full ; among them was a Catholic priest. The poor girl was nearly overcome by the fuss made over her. Some cried; some denounced; some reviled, and the priest used all his art and authority to turn her from her faith. He talked of the fathers, and what they said. To all, Maria replied, "I know nothing about the fathers or grandfathers ; they are dead ; but here is the word of God. That liveth and abideth forever."

CLXXIII.

UNTEMPERED MORTAR.

BECAUSE, even because they have seduced my people, saying, Peace; and *there was* no peace; and one built up a wall, and, lo, others daubed it with untempered *mortar:* say unto them which daub *it* with untempered *mortar*, that it shall fall: there shall be an overflowing shower; and ye, the great hailstones, shall fall; and a stormy wind shall rend *it*. Lo, when the wall is fallen, shall it not be said unto you, Where *is* the daubing wherewith ye have daubed *it?* So will I break down the wall that ye have daubed with untempered *mortar*, and bring it down to the ground, so that the foundation thereof shall be discovered, and it shall fall, and ye shall be consumed in the midst thereof: and ye shall know that I *am* the Lord. Because with lies ye have made the heart of the righteous sad, whom I have not made sad; and strengthened the hands of the wicked, that he should not return from his wicked way, by promising him life; therefore ye shall see no more vanity, nor divine divinations: for I will deliver my people out of your hand: and ye shall know that I *am* the Lord.

HOW TO TRAIN CHILDREN.

A Christian mother, with four sons and three daughters, had the great affliction of knowing that her husband had turned from the faith of his fathers. He was an ardent convert to the new system that he had embraced. He was a man of marked ability. He wrote much and made public addresses. His house was full of his own works. He brought home much company, and religious doctrine was discussed at the table and in the household. But the mother, pained as she was, made no opposition. She looked to God daily for light and strength. Her family grew up in the fear of the Lord. One by one the sons came into church. Not one accepted the system of the father. One day, some Christian friends called on the mother. One of them said, "How is it that all your children have been brought to the Saviour? My husband is not an opposer of religion as yours is. He attends church with me. He is liberal in his support of good things, but he is careless, perhaps indifferent. Yet he has a control over my boys that I can not loosen nor match. What is your secret? do tell." "Well, I have no secret. Perhaps my husband's views of religion have made me more watchful and more careful. I never have opposed my husband. I have never argued with him. I have never been rude. When he talked, I never sent the children from the room; but I have never allowed them to go to bed till in our little room we had all knelt for a word or two of prayer. I have never been so tired or so much in a hurry that I could not read a few words that the blessed Saviour spake. I put the word of the Lord over against the word of man. I never worried my children, nor teased them with matters of religion. I trusted God, and had confidence in prayer, and you see the fruit."

CLXXIV.

IS THINE HEART AS MY HEART?

AND when he was departed thence, he lighted on Jehonadab the son of Rechab *coming* to meet him: and he saluted him, and said to him, Is thine heart right, as my heart *is* with thy heart? And Jehonadab answered, It is. If it be, give *me* thine hand. And he gave *him* his hand; and he took him up to him into the chariot. Finally, brethren, whatsoever things are true, whatsoever things *are* honest, whatsoever things *are* just, whatsoever things *are* pure, whatsoever things *are* lovely, whatsoever things *are* of good report; if *there be* any virtue, and if *there be* any praise, think on these things. Those things, which ye have both learned, and received, and heard, and seen in me, do: and the God of peace shall be with you. That if thou shalt confess with thy mouth the Lord Jesus, and shalt believe in thine heart that God hath raised him from the dead, thou shalt be saved. For with the heart man believeth unto righteousness; and with the mouth confession is made unto salvation. For the Scripture saith, Whosoever believeth on him shall not be ashamed.

SABBATH A DELIGHT.

I WAS trained in a strict school on the Sabbath. Our preparation began on Saturday evening. Our shoes were brushed; our clothes put in order; our dinner cooked overnight; our play-toys hidden, and all entertaining books—few indeed at best—were locked up. Sunday dawned—a day of gloom and restlessness. I would have felt better if I could have gone to the spring for a pail of water; have gone out to fling down a handful of hay for the horse, or run down to poor sick widow Jones, and handed her a few goodies. But no! this was not allowed. "Keep still." "What are you snuffling for?" "Don't scuff with your shoes." "Sit up." "Don't keep giggling." "Now, John, if you don't keep quiet, you shall have to go to bed without your supper." This was a threat that alarmed. Supper, after church, was the principal meal of the day, and as for that, of the week. I found myself growing up with an increasing hatred for God's holy day. It was a burden; there was tyranny about it to me; all seemed glad on the Sabbath but man. The sun shone, oh! how sweetly! The birds sang, oh! how gayly! The brooks ran, and the wind waved the grain. Why then should the day of God be one of gloom and sadness? I resolved that when I was a man, there should be no Sabbaths for me. But God, in great mercy, ordered it otherwise: I became a Christian. I purposed in my heart that the Lord's day should be kept in my house, and should be one of the most blessed of the week. When my children were small, I had a Sunday closet; in it were books, pictures, and small Sunday toys to mark the day. To these were added a small package of candy, with the name of each child on it. Saturday night, the week-days' toys were put away; after dinner on Sunday came the treat. Then the key was given up, and the little ones took the Sunday books and the candy, and we heard nothing of them till supper-time. The happiest day of the week was the Lord's day.

CLXXV.

ABUNDANCE OF MY COMPLAINT.

COUNT not thine handmaid for a daughter of Belial: for out of the abundance of my complaint and grief have I spoken hitherto. Then Eli answered and said, Go in peace: and the God of Israel grant *thee* thy petition that thou hast asked of him. And she said, Let thine handmaid find grace in thy sight. So the woman went her way, and did eat, and her countenance was no more *sad.* I cried unto the Lord with my voice; with my voice unto the Lord did I make my supplication. I poured out my complaint before him; I showed before him my trouble. When my spirit was overwhelmed within me, then thou knewest my path. In the way wherein I walked have they privily laid a snare for me. I *am* the man *that* hath seen affliction by the rod of his wrath. He hath led me, and brought *me into* darkness, but not *into* light. Surely against me is he turned; he turneth his hand *against me* all the day.

THE IRON CAGE.

Among the returned missionaries is a lady of great talent and piety. She has been remarkably successful in awaking a profound interest among the ladies in our churches, in the cause of Foreign Missions. How great soever may have been her success in the foreign field, it is difficult to see how she could do more for the cause of the Divine Master anywhere than she is now doing at home. The incidents related by this devoted woman stir the life-blood. Among these may be named that of "The Man in the Iron Cage." He was a Bramin, devoted and zealous. He proposed to build a tank or cistern, to supply the wants of pilgrims. He made a huge cage to be worn on the head. It was large and heavy; it was not unlike a parrot's cage. The bars were of iron, and the whole weighed a dozen pounds. This unwieldy and heavy appendage was welded on the neck and head. The purpose of the cage was to inflict suffering on the wearer. After the cage was fitted to the neck, the Bramin began his work on the tank. He took a vow that he would wear it till the tank was completed. He worked on day and night. The bars chafed the neck and wore off the skin. The sight was terrible, and the pain excruciating. But the votary worked away, though suffering untold agony. One day, he accepted a small book from the lady missionary. It was the Gospel of John. The book was attended by the Holy Spirit. His eyes were open and his soul saved. But he worked on. He did not cease nor allow the cage to be removed till the elegant cistern was completed. It had been the intention of the Bramins to celebrate the completion of the work by great ceremonies. The work was done at night; the iron cage was filed away; but the converted Bramin had to flee and hide from the indignation of his old friends. The cage is now in America.

CLXXVI.

FEAR HATH TORMENT.

THERE is no fear in love; but perfect love casteth out fear: because fear hath torment. He that feareth is not made perfect in love. We love him, because he first loved us. If a man say, I love God, and hateth his brother, he is a liar: for he that loveth not his brother whom he hath seen, how can he love God whom he hath not seen? And this commandment have we from him, That he who loveth God love his brother also. Finally, my brethren, be strong in the Lord, and in the power of his might. Put on the whole armor of God, that ye may be able to stand against the wiles of the devil. For we wrestle not against flesh and blood, but against principalities, against powers, against the rulers of the darkness of this world, against spiritual wickedness in high *places*. Praying always with all prayer and supplication in the Spirit, and watching thereunto with all perseverance and supplication for all saints.

A BOY'S FAITH.

A LITTLE boy, the son of a minister, had a sore hand. It was very bad; it grew no better under treatment, but rather worse. The doctor said he could do no more; the only thing that could save the lad's life was the amputation of the hand. The day was fixed for the operation. The little fellow was in great distress; not so much at the idea of the terrible pain he would suffer, but at the fearful loss of his hand. He had been trained in the fear of God. He believed in God, and in the power of prayer. He went out alone into the garden. In a retired spot, he fell down on his knees and asked the blessed Saviour to come to his relief and save his poor hand. The next day the physician called. He was astonished as he looked at the hand. It was much better, and amputation was not needful. "Who was your physician?" said the doctor. "I went to the Saviour," was the simple reply, "and asked him to save my hand and heal my wounds, and he came to my relief." Long years after, this little lad became a preacher of the Gospel. On more than one occasion, when preaching on prayer, he would hold up his right hand and say, "Behold the proof that Jesus can answer prayer! He is the same yesterday, to-day, and forever. All glory to the Lamb!"

How strong is often the faith of a child! "Are you not afraid," said a man, "that you will tire out in the long road you have got to travel? You are quite young to be a Christian." "Oh, no! The Bible says Jesus will carry the lambs in his bosom."

CLXXVII.

AGUR'S PRAYER.

TWO *things* have I required of thee; deny me *them* not before I die: remove far from me vanity and lies; give me neither poverty nor riches; feed me with food convenient for me: lest I be full, and deny *thee*, and say, Who *is* the Lord? or lest I be poor, and steal, and take the name of my God *in vain.* Not that I speak in respect of want; for I have learned, in whatsoever state I am, *therewith* to be content. I know both how to be abased, and I know how to abound: everywhere and in all things I am instructed both to be full and to be hungry, both to abound and to suffer need. I can do all things through Christ which strengtheneth me. By him therefore let us offer the sacrifice of praise to God continually, that is, the fruit of *our* lips, giving thanks to his name. But to do good and to communicate forget not: for with such sacrifices God is well pleased.

WORD IN DUE SEASON.

Suddenly a storm came on. A young man, dressed in the style of the day, without an umbrella, made a dart for the church. The pastor was preaching; but he saw the young man enter, and took in the situation at a glance. The visitor paid close attention to the preaching, and kept his seat till the services closed. As the rain came pattering down, the young man delayed awhile. The pastor came down to the pew where he sat, and said, "I am glad to see you in the house of the Lord, even under these circumstances. I hope you will find as good a shelter at the last great day. Remember Him who is a 'covert from the storm,' and do not neglect that shelter 'into which the righteous run and are safe.'" The sermon produced no impression, but the kind personal remarks went home to the heart. Not long after the interview, the young man gave his heart to the Saviour. So the word of God was fulfilled: "A man shall be a hiding-place from the wind, a covert from the tempest, as rivers of water in a dry place, and the shadow of a great rock in a weary land."

CLXXVIII.

NEHEMIAH'S PRAYER.

AND said, I beseech thee, O Lord God of heaven, the great and terrible God, that keepeth covenant and mercy for them that love him and observe his commandments: let thine ear now be attentive, and thine eyes open, that thou mayest hear the prayer of thy servant, which I pray before thee now, day and night, for the children of Israel thy servants, and confess the sins of the children of Israel, which we have sinned against thee: both I and my father's house have sinned. O Lord, I beseech thee, let now thine ear be attentive to the prayer of thy servant, and to the prayer of thy servants, who desire to fear thy name: and prosper, I pray thee, thy servant this day, and grant him mercy in the sight of this man. For I was the king's cupbearer.

PIETY AT THE WASH-TUB.

On one of the side streets of the city lives a washerwoman. Week after week she toils at her tub—the hardest work that the human back can bend to. Sixteen hours a day is her allotted toil. A small room is her home. An old and infirm man, who calls her wife, leans on her for support. At night, bending beneath a heavy load, she bears to her customers the foaming linen, for she is one of the most famous washers in New-York. Our friend is an earnest member of a Christian church. She is a liberal contributor. Out of her penury, she makes donations that would command the approval of the Saviour, were he on earth. One day, the subject of money came up. The church was poor. Over it hung a debt of five hundred dollars—a huge sum for a small poor people. What could be done? The debt must be lifted, or the church be dishonored. Modestly our washerwoman arose and said, "Brethren, I owe all to Jesus. He saved me. He gave for me his own precious blood. He has given me a pleasant home; plenty of work, and health and grace to do it. I have laid up a little money for a rainy day. It all belongs to my blessed Master. I will give one hundred dollars for the cause, and double my subscription for the balance." All hearts were touched; eyes moistened; the company dropped down on the knee to praise the name of the Lord. Each member doubled the subscription. The debt was lifted then and there, but the happiest person that laid her head on a pillow that night was the poor washerwoman of New-York. "She had done what she could."

CLXXIX.

SOLOMON'S PRAYER.

AND Solomon stood before the altar of the Lord in the presence of all the congregation of Israel, and spread forth his hands toward heaven: and he said, Lord God of Israel, *there is* no God like thee, in heaven above, or on earth beneath, who keepest covenant and mercy with thy servants that walk before thee with all their heart: but will God indeed dwell on the earth? behold, the heaven and heaven of heavens can not contain thee; how much less this house that I have builded? Yet have thou respect unto the prayer of thy servant, and to his supplication, O Lord my God, to hearken unto the cry and to the prayer, which thy servant prayeth before thee to-day: and hearken thou to the supplication of thy servant, and of thy people Israel, when they shall pray toward this place: and hear thou in heaven thy dwelling-place: and when thou hearest, forgive.

BUSINESS VALUE OF A SMILE.

A FRIEND of mine runs a large establishment. His employees are mostly women. Many of these are from the lowly ranks of life. Among the girls was one on whose labor an aged mother depended. She came to work promptly on the hour. Her home was far away. It demanded great resolution to get up, get her own and her mother's meal, put things to rights, and reach the mill in season. But cold or warm, in weather wet or dry, Maria was at her post. She never left home without reading a few verses in the Word of God, and a word of prayer.

Maud had a sweet smile on her face, and a kind word for every one. Her good-nature was inexhaustible. She had a helping hand for all. If any one was in trouble, or needed a little aid, or if work perplexed her associates, Maud was looked to for help, and no one came to her in vain.

But work was dull. Times were hard, and the department in which Maria was employed was overloaded. The agent saw he must send some one away. The lot fell on Maria, and one week's notice was given. She made no complaint. She did not even tell her mother, lest it should make her unhappy. She carried her trouble to her Saviour, and felt that he would provide. The day before Maria was to leave, the agent saw how busy she was. Her time was occupied with gathering up her little traps and conveniences, and in leave-taking. Her smile was never brighter, nor her voice more cheery. As the sun went down, the agent called her into the office. He said, "I can't spare you, after all; we want your pleasant smile." And so she staid. "Praise the name of the Lord!" said the happy girl.

CLXXX.

EZRA'S PRAYER.

AND at the evening sacrifice I arose up from my heaviness; and having rent my garment and my mantle, I fell upon my knees, and spread out my hands unto the Lord my God, and said, O my God, I am ashamed, and blush to lift up my face to thee, my God: for our iniquities are increased over *our* head, and our trespass is grown up unto the heavens. Since the days of our fathers *have* we *been* in a great trespass unto this day; and for our iniquities have we, our kings, *and* our priests, been delivered into the hand of the kings of the lands, to the sword, to captivity, and to a spoil, and to confusion of face, as *it is* this day. O Lord God of Israel, thou *art* righteous; for we remain yet escaped, as *it is* this day: behold, we *are* before thee in our trespasses; for we can not stand before thee because of this.

DO QUICKLY.

MEN often push into the Fulton-street meeting as if pursued by some avenger of blood. Men in despair—men on the edge of delirium tremens—men who have been weeks in forming a resolution, come in with a rush. As men and women flocked to the pool of Siloam, fearing that some one would step down before them, so people often crowd the little room of the missionary for aid. Men not sober ask for the pledge. "Now, now! quick, quick!" they cry. "I am afraid it is too late. Give me the pledge, now and here." No other place seems potent under the roof. Consecrated by sixteen years of prayer, they feel that divine help will be granted.

So came a poor, forlorn drinking man one day. He dare not enter; the voice of song was welling up. He leaned on the door-post. He heard requests read for men as miserable as himself. His sins arose as a cloud. He had been a dissolute outcast, profane and drunken, a brawler, a gambler, a hater of religion, and a despiser of God. "Give me the pledge," he said. "Come up, my man," said a kind voice. "Come now, let us kneel down." "No, no. Give me the pledge now." "No; you can't stand alone. The pledge will do you no good unless God aids you." The pledge was bathed in prayer; the man signed it. A good lodging was given him that night. In a few days, he was quite as earnest to be a Christian. The good Master called him, as he called Bartimeus. "*Now I am safe, if Jesus keeps me.*"

Seventeenth Anniversary, Fulton Street Daily Prayer-Meeting, September 23d, 1874.

CLXXXI.

MOSES' PRAYER.

AND Moses said unto the Lord, See, thou sayest unto me, Bring up this people: and thou hast not let me know whom thou wilt send with me. Yet thou hast said, I know thee by name, and thou hast also found grace in my sight. Now therefore, I pray thee, if I have found grace in thy sight, show me now thy way, that I may know thee, that I may find grace in thy sight: and consider that this nation *is* thy people. Who *is* like unto thee, O Lord, among the gods? who *is* like thee, glorious in holiness, fearful *in* praises, doing wonders? Thou stretchedst out thy right hand, the earth swallowed them. Thou in thy mercy hast led forth the people *which* thou hast redeemed: thou hast guided *them* in thy strength unto thy holy habitation. And he said unto him, If thy presence go not *with me*, carry us not up hence. For wherein shall it be known here that I and thy people have found grace in thy sight? *is it* not in that thou goest with us? So shall we be separated, I and thy people, from all the people that *are* upon the face of the earth.

MINISTRY OF A LITTLE GIRL.

KATIE was the youngest member of our household. She took her meals at a little table by herself. She was a devout child, and, like Obadiah, seemed to have " feared the Lord from her youth." She always clasped her hands and said a little grace of her own when her food was ready. One day, an aged relative came to make a visit. As her father was absent, Katie came to the family table. The visitor was not a professing Christian, and there was no one to "ask a blessing." The mother began to pour out the tea, to the dismay of the little girl. "Stop, mother, stop," said Katie. "Somebody must pray." No one responded. The child folded her hands, closed her eyes, and uttered her little thanksgiving to the Giver of all good. All heads were bowed, eyes unused to weep were moistened, and the fruit of that artless trust was seen in the conversion of the visitor, and the turning of more than one of that family to God. "A little child shall lead them."

More than once, in the dark, narrow lanes of London, where poverty has its home, I have seen beggar-girls hold up a piece of bread, lift their eyes heavenward, and say, " The Lord make us thankful."

CLXXXII.

HEZEKIAH'S PRAYER.

AND Hezekiah prayed before the Lord, and said, O Lord God of Israel, who dwellest *between* the cherubim, thou art the God, *even* thou alone, of all the kingdoms of the earth: thou hast made heaven and earth. Lord, bow down thine ear, and hear: open, Lord, thine eyes, and see: and hear the words of Sennacherib, which hath sent him to reproach the living God. Of a truth, Lord, the kings of Assyria have destroyed the nations and their lands, and have cast their gods into the fire: for they *were* no gods, but the work of men's hands, wood and stone: therefore they have destroyed them. Now therefore, O Lord our God, I beseech thee, save thou us out of his hand, that all the kingdoms of the earth may know that thou *art* the Lord God, *even* thou only. The living, the living, he shall praise thee, as I *do* this day: the father to the children shall make known thy truth. The Lord *was ready* to save me: therefore we will sing my songs to the stringed instruments all the days of our life in the house of the Lord.

PRAYER CAN'T WAIT.

FAMILY prayers are often hurried. Haste, irreverence, and tediousness often mark those services that should be tender, genial, and pleasant. Often "family prayers" give way to business, to company, or to personal convenience. Georgie seemed never content to go to bed before devotions were held; so we had our evening service soon after tea. No bat or ball, no truck or sled, no book, toy, or playmate kept our little son from prayers. No one need call him; no admonitions were needed to keep him quiet. The first in his place, he kept his eye on the leader. He knelt reverently, and as the prayer closed, he added "Amen." One night, Georgie was tired. He came to me, and asked to have family prayer that he might go to bed. I was at my desk, writing a letter. I was in some haste to finish it. I said, "Wait a little while, I am busy now. Soon as my letter is done, we will have prayers." "Don't you think, mamma, that prayer is more precious than writing letters, and can't that wait?" I was smitten at once. I arose, took my waiting four-year-old in my arms, planted a kiss on his precious mouth, and led him at once to God in prayer. "Out of the mouth of babes and sucklings thou hast ordained praise."

CLXXXIII.

BOOK OF THE LAW OF THE LORD.

SO they read in the book in the law of God distinctly, and gave the sense, and caused *them* to understand the reading. And there was delivered unto him the book of the prophet Esaias. And when he had opened the book, he found the place where it was written, The Spirit of the Lord *is* upon me, because he hath anointed me to preach the gospel to the poor; he hath sent me to heal the brokenhearted, to preach deliverance to the captives, and recovering of sight to the blind, to set at liberty them that are bruised, to preach the acceptable year of the Lord. And he began to say unto them, This day is this Scripture fulfilled in your ears. And all bear him witness, and wondered at the gracious words which proceeded out of his mouth. And they said, Is not this Joseph's son?

PRAYER IN EXTREMITY.

THE delegates from the Scotch Church to the Presbyterian attended one of the sessions of the Fulton-street meeting. One of the number related this incident, known by him to be true: A little girl was placed in an attic to pass the night. It was a room seldom occupied; but it became necessary to put her in this chamber, to make room for friends who had come unexpectedly to the house. She was awakened in the night by troops of rats running over the bed. The animals were large and bold; they not only chased each other round the room and across the bed, but even across the face of the little girl. Some of the rats took their station on her bosom and looked her fiercely in the face. The little child was terribly frightened and screamed in terror. Her cries did not seem to disturb her visitors; they continued their gambols all the same. She was so far away that the family could not hear her outcries. The child had been trained in the fear of the Lord. She wondered if the Lord would hear her in her extremity, and send her deliverance. She thought over the lessons she had learned in Sunday-school. She remembered that her Heavenly Father heard Joseph in prison, and delivered Daniel from the den of lions. Timid and fearful, she resolved to call upon the Lord. Her prayer was first that the Lord would send her deliverance. If it did not please him to do that, she prayed that he would keep her from harm. While she prayed, a scratching was heard at the door. The little child jumped out of bed, and hurriedly opened the door, when a large cat entered. She was a stranger to the house, but immediately fell upon her enemies. She cleared the room in a trice. The child returned to her bed, and soon fell asleep. She was not disturbed again through the night. In the morning, her deliverer was nowhere to be found. Where she came from or where she went to, no one knows. The child still affirms, and her family believe, as she is a child of undoubted truth and intelligence, that He who shut the mouths of lions when his servant was in peril, had pity on the sufferings of a little girl, heard her prayer, and sent deliverance.

CLXXXIV.

JUDGMENT OF SECRET THINGS.

FOR God shall bring every work into judgment, with every secret thing, whether *it be* good, or whether *it be* evil. But there is a God in heaven that revealeth secrets, and maketh known to the king Nebuchadnezzar what shall be in the latter days. Whither shall I go from thy Spirit? or whither shall I flee from thy presence? If I ascend up into heaven, thou *art* there: if I make my bed in hell, behold, thou *art there.* In the day when God shall judge the secrets of men by Jesus Christ according to my gospel. Therefore judge nothing before the time, until the Lord come, who both will bring to light the hidden things of darkness, and will make manifest the counsels of the hearts: and then shall every man have praise of God.

NICODEMUS'S VISIT TO CHRIST.

It would be interesting to know the exact locality of the interview Nicodemus had with the Saviour. We know why he came by night. He held an eminent position among his people, and the rulers had declared, if any man confessed Christ, he should be turned out of the synagogue. Interested in the teachings of the Saviour, satisfied that he was a teacher sent from God, he was yet not ready to make an open confession of his faith in Christ, and take the consequences.

A man high in authority as a member of the Jewish council, an accredited minister and teacher of the Holy Scriptures, a high official in the synagogue, a devout observer of all the forms and services of his religion, with a high moral character, he was astonished when the Saviour announced to him that he must be born again, or never see the kingdom of our Lord.

We hear little of this eminent man after the interview with the Saviour closed; but what we do hear shows that that interview produced ripe, rich fruits. He was a member of the Great Council who had resolved on the death of the Saviour before it assembled. Yet he was not consenting to the death. He openly defended the Saviour, asking, "Doth our law judge any man before it hear him, and know what he doeth?" In the darkest hour of our Saviour's history, when apostles shrank and the cause seemed hopeless, when the stain of a malefactor rested on the Saviour and his friends were few, Nicodemus joined Joseph of Arimathæa, an honorable counsélor, who also waited for the kingdom of God, and went in boldly unto Pilate and craved the body of Jesus. He made an open profession of his faith in Christ, when he brought a mixture of myrrh and aloes, about one hundred pounds weight, and took the body of Jesus, wound it in linen clothes, with the spices, as the manner of the Jews is to bury. Marveling at the first, at the saying, "Ye must be born again," he found in Christ a personal Saviour, and put to his lips that water of life of which, if a man drink, he shall never thirst.

CLXXXV.

EVIL SPEAKING.

SPEAK not evil one of another, brethren. He that speaketh evil of *his* brother, and judgeth his brother, speaketh evil of the law, and judgeth the law: but if thou judge the law, thou art not a doer of the law, but a judge. But the tongue can no man tame; *it is* an unruly evil, full of deadly poison. Therewith bless we God, even the Father; and therewith curse we men, which are made after the similitude of God. Out of the same mouth proceedeth blessing and cursing. My brethren, these things ought not so to be. *The words* of his mouth were smoother than butter, but war *was* in his heart: his words were softer than oil, yet *were* they drawn swords. And the peace of God, which passeth all understanding, shall keep your hearts and minds through Christ Jesus. Finally, brethren, whatsoever things are true, whatsoever things *are* honest, whatsoever things *are* just, whatsoever things *are* pure, whatsoever things *are* lovely, whatsoever things *are* of good report; if *there be* any virtue, and if *there be* any praise, think on these things.

RICHES TAKE WINGS.

I CAME through the Sound one night. The elegant saloons were crowded. Among the company was a well-known business man. He was celebrated for two things—for his great success in business, and his sharpness in trade. Some called him hard-hearted. He prided himself on keeping the bond, and exacted the covenant from all his creditors. To fail in business was a crime, a crime that ought to be punished. When men, overwhelmed by sudden misfortune, came into his presence to secure a settlement, but little favor was expected. A hundred cents on the dollar was the demand. Though strictly upright, he was unmoved by the misfortunes of others. He believed that no one need fail unless it was through some neglect or criminality of himself. "I have been very successful in business," he said; "I have but two children; I can give both of these an ample fortune; I can settle a fortune on my wife, and then have more left than I can spend through the rest of my days."

Within twelve months, I met the same merchant again on the Sound. I could scarcely recognize him. His tall form was bent. His full, round, and genial bearing had given way to a lean and wasted look. His face was haggard, and even his dress seemed dilapidated. "I have not a dollar in the world," he said. "I put a large sum of money into a railroad, and had to double the sum to save it. Twice I could have got out of the road by paying $100,000, and then would have had a fortune left; but I became infatuated; my judgment seemed to have forsaken me; I hung on until I was overwhelmed with ruin. Then came the sorrow of my life; nobody would help me. Men whose fortunes I had made turned from me. Men who imagined I had been hard with them hastened to make reprisals."

CLXXXVI.

COMFORT OF HOPE.

FOR we are saved by hope: but hope that is seen is not hope: for what a man seeth, why doth he yet hope for? But if we hope for that we see not, *then* do we with patience wait for *it*. Which *hope* we have as an anchor of the soul, both sure and steadfast, and which entereth into that within the vail; whither the forerunner is for us entered, *even* Jesus, made a high priest forever after the order of Melchisedec. Looking for that blessed hope, and the glorious appearing of the great God and our Saviour Jesus Christ; who gave himself for us, that he might redeem us from all iniquity, and purify unto himself a peculiar people, zealous of good works. But this I confess unto thee, that after the way which they call heresy, so worship I the God of my fathers, believing all things which are written in the law and in the prophets: and have hope toward God, which they themselves also allow, that there shall be a resurrection of the dead, both of the just and unjust.

PASTOR'S STORY.

MY only daughter thought she was a Christian when she was six years old. Like Obadiah, she seemed to have feared the Lord from her youth. From her earliest years, she was very reverent; would sit closely at my side at the morning and evening service, and listen with devout attention to religious conversation. At eight years of age, she desired to unite with the church. There was no law in the church on the matter, but a sort of feeling that a child ought to reach the age of twelve years before being admitted to the Communion. I think this impression prevailed from the fact that our Saviour went to the temple when he was twelve years old. Official brethren thought my child too young to make a profession of religion, and that a delay would do her no harm. It was a sad disappointment to the poor child when this decision was announced. "Then I must wait four long years," she said, "before I can testify my love for the Saviour." On Communion Sunday, she spent the day in weeping. The announcement from the pulpit, at any time, that persons who desired to make a profession of religion would meet the committee brought tears into the eyes of my dear child. The period when she would be twelve years of age seemed to be the goal toward which all her life and conversation tended. She counted the years, the months, and the weeks that intervened. And when the day came, and my child stood before the great congregation to witness a good confession, her face was radiant with joy. To the last, she contended that she gave her heart to the Lord when she was six years of age. She gave herself to the work of foreign missions. She died among the valleys of Syria, and her sun went down while it was yet day. It has been a life-long regret with me that I kept her so long from the communion-table. My views on the consecration of children have entirely changed. I would shelter those in the fold who profess to love Christ, and throw around them the loving arms of the Church.

CLXXXVII.

LITTLE FOXES.

TAKE us the foxes, the little foxes, that spoil the vines: for our vines *have* tender grapes. And Jesus said unto him, Foxes have holes, and birds of the air *have* nests; but the Son of man hath not where to lay *his* head. Dead flies cause the ointment of the apothecary to send forth a stinking savor: *so doth* a little folly him that is in reputation for wisdom *and* honor. Behold, we put bits in the horses' mouths, that they may obey us; and we turn about their whole body. Behold also the ships, which though *they* be so great, and *are* driven of fierce winds, yet are they turned about with a very small helm, whithersoever the governor listeth. Even so the tongue is a little member, and boasteth great things. Behold, how great a matter a little fire kindleth! But with me it is a very small thing that I should be judged of you, or of man's judgment: yea, I judge not mine own self. Jesus said unto him, Let the dead bury their dead: but go thou and preach the kingdom of God.

MISSION CHILDREN AND THE LORD'S PRAYER.

We do not give children credit for as much understanding and shrewdness as they possess. Those who have charge of mission work are often astonished at the keenness manifested by the class known as street Arabs. One speaker was greatly astonished when he asked a company of about four hundred children if they knew any thing about the theatre, to have them shout out "Yes, siree!" He was overwhelmed when he asked, "How many of you were ever at the theatre?" to have two hundred hands go up in response. "You said that afore," said a little, ragged newsboy to a speaker, who began to repeat himself. In one of our mission-schools, the Lord's Prayer was the lesson for the day. "Why do we say," said the superintendent, "Our Father in heaven?" "Because it's his headquarters, I guess," said a little fellow whose father had been a soldier. "Why do we pray, 'Give us this day our daily bread'?" "Because we want our bread hot," said a German lad whose father was a baker. "What does this mean, "Forgive us our trespasses, as we forgive those who trespass against us"? "It means, if a feller strikes yer on the one cheek, you must turn the other." "Could you do it?" "Yes, if the boy was bigger nor me." "What does Amen mean?" One boy shouted, "It means to dry up—the minister stops when he says that." If all our schools could give an account of the lessons they learn, they would be well taught.

CLXXXVIII.

CROSS OXEN.

IF an ox gore a man or a woman, that they die: then the ox shall be surely stoned, and his flesh shall not be eaten; but the owner of the ox *shall be* quit. But if the ox were wont to push with his horn in time past, and it hath been testified to his owner, and he hath not kept him in, but that he hath killed a man or a woman; the ox shall be stoned, and his owner also shall be put to death. Withhold not good from them to whom it is due, when it is in the power of thine hand to do *it*. Say not unto thy neighbor, Go, and come again, and to-morrow I will give; when thou hast it by thee. Withdraw thy foot from thy neighbor's house; lest he be weary of thee, and *so* hate thee. *Let* love be without dissimulation. Abhor that which is evil; cleave to that which is good. *Be* kindly affectioned one to another with brotherly love; in honor preferring one another.

SAW IT IN HIS FACE.

WE often read the character of men in their faces. If they are kind and intelligent, or coarse and brutal, it is easily detected. Even the animal creation can read whether good-nature or anger possesses a person. A neighbor was given to the intoxicating cup. He was a lumberman—when he worked

—and spent a portion of each year camping out in the woods. He was a stout, strong, able-bodied man, and earned a good living when he was sober. His habits of drinking grew upon him. His home was the abode of poverty and wretchedness. The wife was broken-hearted, discouraged, and her days and nights were filled with suffering. It was a relief to have the man depart for the camp. He was almost worthless as a lumberman. He spent a large part of his time and most of his wages in drinking. As his habits of intemperance increased, his ability to work decreased. At the end of the season, he came home ragged, dirty, brutal. His coming filled the household with terror. His wife trembled as she heard his foot on the step-stone. His children fled from his presence, and hid till they knew whether he was drunk or sober. Even his dog hid himself in the wretched shed which was called a barn. One winter, while the man was lumbering, a clergyman, in search of health, camped out in the woods near the encampment of the lumbermen. He was fond of athletic sports. He was a boatman, a walker of great endurance, and his rowing was worthy of a regatta. He kindled his own fires, and cooked his own food. He made the acquaintance of the hardy lumbermen, and talked to them round their camp-fires at night on every subject but religion. He secured the confidence of the men, and invited them over to his quarters for divine service on Sunday. Most of them came. A sensible discourse was preached, after which a substantial meal was prepared for the visitors. After a while, the temperance pledge was introduced. The first to sign it was the man we have referred to. For two months, he was true to his pledge. The camp broke up, and he started for home. The first to meet him was his dog, who saw the pledge in his face, and knew that his master would beat him no more. His wife was astonished. His children came from their hiding-places, and joy reigned in that family.

CLXXXIX.

ANCHORS OUT OF THE STERN.

THEN fearing lest we should have fallen upon rocks, they cast four anchors out of the stern, and wished for the day. And as the shipmen were about to flee out of the ship, when they had let down the boat into the sea, under color as though they would have cast anchors out of the foreship, Paul said to the centurion and to the soldiers, Except these abide in the ship, ye can not be saved. Then the soldiers cut off the ropes of the boat, and let her fall off. His mother saith unto the servants, Whatsoever he saith unto you, do *it*. And there were set there six waterpots of stone, after the manner of the purifying of the Jews, containing two or three firkins apiece. Jesus saith unto them, Fill the waterpots with water. And they filled them up to the brim. The Lord is not slack concerning his promise, as some men count slackness ; but is longsuffering to us-ward, not willing that any should perish, but that all should come to repentance.

A SCOTCHMAN OUTWITTED.

A WELL-KNOWN Scotch gentleman related this incident in the meeting. It was published in a Scottish religious journal, the editor vouching for the truth of the narrative. A gentleman in Glasgow owned a very intelligent Newfoundland dog. He accompanied his master wherever he went, and was his inseparable companion in his visits and to church. One evening, the gentleman went out to visit a neighbor. The dog attended him. It was quite late when the gentleman started for home, and, to his surprise, his dog could not be found. After the family had retired to bed, there was a great noise in the kitchen. It was supposed that burglars were robbing the house. Soon there was a crash and a smash like the breaking in of a window, and then all was still. The morning revealed the mystery. The dog had fallen asleep under the table. He was sensible that his master had gone home, and the noise heard was the attempt of the dog to make his escape. As there was no other way to get out, the sagacious animal went through the window, taking the glass and frame with him. It was a long time before his master visited that house again. When he did, his dog accompanied him, and the animal found his way through the open door of the kitchen to his old hiding-place under the table. It was late when the master started for home. But neither his hat nor cane could be found. After a long search, the dog was discovered fast asleep under the table; one paw was in his master's hat, the other rested on his master's cane. How he obtained possession of these articles, no one could tell. He remembered his last visit to the place, and how scurvily he was treated. The sagacious creature resolved not to be left behind the next time. He knew that his master could not go home without his hat and cane, and that he would be quite likely to be awakened up when his owner got ready to walk. His plans were acutely laid, and if he had possessed reason, he could not have done better.

CXC.

WENT TO THEIR OWN COMPANY.

AND being let go, they went to their own company, and reported all that the chief priests and elders had said unto them. And when they heard that, they lifted up their voice to God with one accord, and said, Lord, thou *art* God, which hast made heaven, and earth, and the sea, and all that in them is. And as they went through the cities, they delivered them the decrees for to keep, that were ordained of the apostles and elders which were at Jerusalem. And so were the churches established in the faith, and increased in number daily. And a vision appeared to Paul in the night; there stood a man of Macedonia, and prayed him, saying, Come over into Macedonia, and help us. And after he had seen the vision, immediately we endeavored to go into Macedonia, assuredly gathering that the Lord had called us for to preach the gospel unto them. Therefore loosing from Troas, we came with a straight course to Samothracia, and the next *day* to Neapolis; and from thence to Philippi, which is the chief city of that part of Macedonia, *and* a colony: and we were in that city abiding certain days. And on the Sabbath we went out of the city by a river side, where prayer was wont to be made; and we sat down, and spake unto the women which resorted *thither*.

THE SAVIOUR AT WORSHIP.

We know little of the childhood of our Lord. His home life is nearly a blank, from the moment Simeon took the child Jesus in his arms, in the temple, to the hour of his baptism. A glimpse here and there of the boy-life of the Son of God is all we have. We know that he grew good as he grew tall. He grew wise as he grew old; and all the way up, such was his life, that men loved and God approved. As the Bible puts it, "He grew in wisdom and in stature, and in favor with God and man." He was learned, as a child, in the Holy Scriptures. At twelve years of age, he discussed divine things with the doctors and the lawyers. He astonished the wise with his understanding and answers. He was a regular attendant on divine worship. It was his custom to go into the synagogue on the Sabbath-day. He joined the multitude who kept the great festivals of his nation.

If there was one family in Judea that did not need the aid of Sabbath worship, it was the family in Nazareth in which the child Jesus was brought up. Joseph is pronounced, by the inspiration of God, a just man. He was just to his own household, and was not willing to put his espoused wife to an open shame. Mary was selected for her high mission, for her spotless purity and humble piety. Her heroic song at the Annunciation shows her humility and her unblenching dependence on God. When the path of shame, derision, scorn, perhaps death, was open before her, she responded with unfaltering faith, "Behold the handmaid of the Lord, be it unto me according to thy word." Her Son, our Saviour, was learned above all his teachers. He stood up to read the word of the Lord, at the opening of his ministry. He expounded the Scripture as referring to himself. Men wondered, and were astounded, for he had never known his letters. Taught by God, he could have been the wisest of all instructors in his own household.

CXCI.

LET HIM ALONE.

EPHRAIM *is* joined to idols: let him alone. Their drink is sour: they have committed whoredom continually: her rulers *with* shame do love, Give ye. The wind hath bound her up in her wings, and they shall be ashamed because of their sacrifices. And the Lord God said, *It is* not good that the man should be alone; I will make him a help meet for him. And there was in their synagogue a man with an unclean spirit; and he cried out, saying, Let *us* alone; what have we to do with thee, thou Jesus of Nazareth? art thou come to destroy us? I know thee who thou art, the Holy One of God. The ungodly *are* not so: but *are* like the chaff which the wind driveth away. Therefore the ungodly shall not stand in the judgment, nor sinners in the congregation of the righteous. And if the righteous scarcely be saved, where shall the ungodly and the sinner appear? Wherefore, let them that suffer according to the will of God commit the keeping of their souls *to him* in well doing, as unto a faithful Creator.

ROBERT LENNOX AS AN USHER.

THAT portion of New-York who put on Christ are very devoted. It costs something to be a Christian in the great city of Mammon. The rush of business is so fierce, the rivalry of gain so hot, the current of fashion so impetuous, that it takes character and principle to be a Christian. The rich professors are princely givers. The leading lawyers, merchants, and master-builders are found in the Sunday-school, in mission work, and wherever toil for the Master is the most unwelcomed. So it has always been.

When the first Christian church was established in the city, little colonies were dotted round about. Communipaw, Wallabout, Harlem, and even Westchester sent delegates to the house of the Lord on Sunday. The farthest away were in Westchester. The worshipers walked the whole distance to church. They were too conscientious to break the Sabbath. They left on Saturday afternoon, that they might reach the old Fort at the Battery, where the church was, before midnight. They left, on their return home, after twelve o'clock at night on Sunday. They beguiled the long way by devout conversation, and by singing the hymns of Marot. They reached home in season to begin an early day's work on Monday morning.

Many years ago, the First Presbyterian Church stood on Wall street, and Mr. Lennox assumed the position of usher. He made it his especial business to welcome strangers. One morning, he saw a timid young person looking anxiously round, as if for a seat. "Are you a stranger?" "I am." "Come with me, and I will give you a seat." The next day, the young man took a letter that he had to the store of a merchant. "Can I get a small bill of goods to begin business with?" "I will trust any body with a bill of goods that Robert Lennox invites into his pew." "I owe all my success in life," said Jonathan Sturges, "to the invitation of Robert Lennox to sit in his pew."

CXCII.

OPEN-HANDED.

THERE is that scattereth, and yet increaseth; and *there is* that withholdeth more than is meet, but *it tendeth* to poverty. The liberal soul shall be made fat: and he that watereth shall be watered also himself. He that withholdeth corn, the people shall curse him: but blessing *shall be* upon the head of him that selleth *it*. If my land cry against me, or that the furrows likewise thereof complain; if I have eaten the fruits thereof without money, or have caused the owners thereof to lose their life: let thistles grow instead of wheat and cockle instead of barley. The words of Job are ended. Upon the first *day* of the week let every one of you lay by him in store, as *God* hath prospered him, that there be no gatherings when I come. And when I come, whomsoever ye shall approve by *your* letters, them will I send to bring your liberality unto Jerusalem.

MINISTER'S LOAD OF HAY.

THERE is great philosophy as well as religion in the command to be tender and affectionate toward ministers of religion, and to esteem them very highly in love for their works' sake. The draft of the ministry is directly on the nerves.

Besides his own sorrows and woes and trials, he has those to bear which are common to the people of the Lord. He is liable to discouragement. It is said of our Lord, in the prophecy, that he should not be discouraged. Without the divine aid that sustained the Saviour, the ministers of the word have the work to do that filled the Saviour hands. A kind word, a grasp of the hand, a pleasant utterance, "I thank you for that sermon," would encourage a pastor very greatly. The little token of affection sent by the Philippians to Paul in chains has been made memorable by the pen of inspiration. "I am full," said St. Paul, "having received of Epaphroditus the things which were sent from you, an odor of a sweet smell, a sacrifice acceptable, well pleasing to God."

One of our pastors is settled over a country charge. His salary is not large, but it seems a great sum to toilers of the sea, and farmers who work hard for a little money. The parish was wealthy in lands, stock, and crops. One day, the pastor said to a visiting friend who was to preach for him, "I am nearly discouraged. My small salary is paid promptly, but my people do little else. My brethren in the ministry around me are constantly receiving little tokens of regard from their people. A load of hay, a bag of oats, and fruits are often donated. I don't think my people care much about me, or they would not neglect me." "Would you like a load of hay?" said the visiting brother. "If you would, I will draw one into your barn." Satisfied that the parish was thoughtless rather than intentionally indifferent, the preacher made an adroit allusion to little attentions which pastors need, and illustrated his subject by showing how easily a congregation could show its regard for its pastor. A load of hay came before the week was out. The aroma of that sermon abides in the parish to this day. There are

"Evils wrought for want of thought,
As well as want of heart."

CXCIII.

I WILL GIVE YOU REST.

COME unto me, all *ye* that labor and are heavy laden, and I will give you rest. For we which have believed do enter into rest, as he said, As I have sworn in my wrath, if they shall enter into my rest: although the works were finished from the foundation of the world. For he spake in a certain place of the seventh *day* on this wise, And God did rest the seventh day from all his works. And in this *place* again, If they shall enter into my rest. Forasmuch then as the children are partakers of flesh and blood, he also himself likewise took part of the same; that through death he might destroy him that had the power of death, that is, the devil; and deliver them, who through fear of death were all their lifetime subject to bondage. For verily he took not on *him the nature of* angels; but he took on *him* the seed of Abraham. Wherefore in all things it behooved him to be made like unto *his* brethren, that he might be a merciful and faithful high priest in things *pertaining* to God, to make reconciliation for the sins of the people.

"DO YOU WANT A BOY, SIR?"

A MINISTER died, and left two children, a boy and a girl. The widow had only a small pittance to live upon. She was often in great fear that her children would not have bread. When her son reached the age of ten years, he refused longer to be a burden to his mother. The lad resolved to try his fortune in the great mart of trade. He had a distant relative in New-York who offered the boy a home until he could get employment. The lad kissed his mother good-by, and started out on foot to make, as he said, a man of himself. It was no easy thing to find a position. Bad business was easy to be had. Doors stood wide open where bad men congregate, and the boy had many chances to work round in bar-rooms, and wait and tend where liquor was sold. The banks were all full; the insurance companies did not need any one, and to the oft-repeated question, "Do you want a boy, sir?" the dry-goods men shook their heads, and said, "No; we have all the help we need." But Charlie was not discouraged.

One day, he crossed the threshold of a well-known business-man. He found the merchant reading the morning paper, and said to him, "Do you want a boy, sir?" The gentleman looked at him, and said, "What can you do?" "I can do any thing that can give me an honest living." "Well, take these boots down-stairs and black them." Charlie was at home blacking boots; he had been trained to it. His father used to say that blacking ministers' boots was washing disciples' feet. The boy soon returned. The handsome polish on the boots attracted attention, and the merchant said, "Why, my boy, you have done those very well." "Mother told me always to do well whatever I did." "Come here to-morrow morning, and I will try you, my lad." He became a success; stood high as a merchant; became a bank president, and his name is among the most eminent and honored of the merchant princes of the city.

CXCIV.

MONEY FOR WHAT IS NOT BREAD.

WHEREFORE do ye spend money for *that which is* not bread? and your labor for *that which* satisfieth not? hearken diligently unto me, and eat ye *that which is* good, and let your soul delight itself in fatness. Be not among winebibbers; among riotous eaters of flesh: for the drunkard and the glutton shall come to poverty: and drowsiness shall clothe *a man* with rags. Again, the kingdom of heaven is like unto a merchantman, seeking goodly pearls: who, when he had found one pearl of great price, went and sold all that he had, and bought it. Get wisdom, get understanding: forget *it* not: neither decline from the words of my mouth. Forsake her not, and she shall preserve thee: love her, and she shall keep thee. Wisdom *is* the principal thing; *therefore* get wisdom: and with all thy getting get understanding.

MANUFACTURER AND HIS MEN.

WE have full ten thousand young men in New-York. Many stores employ from two to three hundred each. Put the business young men in a line, from the Battery up Broadway, and they would outnumber the National Guard. In lower New-York, the great boarding-houses are crowded with young clerks, salesmen, students of law, and those who are to be our judges, merchants, and master-builders in a few years. But where are these young men on the Lord's day? How many of them have seats in our costly up-town churches? How many of our merchants feel charged with the spiritual interests of the young men who are serving them? How many of our merchant princes stand at the church-door as Robert Lennox did, and welcome the young to the best seats?

The old-style men are not all dead. There is a manufacturer in New-York who employs one hundred men. A great many of these are old-country men, Scotch, Irish, and English. They are in humble positions, and live in the lowly dwellings and tenements around the Fulton-street Church. One day, the manufacturer came down to Fulton street to prefer a request. He said, "I want to come down to this church on Sunday when your Sunday-school meets. I wish to invite all my employees to meet me here in the afternoon, to study the Word of the Lord. I want to form my men into a Bible-class, and teach them myself. I look after their temporal interests: I do not neglect them when they are sick, nor desert them when they are feeble. I give them fair wages, and treat them justly. They have confidence in me. I try to live my religion, so that I need not be ashamed to meet my men anywhere." The request was cheerfully granted. The first Sunday, about fifty men accepted the invitation of their employer, and filed into the old church, and became students of the Word of the Lord. The sight was a most interesting and suggestive one, showing how Christian men can interest themselves in the spiritual welfare of their employees.

CXCV.

BE SOBER.

WHEREFORE let us not sleep, as *do* others; but let us watch and be sober. For they that sleep sleep in the night; and they that be drunken are drunken in the night. But let us, who are of the day, be sober, putting on the breastplate of faith and love; and for a helmet, the hope of salvation. But speak thou the things which become sound doctrine: that the aged men be sober, grave, temperate, sound in faith, in charity, in patience. The aged women likewise, that *they be* in behavior as becometh holiness, not false accusers, not given to much wine, teachers of good things; that they may teach the young women to be sober, to love their husbands, to love their children, *to be* discreet, chaste, keepers at home, good, obedient to their own husbands, that the word of God be not blasphemed. But the end of all things is at hand: be ye therefore sober, and watch unto prayer. And above all things have fervent charity among yourselves: for charity shall cover the multitude of sins.

WORK AMONG THE LOWLY.

LORD SHAFTESBURY has spent a long life in labor among the lowly. As Lord Ashley, he entered the House of Commons. The young noblemen of his age and rank were little given to religion or works of philanthropy. Sporting, racing, gaming, and drinking, with a gay and fast career, marked their life. Lord Ashley became a Christian in early life. He resolved to bind himself up with the poor, the down-trodden, and the helpless. He resolved to rescue the children of London from ignorance, want, and crime. Lord Ashley stood at the door of the House of Commons, hat in hand. He begged of the Lords and the Commoners money to found ragged schools. His appeals were met with sneers, taunts, and gibes, accompanied with the toss of a shilling, sometimes a guinea. Now the great Ragged-School system commands the patronage of the Queen. He got through the Parliament a law to protect the little sweeps. Amid derision and laughter, he broke up the white slavery of the factory children. So many square feet of air and light were allowed to each British workman. Under this law, the rookeries and vile dwellings of the working people came down. Lines of tenements, comfortable and wholesome, were erected under the eye of Shaftesbury himself. And Peabody, with his splendid dwellings for the London poor, only imitated what Shaftesbury had done twenty years before. Window-gardens for the laborers came next. Theatre-preaching for the masses who would not go into the chapels has become a fixed institution for the metropolis. Then came that pride of London —the Boot-Black Brigade. Underlying all this work has been deep religious principle. The proudest memorial of Lord Shaftesbury will be, when he passes away, that, during the thirty years of his public life, he has devoted his youth and manhood, his wealth and renown, to lift up the down-trodden, relieve the oppressed, comfort the poor, change the laws of the land that were hurtful, and restore the alienated working-people of London to the altars of religion and to the Cross.

CXCVI.

ELOQUENT IN THE SCRIPTURES.

AND a certain Jew named Apollos, born at Alexandria, an eloquent man, *and* mighty in the Scriptures, came to Ephesus. And when he was disposed to pass into Achaia, the brethren wrote, exhorting the disciples to receive him: who, when he was come, helped them much which had believed through grace: for he mightily convinced the Jews, *and that* publicly, showing by the Scriptures that Jesus was Christ. And I, brethren, when I came to you, came not with excellency of speech or of wisdom, declaring unto you the testimony of God. For I determined not to know any thing among you, save Jesus Christ, and him crucified. For *his* letters, say they, *are* weighty and powerful; but *his* bodily presence *is* weak, and *his* speech contemptible. Let such a one think this, that, such as we are in word by letters when we are absent, such *will we be* also in deed when we are present.

THE ANNUNCIATION.

IN the town of Nazareth lived a woman named Anna. She was probably a widow. She was of the royal line of David. Had the kingly line been unbroken, Anna and her daughter Mary would have dwelt in the palaces of kings. Visions of royal greatness did not disturb that humble home. The daughter was distinguished for her humble piety and devotion. Her ambition was to serve well the God of her fathers, and be among her kindred the joyful mother of children. She was affianced to a man in humble life, a carpenter by trade, but one pronounced by the inspiration of God as a just and honorable man. To that hillside cottage Gabriel, who stood in the presence of the Most High, came as a messenger from God. Mary's heart died within her as she received the salutation of the angel, "Hail, thou highly favored of God, forever blessed among women." The mission to which she was called was revealed to her. Who would believe her story of the visit of Gabriel? How could she meet the eye of Joseph? Hesitating not one moment, however, she bowed her head, exclaiming, "Behold the handmaid of the Lord. Be it unto me according to thy word." Her ecstatic song shows her abiding confidence in the God of her fathers. To some one the great secret must be confided. Not to Anna; not to Joseph. Far away was the memorable city of Hebron, on the plains of Mamre. There dwelt a kinswoman, Elizabeth by name. To her she could tell the great story of Gabriel's message. On foot and alone, Mary traveled on to the home of Zacharias and Elizabeth. On the aged bosom of her kinswoman she could press her aching head, and into her sympathetic ear pour the great secret, which to that hour had been told to no one. Weary with travel, with a heart almost bursting with anxiety, full of astonishment that she, an humble maiden of Judea, should be elected to so great an honor, Mary crossed the threshold of the aged saint. Before she could speak, the salutation of Elizabeth thrilled Mary's soul: "Hail, thou highly favored; blessed art thou among women, blessed is she that believed."

CXCVII.

MAN OF GOD PERFECT.

ALL Scripture *is* given by inspiration of God, and *is* profitable for doctrine, forre proof, for correction, for instruction in righteousness: that the man of God may be perfect, thoroughly furnished unto all good works. Therefore leaving the principles of the doctrine of Christ, let us go on unto perfection; not laying again the foundation of repentance from dead works, and of faith toward God. Jesus saith unto them, Did ye never read in the Scriptures, The stone which the builders rejected, the same is become the head of the corner: this is the Lord's doing, and it is marvelous in our eyes? Stand therefore, having your loins girt about with truth, and having on the breastplate of righteousness; and your feet shod with the preparation of the gospel of peace; above all, taking the shield of faith, wherewith ye shall be able to quench all the fiery darts of the wicked. And take the helmet of salvation, and the sword of the Spirit, which is the word of God.

RELIGIOUS AFFECTION.

NAOMI, a widow, longed for her home and kindred in Bethlehem. Moab, to which she had fled to escape the famine, furnished a grave for her husband and her two sons. Moab had now no charms for her. She resolved to return to her own kindred. "Call me not Naomi," she said; "call me Mara; for the Almighty hath dealt very bitterly with me." Three widows met under one tent, Naomi and her two daughters-in-law, Ruth and Orpah. Seeking the land of her fathers, Naomi had not the heart to take from their kindred and their altars the young women who loved her for the sake of the dead. She bade them return to their own houses, adding the benediction, "The Lord deal kindly with you, as ye have dealt with the dead and with me." Orpah loved Naomi with a deep and tender love; but it was natural affection simply, and could be overborne. But Ruth was bound to Naomi, not only by natural but by religious affection. "Entreat me not to leave thee, or return from following after thee. For whither thou goest, I will go; where thou lodgest, I will lodge; thy people shall be my people, and thy God my God; where thou diest, I will die, and there will I be buried." Along the highway, along toward the Holy Land, matron and maiden trod, footsore and weary. The coming of Naomi had reached the city of David. All the city was moved at her approach, and came out to meet her. Friends were raised up on every side; the great lord of the place welcomed Ruth to his gleaning-fields. "It hath been fully shown me," he said, "all that thou hast done unto thy mother-in-law since the death of thy husband; and how thou hast left thy father and thy mother, and the land of thy nativity, and art come unto a people whom thou knewest not heretofore."

CXCVIII.

HIDING-PLACE FROM THE WIND.

AND a man shall be as a hiding place from the wind, and a covert from the tempest ; as rivers of waters in a dry place, as the shadow of a great rock in a weary land. And the rain descended, and the floods came, and the winds blew, and beat upon the house ; and it fell : and great was the fall of it. And it came to pass, when Jesus had ended these sayings, the people were astonished at his doctrine : for he taught them as *one* having authority, and not as the scribes. Oh that *men* would praise the Lord *for* his goodness, and *for* his wonderful works to the children of men ! Let them exalt him also in the congregation of the people, and praise him in the assembly of the elders. He turneth rivers into a wilderness, and the watersprings into dry ground ; for ye were sometime darkness, but now *are ye* light in the Lord : walk as children of light ; (for the fruit of the Spirit *is* in all goodness and righteousness and truth ;) proving what is acceptable unto the Lord.

SABBATH NOT REPEALED.

MANY contend that our Lord in spirit, if not in words, repealed the Sabbath of the olden time. That God established the Sabbath no one doubts. There is no limitation to the Sabbath; it applies to the race. The reason given for its original appointment, that God rested from all his labors on the Sabbath-day, and hallowed it, will remain till the end of time as a reason why the Sabbath should be kept. No man can put his finger on a line in the New Testament that repeals directly or indirectly the Sabbath of God's appointment. The Sabbath is not impracticable. It can be kept as easily as it could be observed in Eden, or by the tribes in the wilderness. In the Mosaic law, it is found in the centre of a moral code, every precept of which is binding on the nations of the earth to-day. Our Lord arose from the dead on the special day the Lord had made. The apostles met for worship on the first day of the week. On the one or two occasions in which our Lord seemed to violate the strictness of the Jewish Sabbath, he vindicated his conduct because the occasion was an extraordinary one. He cited the case of David, who, in a case of life and death, received from the high-priest the showbread, which it was not lawful for him to eat. At the close of his ministry, our Lord taught that there would be so much conscience in the church in regard to the Sabbath, forty years after his death, that Christians to save their lives would travel only a Sabbath-day's journey on the Lord's day—a distance of three miles—or from one synagogue to another. Hence the words: "Pray ye that your flight be not on the Sabbath-day." As the Sabbath was made for man, and not for a nation or a tribe; has never been repealed; could not expire by limitation, but would always be binding; is not only not impracticable, but adds to the value of a man and a nation, and benefits the race physically, intellectually, and morally, the command will always be binding on all the nations of the earth: "Remember the Sabbath-day, to keep it holy."

CXCIX.

HELP THOSE WOMEN.

AND I entreat thee also, true yoke-fellow, help those women which labored with me in the gospel, with Clement also, and *with* other my fellow-laborers, whose names *are* in the book of life. And when he had considered *the thing*, he came to the house of Mary the mother of John, whose surname was Mark; where many were gathered together praying. And as Peter knocked at the door of the gate, a damsel came to hearken, named Rhoda. And when she knew Peter's voice, she opened not the gate for gladness, but ran in, and told how Peter stood before the gate. And they said unto her, Thou art mad. But she constantly affirmed that it was even so. Then said they, It is his angel. Then Peter arose and went with them. When he was come, they brought him into the upper chamber: and all the widows stood by him weeping, and showing the coats and garments which Dorcas made, while she was with them. But Mary stood without at the sepulchre weeping: and as she wept, she stooped down, *and looked* into the sepulchre.

THE SABBATH NOT MOSAIC.

MEN might just as well argue that the command against idolatry was Mosaic; that it was only wrong to steal and commit perjury while the dispensation of Moses was in force. The moral precepts of the law were not Mosaic. It was as wrong to steal, to do violence, and to commit crime before Moses was born, as it was after the tables of the law had been written with the finger of God. Centuries before Moses was born, the Sabbath, as a positive law, was made and observed. It was the crown of creation, and God sanctified the Sabbath as holy unto his own service. He put the seal of his divine sovereignty on the Sabbath in the wilderness, by the miracle of the manna. Six days the manna must be gathered fresh. But double the quantity was gathered on the sixth day, and it was kept from putrefaction by the interposition of God. And the people were distinctly notified that on the seventh day, which is the Sabbath, no manna should be found in the field. Placed in the law, the Sabbath is not introduced as a strange institution, but one with which the people were familiar. Hence the simple command: "Remember the Sabbath-day, to keep it holy." Isaiah, who saw the glory of the Lord, and spake of him seven hundred years before his coming, predicted that when the Messiah's kingdom should fill all the earth, and the people be holy, the Sabbath would be universally observed as a day of rest and service, "from sea to sea, and from the river unto the ends of the earth." In the new dispensation, the Holy Spirit was poured out on the Sabbath. The foundations of the church at Philippi were laid at the river-side; prayer-meeting held on the Sabbath; and when St. John beheld the Lord robed in his majesty on the Isle of Patmos, he was in the spirit on the Lord's day. While justice, honesty, truth, and fair dealing will be required of men, the Sabbath will be binding on all the nations of the earth.

CC.

ABUNDANCE OF PEACE.

IN his days shall the righteous flourish; and abundance of peace so long as the moon endureth. He shall have dominion also from sea to sea, and from the river unto the ends of the earth. Arise, shine; for thy light is come, and the glory of the Lord is risen upon thee. For, behold, the darkness shall cover the earth, and gross darkness the people: but the Lord shall arise upon thee, and his glory shall be seen upon thee. And the Gentiles shall come to thy light, and kings to the brightness of thy rising. Rejoice ye with Jerusalem, and be glad with her, all ye that love her: rejoice for joy with her, all ye that mourn for her: that ye may suck, and be satisfied with the breasts of her consolations; that ye may milk out, and be delighted with the abundance of her glory. For thus saith the Lord, Behold, I will extend peace to her like a river, and the glory of the Gentiles like a flowing stream: then shall ye suck, ye shall be borne upon *her* sides, and be dandled upon *her* knees.

WOMEN AT THE SEPULCHRE.

THE Jewish law accounted a man accursed of God who had been crucified. He was not allowed a burial in the family tomb, nor in any tomb wherein man had been laid. But for the rich disciple, Joseph of Arimathea, the prophecy could hardly have been fulfilled: "He shall make his grave with the rich in his death." The mother of our Lord, a poor, lone widow, could furnish her son with no fitting sepulchre. His friends were few, and, with one or two solitary exceptions, none were rich. But Joseph had hewn a tomb out of the solid rock. He builded better than he knew. In that tomb no man had been laid. Boldly he went to Pilate, and begged the body of Jesus. Nicodemus joined Joseph at the cross. They lowered the body, wrapped it in linen cloth, "with myrrh and aloes, according to the manner of the Jews." As the sun lingered on dome and minaret, Jesus was borne to his burial "in a new sepulchre wherein was man never yet laid."

A few women beheld where he was laid. They kept watch and ward lest the body should be taken away, or the tomb be unmarked. These faithful women had learned nothing from their Lord that withdrew from the Sabbath its sacred character. After marking the exact place where the body was laid, these holy women felt that even affection must give place to duty. Leaving the sepulchre, as the "preparation of the Sabbath drew on," "they returned to their homes and prepared spices and ointments; and rested the Sabbath-day, according to the commandments." The women knew nothing of the Resurrection. But they knew that, at the expiration of three days, the guard would be withdrawn, the seal broken, and the body of their Lord delivered to his friends, that it might be embalmed and affection do its fitting work. Judas had gone to confusion and suicide. Peter wept over his cowardice and desertion. The disciples were hidden. But woman, with unblenching faith, stood by him to the last.

"Not she with traitorous kiss the Saviour stung;
Not she denied him with unhallowed tongue.
She, when apostles shrank, could dangers brave;
Last at the cross, and earliest at the grave."

CCI.

KEPT BACK PART OF THE PRICE.

BUT a certain man named Ananias, with Sapphira his wife, sold a possession, and kept back *part* of the price, his wife also being privy *to it*, and brought a certain part, and laid *it* at the apostles' feet. But Peter said, Ananias, why hath Satan filled thine heart to lie to the Holy Ghost, and to keep back *part* of the price of the land? I beseech you therefore, brethren, by the mercies of God, that ye present your bodies a living sacrifice, holy, acceptable unto God, *which is* your reasonable service. For he that is called in the Lord, *being* a servant, is the Lord's freeman: likewise also he that is called, *being* free, is Christ's servant. Ye are bought with a price; be not ye the servants of men. Blessed *be* the God and Father of our Lord Jesus Christ, which according to his abundant mercy hath begotten us again unto a lively hope by the resurrection of Jesus Christ from the dead.

A MEEK AND QUIET SPIRIT.

THERE is a sense of shame, even a loathing, that comes over a sensitive, refined, and religious mind when satisfied that the husband and father is a confirmed drunkard. Men often contract habits of drunkenness after they are married. Genial, jovial, light-hearted men, as years increase, drift into intemperance from the social cup. Many disguise the fatal habit till after the bridal vow has been said. Ought a woman be compelled to bear the disgrace, the insult, the ignominy, and the want that attends drunkenness? As a general rule, no. And yet there are various forms of heroism, suffering for Christ's sake, and even martyrdom. A wife who, from regard to her children, her friends, or her husband, bears the heavy burden laid upon her, is as truly a missionary as if she laid her bones to rest beneath the hot sands of Africa.

A company of men were assembled in the bar-room. It was a late hour. One of them was a young man on whom the grip of the wine-cup was strong. The young man boasted that his wife was the best-tempered woman in the town. "Late as it is, I can take you all home to my house, and call my wife up, and, without a murmur of complaint, she will get you a neat supper." Bets were laid, and the party started for the young man's home. The wife was aroused. The sudden call for supper was cheerfully met. The men were astonished at the quiet and even cheerful way that the wife complied with the wishes of her husband. The men could eat nothing. They were so won by the meek and patient spirit of the woman, that they made a plain confession of the bet, and the purpose for which they came. "How could you," they said, "comply with so unreasonable a request so kindly?" "Well, I took my husband for better or worse. In the main, I think he means well. I hope to win him to better things. At least, there shall be nothing in his home, if I can prevent it, to drive him to the dram-shop." Four temperance pledges were signed that night. The woman saved her husband and his companions.

CCII.

NOT FOR THESE ALONE.

NEITHER pray I for these alone, but for them also which shall believe on me through their word. And when he cometh home, he calleth together *his* friends and neighbors, saying unto them, Rejoice with me; for I have found my sheep which was lost. I say unto you, that likewise joy shall be in heaven over one sinner that repenteth, more than over ninety and nine just persons, which need no repentance. But he answered and said, It is not meet to take the children's bread, and to cast *it* to dogs. And she said, Truth, Lord: yet the dogs eat of the crumbs which fall from their master's table. Thou preparest a table for me in the presence of mine enemies: thou anointest my head with oil; my cup runneth over. Surely goodness and mercy shall follow me all the days of my life: and I will dwell in the house of the Lord forever.

"YOU HAVE GOT GOOD BLOOD IN YOU."

In one of the small inland towns on Long Island, there dwelt a family of pious but humble people. One Monday morning, there was sorrow in that household. The oldest son, James, was to leave the old homestead, and go to the great city to learn a trade. James must look out for himself. His father and mother had quite as much as they could do to earn their own livelihood. A stout, robust, energetic boy could not expect to be always tied to his mother's apron-strings. The lad selected the trade of a printer. The wagon was at the door, and the few clothes that belonged to the lad were packed with a mother's care, and already in the carriage. But "prayer and provender hinder no man's journey," saith the Scotch proverb. And this family could not separate without a word of prayer. The mother, singularly gifted, led the devotions. Her prayer was full, rich, tender, and almost prophetic. It followed the boy till the frosts of more than sixty years whitened his brow. But this was not enough. The mother followed her son till he was seated in the wagon. Taking his hand, she said, "James, remember you have got good blood in you; don't disgrace it." These words burnt into the soul of the boy; he knew their full import: the blood of honest toil, fair dealing, of exact truth, of humble faith. Better this inheritance than fame, wealth, and worldly honor. Like the gift of wisdom given to Solomon, it included all else in humble toil, in menial work. Amid many temptations, surrounded by gay and dissolute associates, the Long Island boy worked steadily on. With every upward step, he heard the ringing words, "James, you have got good blood in you; don't disgrace it." Nor did he. Man, merchant, mayor, everywhere he was a man of God, a decided Christian.

CCIII.

THE SPIRIT OF FEAR.

FOR God hath not given us the spirit of fear; but of power, and of love, and of a sound mind. Be not thou therefore ashamed of the testimony of our Lord, nor of me his prisoner: but be thou partaker of the afflictions of the gospel according to the power of God. Let us therefore come boldly unto the throne of grace, that we may obtain mercy, and find grace to help in time of need. Being confident of this very thing, that he which hath begun a good work in you will perform *it* until the day of Jesus Christ. Keep yourselves in the love of God, looking for the mercy of our Lord Jesus Christ unto eternal life. To the only wise God our Saviour, *be* glory and majesty, dominion and power, both now and ever. Amen.

CAN THE OUTCAST BE RECLAIMED?

MAYOR HARPER was one of the most humane and philanthropic of men. His heart was large, his purse long, and his charities unbounded. One day, there were brought before him a company of young women, arrested on the street by the police. One of the number, quite young, attracted the attention of the mayor. He took the girl into his private office, and learned her history. She came from one of the New-England States. She had a respectable and sorrowing home. Her father and mother had not the slightest idea where she was or what she was doing. She graduated a few months before, with high honors, at a celebrated academy, and came almost direct to New-York. That she had been betrayed and abandoned she admitted, but refused to name the person who had left her to want and sorrow.

To all entreaty to go home, she had but one answer, "Never! My mother would not forgive me. I should be the scorn and derision of my acquaintances and kinsfolk; a menial where once I reigned a queen. I have chosen my path, and must walk in it," she said.

But the good mayor was certain that something better was in store for her. In answer to the question, "What can you do?" she replied, "Almost any thing. I am a capital housekeeper, and know housewifery in all its branches. I am an expert seamstress. I have had a fine musical education, and my voice alone ought to earn me an excellent livelihood." "And all this," said the mayor, "you are ready to throw to the winds for the precarious and dissolute life of a tramp?"

"I am compelled to do this," was the reply, "or starve. All my gifts and accomplishments will not earn me a bit of honest bread. No one will believe in me; no one trust me; nor are my sighs or prayers heeded." Looking Mr. Harper square in the face, she said, "Sir, you have a number of daughters. Some one must attend them, make their clothes, and array them. Would you trust me as a companion to your daughters?" The mayor hesitated. "You need not speak; I know what you would say. If a man as kind as you hesitate, what can I expect of the world?" Without one word more, she walked from the office.

CCIV.

GARDEN OF EDEN.

AND the Lord God planted a garden eastward in Eden; and there he put the man whom he had formed. And out of the ground made the Lord God to grow every tree that is pleasant to the sight, and good for food; the tree of life also in the midst of the garden, and the tree of knowledge of good and evil. And the Lord God commanded the man, saying, Of every tree of the garden thou mayest freely eat: but of the tree of the knowledge of good and evil, thou shalt not eat of it: for in the day that thou eatest thereof thou shalt surely die. Therefore the Lord God sent him forth from the garden of Eden, to till the ground from whence he was taken. So he drove out the man: and he placed at the east of the garden of Eden cherubim, and a flaming sword which turned every way, to keep the way of the tree of life. But I fear, lest by any means, as the serpent beguiled Eve through his subtilty, so your minds should be corrupted from the simplicity that is in Christ.

BE COURTEOUS.

In the city of Philadelphia, a large machine-shop was located. It was quite celebrated for the construction of locomotives and ingenious machinery. One day, two gentlemen called and asked to see the proprietor. He was away. A young man of more than ordinary intelligence represented the house. The strangers were from abroad. They wanted to walk through the workshop and examine the machinery.

The young attendant said that the proprietor was away. He knew he would be only too well pleased to have any foreigner see all there was to be seen, and proposed to accompany the visitors in their tour of inspection. This he did. He withheld nothing from his attendants. He explained the working of the machinery, and said openly what many manufacturers prefer to keep secret.

The tour finished, the strangers expressed not only their gratification, but their surprise that all the secrets of the shop should have been laid open. And the gentlemen related the difficulty they met with in other manufactories. The young man said that the proprietor relied more on the excellence and cheapness of the work than he did on the machinery he employed. The gentlemen talked together apart a little while, and then, handing the young man a card, asked him to call at a well-known hotel in the evening. With this, they took their leave.

The young man kept the appointment. He found the gentlemen in elegant quarters. They were Russian noblemen. They came to America at the command of the Czar. They came to inspect our railroad machinery, with a view to build the great Russian roads. Pleased with the courtesy and intelligence of the young mechanic, they made him a lucrative offer to attend them to Russia. He closed the contract. He rendered honorable service, made his own fortune, and made the name of American mechanism honorable in foreign lands. He found a business value in the command of the apostle, "BE COURTEOUS."

Second Story Room in the Consistory Building.

CCV.

GARDEN OF GETHSEMANE.

WHEN Jesus had spoken these words, he went forth with his disciples over the brook Cedron, where was a garden, into the which he entered, and his disciples. And Judas also, which betrayed him, knew the place: for Jesus ofttimes resorted thither with his disciples. And they came to a place which was named Gethsemane: and he saith to his disciples, Sit ye here, while I shall pray. And he taketh with him Peter and James and John, and began to be sore amazed, and to be very heavy; and saith unto them, My soul is exceeding sorrowful unto death: tarry ye here, and watch. And he went forward a little, and fell on the ground, and prayed that, if it were possible, the hour might pass from him. And he said, Abba, Father, all things *are* possible unto thee; take away this cup from me: nevertheless, not what I will, but what thou wilt. And he cometh unto the disciples, and findeth them asleep, and saith unto Peter, What, could ye not watch with me one hour? Watch and pray, that ye enter not into temptation: the spirit indeed *is* willing, but the flesh *is* weak.

ORPHANS TAKE RANK.

ONE of the marvels of England is the orphan establishment of George Müller. In the Downs near Bristol, Mr. Müller has spent nearly thirty years of his life. He began his work among orphan children in the streets of Bristol. His love for vagrant boys and girls made him unpopular as a missionary of the Church. As he would not abandon this work, his salary was stopped. He resolved never more to rely on man for his support. Without a dollar of his own, without a patron or friend, he gathered six children into a little room and began his life-work. He has now seven stone buildings—each perfect in itself, finely walled in—with lodge, play-grounds, and every convenience ; each house capable of accommodating 500 children. The buildings, of stone, are equal to any public buildings or hospitals in the country. The ventilation, heating, and domestic arrangements are so perfect, that the Queen has sent to Mr. Müller her chief steward, to learn how to heat her palaces. Mr. Müller is no fanatic; his executive force is amazing; he could run the British Government. Gentle as a woman to the orphans under his care, he is a Martinet to outsiders. His rules are like those of the Medes and Persians. One day, a nobleman drove up and desired to go through the building. He was politely informed by the porters that it was not visiting-day. "Oh! that is all very well; take my card up to Mr. Müller, and tell him that Lord —— wishes to go through his buildings." "It would be no use," was the reply; "dukes and lords are of no account; orphans take rank here." In a pet, his lordship said, "Tell Mr. Müller he has lost 500 pounds by the silly enforcement of his rules." "I will deliver your message," said the lady. "I know what the answer of Mr. Müller will be. He will wish me to say to you, that if the Lord wishes him to have your money, he knows best how to draw it from you." But Mr. Müller did not lose the 500 pounds.

CCVI.

GARDEN OF THE SEPULCHRE.

THE first *day* of the week cometh Mary Magdalene early, when it was yet dark, unto the sepulchre, and seeth the stone taken away from the sepulchre. Then she runneth, and cometh to Simon Peter, and to the other disciple, whom Jesus loved, and saith unto them, They have taken away the Lord out of the sepulchre, and we know not where they have laid him. Now in the place where he was crucified, there was a garden; and in the garden a new sepulchre, wherein was never man yet laid. But Mary stood without at the sepulchre weeping: and as she wept, she stooped down, *and looked* into the sepulchre. Jesus saith unto her, Woman, why weepest thou? whom seekest thou? She, supposing him to be the gardener, saith unto him, Sir, if thou have borne him hence, tell me where thou hast laid him, and I will take him away. Jesus saith unto her, Mary. She turned herself, and saith unto him, Rabboni; which is to say, Master.

SPURGEON'S TACT.

WISE men differ in regard to the secret of Spurgeon's success. He came to London a mere boy. He took a congregation, weakened almost to dissolution, and made it one of the strongest in the world. His audience from 50 ran up to 5000. He is as popular to-day as he was ten years ago. Some attribute his success to his deep piety; to his ringing voice and clear enunciation; to his executive force; to his wit, humor, and tact; to his humanity; to his deep acquaintance with the fathers. Perhaps all this enters into his success. His great ability comes out in the building of the huge tabernacle, in the immense revenue, and the exactness with which the financial and spiritual affairs of his church are run. The work he performed while gathering funds for the tabernacle was simply amazing. He preached everywhere where they would give him a collection. He preached nearly every night, from the laying of the corner-stone to the dedication. In one of his journeys, he spent the Sunday in Bristol. He preached in the morning to an immense throng. He had two invitations to dinner. The one was from a poor but sincere and devoted Christian, who lived in humble style on a retired street. He had been a member of the New-Park Church in other days. The other invitation came from a wealthy manufacturer residing just outside the city. He occupied an elegant mansion, and entertained his guests with a generous hospitality. As he was to receive the great London preacher, he made great preparations. Distinguished friends were to be guests with Mr. Spurgeon. To the astonishment and indignation of the wealthy host, Mr. Spurgeon decided to take dinner in the quiet home of his poor parishioner. The disappointed host expressed his feelings. He felt slighted, and did not care who knew it. Besides the entertainment provided for the London preacher, he had a check of 100 pounds for the new tabernacle. But not a cent of it should Mr. Spurgeon receive. All this was told to Mr. S. He made no comment. He preached in the evening, and went his way home. When the corner-stone of the new tabernacle was laid, the cashier of the Bristol manufacturer laid on it 100 pounds, accompanied by the message, "Tell Mr. Spurgeon that I honor his principle. I believe him to be truly a Christian minister, for he was not afraid to keep the Sabbath unto the Lord."

CCVII.

JESUS AND THE WORKSHOP.

IS not this the carpenter's son? is not his mother called Mary? and his brethren, James, and Joses, and Simon, and Judas? And his sisters, are they not all with us? Whence then hath this *man* all these things? Now we command you, brethren, in the name of our Lord Jesus Christ, that ye withdraw yourselves from every brother that walketh disorderly, and not after the tradition which he received of us. For yourselves know how ye ought to follow us: for we behaved not ourselves disorderly among you; neither did we eat any man's bread for nought; but wrought with labor and travail night and day, that we might not be chargeable to any of you. Not slothful in business; fervent in spirit; serving the Lord. I have showed you all things, how that so laboring ye ought to support the weak, and to remember the words of the Lord Jesus, how he said, It is more blessed to give than to receive.

QUICK AND POWERFUL.

A PROTRACTED meeting was held in a town, that attracted much attention. Crowds came in from the region round about, and many turned unto the Lord. A farmer, a very worldly-minded man, was greatly exercised about the meetings. He believed in the literal command, "Six days shalt thou labor." He was offended at the fanaticism which could devote working days to religion. More than all, his family became interested in the work of grace. In following out his plans, it became necessary that he should spend a day in ploughing in the vicinity of the meetings. He was not a Christian, but he was not an opposer of religion. He attended church regularly, paid his subscription, and was a regular supporter of religion. He did not want any revival. The old-fashioned way of seeking the Lord suited him. When he saw the crowd around the church, looked at the well-known teams hitched in the shed and at the fences, and as the singing was wafted over the field where he was at work, he was stirred up marvelously. The windows of the church were opened, and a sentence or two of the sermon struck his ear. The voice of the preacher was sonorous and clear. As the farmer came up and turned his furrow, he heard again and again the text repeated, "Turn ye to the stronghold," "Turn ye to the stronghold." So again and again he heard that invitation, which sometimes sounded like a warning. The word finally took effect. The plough was left on the furrow; the oxen were unhitched and unyoked, and seemed to look with astonishment, as they cropped the grass, that the burden was lighter for an hour. In his working clothes, the farmer stood in the vestibule of the church, leaning, with a sad expression, on the lintel of the door. He rose with those who asked for prayers. He went from his labor a renewed man. The golden text in that family is, "Turn ye to the stronghold, ye prisoners of hope."

CCVIII.

INTIMATIONS OF THE SPIRIT.

HE saw in a vision evidently about the ninth hour of the day, an angel of God coming in to him, and saying unto him, Cornelius. And when he looked on him, he was afraid, and said, What is it, Lord? And he said unto him, Thy prayers and thine alms are come up for a memorial before God. And a vision appeared to Paul in the night; there stood a man of Macedonia, and prayed him, saying, Come over into Macedonia, and help us. And after he had seen the vision, immediately we endeavored to go into Macedonia, assuredly gathering that the Lord had called us for to preach the gospel unto them. And I said, What shall I do, Lord: and the Lord said unto me, Arise, and go into Damascus; and there it shall be told thee of all things which are appointed for thee to do. And Ananias went his way, and entered into the house; and putting his hands on him said, Brother Saul, the Lord, *even* Jesus, that appeared unto thee in the way as thou camest, hath sent me, that thou mightest receive thy sight, and be filled with the Holy Ghost.

ASKING AMISS.

MANY prayers are unanswered. People ask and receive not, because they ask amiss. The prayer of Abraham for Sodom, Elijah for the Shunamite boy, Hezekiah's prayer, with all the prayers in the New Testament—Lord, come down ere my son die; Son of David, have mercy on me; Lord, save, or I perish; Remember me—these are specimens of effectual prayer. The direction of St. James by which the prayer of faith may heal the sick, show how personal prayers may be. Müller, that remarkable man of God, who for thirty years has maintained his great institutions, and has fed, clothed, and educated thousands of orphan children, having no resource but prayer—no patron, no fund, no banker—is distinguished for the directness of his prayers. When he prays for his friends, he calls them by name. If he wants wood, bread, shoes, clothes, money, he asks for the exact thing that he needs. One source of Spurgeon's great power is his public prayers. Preaching to 25,000 in Agricultural Hall, he melted the whole audience to tears by his prayers.

The other day, a man came into Fulton-street meeting to give thanks to the name of the Lord. He had been delivered from a great strait. He was a lawyer, and had certain important papers in his possession. They concerned the settlement of an estate. The business was to be closed at nine o'clock that morning. On returning to his office the afternoon before, his papers were missing. He searched for them high and low. They were not to be found anywhere. He was nearly frantic. If the papers were not found before nine o'clock in the morning, his clients would be damaged and his reputation suffer. He had no recourse but to God. He spent a large part of the night in prayer. His burden was that God would help him in his distress and bring him relief before the appointed hour. He went to his office early. At a quarter to nine, a stranger came in, handed him an envelope, and passed out without speaking. Every paper was found intact.

CCIX.

THAT ROCK WAS CHRIST.

AND did all drink the same spiritual drink; for they drank of that spiritual Rock that followed them: and that Rock was Christ. And were all baptized unto Moses in the cloud and in the sea; and did all eat the same spiritual meat. O that they were wise, *that* they understood this, *that* they would consider their latter end! How should one chase a thousand, and two put ten thousand to flight, except their Rock had sold them, and the Lord had shut them up? And I say also unto thee, That thou art Peter, and upon this rock I will build my church; and the gates of hell shall not prevail against it. And I will give unto thee the keys of the kingdom of heaven: and whatsoever thou shalt bind on earth shall be bound in heaven; and whatsoever thou shalt loose on earth shall be loosed in heaven.

ABUNDANTLY PARDON.

I WAS standing in the anteroom at the White House with a crowd of persons waiting for admission to the President's room. It was a short time before Mr. Lincoln's death. Among the crowd, I noticed an old man; his face furrowed with care, and his expression sad in the extreme. His dress indicated deep poverty. He wore a suit of home-made clothes, of the style known as Kentucky jeans. He took his position in front of the door leading to the President's room, and there he stood during the weary hours of watching and waiting known to the frequenters of that antechamber. Struck with the sorrow and apparent helplessness and hopelessness of the man, I went up and spoke to him. He had a sad story to tell. Two sons had been killed in the war. His only remaining child was under the sentence of death, and in ten days he would die. The general of the division, the judge-advôcate, with the leading officers, had signed a recommendation for mercy. The President had promised to look at his papers, and he had been in attendance day by day, waiting with that sickness of heart which attends hope deferred. Just then, the messenger opened the President's door and said, "No more interviews to-day, gentlemen." The old man gave a groan, and would have fallen to the floor if I had not supported him.

Placing him in a chair, I slipped round through the private secretary's chamber, and found Mr. Lincoln, hat in hand, ready to go out with the committee. I knew one of Mr. Lincoln's peculiarities. Whoever got his ear would be heard through. I made a dash for him in spite of the committee. "You must hear this old man five minutes," I said, "or his son will be unjustly shot, and his blood will be on your hands." With some impatience, he said, "Well, bring him in here." The sorrow-stricken father bowed low and said, "Spare my boy, for he does not deserve to die." Retiring from the crowd, Mr. Lincoln took the papers, read them carefully, and said, "This is a hard case." There was perfect silence in the room. "Bring me a pen," he said. I did not wait for a second order; there was life and death in the message. He signed the pardon, for the judge-advocate had prepared the document in advance. The President had hardly lifted the pen from the paper before the old spirit came over him. As he put the pardon into the hands of the father, he said, "Now, old man, run for your life, or your boy will be shot before you get home."

CCX.

DESPISERS AND REJECTERS.

BEHOLD, ye despisers, and wonder, and perish: for I work a work in your days, a work which ye shall in no wise believe, though a man declare it unto you. He answered and said unto them, Well hath Esaias prophesied of you hypocrites, as it is written, This people honoreth me with *their* lips, but their heart is far from me. This know also, that in the last days perilous times shall come. For men shall be lovers of their own selves, covetous, boasters, proud, blasphemers, disobedient to parents, unthankful, unholy. Or despisest thou the riches of his goodness and forbearance and longsuffering; not knowing that the goodness of God leadeth thee to repentance? But, after thy hardness and impenitent heart, treasurest up unto thyself wrath against the day of wrath and revelation of the righteous judgment of God. But a certain fearful looking for of judgment and fiery indignation, which shall devour the adversaries.

TRAIN UP A CHILD.

A Christian woman was left with five boys. She kept her household together, held her influence without slackening over her sons, and increasing years only seemed to make the mutual attachment stronger. Each son, after obtaining a good education, went into business, and is to-day among the most successful traders of the land. Her friends were anxious to know how she could train and control her five sons, keep them at home, and have that home so happy and attractive. From time to time, persons inquired of the mother how she managed. She said, "I have but little to tell. The loss of my husband was a sore one to me, and I felt keenly the great responsibility of bringing up my children. I established relations of confidence between my sons and myself. They agreed to tell me every thing they did and wherever they went. Whatever they made their minds up to do, whether I approved it or not, they promised to let me know. Whatever company they kept, whatever pastimes, games, or amusements they resolved to indulge in, they would have their recreation and their company in my own house. If they would smoke or play cards, or go with persons whom I thought not proper, I thought it safer to have the annoyance at home than to expose my sons abroad. I tried to make the Sabbath a pleasant day, and so mark it that it would not be a weariness. When my boys were too young to understand what the day meant, I had books and pictures and toys that were never used except on the Lord's day. On Saturday night, the playthings of the week were gathered and put away. On Sunday morning, the key of the Sunday closet was given to the children, with the injunction to make no noise. When they became weary and nervous, and reading and singing would not do, I sent them out on little errands of mercy. Sometimes they fed the horse or drew a pail of water. I timed my religious instruction somewhat to the frame of mind of my boys. The Sabbath with us has always been a delight. My children are all in the kingdom, and the Lord has blessed me in my household as he blessed Naomi in Ruth."

CCXI.

ARMOR OF GOD.

PUT on the whole armor of God, that ye may be able to stand against the wiles of the devil. Wherefore take unto you the whole armor of God, that ye may be able to withstand in the evil day, and having done all, to stand. The night is far spent, the day is at hand: let us therefore cast off the works of darkness, and let us put on the armor of light. Let us walk honestly, as in the day; not in rioting and drunkenness, not in chambering and wantonness, not in strife and envying. Praying always with all prayer and supplication in the Spirit, and watching thereunto with all perseverance and supplication for all saints. Then goeth he, and taketh *to him* seven other spirits more wicked than himself; and they enter in, and dwell there: and the last *state* of that man is worse than the first.

THE OX-OWNER.

A COARSE, brutal, revengeful man is a curse to his household. A farmer, who had by hard labor and economy acquired considerable wealth, was everywhere distinguished for his violent temper. When he came in from the field, his step sent a thrill through the house. His boys kept out of his way, and his girls trembled in his presence. The softening refining influence of the Sabbath had no effect on him. He seldom visited the house of God; and though he did not work on the Lord's day, he spent the sacred hours in secular things. He salted his cattle; looked after his fences; tramped round the fields; watered his stock; brushed up the barn, and did little odd chores which a farmer does not place under the head of labor.

Death came into the neighborhood, and the man went with his family to the funeral. A stranger preached, and the text arrested attention—"The ox knoweth his owner, and the ass his master's crib: but Israel doth not know, my people doth not consider." Some time afterward, the farmer was ploughing in his field. One of the oxen got his foot over the chain, and the owner, becoming enraged, commenced beating the ox with his goad. The cattle ran away, and were chased round the field, and finally cornered. Chaining them to a tree, the man, whose temper was at white heat, beat the offending ox most cruelly. He became exhausted. Passing the head of the ox, as he paused in his brutal beating, the animal that had been so cruelly treated, trembling with pain, and with moistened eye, ran out his tongue and licked the sleeve of the cruel owner. The supplicating look of the ox, and his piteous pleading smote the heart of the cruel man. The text at the funeral flashed upon him—"The ox knoweth his owner, . . . but my people do not consider." He sat down on the wall, and looked steadily at the ox. Tears moistened his eyes, and he was ready to ask pardon of the injured animal. He knelt on a pile of stones, and asked God to forgive him and help him to control his temper. He wrestled till the victory came; and what sermons and religious services failed to do, the piteous pleading of an ox accomplished. House, home, children, cattle, and friends were all the better for that hour of consecration.

CCXII.

FATHERLESS AND WIDOWS.

PURE religion and undefiled before God and the Father is this, To visit the fatherless and widows in their affliction, *and* to keep himself unspotted from the world. A father of the fatherless, and a judge of the widows, *is* God in his holy habitation. He doth execute the judgment of the fatherless and widow, and loveth the stranger, in giving him food and raiment. If I have withheld the poor from *their* desire, or have caused the eyes of the widow to fail; if I have lifted up my hand against the fatherless, when I saw my help in the gate: *then* let mine arm fall from my shoulder blade, and mine arm be broken from the bone. Remember, O Lord, what is come upon us: consider, and behold our reproach. Our inheritance is turned to strangers, our houses to aliens. We are orphans and fatherless, our mothers *are* as widows.

APOSTOLIC PRAYER-MEETING.

PERHAPS much of the success of the daily prayer-meeting has been due to its apostolic character. From the few hints thrown out in the New Testament, we learn something of the nature of an apostolic prayer-meeting. The Fulton-street service resembles these ancient gatherings, if the hints in the

New Testament can guide us. It is evident that the whole church anciently came together for prayers. The disciples had a set time for assembling, and at these gatherings the weekly offerings were to be made. The place of prayer was well known, and the upper room chosen was where the apostles abode. There was unity in the gathering; for those who assembled continued steadfast in the apostles' doctrine; enjoyed fellowship one with another; often met for the breaking of bread, and were with one accord in prayer and supplication. There was great variety in the service. Every one took part. Psalms were sung; doctrines taught; scriptures interpreted; tongues revealed, and the whole church edified. Into this assembly came the heathen and the unbeliever. The service was so impressive as to affect idolaters. Those who came into the prayer-meeting were convinced of all, judged of all. The secrets of the heart were made manifest. The unbeliever fell on his face, worshiped God, and reported that God was among that people of a truth.

It is clear that in an apostolic prayer-meeting there was no stupidity or dullness. One or two men did not run the meeting with prayer or talk. "Every one of you hath a psalm, a doctrine." The song of praise was not a mere wedge to keep the services apart—a time for the pastor to scribble his notes, or the sexton to do odd jobs about the church—but the psalm was as much a part of the devotions as the prayer or supplication. The brethren, when they came together, brought something to add to the common stock. All could not pray; all could not sing; all could not teach; all could not interpret; but each could do something; and, as at a picnic, at which every one feels bound to make some contribution, each one who attended the prayer-meeting made an offering for general edification. Soundness in doctrine, Christian fellowship, unity in worship, varied song, and offerings from the land and the sea have made the Fulton-street prayer-meeting a power owned of the Lord.

CCXIII.

ALWAYS GIVING THANKS.

EVERY man according as he purposeth in his heart, *so let him give;* not grudgingly, or of necessity: for God loveth a cheerful giver. And God *is* able to make all grace abound toward to you; that ye, always having all sufficiency in all *things*, may abound to every good work. Oh that *men* would praise the Lord *for* his goodness, and *for* his wonderful works to the children of men! And let them sacrifice the sacrifices of thanksgiving, and declare his works with rejoicing. Speaking to yourselves in psalms and hymns and spiritual songs, singing and making melody in your heart to the Lord; giving thanks always for all things unto God and the Father in the name of our Lord Jesus Christ. Let them praise his name in the dance: let them sing praises unto him with the timbrel and harp. For the Lord taketh pleasure in his people: he will beautify the meek with salvation. *Let* the high *praises* of God *be* in their mouth, and a twoedged sword in their hand.

WHITE-HORSE FAIR.

A YOUNG Christian woman found herself in possession of a fortune. A portion of it she resolved to spend for religion and humanity. She made two or three rules to guide her life, one of which was that she would never see suffering or sorrow or want without attempting to afford relief. Her resolution extended to the dumb creation. A neighbor had a white horse, celebrated principally for the long years of service he had given to the family. He was a horse of all work—good at the plough, in the hay-cart, and on the road. He jogged along steadily and without complaint from dawn till dark. Old age came upon him; his eye grew dim; his uncertain limbs made him stumble; and as he was no longer able to serve, he was turned out into the roadside to crop the scant herbage or starve.

The attention of the young woman was frequently drawn to the neglected animal. The horse seemed to have an instinct that a kind heart dwelt beneath her roof. Sometimes his head would rest on the stone wall, over which he would gaze anxiously into the green paddock. A thought struck the young woman. Why not have a fair for Old Whitey; raise a little fund, that should be devoted to good pasturage and kind care for the horse while he lived? To think was to do. The young of the town entered heartily into the arrangement. Donations poured in on every side. The fair proved a great success. The horse was placed in comfortable quarters, and received considerate care till he died. The act was a Christian one. It not only relieved the sufferings and provided for the wants of a faithful beast, but it was a living lesson of humanity and tenderness, to which the whole town gave heed. A merciful man regardeth the life of his beast. And this lesson carried with it an impression long enduring on the town.

CCXIV.

EXCELLENCY OF THE KNOWLEDGE.

YEA, doubtless, and I count all things *but* loss for the excellency of the knowledge of Christ Jesus my Lord: for whom I have suffered the loss of all things, and do count them *but* dung, that I may win Christ. Beloved, now are we the sons of God, and it doth not yet appear what we shall be: but we know that, when he shall appear, we shall be like him; for we shall see him as he is. Giving thanks unto the Father, which hath made us meet to be partakers of the inheritance of the saints in light: who hath delivered us from the power of darkness, and hath translated *us* into the kingdom of his dear Son. They shall not hurt nor destroy in all my holy mountain: for the earth shall be full of the knowledge of the Lord, as the waters cover the sea. For we are his workmanship, created in Christ Jesus unto good works, which God hath before ordained that we should walk in them.

SPURGEON AND HIS DEACONS.

THE church organization in London over which Mr. Spurgeon presides is a very peculiar establishment. Few ministers have the advantages that Spurgeon claims. He is the head of his church, and his elders and deacons are merely assistants. The great Tabernacle was built by his own labors, and is controlled solely by himself. He can open and shut it as he pleases. The revenue is in his own hands for disposal. His officials give a receipt for every dollar they expend. If there is any trouble in the congregation, the disaffected leave, but the preacher remains. His elders and deacons, as a sort of body-guard, attend the preacher to the pulpit, and surround him while he dispenses the word of Life. In his early ministry, as the church grew and began to be a power in the city, there was a little conflict between Mr. Spurgeon and his officials. He felt hampered by their opposition to his measures, and chafed under the restraint put upon him. Resolving to settle the conflict once for all, Mr. Spurgeon called a meeting of the church. The attendance was very large. He came in at the usual time, with the official brethren in attendance. They had not the slightest idea of the business to be laid before the meeting. After the usual exercises, Mr. Spurgeon arose, and gave a detailed account of his ministry; his early coming; the weak and feeble congregation that met him; the marvelous growth and strength of the Church; the revivals with which he had been favored. He then revealed the opposition of the deacons to his work and style of doing things, and told the church plainly that it must then and there choose between him and the official board. If they wished him to remain, they must muzzle the deacons; but, one way or the other, the question must be decided that night. His appeal to the church created intense excitement. The deacons were dumbfounded. The church by a rising vote unanimously sustained the pastor; and from that hour to to this, though years have rolled between, the wish of Mr. Spurgeon has been law to the church. To his ability to carry out the plans he thought for the best good of the church, free and untrammeled, he attributes, in a large measure, his eminent success.

CCXV.

GROUNDED AND SETTLED

IF ye continue in the faith grounded and settled, and *be* not moved away from the hope of the gospel, which ye have heard, *and* which was preached to every creature which is under heaven; whereof I Paul am made a minister. Rooted and built up in him, and stablished in the faith, as ye have been taught, abounding therein with thanksgiving. Till we all come in the unity of the faith, and of the knowledge of the Son of God, unto a perfect man, unto the measure of the stature of the fullness of Christ. And this I say, lest any man should beguile you with enticing words. That ye might walk worthy of the Lord unto all pleasing, being fruitful in every good work, and increasing in the knowledge of God; strengthened with all might, according to his glorious power, unto all patience and longsuffering with joyfulness.

LORD ASHLEY AND THE COMMONS.

FEW names stand higher in London to-day than that of Lord Shaftesbury. He leads the evangelical party, which, as against ritualism, is a power. He is at the head of the missionary movements, the circulation of the Bible, and the great reforms of the age. He began his religious life at an early age. When most of the young noblemen were spending their time in gaming, horse-racing, and dissipation, Lord Ashley consecrated himself to the service of the Lord. The great movements to help and save the lowly were not then in use. There were no common schools. Even the refuges known as reformatories could not be entered without a commitment from a magistrate. The children of the poor, without schooling or employment, were turned into the street to run wild till some trivial crime was committed, and then they were sent to Bridewell or a refuge. Lord Ashley felt that something could be done to rescue these children from ignorance, idleness, and crime. The government could do nothing; an appeal must be made to private charity. All unaided and alone, Lord Ashley undertook the work. He stood at the door of the House of Commons, hat in hand, and begged donations to relieve the hungry and ragged lads in the streets. Some gave sovereigns, some shillings, and others gave sneers. But the young nobleman was not diverted from his course. He persevered. He founded the ragged-schools of London. He rescued thousands from want and woe. He formed the Boot-Black Brigade, now so famous in the city, and gave employment to hundreds. From a small beginning a mighty institution has risen.

CCXVI.

GLORY IN THEIR SHAME.

FOR many walk, of whom I have told you often, and now tell you even weeping, *that they are* the enemies of the cross of Christ: whose end *is* destruction, whose God *is their* belly, and *whose* glory *is* in their shame, who mind earthly things. But these speak evil of those things which they know not: but what they know naturally, as brute beasts, in those things they corrupt themselves. Wo unto them! for they have gone in the way of Cain, and ran greedily after the error of Balaam for reward, and perished in the gainsaying of Core. Having eyes full of adultery, and that can not cease from sin; beguiling unstable souls: an heart they have exercised with covetous practices; cursed children. For when they speak great swelling *words* of vanity, they allure through the lusts of the flesh, *through much* wantonness, those that were clean escaped from them who live in error.

LORD SHAFTESBURY ON WINDOW-GARDENS.

In his work among the lowly, Lord Shaftesbury believed that the ministry of the beautiful was a power. The homes of London workmen were poor indeed. Could not there be some invention by which flowers and plants, and even fruits, could be cultivated. The blank and dingy room in which the poor man lived, could not this be made cheerful? So window-gardens were invented. These were simply boxes made to set on the window-sill, filled with rich earth, and planted with choice seeds. The plan was a success beyond the most sanguine hope. Gardens in the windows multiplied; none were so poor as to be shut out from these cheery influences; any workman could have a garden for the asking. Fine mould and rare seeds were dealt out without cost to all who came for them. Hours spent in the public beer-gardens were now devoted to window-gardens. A healthy rivalry sprang up between workmen as to who should raise the richest flowers and have the greatest variety. The great patron of the workingman arranged a horticultural show. Side by side with the flowers that bloomed in the hot-house or on the immense lawns of the wealthy, stood the fragrant plants raised in the humble home of the London poor. The show was an elegant success. The nation was surprised at the display. With the flowers came a tidy hearthstone, clean and happy children, a bountiful table filled with the money saved from the "public." From the flower-garden to the chapel the step was an easy one, and the blushing rose and blooming lily became means of grace.

CCXVII.

IMAGE OF THE INVISIBLE.

WHO being the brightness of *his* glory, and the express image of his person, and upholding all things by the word of his power, when he had by himself purged our sins, sat down on the right hand of the Majesty on high. For by him were all things created, that are in heaven, and that are in earth, visible and invisible, whether *they be* thrones, or dominions, or principalities, or powers: all things were created by him, and for him: and he is before all things, and by him all things consist. For this cause I bow my knees unto the Father of our Lord Jesus Christ, of whom the whole family in heaven and earth is named, that he would grant you, according to the riches of his glory, to be strengthened with might by his Spirit in the inner man; to the intent that now unto the principalities and powers in heavenly *places* might be known by the church the manifold wisdom of God.

HOW MÜLLER PAID HIS SALARY.

GEORGE MÜLLER came to England from Germany. After his conversion, he devoted himself to the work of missions. The field was larger in England, so he left Germany for London. He began his work in the old town of Bristol. He was in the employ of the Church Evangelical Society. His work was the ordinary kind: he was to distribute Bibles and religious books; he must visit the sick; hold meetings from time to time, and do all in his power to save souls. The streets of Bristol were full of boys and girls running wild. There were no free schools for children; no employment could be had. Vagrancy became a trade, and idleness a calling. Müller's heart was touched; his pity was especially called for toward orphan children, who ran about the streets hungry, friendless, and forlorn. He made an attempt to rescue this class. He gathered a few into a small room, and began to instruct them. But food must be had, clothing was needed, and temporal wants must be met as well as the intellect and the soul.

The new work reaching London, it was not approved. Teaching little street Arabs, feeding and clothing the poor little urchins, might be well enough, but that was not the work assigned to the missionaries of the society. Mr. Müller was ordered to dismiss his school, and turn the children out into the street from whence he took them. This he declined to do. His salary was then stopped. From that moment, Mr. Müller resolved never again to trust man for his daily bread. A whole generation has passed away since that resolution was made. God has been his bountiful provider.

CCXVIII.

FERVENT LABOR IN PRAYER.

I THANK God, whom I serve from *my* forefathers with pure conscience, that without ceasing I have remembrance of thee in my prayers night and day. For ye remember, brethren, our labor and travail: for laboring night and day, because we would not be chargeable unto any of you, we preached unto you the gospel of God. And we beseech you, brethren, to know them which labor among you, and are over you in the Lord, and admonish you; and to esteem them very highly in love for their work's sake. *And* be at peace among yourselves. Night and day praying exceedingly that we might see your face, and might perfect that which is lacking in your faith? For ye had compassion of me in my bonds, and took joyfully the spoiling of your goods, knowing in yourselves that ye have in heaven a better and an enduring substance.

HOMES OF THE LONDON POOR.

PEABODY in London has reared his monument. He has bound himself up with the London poor. As a philanthropist, his name must be immortal. The long rows of convenient dwellings, full of comfort and elegance, put within the reach of honest industry, speak his praise. But this beneficent plan did not originate with the munificent banker. Years before, the work was begun by a company of religious men. They sought to give comfortable homes to the poor, and to do it for the Saviour's sake.

No part of the world had such wretched, miserable dwellings as London. A law passed Parliament allowing every workingman so many square feet of light and air. Old rookeries came down; ill-ventilated dwellings were removed; narrow lanes were widened. The police who executed the law had their clothes ruined; the vermin rained down on them. The heated furnace was needed to consume the filth.

New and comfortable houses spread out on all sides. These were private enterprises. It was not expected that any pecuniary gain would result from this investment. Lines of houses were bought and pulled down; new and wide streets were opened; old rookeries disappeared, and lofty dwellings took their places. It was soon found that the work was not only one of humanity; it proved to be also one of profit. From this work of Christian philanthropy, Peabody got his idea of an investment that should repay all the expenditure. The profit added to the original outlay would perpetuate and increase the benefaction to coming generations.

CCXIX.

DEACONS.

WHEREFORE, brethren, look ye out among you seven men of honest report, full of the Holy Ghost and wisdom, whom we may appoint over this business. But we will give ourselves continually to prayer, and to the ministry of the word. And Philip said, If thou believest with all thine heart, thou mayest. And he answered and said, I believe that Jesus Christ is the Son of God. And the word of God increased; and the number of the disciples multiplied in Jerusalem greatly; and a great company of the priests were obedient to the faith. And Stephen, full of faith and power, did great wonders and miracles among the people. Paul and Timotheus, the servants of Jesus Christ, to all the saints in Christ Jesus which are at Philippi, with the bishops and deacons: grace *be* unto you, and peace, from God our Father, and *from* the Lord Jesus Christ.

ELEGANT LITERATURE.

NOTHING is more corrupting than bad poetry, unless it be impure pictures. Paternoster Row is crowded with prints. Lines of unemployed men and women hang round the windows looking at them. What is true of London is true of the leading cities of England: the working people of England are especially fond of pictures. It occurred to some far-seeing, liberal people that it would be a good thing to form a society to produce attractive pictures and prints, and sell them cheap. It was useless to declaim against impure cuts, if there were none of an elevated character to take their places. If a workingman could take home an agricultural cut, a print of a horse or some animal, the likeness of some eminent man who had worked his way up from humble life, and get these refining and elevating pictures cheaper than was the cost of impure prints, he would at once secure such treasures.

No common pictures were sent out. The best artists were employed. Men gave large sums to have these elegant prints put at the price of common and debasing ones. The scheme worked like a charm. New picture societies sprang up in all the cities of the kingdom. The dealers in coarse and debasing pictures were made allies. As a specimen, a committee called at a store in Bristol, where a large trade in prints for popular use was carried on. "What do you make on your stock?" "Twenty-five per cent." "Will you change your style, if we will guarantee you a profit of fifty per cent?" "Be sure I will." A bargain was struck, and an immense sale was the consequence. Impure prints have been nearly driven from the show-windows.

CCXX.

TRODDEN UNDER FOOT.

OF how much sorer punishment, suppose ye, shall he be thought worthy, who hath trodden under foot the Son of God, and hath counted the blood of the covenant, wherewith he was sanctified, an unholy thing, and hath done despite unto the Spirit of grace? He therefore that despiseth, despiseth not man, but God, who hath also given unto us his Holy Spirit. Then Paul and Barnabas waxed bold, and said, It was necessary that the word of God should first have been spoken to you: but seeing ye put it from you, and judge yourselves unworthy of everlasting life, lo, we turn to the Gentiles. *It is* a faithful saying: For if we be dead with *him*, we shall also live with *him:* if we suffer, we shall also reign with *him:* if we deny *him*, he also will deny us: if we believe not, *yet* he abideth faithful: he can not deny himself.

THE FARMER AND HIS POTATOES.

WE live in the reign of the Holy Spirit. There are diversities of operations: sometimes men are called into the kingdom by one instrumentality, sometimes by another. John was not called as was Zachary; nor was Matthew called as was Philip. Two men to day seldom enter the church under exactly the same influences. Some men have their attention arrested in the flush of trade and turmoil of business; another in the repose of a sick-room. Death calls one man to the Saviour; the birth of a child another. An earnest sermon saves one soul; another is saved by a sermon heard in childhood, or a text hidden away for years.

A farmer was noted for his worldly spirit and bad temper. He toiled early and late; he added field to field and farm to farm. His family stood in awe of his violent temper, and when his children were young, they ran and hid when they heard the footsteps of their father. His temper was not only bad, but he was terribly profane. It was really awful to hear him take God's name in vain.

One day, he was at work a mile away. He had to ascend a very rugged, tedious hill to reach home. He had a large wagon full of potatoes, drawn by two horses. The farmer walked at the heads of the horses. The jostling of the road jarred out the tail-board. Slowly but surely, the load ran through all unobserved. Reaching the summit of the hill, he looked back and saw his load strewed from the bottom to the top of the road. All looked for a profane outburst. He said not a word. He reloaded, sought his home, and that night gave his heart to God.

CCXXI.

WHAT IS YOUR LIFE?

GO to now, ye that say, To-day or to-morrow we will go into such a city, and continue there a year, and buy and sell, and get gain: whereas ye know not what *shall be* on the morrow. For what *is* your life? It is even a vapor, that appeareth for a little time, and then vanisheth away. *As* the cloud is consumed and vanisheth away; so he that goeth down to the grave shall come up no *more.* He shall return no more to his house, neither shall his place know him any more. The days of our years *are* threescore years and ten; and if by reason of strength *they be* fourscore years, yet *is* their strength labor and sorrow; for it is soon cut off, and we fly away. Who knoweth the power of thine anger? even according to thy fear, *so is* thy wrath. So teach *us* to number our days, that we may apply *our* hearts unto wisdom. For the Son of man shall come in the glory of his Father, with his angels; and then he shall reward every man according to his works.

GIVE THYSELF WHOLLY TO THEM.

VERSATILITY in talent is an accomplishment, but success in life usually attends the close adherence to one settled line of action. "Jack-at-all-trades and good at none" is a proverb old and true. The great number of traders go under; the few have permanent prosperity. This is true of all lands and of all ages—of cities and nations, as well as of persons. In most cases, the ruin comes from a multiplicity of engagements and pursuits. In business, most men who fail are engaged on side issues and outside things. A successful merchant makes a venture on stocks, and locks up money in the street that he will need when a panic strikes him. A manufacturer with a balance of $30,000 buries it in real estate. Nor can the ministry do better. "Give thyself wholly to thy work," is an apostolic command, as well as a maxim of prudence. Few men do well as pastors, who give their strength to trade—to stocks, to editorship, or to authorship. One of the best-known pastors had an elegant settlement; he had a large fortune; he kept an open-handed hospitality. He wanted a wider field. He took to editing; that was not enough. He took his own money, and that of his friend, and went West to found a religious colony. He bought land right and left; laid the foundation for a city—a college and a church. The whole thing came to naught. He buried the money of his friend; lost all his own property; beggared his wife and children; was accused of fraud, a passed the closing years of his life under a cloud.

CCXXII.

PARTAKERS OF SUFFERING.

BUT rejoice, inasmuch as ye are partakers of Christ's sufferings; that, when his glory shall be revealed, ye may be glad also with exceeding joy. Wherefore, let them that suffer according to the will of God commit the keeping of their souls *to him* in well doing, as unto a faithful Creator. Yet if *any man suffer* as a Christian, let him not be ashamed; but let him glorify God on this behalf. Who, when he was reviled, reviled not again; when he suffered, he threatened not; but committed *himself* to him that judgeth righteously: who his own self bare our sins in his own body on the tree, that we, being dead to sins, should live unto righteousness: by whose stripes ye were healed. For ye were as sheep going astray; but are now returned unto the Shepherd and Bishop of your souls.

COALS OF FIRE ON THE HEAD.

A COMPANY of lads belonged to a Sunday-school; they were a sharp, bright, crisp set, full of fun and frolic, but no worse than boys average. One of the number found his associates in a cluster they had assembled after school, bent on mischief. But the mischief had a spice of justice in it. On the outside of the village was a small hut. It was the home of a poor woman who went out washing day by day. Her hut was a poor one. The snow was banked up to the doorstone. The path to the well was unshoveled. A little green wood lay under the snow, partly covered by a broken shed-roof. The old woman had offended the boys. She saw them in some mischief, and told on them. In their language, they "meant to be even with her." And this was the purpose of the gathering. The boys proposed to go down to the hut, climb up on the roof, put a board on the chimney, and to "smoke the old woman out." One of the boys thought the better way would be to "heap coals of fire on the old woman's head." "How is that! how is that!" shouted the lads. So the plan was laid. The boys were to provide themselves with axes and shovels, make paths to the shed and the well, cut up the wood, haul on a sled some dry stuff, make a fire, and then hide and wait the return of the owner. As planned, so was it done. The boys worked with a will: the paths were made; the wood was cut; the kindlings brought; the fire made. The heroic boy who planned the revenge did more. He let his mother into the secret. A basket of good things was sent down, and the table was spread. Homeward the poor woman came after the toils of the day. Amazed, she looked on the paths, the pile of wood, the glowing fire, and the well-spread table. The boys could hold in no longer; they shouted, "Jimmie did it"—"Coals of fire!"

CCXXIII.

WALKING IN THE TRUTH.

I HAVE no greater joy than to hear that my children walk in truth. Let us therefore, as many as be perfect, be thus minded : and if in any thing ye be otherwise minded, God shall reveal even this unto you. Nevertheless, whereto we have already attained, let us walk by the same rule, let us mind the same thing. I have not sat with vain persons, neither will I go in with dissemblers. I have hated the congregation of evil doers ; and will not sit with the wicked. I will wash mine hands in innocency : so will I compass thine altar, O Lord. Then Jesus said unto them, Yet a little while is the light with you. Walk while ye have the light, lest darkness come upon you : for he that walketh in darkness knoweth not whither he goeth.

PREMIER AND GAMING.

MEN who make their mark in the world are usually distinguished for firmness of character. As in war, he that ruleth his own spirit is a mighty man, so, in morals and trade, a man to succeed must have pluck. The great Pitt came on the theatre of public life at a stirring time. Drinking and gaming were the common vices of the day, and these were nearly universal. Neither the one nor the other harmed a man's political prospects, so far as reputation went. That young men should drink and gamble was as much expected as that they should be young men. It was a common thing for eminent men on both sides to be unfit to make a motion in Parliament. Young Pitt saw the future that was before him. Between him and eminence was a great gulf: that was gambling. Impetuous, impatient, he knew how fascinating the passion for play was. Once the mastery over him, and he was ruined. One night he went home from play. He had been plunging deep into the vortex. One night more, and he would be a slave to the dice. Yet he was master. That night must decide between the chair of a premier and the shame of a gambler. He took his resolution at once: "I will never play more," he said. He kept the resolution to the end. The heroism and courage that enabled him to conquer himself helped him over all the difficulties that stood between him and the great ambition he had marked for his own. "He that ruleth his own spirit is mightier than he that taketh a city."

CCXXIV.

OLD AGE.

CAST me not off in the time of old age; forsake me not when my strength faileth. And *even* to *your* old age I *am* he; and *even* to hoar hairs will I carry *you:* I have made, and I will bear; even I will carry, and will deliver *you.* For it came to pass, when Solomon was old, *that* his wives turned away his heart after other gods: and his heart was not perfect with the Lord his God, as *was* the heart of David his father. For a thousand years in thy sight *are but* as yesterday when it is past, and *as* a watch in the night. Whoso mocketh the poor reproacheth his Maker: *and* he that is glad at calamities shall not be unpunished. Children's children *are* the crown of old men; and the glory of children *are* their fathers. The days of our years *are* threescore years and ten; and if by reason of strength *they be* fourscore years, yet *is* their strength labor and sorrow; for it is soon cut off, and we fly away.

DANIEL AND HIS PLEDGE.

Daniel was born in slavery. He was tenderly nurtured, and trained in the fear of God. Among the captives of Judah, he was selected for the perilous favor of the king and of the court. As he was to stand in the king's presence and serve him, his life and training were to be carefully regarded. It was the royal order that Daniel and his brethren should be fed from the royal table, " eat of the king's meat, and drink the king's wine" daily. He was chosen for his beauty and wisdom. "There was no blemish in him." "He was well favored and skillful in all wisdom, and cunning in knowledge, and understanding science, and had ability to stand in the king's palace." Daniel had ever before him the fear of God. The society of the court and the style of living appointed were perilous to a young man who had so many elements for a gay and dissipated career. Daniel knew that a life such as he was expected to live, with its dissipations and luxuries, was full of peril. There was but one way to avoid those evils. That way he selected, and that path he trod. "He purposed in his heart that he would not defile himself with the portion of the king's meats, nor with the wine which he should drink." Three years of such a life of dissipation that the young Hebrew was to lead would be destructive to his moral and religious character. Therefore he would none of it. The heroism of the young slave, that led him to adhere to the simple diet of his own people, that of " pulse and water ;" that enabled him to pass by untasted the heating viands of the royal steward ; that helped him to avoid that fatal glance of the wine-cup that has stung so many ; that heroism bore him onward to high honor and renown, gave him favor with the captors of his people, and elevated him to the position of prime minister of the kingdom.

CCXXV.

YOUR ADVERSARY THE DEVIL.

BE sober, be vigilant; because your adversary the devil, as a roaring lion, walketh about, seeking whom he may devour; whom resist steadfast in the faith, knowing that the same afflictions are accomplished in your brethren that are in the world. He that committeth sin is of the devil; for the devil sinneth from the beginning. For this purpose the Son of God was manifested, that he might destroy the works of the devil. Ye are of *your* father the devil, and the lusts of your father ye will do: he was a murderer from the beginning, and abode not in the truth, because there is no truth in him. When he speaketh a lie, he speaketh of his own: for he is a liar, and the father of it. Forasmuch then as the children are partakers of flesh and blood, he also himself likewise took part of the same; that through death he might destroy him that had the power of death, that is, the devil.

THE CURSE OF ORLEANS.

SOME men never succeed, neither in church nor state; neither in religious nor secular life. This feature results not from want of success, nor from indolence, nor for lack of zeal. Some people who have the least success have the most zeal. We see men in trade whose whole life has been a failure, that are equaled by few in their endeavors to achieve success. In the church, the most zealous and untiring are not the most useful. And the reason is obvious: people who have talent and piety mix up with these elements which neutralize or destroy.

The famous Orleans family was celebrated for the great talent and the great misery of its members. Its wealth, honor, social position, and great talent seemed only a curse, and not a blessing. The Duchess of Orleans used to account for the misfortunes of her household by a fable which she used to repeat:

"A princess was born to a house. Several fairies were called to the birth. All came with gifts. One brought beauty, wisdom, wealth, position, talent. One of the sisters, not invited, came at last; she brought no gift; she could not undo what her sisters had done, nor recover one of the gifts donated. But she did what was worse. She mingled a curse with every blessing, and stirred up sorrow and shame with every gift."

A well-ordered, well-balanced Christian character can alone make a useful Christian. Zeal with knowledge, faith with work, alone will lead to a growth to the full stature of Christian manhood.

CCXXVI.

SERVANTS OF CORRUPTION.

WHILE they promise them liberty, they themselves are the servants of corruption: for whom a man is overcome, of the same is he brought in bondage. For if after they have escaped the pollutions of the world through the knowledge of the Lord and Saviour Jesus Christ, they are again entangled therein, and overcome, the latter end is worse with them than the beginning. And shall receive the reward of unrighteousness, *as* they that count it pleasure to riot in the daytime. Spots *they are* and blemishes, sporting themselves with their own deceivings while they feast with you. But every man is tempted, when he is drawn away of his own lust, and enticed. Then when lust hath conceived, it bringeth forth sin; and sin, when it is finished, bringeth forth death.

A MIDNIGHT INTERVIEW.

OUR Lord must have been one of the busiest of men. People trod one upon another to be near him. The roofs of dwellings were removed that the sick might be laid before him. His abode was hidden from men, and to be alone with God in prayer, he had to arise "a great while before day." In the solitude of the mountain he had his closet of prayer. And the watchman on Zion could have seen the Son of God, as he went up the Mount of Olives while it was yet dark, brushing the dew from the grass with his seamless robes, as he went up to pray.

The sanhedrim was the high court of the Jews. The eminent of the nation were members. The reception or rejection of Jesus, as the prophet of God, lay largely with this council. Outwardly, the sanhedrim gave voice against Jesus. It publicly proclaimed to the population that the prophet of Nazareth was a madman, a deceiver, an agent of Beelzebub, the prince of devils, and one to whom the faithful should not listen. Inwardly, the rulers knew that the man of Nazareth was a prophet of the Most High, for "no man could do the miracles that he did, except God was with him."

Amid the night-watches, there came to Jesus a member of the supreme council. He came with confession on his lip; he came as a disciple; he came to learn something of that wonderful system of grace that Jesus taught. He went out a changed man. He learned that he was a sinner; that no pride of birth or ancestry could save. Each for himself must be born of the Spirit. In the council, when Jesus had none to speak for him, he lifted up his voice. He made a public profession of his faith in the Son of God, when he stood by Joseph, as he begged the body of Pilate, and joined in the honors of embalming with the spices.

CCXXVII.

UNLEARNED AND UNSTABLE.

AND account *that* the longsuffering of our Lord *is* salvation; even as our beloved brother Paul also according to the wisdom given unto him hath written unto you; as also in *his* epistles, speaking in them of these things; in which are some things hard to be understood, which they that are unlearned and unstable wrest, as *they do* also the other Scriptures, unto their own destruction. He answered and said unto them, Because it is given unto you to know the mysteries of the kingdom of heaven, but to them it is not given. Let a man so account of us, as of the ministers of Christ, and stewards of the mysteries of God. But blessed *are* your eyes, for they see: and your ears, for they hear. For verily I say unto you, That many prophets and righteous *men* have desired to see *those things* which ye see, and have not seen *them;* and to hear *those things* which ye hear, and have not heard *them.*

OLD WHITEY AT THE CAPITAL.

WHEN General Taylor came to the White House, he brought in his train his war-horse, known as "Old Whitey." He had borne his master through all the perils of the Mexican war, and when the high honors of the nation were conferred on the general, the old war-steed was not forsaken. The horse was made to feel at home in the paddock on the east side of the White House. There the small chubby steed could be seen feeding in quietness, day after day. The horse was blind and lame, but his hearing was acute: he knew the voice of his master, and came daily at his call; but to all other voices he was deaf as an adder. Dull, and seemingly lifeless, he was indifferent to all surroundings. But the love of the military never died out in the old horse. Like the war-horse of the Bible, Old Whitey snuffed the battle afar. He could hear a fife and a drum blocks away. A band made him nearly wild. When the government troops moved from one part of the city to the other, it was the custom to pass the field and salute the old horse. All military visitors came up to the field and paid the horse a salute. A loud snort answered the bugle of flying-artillery. He knew every note, and put himself in position at every blast. He took the review in good earnest. Taking position, he accepted the salute; and when the grand rounds were marched, Old Whitey was in his glory; he would snort, elevate head and tail, dart round the enclosure, and seem wild with delight. Crowds filled the avenue to see the old war-horse recall the days of his stirring life. He who taught men by the ravens, the storks of the air, and birds who have nests in the trees, could give us a lesson of integrity and devotedness from the white horse at the capital.

CCXXVIII.

COMMON SALVATION.

BELOVED, when I gave all diligence to write unto you of the common salvation, it was needful for me to write unto you, and exhort *you* that ye should earnestly contend for the faith which was once delivered unto the saints. For mine eyes have seen thy salvation, which thou hast prepared before the face of all people; a light to lighten the Gentiles, and the glory of thy people Israel. In that day shall this song be sung in the land of Judah: We have a strong city; salvation will *God* appoint *for* walls and bulwarks. I will trust, and not be afraid; for the Lord JEHOVAH *is* my strength and *my* song; he also is become my salvation. Therefore with joy shall ye draw water out of the wells of salvation. For we are unto God a sweet savor of Christ, in them that are saved, and in them that perish: to the one *we are* the savor of death unto death; and to the other the savor of life unto life. And who *is* sufficient for these things?

JOHNSON AND THE WINE-CUP.

JOHNSON was not a model man in many things, but he had some traits worthy of commendation. He was a fast friend, and kind to the poor and needy. He had known want; he had been humbled by poverty, and in better days he had an open hand for those in want. The common drink of the day was wine and ale. Deep drinking, like deep gaming, was common. But Johnson passed the wine-cup by, and refused to touch the tankard. He was held back by no scruples. A teetotaller in practice, he was not so in theory. But Johnson or the wine-cup must be master. "Drink a *little* wine, Dr. Johnson," said a friend. "I can not," was the reply; "I can drink a great deal; I can drink none at all, but I can not drink a little." Such conduct was heroic. A drunkard's doom would have been Johnson's had he not conquered. But pure, high resolution saved him.

"I AM a Christian, sir," said a young lady at a fashionable watering-place. An evening's pastime had been agreed upon. A part was assigned to this young person. She thought the amusement not proper for one professing godliness. She declined to attend. To an earnest entreaty, she made the simple reply, "No, I am a Christian. The recreation, in my judgment, is not a consistent one, and I can not participate." The most worldly commended the courage of the young woman. "Cleanse thou me from secret faults; let them not have dominion over me." When to these petitions we join a heroic courage that will make us bold for the truth. then may we hope for victory.

CCXXIX.

ETERNAL CITY.

AND there shall be no night there, and they need no candle, neither light of the sun ; for the Lord God giveth them light: and they shall reign forever and ever. And I John saw the holy city, new Jerusalem, coming down from God out of heaven, prepared as a bride adorned for her husband. And I looked, and, lo, a Lamb stood on the mount Zion, and with him a hundred forty *and* four thousand, having his Father's name written in their foreheads. Great *is* the Lord, and greatly to be praised *in* the city of our God, in the mountain of his holiness. Beautiful for situation, the joy of the whole earth, *is* mount Zion, *on* the sides of the north, the city of the great King. For we that are in *this* tabernacle do groan, being burdened: not for that we would be unclothed, but clothed upon, that mortality might be swallowed up of life.

NIGHT AT A FARO-BANK.

WILBERFORCE, when a young man, was gay, worldly, and dissipated. He ran the whole career of the young men of the age. Gaming, that sweeps into the vortex of ruin so many youth, seized him. Night after night, he was found deeply immersed in play. His conscience often troubled him, but he rushed wildly on. One night, he was induced to keep the bank. Then his eyes were opened for the first time to the great horrors of play. He saw how men lost their thousands at a sitting; how young men, with prospects far brighter than his, went out of the room to suicide or dishonor. Amid the rattle of the dice, the call of the card-table, the glare of the room, the shout of despair, he vowed never to gamble again. With him, to make a resolution was to keep it. From that moment to the day of his death, Wilberforce kept the vow he made under such strange surroundings.

Changing his pastimes, he changed his associates. A new life opened to him; and not long after that night at the faro-bank, Wilberforce gave his heart to Jesus, and devoted his life to the service of the Lord.

How strangely God calls people to his service! The woman of Samaria, at the well-curb; Matthew, from the custom-house; Zaccheus, from the sycamore; Bartimeus, from the hillside; Whitfield, from an ale-house, and Wilberforce, from a faro-bank; "that he might make known the riches of his glory on the vessels of mercy, which he had afore prepared unto glory." "He that glorieth, let him glory in the Lord."

CCXXX.

GLORY TO THE LAMB.

LET us be glad and rejoice, and give honor to him: for the marriage of the Lamb is come, and his wife hath made herself ready. And to her was granted that she should be arrayed in fine linen, clean and white: for the fine linen is the righteousness of saints. And he saith unto me, Write, Blessed *are* they which are called unto the marriage supper of the Lamb. And he saith unto me, These are the true sayings of God. Saying with a loud voice, Worthy is the Lamb that was slain to receive power, and riches, and wisdom, and strength, and honor, and glory, and blessing. And every creature which is in heaven, and on the earth, and under the earth, and such as are in the sea, and all that are in them, heard I saying, Blessing, and honor, and glory, and power, *be* unto him that sitteth upon the throne, and unto the Lamb forever and ever.

LOYOLA'S DISCIPLINE.

"The children of the world are wiser in their generation than the children of light." To the Church of Rome has been accorded such a wisdom in a marvelous degree. That Church has a place for all workers. She has workers for all places. The talent in one place that is needed in another, is at once moved to the desired position. The grave and the gay, the young and the old, the recluse and the worldly, the ascetic and the scientist, have a use in the Roman communion. One generation enters into the labors of the past, and does work that is to run on to coming ages.

The Army of Jesus, as the Jesuits are called, are a consummate organization. The cardinal virtue is obedience. The order owe allegiance only to its head. It knows no sovereign but the pope. No family or national tie can interfere with the obligation the members of the order owe to the chief. The bishop of each diocese can say whether or not a society shall work in his jurisdiction. But once admitted, the bishop has no control over the manner in which the Jesuit chief shall do his work.

Loyola, the founder, was a cavalier. He received wounds that incapacitated him for gay and festive life, and he turned his attention to the church. He obtained such command over his appetites and passions that he was absolutely superior to his nature. To show a libertine that he could reform, Loyola stood for two hours in a pond of frozen mud, with the water up to his chin, on a bitter cold day. From a despised company of three persons, over and over rejected by the pope, the order swelled to gigantic proportions, and became the terror of kings. Not a Catholic nation has existed that has not been compelled to banish the Jesuits.

CCXXXI.

RAIN ON MOWN GRASS.

HE shall come down like rain upon the mown grass: as showers *that* water the earth. For I will pour water upon him that is thirsty, and floods upon the dry ground: I will pour my Spirit upon thy seed, and my blessing upon thine offspring: and they shall spring up *as* among the grass, as willows by the watercourses. Repent ye therefore, and be converted, that your sins may be blotted out, when the times of refreshing shall come from the presence of the Lord. Then they that gladly received his word were baptized: and the same day there were added *unto them* about three thousand souls. And they continued steadfastly in the apostles' doctrine and fellowship, and in breaking of bread, and in prayers. And fear came upon every soul: and many wonders and signs were done by the apostles. But in the last days it shall come to pass, *that* the mountain of the house of the LORD shall be established in the top of the mountains, and it shall be exalted above the hills; and the people shall flow unto it.

ASTOR AND THE LINDEN-TREE.

Few men earned their fortune more really than did John Jacob Astor. He swelled-his fortune to huge dimensions by extraordinary diligence and thrift; but the fortune itself was gathered by patient toil and hardy endurance. His habits were simple; his style of life plain. Day and night he was at his post. With his own hands he toiled, with his own eyes he oversaw his business. He bought and sold on his own judgment, and that seldom led him astray. He was in no haste to be rich. His word at the start was as good as his bond. His early domestic attachments kept him from expensive and ruinous associates. No man owed more to his wife than did the elder Astor. Her industry, her frugality, her sound judgment, more than once stood her husband in good stead. "The heart of her husband safely trusted in her. She did him good, and not evil, all the days of her life." To a resolution made in the fatherland, Mr. Astor owed much of his success. He resolved to emigrate to America, and seek his fortune in a foreign clime. He had few worldly possessions. These were tied up in a bundle, and hung on a stick across the shoulder. He trod on foot from his home to the seaport from which he was to sail. As he crossed the boundary of his province, he paused under a linden-tree, and formed three resolutions: He would be industrious; he would not drink; he would never gamble. These he kept to his death. They were supplemented by others which keep company with such resolutions, as mercy and peace embrace each other. Kept in the way of truth and rectitude, his step was strong and his way upward.

CCXXXII.

TO THE CHURCHES.

I AM Alpha and Omega, the first and the last: and, What thou seest, write in a book, and send *it* unto the seven churches which are in Asia; unto Ephesus, and unto Smyrna, and unto Pergamos, and unto Thyatira, and unto Sardis, and unto Philadelphia, and unto Laodicea. Fear none of those things which thou shalt suffer: behold, the devil shall cast *some* of you into prison, that ye may be tried; and ye shall have tribulation ten days: be thou faithful unto death, and I will give thee a crown of life. I know thy works, and where thou dwellest, *even* where Satan's seat *is:* and thou holdest fast my name, and hast not denied my faith, even in those days wherein Antipas *was* my faithful martyr, who was slain among you where Satan dwelleth. Thou hast a few names even in Sardis which have not defiled their garments; and they shall walk with me in white: for they are worthy.

COMFORTED OF GOD.

A MARVELOUS passage is that: "That we may be able to comfort them which are in any trouble, by the comfort wherewith we ourselves are comforted of God." Our High Priest is merciful and compassionate, because he hath borne our griefs, and been both afflicted and comforted of God. A church called a pastor. He was talented and eloquent. He seemed to lack tenderness. At the sick-bed, and at a funeral, he seemed to lack heart. What he said was well enough, but he had no sympathy. This was accounted for in various ways. Some thought he was too intellectual to be touched with the common woes of life; others said his health was too robust; while not a few thought that the furnace of affliction would alone melt his unsympathizing heart. Having never been comforted of God in his sorrows, he could not "comfort others in any trouble." But his time came at last. Sorrows, that "come not in single spies, but in battalions," crossed his threshold. A babe was born, and died in a day. His poor feeble wife seemed to be dying. His only child lay in convulsions. No help was at hand. The pastor was mute and submissive. His child lay in his arms, and expired in a fit. He closed its eyes, and laid it beside its mother. The storm passed, and left a wreck behind. From that hour, the pastor was a changed man. He was tender, sympathetic, and considerate. He was the comforter of the afflicted, for he himself had been comforted of God. His mission seemed to lie among the poor little children of want and sorrow. It was his delight to point to Jesus, as the merciful and compassionate, who can have compassion. "For that He himself also is compassed with infirmity."

CCXXXIII.

COLD OR HOT.

I KNOW thy works, and charity, and service, and faith, and thy patience, and thy works; and the last *to be* more than the first. I counsel thee to buy of me gold tried in the fire, that thou mayest be rich; and white raiment, that thou mayest be clothed, and *that* the shame of thy nakedness do not appear, and anoint thine eyes with eyesalve, that thou mayest see. And to the angel of the church in Philadelphia write: These things saith he that is holy, he that is true, he that hath the key of David, he that openeth, and no man shutteth; and shutteth, and no man openeth. I know thy works, that thou art neither cold nor hot: I would thou wert cold or hot.

BRAMIN AND MICROSCOPE.

"He that increaseth knowledge, increaseth sorrow." So men find it in all ages. One of our missionaries took with him to his field of labor a microscope. He thought it would aid him in his work. The Bramins are not allowed to eat or drink any thing that has life in it. Could the missionary show the heathen that it was impossible to keep the law of his religion, he would turn to the true God. The water used for religious as well as for domestic uses was impure. To show this would bring the worshipers to the cross. One day, the missionary invited a Bramin to a conference. He took some pure water ; put it under the glass ; asked the teacher to look. Horror of horrors! the water was alive ; it was full of unclean beasts and reptiles. He was filled with consternation. "May I see that curious instrument?" It was handed to him. "Are there more in this country?" "No; this is all." In a moment, the Bramin dashed the microscope on to a stone, and it scattered in a hundred pieces. "You have moved both my soul and my peace of mind. I shall never know joy any more; but you shall not harm my people. They will not believe what you say. They will cleave to their religion, and die in the comfort that offers." And he turned, and went his way. He had increased knowledge, and, added to that, profound sorrow. Blessed are those that secure that wisdom that consists in the fear of the Lord! His merchandise is better than the merchandise of silver, and his gain than fine gold.

CCXXXIV.

SOUNDED OUT THE WORD OF THE LORD.

FOR from you sounded out the word of the Lord not only in Macedonia and Achaia, but also in every place your faith to God-ward is spread abroad; so that we need not to speak any thing. Therefore, saith he unto them, The harvest truly *is* great, but the laborers *are* few: pray ye therefore the Lord of the harvest, that he would send forth laborers into his harvest. The Spirit of the Lord *is* upon me, because he hath anointed me to preach the gospel to the poor; he hath sent me to heal the broken-hearted, to preach deliverance to the captives, and recovering of sight to the blind, to set at liberty them that are bruised, to preach the acceptable year of the Lord.

HAMILTON AND DR. MASON.

ALEXANDER HAMILTON and Dr. John Mason were fast friends. In times that tried men's souls, these eminent men took counsel together. They often went to the house of God in company. Dark and stormy were some of those days. The friends of freedom were not agreed. At one time, anarchy seemed probable, and even Washington trembled for the ark of freedom. Hamilton was called to the seat of government. It was not an easy thing to frame a constitution that should conciliate all sections and harmonize rival factions. North and South were disunited. Radical men and conservative men both wanted the government, and there were factions even in the Cabinet and under the eye of Washington, nor did the cabals spare the chief himself. One day, Dr. Mason was walking down Broadway. He met General Hamilton, fresh from his labors in behalf of the Federal Constitution. "Have you read the new constitution?" said General Hamilton to the preacher. "I have." "And how do you like it?" "Why, general, you have left God wholly out of it." "So we have! Well, we forgot it, and I am sorry." And so nations forget God? Sorrow and despair await all such. God's word reads: "The wicked shall be turned into hell, and all the nations that forget God." So perished the Egyptians; so fell Sodom and Gomorrah: for their sins were "pride, fullness of bread, and abundance of idleness." So perished Corah; so Keshon was swept away; Sisera and his hosts. Nebuchadnezzar found to his cost that the Most High ruled among the nations. And when "Herod, Pontius Pilate, Caiaphas, and the Jews" arrayed themselves against the child Jesus, he that sitteth in the heavens laughed. The Lord had them in derision.

CCXXXV.

CONTRARY TO ALL MEN.

WHO both killed the Lord Jesus, and their own prophets, and have persecuted us; and they please not God, and are contrary to all men: and some believed the things which were spoken, and some believed not. That ye may walk honestly toward them that are without, and *that* ye may have lack of nothing. And that we may be delivered from unreasonable and wicked men: for all *men* have not faith. For John came neither eating nor drinking, and they say, He hath a devil. The Son of man came eating and drinking, and they say, Behold a man gluttonous, and a winebibber, a friend of publicans and sinners. But wisdom is justified of her children. And when they found them not, they drew Jason and certain brethren unto the rulers of the city, crying, These that have turned the world upside down are come hither also.

"WE HAVE MET THE ENEMY."

All nations have their banners. Many have mottoes, battle-cries, watchwords, and symbols that are worth a thousand men. It was so in the time of Deborah, and with these she rallied a host in a time of national apathy, when among ten thousand there was not one spear or shield. In the war of 1812, the Americans had no navy. The government was pitted against the proudest and ablest nation, whose sails whitened all seas, and the keel of whose commerce fretted the waters of all climes. The little navy grew with the exigencies of the hour. When the war broke out, the oaks were growing in the forests; these were cut down, hewn into ship-timber, and this constructed into vessels of war to defend the American flag.

On the shores of the great lakes, Commodore Perry superintended the construction of a fleet. He put that fleet in motion, and did valiant service. In a severe battle, he was victorious. He sent the result to the United States Government in a trite motto, that was afterward made a symbol of victory—"We have met the enemy, and he is ours."

St. Paul seems to have somewhat such an idea when, making an inventory of the Christian inheritance, he says to the believer, "Death is yours." "O death, where is thy sting? "O grave, where is thy victory?" "Thanks be unto God who giveth us the victory." The believer is no longer under bondage to the fear of death; to the Christian he is a conquered foe. As he crosses the flood he shouts, "We have met the enemy; he is ours. Thanks be to God!"

CCXXXVI.

HONEST TOIL.

IN the sweat of thy face shalt thou eat bread, till thou return unto the ground; for out of it wast thou taken: for dust thou *art*, and unto dust shalt thou return. And that ye study to be quiet, and to do your own business, and to work with your own hands, as we commanded you; that ye may walk honestly toward them that are without, and *that* ye may have lack of nothing. Then I looked on all the works that my hands had wrought, and on the labor that I had labored to do: and, behold, all *was* vanity and vexation of spirit, and *there was* no profit under the sun. Wherefore we labor, that, whether present or absent, we may be accepted of him. For we must all appear before the judgment-seat of Christ.

MEN OF ISSACHAR.

In the day of battle, all Israel was called to the fight. Israel had no standing army. The ark of God was in the keeping of the nation. When enemies rallied, and valiant men smote the people sore, all the tribes and all the families contributed men and arms to do good service in the national cause.

In the time of general calamity, the nation was called upon to send up valiant men for the battle. The nation responded nobly; some tribes sent forth a thousand men; some sent forth ten thousand. "From day to day, there came to the king men of might to help him, until it was a great host, like the host of God." But the children of Issachar were a feeble flock. About two hundred was the contribution. But this contribution was more than all Israel. These two hundred were the brains of the army. They made the war council of the king. Their rank and service is thus worded: "And of the children of Issachar, which were men that had understanding of the times, to know what Israel ought to do: the heads of them were two hundred, and all their brethren were at their commandment."

God can save by many or by few. The three hundred of Gideon's band are better than ten thousand, when God leads. The word of Moses is superior to the forces of Pharaoh—"two can chase a thousand, and two put ten thousand to flight." The sling-stone of David is worth all the armor of Goliath. The peasant King who rides into Jerusalem on the foal of an ass can make the kings of the earth quail, and break nations to pieces as a potter's vessel is broken.

CCXXXVII.

MYSTERY OF INIQUITY.

FOR the mystery of iniquity doth already work: only he who now letteth *will let*, until he be taken out of the way. And then shall that Wicked be revealed, whom the Lord shall consume with the spirit of his mouth, and shall destroy with the brightness of his coming. Let no man deceive you by any means: for *that day shall not come*, except there come a falling away first, and that man of sin be revealed, the son of perdition; who opposeth and exalteth himself above all that is called God, or that is worshiped; so that he as God sitteth in the temple of God, showing himself that he is God. And they cast dust on their heads, and cried, weeping and wailing, saying, Alas, alas, that great city, wherein were made rich all that had ships in the sea by reason of her costliness! for in one hour is she made desolate.

DRUNKARD'S DOOM.

A MAN came into the meeting one night. He was the mere wreck of a man. Satan had been a hard master. He had written his name, as owner, on all the lineaments of the man's face. Young in years, he was prematurely aged. "I want to sign the pledge; I do not want a drunkard's doom." "What do you know about a drunkard's doom?" said the missionary. The man repeated, "No drunkard can inherit the kingdom of God." "Where did you learn that; have you been in church lately?" "No, I have not been inside a church for years. No one has spoken to me. I have seen no pastor, nor has any one talked to me about my soul. I was not always what you see me. I had a happy childhood. The fear of God was in my mother's household. I studied the Bible at my mother's knee. Among the fears of my sainted mother was that I should love the wine-cup. She grouped the texts, spoke of the sin of drunkenness, and I committed them to memory. Strange that the vice she feared the most—the one she most faithfully warned me against—should be the vice that wound its subtle links about me! But so it was. I married, and had a home. But my love of drink was a curse amid all my home blessings. My wife suffered all but death, and then left me. I went from bad to worse. But in all my disgrace, never for one moment did I forget the text, 'No drunkard shall inherit the kingdom of God.' It flamed on the walls of my bed-room; it flared over the doorway of my drinking-saloon; it sounded in my ears at midnight. I have come here to be free from it. Give me the pledge! give me your prayers! I want to *escape a drunkard's doom.*"

CCXXXVIII.

DISORDERLY WALKING.

FOR we hear that there are some which walk among you disorderly, working not at all, but are busy-bodies. For yourselves know how ye ought to follow us: for we behaved not ourselves disorderly among you; neither did we eat any man's bread for nought; but wrought with labor and travail night and day, that we might not be chargeable to any of you. Give them according to their deeds, and according to the wickedness of their endeavors: give them after the work of their hands; render to them their desert. Because they regard not the works of the LORD, nor the operation of his hands, he shall destroy them, and not build them up. And the very God of peace sanctify you wholly; and *I pray God* your whole spirit and soul and body be preserved blameless unto the coming of our Lord Jesus Christ.

ALL FOR JESUS.

SOME cases seem too hard for the Lord. "Can God work miracles in these days?" men ask; "can the Ethiopian change his skin, or the leopard his spots?" If not, then some sinners can not come to God. But there is balm in Gilead. The publican was pardoned. The children's bread has been cast to dogs. Many Magdalens can sit at Jesus' feet. The woman that is a sinner can break the box of fragrant ointment on the feet of the Son of God. The woman of Samaria can lead a whole city to exclaim, "We know this is indeed the Christ, the Saviour of the world!" The blasphemer and the thief, who on the cross admitted that he was justly condemned, could hear the sentence of pardon sounding out in the words, "To-day thou shalt be with me in paradise."

The same grace to-day abounds toward sinners. In the city of New-York lived a woman noted for her bad deeds. Her house was one of the most noted of those that "lead to hell, going down to the chambers of death." Her dwelling was a palace; its sumptuous adornments were on the lips of hundreds. The young and the fair came into her net, and the attraction of the place was equaled by few others. It became known that the woman proposed to throw up her vile trade. The place, its repute and garniture had a commercial value. Many sought the lease. The establishment would have commanded a great sum. All flattering offers were declined. The house was let for business, with a contract that it should never be let for lodging. The woman called her girls together; begged them to abandon their life; agreed to support them six months and see they did not want. She had been called by the Saviour, and left all and followed him.

CCXXXIX.

SWEET WATER AND BITTER.

DOTH a fountain send forth at the same place sweet *water* and bitter? Can the fig tree, my brethren, bear olive berries? either a vine, figs? so *can* no fountain both yield salt water and fresh. Out of the same mouth proceedeth blessing and cursing. My brethren, these things ought not so to be. But if ye have bitter envying and strife in your hearts, glory not, and lie not against the truth. Faithful *are* the wounds of a friend; but the kisses of an enemy *are* deceitful. He that justifieth the wicked, and he that condemneth the just, even they both *are* abomination to the Lord. Woe unto them that call evil good, and good evil; that put darkness for light, and light for darkness; that put bitter for sweet, and sweet for bitter! Woe unto *them that are* wise in their own eyes, and prudent in their own sight! Woe unto *them that are* mighty to drink wine, and men of strength to mingle strong drink.

OVER THE FALLS.

MEN run into temporal temptation as they run into moral. Men are rash in the things of this life, as they are in things that pertain to their eternal peace. "Lead us not into temptation," is a prayer needed for the body as for the soul. One day, a crowd of men lined the shores of the Niagara River, above the falls. Each train of cars that arrived came loaded down with hundreds of the curious and the sympathetic, and these swelled the great company. The telegraph thrilled the country with the news, "A man going over the falls! a man going over the falls!" And to see the terrible sight, men and women crowded into the town. Ten thousand eyes rested on the little rocky island in the centre of the great cataract. Far above the falls, amid the rapids, was a ferry. Daring men crossed over, but strong arms, a full breath, and a steady nerve were needful for a safe passage, always perilous. Many crossed in safety. One morning, a young man, from mere bravado or foolhardiness, resolved to tempt the terrible danger. Brave old boatmen warned him that the feat was full of peril. The current was strong and treacherous. Once on the wave, he would have to row for life, and few could tell which way the boat would head. But all remonstrance was vain. He launched his boat, and in a moment the powerful current bore him on to the falls. The boat struck on the little island, and went to pieces. The man clung to the rocks and shouted for help. But no help came. For twenty-four hours, he hung on for life. Hundreds in the crowd would have risked all to save him. One princely man offered five thousand dollars to any one who would go to his rescue. Gradually his strength yielded. At last, his hold gave way. The mighty current bore him on swiftly to ruin. In the sight of thousands, he leaped into the air, shouted a death-cry, and passed away forever.

CCXL.

NOTHING WAVERING.

BUT let him ask in faith, nothing wavering. For he that wavereth is like a wave of the sea driven with the wind and tossed. For in many things we offend all. If any man offend not in word, the same *is* a perfect man, *and* able also to bridle the whole body. If any of you lack wisdom, let him ask of God, that giveth to all *men* liberally, and upbraideth not; and it shall be given him. Be not carried about with divers and strange doctrines: for *it is* a good thing that the heart be established with grace; not with meats, which have not profited them that have been occupied therein. Cast not away therefore your confidence, which hath great recompense of reward. For ye have need of patience, that, after ye have done the will of God, ye might receive the promise. Wherefore we receiving a kingdom which can not be moved, let us have grace, whereby we may serve God acceptably with reverence and godly fear.

EPHESIAN BOOKS.

What men want of religion who do not believe it and are not sincere in their love to Christ, is a marvel. Even in Moses' time, when men suffered affliction for the faith of God, there were false prophets among the people. Under the eye of the Saviour, there were wolves in sheep's clothing. Men made long prayers while they devoured widows' houses. In the church of the apostles, there was a Judas, a Simon Magus, and an Ananias. But when men test these sincerely, by martyrdom, imprisonment, or the loss of their worldly goods, there is little doubt that they are true witnesses for the Lord. The early disciples sold their possessions, and laid the price at the apostles' feet, to relieve their poor brethren. This is one of the fruits of the outpouring of the Spirit at the day of Pentecost. That men were possessed of devils in the time of the apostles, no one can doubt who believes the Bible. The apostles boasted that "even spirits were subject to them," in the name of the Lord. Men attempted to "call over people possessed" the name of the Lord. The maddened spirits leaped on the pretenders, who "fled from their presence naked and wounded." Among the enemies of the Gospel were men eminent in the magic art. These, like Jannes and Jambres, before Moses, withstood the truth. Men were learned in the black art, and led captive the people. But the word of God was not bound. It was quick and prompt, and valiant in its war with spiritual wickedness in high places. It assailed the high places of Satan; held captive his chief allies. "Many of them which used curious arts, believed and confessed. They brought their books together, and burned them before all men; and they counted the price of them, and found it fifty thousand pieces of silver. So mightily grew the word of God and prevailed."

CCXLI.

UNRULY MEMBER.

BEHOLD, we put bits in the horses' mouths, that they may obey us; and we turn about their whole body. Behold also the ships, which though *they be* so great, and *are* driven of fierce winds, yet are they turned about with a very small helm, whithersoever the governor listeth. Even so the tongue is a little member, and boasteth great things. Behold, how great a matter a little fire kindleth! And the tongue *is* a fire, a world of iniquity: so is the tongue among our members, that it defileth the whole body, and setteth on fire the course of nature; and it is set on fire of hell. For this shall every one that is godly pray unto thee in a time when thou mayest be found: surely in the floods of great waters they shall not come nigh unto him. Thou *art* my hiding place; thou shalt preserve me from trouble; thou shalt compass me about with songs of deliverance. Selah.

PRAYER AND A LAWSUIT.

MEN read the story of Peter's deliverance from prison in answer to the prayer of the faithful, and profess to believe it. Yet they stagger and stumble at answers to prayer which occur in our own times, and receive with distrust those instances of marvelous deliverance which God vouchsafes to his people in this present hour. A short time since, a young lawyer appeared in Fulton-street meeting. He told a simple, touching story of great faith and great deliverance. He was counsel for a young man incarcerated in a Jersey prison. The young lawyer said, "My heart died within me when I saw the array of counsel read the proof on which the prosecution relied, and the slender defense I could put forth. Believing in prayer, and as I seemed to have no other refuge, I came to this meeting, and laid the case of the poor prisoner before you. The burden of my prayer was that God would appear for his deliverance, and open a way for his escape, that, if innocent, it might be made manifest, and he be saved from the brand of a felon, and an honored home be saved from disgrace. I well remembered how you prayed; how fervent, how affectionate, and how effectual it seemed to me. The corporation was represented by able legal talent. It filled the court-room with prominent citizens, and brought its wealth and social influence to bear against the young man at the bar. On my conscience, I had to say that if I was on that jury, on that proof I should have to bring in the verdict of guilty. I made a very short opening, and then placed my client on the stand. He told a straightforward, simple, touching story. The cross-examination failed to shake his story in the least. The judge charged strongly against the prisoner, and on the proof could do nothing else. As the jury drifted out, the lawyers said, 'Poor fellow! he is in for it; nothing can save him from State prison.' In a few moments, the jury returned, and astonished every body by rendering a verdict—'Not guilty!' The prisoner wept like a child. 'How could you bring in such a verdict in the face of such testimony?' said a man to one of the jurors. 'I can not tell, except that his simple story carried us all with him.'"

CCXLII.

DOUBLE-MINDED.

A DOUBLE-MINDED man *is* unstable in all his ways. The spirit of man *is* the candle of the Lord, searching all the inward parts of the belly. The sacrifice of the wicked *is* abomination: how much more, *when* he bringeth it with a wicked mind? Hearken, my beloved brethren, Hath not God chosen the poor of this world rich in faith, and heirs of the kingdom which he hath promised to them that love him? But ye have despised the poor. Do not rich men oppress you, and draw you before the judgment seats? Again, a new commandment I write unto you, which thing is true in him and in you: because the darkness is past, and the true light now shineth. He that saith he is in the light, and hateth his brother, is in darkness even until now. And every man that hath this hope in him purifieth himself, even as he is pure. Whosoever committeth sin transgresseth also the law: for sin is the transgression of the law.

TUFTED SAND-BANK.

Out in the ocean, sixty miles from land, is a tufted sand-bank. Nantucket is a quaint old place; men who visit it seem to be thrown back at least fifty years. Once it was a place of great trade. There dwelt merchants whose names were good on the Thames and among the dikes of Holland; sea-captains famous for voyages that consumed four or five years had here their homes. The gigantic whale-fishing was nearly monopolized by the people of Nantucket. It has been long asserted that the women of the island have been among the most intelligent females of the land. While the husbands and fathers, the brothers and the lovers were pursuing their gigantic game in the Pacific, the women tarried by the stuff, educated the children, took care of the household, and carried on a correspondence with all parts of the globe. In one of the plain, unpretending houses on the island dwelt a man with his wife and daughter. He was fond of astronomy, and trained up his daughter to love the same pursuit. She was eminently domestic, and took the care of the house from the shoulders of an infirm mother. In the daytime, she swept the house and made it bright and clean. At night, she swept the heavens and aided her father in his studies. She was a favorite with the boys and girls of the town; she mended their whips, their tops, and other toys; she kept an arsenal to repair damages that childhood is heir to. The king of Denmark promised a gold medal to any one who would discover a telescopic comet. Our fair friend entered the contest for the prize. Kings and nobles were her competitors, but she bore off the palm.

CCXLIII.

WITHOUT THE CAMP.

WHEREFORE Jesus also, that he might sanctify the people with his own blood, suffered without the gate. Let us go forth therefore unto him without the camp, bearing his reproach. Who through faith subdued kingdoms, wrought righteousness, obtained promises, stopped the mouths of lions, quenched the violence of fire, escaped the edge of the sword, out of weakness were made strong, waxed valiant in fight, turned to flight the armies of the aliens. For I know that this shall turn to my salvation through your prayer, and the supply of the Spirit of Jesus Christ, according to my earnest expectation and *my* hope, that in nothing I shall be ashamed, but *that* with all boldness, as always, *so* now also Christ shall be magnified in my body, whether *it be* by life, or by death. For here have we no continuing city, but we seek one to come. By him therefore let us offer the sacrifice of praise to God continually, that is, the fruit of *our* lips, giving thanks to his name.

AFTER MANY DAYS.

DURING our civil war, a regiment was quartered at Harlem. The colonel was a very smart, energetic man, but cared little for religion or religious things. Late on Saturday, he received orders to move his column early on Monday toward the Potomac. The suddenness of the order affected him. He was impressed with the idea that he should never return. Contrary to his usual custom, he thought he would visit, with his friends, the house of the Lord on Sunday morning. A very earnest sermon was preached by a stranger, and the colonel was visibly affected. He bade farewell to his friends the next morning, and, like a patriot, met his duty promptly and cheerfully. The sermon he heard followed him to his camp. Amid the stirring scenes of a soldier's life, he found peace in believing. He enlisted under the banner of the Prince of Peace, and resolved to be a true soldier to his new Captain.

Again an order reached him on Saturday. He was ordered to the front. A battle was imminent, and he would probably have to lead his column into the strife. He was anxious to make a profession of religion. He wanted to bear public testimony to the loving-kindness of the Saviour who had been so merciful to him. The only minister in the neighborhood was a poor colored preacher who had been a slave. His church was small and poor, and made up principally of emancipated bondmen and bondwomen. He sought out the preacher, and made known his desire to profess Christ before he went into battle. The preacher told him that he was to baptize two colored women the next day. If the colonel would be at the church that night, and relate his experience, he might join the little company the next day at the river-side. He joyfully accepted the proposal. In the presence of a dozen or more of the humblest of the Lord's people, he gave the reason of the hope that was in him, and was baptized in the Potomac. Amid the noise and confusion and bustle of the preparation for the march, the colonel sat down and related his profession of faith in Christ, and sent it in a letter to a Christian friend in New-York. He went into the conflict the next morning, and never came out. He died a Christian soldier, to be more than conqueror through Him that loved him.

CCXLIV.

"LET HER DRIVE."

AND when the ship was caught, and could not bear up into the wind, we let *her* drive. And the third *day* we cast out with our own hands the tackling of the ship. And when neither sun nor stars in many days appeared, and no small tempest lay on *us*, all hope that we should be saved was then taken away. But Peter said unto him, Thy money perish with thee, because thou hast thought that the gift of God may be purchased with money. Thou hast neither part nor lot in this matter: for thy heart is not right in the sight of God. Repent therefore of this thy wickedness, and pray God, if perhaps the thought of thine heart may be forgiven thee. For I perceive that thou art in the gall of bitterness, and *in* the bond of iniquity. As long as it lieth desolate it shall rest; because it did not rest in your Sabbaths, when ye dwelt upon it. And upon them that are left *alive* of you I will send a faintness into their hearts in the lands of their enemies; and the sound of a shaken leaf shall chase them; and they shall flee, as fleeing from a sword; and they shall fall when none pursueth. Therefore I will be unto them as a lion: as a leopard by the way will I observe *them:* I will meet them as a bear *that is* bereaved *of her whelps,* and will rend the caul of their heart, and there will I devour them like a lion: the wild beast shall tear them.

NUTS AND RAISINS.

THE habits of youth cling to a man, even in the sere and yellow leaf of autumn. This fact is recognized in the Bible. "Remember now thy Creator in the days of thy youth, before *the evil days come.*" "Train up a child in the way he should go, and *when he is old* he will not depart from it." Men who swore in youth—broke the habit in manhood—have returned to it in old age. Reformed men, who, in youth, drank deep, have gone down to a drunkard's grave and doom by the force of an early habit. English statesmen, who brought with them from beyond the Tweed a brogue, cured it by culture, spoke pure English in manhood, and in advanced years went back to the old custom.

A boy is the type of a man. Education may do much; grace may do much. But the marked characteristics of boyhood come out in manhood. A fair boy, a manly boy, or a mean, tricky, white-livered boy, usually carry those traits through life.

A business man was noted for his parsimony. He was mean in small things and in large, in high things and in low. The half cent always turned to his side of the bargain. But it was noted that this trait cost him more than it brought. One day, a friend was in conversation with another person. The name of this man was mentioned. "Do you know him?" "Know him! I went to school with him." "What kind of a boy was he?" "He was one of the meanest fellows in town. He used to sneak behind the school-house to eat his nuts and raisins, so as not to give the fellows any." As was the boy, so was the man. "Thy servant has served the Lord from his YOUTH."

CCXLV.

NEED OF PATIENCE.

FOR ye have need of patience, that, after ye have done the will of God, ye might receive the promise. Knowing *this*, that the trying of your faith worketh patience. But let patience have *her* perfect work, that ye may be perfect and entire, wanting nothing. Take, my brethren, the prophets, who have spoken in the name of the Lord, for an example of suffering affliction, and of patience. Behold, we count them happy which endure. Ye have heard of the patience of Job, and have seen the end of the Lord; that the Lord is very pitiful, and of tender mercy. Be patient therefore, brethren, unto the coming of the Lord. Behold, the husbandman waiteth for the precious fruit of the earth, and hath long patience for it, until he receive the early and latter rain. But call to remembrance the former days, in which, after ye were illuminated, ye endured a great fight of afflictions; partly, whilst ye were made a gazing-stock both by reproaches and afflictions; and partly, whilst ye became companions of them that were so used. For ye had compassion of me in my bonds, and took joyfully the spoiling of your goods, knowing in yourselves that ye have in heaven a better and an enduring substance. Cast not away therefore your confidence, which hath great recompense of reward.

PROFANE AT SIXTY.

In one of our churches was a man in whose mouth guile was never found. He was especially pure in utterances and guarded in his remarks. He seemed to have put a guard on his mouth, lest he should sin with his tongue.

He was taken down with a brain-fever. In the midst of his delirium, he used the most awful profanity that could be conceived. He swore terribly and constantly. His oaths were simply blasphemies. His family, his pastor, and his brethren of the church were both astounded and ashamed. Was the good brother a life-long hypocrite? Were his guarded utterances a pretense? Under the guise of fervent piety, was he a blasphemer? The disease passed away, and the sick man came forth and was seen in his accustomed places. He was the same quiet, pure-spoken, and cautious man that he was before.

At length, some of his friends spoke to him about his sickness; they told him how troubled they had been on account of his profanity. The poor man was overwhelmed with shame and sorrow. "Alas! my brethren, alas! what has sin done for me! I was an ungodly boy; I passed my youth in folly and dissipation; my besetting sin was profanity; I swore more than all my associates. It is now nearly forty years since I spake an oath or uttered a profane word. I supposed that the habit was gone from me; but behold, the stain of sin, the leprosy is still in my blood. Grace has done great things for me, it has kept me back from presumptuous sins. But it has not, it seems, cleansed me from secret faults. The tiger is chained, but he is alive. Oh! had I given my youth to Jesus, and prayed when I was swearing, this terrible despair would not have come on me."

CCXLVI.

STONE OF STUMBLING.

UNTO you therefore which believe *he is* precious: but unto them which be disobedient, the stone which the builders disallowed, the same is made the head of the corner, and a stone of stumbling, and a rock of offense, *even to them* which stumble at the word, being disobedient: whereunto also they were appointed. Wherefore lay apart all filthiness and superfluity of naughtiness, and receive with meekness the engrafted word, which is able to save your souls. But be ye doers of the word, and not hearers only, deceiving your own selves. For if any be a hearer of the word, and not a doer, he is like unto a man beholding his natural face in a glass: for he beholdeth himself, and goeth his way, and straightway forgetteth what manner of man he was. But the wisdom that is from above is first pure, then peaceable, gentle, *and* easy to be entreated, full of mercy and good fruits, without partiality, and without hypocrisy.

WATERS OF BETHLEHEM.

THE battle waxed hot. The Philistines and their mighty men of war held Bethlehem for a garrison. Now David was in the cave of Adullam. Then came to him three of the thirty chiefs in the harvest-time, and dwelt with David. And David longed, and cried, "Oh! that one would me give drink of the water of the well of Bethlehem which is by the gate!" "And the three mighty men brake through the host of the Philistines, and drew water out of the well of Bethlehem that was by the gate, and took it, and brought it to David; nevertheless he would not drink thereof, but poured it out before the Lord."

This little incident is in the midst of the account of the valiant men who aided David in setting up his kingdom, by whose valor the kingdom of Saul grew weaker, and the house of David grew stronger and stronger. To their bravery and heroism David owed his success. When the three mighty men broke through the hosts of Philistines, and took their lives in their hands, and bore the water to their chief, David would not use it, much as he longed for it. It was the price of blood. The valiant men jeopardized their lives to obtain it. It was too precious for men to drink; so David poured it out as an offering to the Lord.

Then there was the son of Jehodiah, the son of a valiant man of Kabdiel. He went down into a pit, and slew a lion when he was fierce from confinement and hunger. He did this in the time of "snow." Single-handed men fought against thousands, and God gave the victory. Such valiant men the Church always needs.

CCXLVII.

GOOD LIKE A MEDICINE.

A MERRY heart doeth good *like* a medicine: but a broken spirit drieth the bones. A merry heart maketh a cheerful countenance: but by sorrow of the heart the spirit is broken. All the days of the afflicted *are* evil: but he that is of a merry heart *hath* a continual feast. Go thy way, eat thy bread with joy, and drink thy wine with a merry heart; for God now accepteth thy works. I said in mine heart, Go to now, I will prove thee with mirth; therefore enjoy pleasure: and, behold, this also *is* vanity. I said of laughter, *It is* mad: and of mirth, What doeth it? Even in laughter the heart is sorrowful; and the end of that mirth *is* heaviness.

JOINT OF MEAT.

THE character of men is known by small things. Cuvier, the great naturalist, could make up an animal out of a single bone. If he found one thing, he would find another and another. Each bone would fit, and so the whole animal world be produced. Cuvier could tell the latitude in which the animal lived, its habits, its food, and could classify it. He did this on the principle of comparative anatomy.

Men are known also by some act. Dr. Johnson was asked to review a book. His review was not favorable. The author was very indignant, and called on the doctor. "You could not, sir, have read my book with care, or you would have come to conclusions quite different." Dr. Johnson admitted that he had not read the book through. He denied that a man was obliged to eat a whole joint of meat to know whether or not it was tainted.

Young men are not aware how much character is revealed by small things. Indeed, character is made up of small things. Traits, like families, dwell together. A single word tells a volume; a book on a table, the company of one person, the avowal of opinions, reveal a whole class. Young men fall under suspicion, and suffer long before they have an idea that any one knows their habits. The merchant who drew his account out of a bank on Monday, because he saw the cashier in questionable company on Sunday, was wise. What a man does, what he does not, the company he keeps, the company he avoids, his style of living, the garniture of his rooms, are vived with the revelation of character. "The ointment of the right hand bewrayeth itself."

CCXLVIII.

DRAWN AWAY OF HIS OWN LUST.

BUT every man is tempted, when he is drawn away of his own lust, and enticed. Then when lust hath conceived, it bringeth forth sin; and sin, when it is finished, bringeth forth death. Blessed *is* the man that endureth temptation: for when he is tried, he shall receive the crown of life, which the Lord hath promised to them that love him. Let no man say when he is tempted, I am tempted of God: for God cannot be tempted with evil, neither tempteth he any man. And came and preached peace to you which were afar off, and to them that were nigh. For through him we both have access by one spirit unto the Father. And this know, that if the goodman of the house had known what hour the thief would come, he would have watched, and not have suffered his house to be broken through. Be ye therefore ready also: for the Son of man cometh at an hour when ye think not.

CALL OUT THE SAINTS.

BAD men pretend that religion does not make men better. They say that a man can be just as good without being a professing Christian, as he can if he take on him the vows of religion. All the while, these men keep their eyes on professors. They demand of them a higher style of morality. They condemn members of the church for conduct in which they themselves indulge. When censured for their inconsistency, they reply, "Oh! I don't profess any thing; that man does." Some object to religion, that it makes men effeminate. But the bravest of troops and the most victorious of soldiers have been religious men. Men are hard to meet, and dangerous to contend with, who sing the psalms of David as a battle-cry; who hang the Bible to their horses' bridles; who mount with prayer, and shout to the host, "The sword of the Lord and Gideon!"

General Havelock commanded a corps of religious men. The troops drank no intoxicating drinks; they swore no oaths. The morning and evening were saluted with prayer. The cant name given to this corps was "The Saints." More than this, the general was the chaplain. On the Lord's day, the regiment formed a hollow square, and the commander preached. All this was told to the government at London. A commission was sent to inquire into these strange doings. The report came that the charges were all true: the Saints prayed and the commander preached. "But," it was added, "no troops in India are as well drilled, as well equipped, as efficient. In time of trouble, the cry is, 'Bring out the Saints. They are never drunk. Havelock never blunders.'" It was added, as if prophesied, "Should trouble arise in India, Havelock's corps will be the main reliance of the government."

CCXLIX.

DRAW NIGH TO GOD.

DRAW nigh to God, and he will draw nigh to you. Cleanse *your* hands, *ye* sinners; and purify *your* hearts, *ye* double-minded. Be afflicted, and mourn, and weep: let your laughter be turned to mourning, and *your* joy to heaviness. Humble yourselves in the sight of the Lord, and he shall lift you up. Neither give place to the devil. Let him that stole steal no more: but rather let him labor, working with *his* hands the thing which is good, that he may have to give to him that needeth. Wherefore he saith, God resisteth the proud, but giveth grace unto the humble. Behold, the hire of the laborers who have reaped down your fields, which is of you kept back by fraud, crieth: and the cries of them which have reaped are entered into the ears of the Lord of Sabaoth. Ye have lived in pleasure on the earth, and been wanton; ye have nourished your hearts, as in a day of slaughter. Ye have condemned *and* killed the just; *and* he doth not resist you.

CLEAN THE DOOR-STEP.

An English workman and his wife lived an unhappy life. The woman was a scold. Her person was untidy, and her house the abode of disorder and negligence. Some good women got up a tea-meeting, and the workman and his wife were of the company. The next day, the benevolent women took a run among the families of the invited. In their rounds, they came to the home referred to. It was a loathsome place. Squalid poverty and filth met the eye everywhere. The children were offensive, and the woman, stout and strong, but clearly disheartened, sat composedly in the midst of the disorder. She gave her visitors a sullen welcome, evidently ashamed to have the ladies look on the squalid poverty in which she lived. The visitors were practical women. In reply to the inquiry, "Why not clean up?" the woman said, "What's the use; Jim spends all his time in the ale-house. He don't know dirt from cleanliness. He does but little else than drink and swear. I have to support the family, and I have no time to clean my own room." In the meantime, the ladies began to put things to rights and tidy up matters. The poor woman was surprised with the ease her visitors went to work, and how little trouble it was to make things tidy. They persuaded her to clean her children; make herself look decent; sweep up the room, and even clean the door-step. Her work done, the wife waited for her husband. He came in due time. Somehow he forgot to stop at the tavern. He was sober for once in his life. He drew near to a clean door-stone, whitened after the manner of English door-stones. He thought he had made a mistake. He leaped over the stone, that he might not soil it. On opening the door, he found a clean room, well-dressed children, and a tidy wife. "Come in, Jim; this is all for you." He turned and fled. Soon he came back with his arm full of goods. He sat down to a fine tea. The clean door step began a new life.

CCL.

SLANDERERS.

TAKE ye heed every one of his neighbor, and trust ye not in any brother: for every brother will utterly supplant, and every neighbor will walk with slanders. And they will deceive every one his neighbor, and will not speak the truth: they have taught their tongue to speak lies, *and* weary themselves to commit iniquity. Speak not evil one of another, brethren. He that speaketh evil of *his* brother, and judgeth his brother, speaketh evil of the law, and judgeth the law: but if thou judge the law, thou art not a doer of the law, but a judge. There is one lawgiver, who is able to save and to destroy: who art thou that judgest another? I speak after the manner of men because of the infirmity of your flesh: for as ye have yielded your members servants to uncleanness and to iniquity unto iniquity; even so now yield your members servants to righteousness unto holiness. *It is* better to hear the rebuke of the wise, than for a man to hear the song of fools.

ON THE SLOPE.

COLONEL WILLIAM ALEXANDER, who has just gone to his home, used to relate an incident in the life of his father. A stout defender of the truth, in his way, he was by no means sectarian. He did not approve of Dr. Miller's attack on the Episcopalians. Though that body held many things Dr. Alexander did not approve, he thought it better for Christians to use their guns against a common enemy than to use them against one another. As he drew near the grave, his catholicity increased. One day, he called his son to his bedside. He said, "My son, I have been a great controversialist all my days, and have stoutly contended for what I believed to be the faith once delivered to the saints; but my work is nearly done; I reached the summit long ago, and began the descent on the western slope. I am nearing the shore. I see the bold waters as they roll along, and must soon step into the turbid tide. I want to say to you, my son, in view of death and judgment, that all my theology is summed up in this: 'This is a faithful saying, and worthy of all acceptation, that Jesus Christ came into the world to save sinners; of whom I am chief.'" And clasping the cross in his hand, and confident of the Saviour's presence, he departed to be with God.

"I saw one hanging on the tree,
In agony and blood;
He fixed his dying eyes on me,
As near the cross I stood."

CCLI.

PRAISE IS COMELY.

REJOICE in the Lord, O ye righteous: *for* praise is comely for the upright. Praise the Lord with harp: sing unto him with the psaltery *and* an instrument of ten strings. Offer unto God thanksgiving; and pay thy vows unto the Most High: and call upon me in the day of trouble: I will deliver thee, and thou shalt glorify me. Violence shall no more be heard in thy land, wasting nor destruction within thy borders; but thou shalt call thy walls Salvation, and thy gates Praise. Thy sun shall no more go down; neither shall thy moon withdraw itself: for the Lord shall be thine everlasting light, and the days of thy mourning shall be ended. Praise waiteth for thee, O God, in Zion: and unto thee shall the vow be performed.

SUNDAY-SCHOOL CHILD AND PRAYER.

A LITTLE girl was brought into one of our mission Sunday-schools. She was prematurely old; the lines of sorrow were furrowed on her face. She was poorly clad, and want and suffering had left their mark on her.

She was welcomed by a kind-hearted teacher. A kind word was a stranger to this little sufferer. She looked at the genial, well-dressed lady as she would on a being from another world, and wondered whether she would ever swear at her, beat her, and send her hungry to bed. A few weeks made a great change in her young life. Good and warm clothing was provided for her. Kind friends called upon her at her home. Her poor sick mother was made comfortable. Even her miserable father seemed to be touched, and promised to turn from his cups.

One day, he came to the school-teacher, his little girl by the hand. "I came," he said, "to thank you for what you have done for my child; she has been a blessing to us all. Under your influence, I was induced to sign the pledge. That was a happy day in my house. I got work at once. I brought my earnings to my family instead of leaving them in the till of the rum-seller. But this did not satisfy my child. 'Pray, father; won't you please pray?' was her burden morning and night. So I have come with her to-day to the Sunday-school, to see if I can learn something about that Jesus of which my child talks so much." "Come, and welcome," was the response; "come, and welcome to the Saviour."

CCLII.

MISSION OF OUR LORD.

TO proclaim the acceptable year of the Lord, and the day of vengeance of our God; to comfort all that mourn; to appoint unto them that mourn in Zion, to give unto them beauty for ashes, the oil of joy for mourning, the garment of praise for the spirit of heaviness; that they might be called Trees of righteousness, The planting of the Lord, that he might be glorified. Then Peter said, Silver and gold have I none; but such as I have give I thee: In the name of Jesus Christ of Nazareth rise up and walk. And that he might reconcile both unto God in one body by the cross, having slain the enmity thereby: but ye *are* a chosen generation, a royal priesthood, a holy nation, a peculiar people; that ye should show forth the praises of him who hath called you out of darkness into his marvelous light: which in time past *were* not a people, but *are* now the people of God: which had not obtained mercy, but now have obtained mercy.

POWER OF PRAISE.

AMONG the great services rendered to the church by the Fulton-street Prayer-meeting, the subject of praise is not the least. It is conceded on all hands, that much of the power of this meeting consists in the short, crisp, energetic sayings which have always marked the meetings. The most hearty and earnest Christians attend these meetings. This class know well the old familiar hymns of the fathers. The tunes are not the new-fangled ones made of inverted drinking-songs and ballads, sanctified by alteration. They are the solid melodies that warmed the heart of Scotia's bard; tunes that gave English Christians courage when they resisted the oppressions of Laud and Bonner. These are sung with the spirit and with the understanding. Short as the prayers are, and brief as are the exhortations, a verse or two of sacred song separate these services.

For long years, singing was considered in divine worship a luxury that should not be too freely enjoyed. It was too buoyant, too ecstatic, too joyous for ordinary use, when sinful mortals drew near to God. It was dealt out in homœopathic measure. Some churches had very little singing, and some none at all. If the time was short, the hymn was shortened, the sermon never. A prominent church still stands in Rhode Island, in which a hymn of praise was not sung in public worship for a hundred years. Music was introduced at last, with much misgiving and many fears. One hymn a day was all that was thought safe. This was too much for tender consciences: before the psalmody began, simple as it was, men and women arose from their seats, went outside, and stood in a north-east gale till the psalm was over. The church, having a regard for tender consciences, voted that Christians who could not conscientiously listen to the music might go out-door and stand in the cold, without being subject to discipline. The power of sacred song as seen in Fulton-street meeting is now accepted all over the land.

CCLIII.

GRACE ABUNDANT.

AND the grace of our Lord was exceeding abundant with faith and love which is in Christ Jesus. This *is* a faithful saying, and worthy of all acceptation, that Christ Jesus came into the world to save sinners; of whom I am chief. According to the glorious gospel of the blessed God, which was committed to my trust. And I thank Christ Jesus our Lord, who hath enabled me, for that he counted me faithful, putting me into the ministry; who was before a blasphemer, and a persecutor, and injurious: but I obtained mercy because I did *it* ignorantly in unbelief. For the grace of God that bringeth salvation hath appeared to all men, teaching us that, denying ungodliness and worldly lusts, we should live soberly, righteously, and godly, in this present world. Who gave himself for us, that he might redeem us from all iniquity, and purify unto himself a peculiar people, zealous of good works.

AND THE PRISONERS HEARD.

Two burglars started out on a thieving expedition. They were very expert in their profession. They were the desperate men of the city, well known to the police, daring and unscrupulous. They would serve well as a type of hardened and abandoned men, upon whom all good influences would be lost.

They planned an attack on an up-town house. They rifled it from bottom to top, with the exception of the upper story. Supposing the house to be emptied, they set fire to the central room. A poor woman, who had the care of the building, was asleep in an upper room with a child. As the burglars were departing, they heard the child cry. One of them turned back, went up-stairs, rescued both woman and child, and brought the little one away in safety. He was arrested and sent to prison. Some time afterward, he was visited by one of his comrades, who said to him, "Jim, if you had let that brat alone, you would not have been caught." "I know it," was the reply, "but I would do it again."

A commotion as great as that produced in the jail at Philippi, when Paul and Silas sang praises to God, and the prisoners heard, is often produced in our prisons under the ministry of the Word. Those who have spoken on Blackwell's Island to the seven hundred convicts gathered in the chapel on the Lord's day, have often seen an impression produced, as the simple story of the cross was told, far exceeding the ordinary impressions in our churches on Sunday. Men file in, apparently of the most daring of their class, some in fetters, some in chains, some bearing aloft an iron ball quite equal to their strength, some muffled with irons to keep them from biting. Yet these desperate fellows who clank their chains during divine service listen attentively to the words of Jesus, and weep as his dying love for sinful men is portrayed.

In one of our prisons was a maniac, fierce, uncontrollable, and dangerous. He was chained to the floor, or he would have dashed his brains out against the wall. He tore his bed and clothing into rags, and his food had to be pushed to him through a hole in the wall. A minister visited him one day, and sang of the compassion of Christ. At first the prisoner was defiant; then his muscles relaxed; then he lay quiet as a child; then, as the song closed, with a feeble, plaintive utterance he said, "More—more—sing more."

CCLIV.

CHILDREN IN THE MARKETS.

BUT whereunto shall I liken this generation? It is like unto children sitting in the markets, and calling unto their fellows, and saying, We have piped unto you, and ye have not danced; we have mourned unto you, and ye have not lamented. Saying, Go unto this people, and say, Hearing ye shall hear, and shall not understand; and seeing ye shall see, and not perceive: for the heart of this people is waxed gross, and their ears are dull of hearing, and their eyes have they closed. He that receiveth you receiveth me; and he that receiveth me receiveth him that sent me. He that receiveth a prophet in the name of a prophet shall receive a prophet's reward; and he that receiveth a righteous man in the name of a righteous man shall receive a righteous man's reward. And whosoever shall give to drink unto one of these little ones a cup of cold *water* only in the name of a disciple, verily I say unto you, he shall in no wise lose his reward.

VOICE OF SONG.

THE old church stands in the noisy centre of trade. The great crowd rush along the highway. Teams in countless numbers rattle over the pavement. But above the rattle, the roar, and the confusion can often be heard the song of praise. Every day numbers come into the room, or fill the vestibule to hear the hymn of praise that rolls forth into the street.

Among the crowd of lookers-on, there stood, one day, a young man. He had a fine forehead ; his look indicated intelligence, but his dress was seedy. His general outlook was that of dilapidation. But he was absorbed in the meeting ; his face flushed as request after request was read. Some of them seemed to cover his case. He was especially taken by those that related to the rescue and reform of the young. He wrote on his knee a hasty note, and sent it to the leader. He then went in and took a seat. Soon a request was read : "A young man, present in this meeting, asks the prayers of God's people, that he may be saved, and saved now, from both the appetite and the slavery of strong drink." The meeting was well kept up; fervent prayer was called forth. The young man bowed himself before God. He went out a free man in the Lord.

He was the son of a doctor. He had been finely educated; but he took to the wine-cup. He ran through a fine property. He flung away a fine practice. All vows of amendment and resolutions to reform had been of no avail. Destitute and dishonored ; penniless, and with no friend to help, he was on his way to the East River, to end his miserable life. That song arrested him. He anchored in Christ.

CCLV.

PILLOWS TO ARMHOLES.

WOE to the *women* that sew pillows to all armholes, and make kerchiefs upon the head of every stature to hunt souls! Will ye hunt the souls of my people, and will ye save the souls alive *that come* unto you? Now we exhort you, brethren, warn them that are unruly, comfort the feeble-minded, support the weak, be patient toward all *men*. See that none render evil for evil unto any *man;* but ever follow that which is good, both among yourselves, and to all *men*. For this is the will of God, *even* your sanctification, that ye should abstain from fornication; that every one of you should know how to possess his vessel in sanctification and honor; not in the lust of concupiscence, even as the gentiles which know not God.

"IS THAT THE WAY YOU PRAY?"

SOME trivial thing maddened a man. He broke out in the foulest and most blasphemous words. He invoked on his own soul the most dire curses. He called down the vengeance of God on the body and soul of the person with whom he was angry. Passing along at that time was a neighbor ; he was a genial, warm-hearted man. His face was a benediction, and his tongue was the law of kindness. He knew how good a word was spoken in due season. His words, like the wise man's, were as nails and as gourds. Fitly chosen were his utterances, even as apples of gold in baskets of silver. He paused a moment until the profane man was out of breath. He said to the blasphemer, "Is that the way you pray ? Suppose God should answer your prayer, what then?" and he passed on. The profane man was struck dumb. He groaned with terror. At length he spoke to himself, "Am I a man of prayer ? Am I calling on God ? Is that idle and wicked habit of mine an appeal to God? Suppose he should answer. Suppose he should hear me as he heard the profane men of Sodom, and come down to see how great my wickedness is." He knelt down and prayed, "O blessed Lord, help me! help me to pray as I ought. God be merciful to me a sinner." That prayer the good Lord heard. Like the madman among the tombs, he was changed at once. He honored the name of the Most High. He used his tongue to praise the Lord ; he filled his house with the tones of song. "A word in due season, how good is it."

CCLVI.

NAIL IN THE SURE PLACE.

AND I will fasten him *as* a nail in a sure place; and he shall be for a glorious throne to his father's house. And they shall hang upon him all the glory of his father's house, the offspring and the issue, all vessels of small quantity, from the vessels of cups, even to all the vessels of flagons. And Jesus returned in the power of the Spirit into Galilee: and there went out a fame of him through all the region round about. And he taught in their synagogues, being glorified of all. For God hath not called us unto uncleanness, but unto holiness. He therefore that despiseth, despiseth not man, but God, who hath also given unto us his Holy Spirit. But as touching brotherly love ye need not that I write unto you: for ye yourselves are taught of God to love one another. (For we walk by faith, not by sight.) We are confident, *I say*, and willing rather to be absent from the body, and to be present with the Lord.

MINISTERIAL HUMOR.

"A MERRY heart doeth good like a medicine." The Bible makes a wide difference between the "laughter of fools" and the wit of the wise; between the buffoonery of the pot, and the cheer of a well-ordered home; between the laughter that is mad and the mirth that promotes good digestion. No class of men, as a class, have a higher fund of humor than ministers The man that never makes an audience smile seldom moves men to tears. The great master of pulpit eloquence (Spurgeon), whose roll of converts is longer than that of any other minister in the world, is celebrated for his humor. He keeps it neither out of his sermons nor out of his prayer-meetings. The early pastors of New England, whose term of office was for life, were celebrated for their wit. They were practica men. They understood human nature well. They were able to found both church and state. They tilled the ground and ate the fruit thereof. The best business men in the land, the most beneficent inventors, the most skillful navigators, the most successful of merchants, have come from the parsonage. The social life founded on the Bible is the best and most cheery. It is not a gloomy system. Home under its power is not bare and unsightly. The homes that are elegant, tasteful, full of virtue and music, full of song and grace, are the homes of the Bible. In these, "our sons are as plants grown up in their youth, and our daughters as corner-stones polished after the similitude of a palace."

CCLVII.

SPEAKING AGAINST GOD.

AND he shall speak *great* words against the Most High, and shall wear out the saints of the Most High, and think to change times and laws: and they shall be given into his hands until a time and times and the dividing of time. But the judgment shall sit, and they shall take away his dominion, to consume and to destroy *it* unto the end. And at the end of the days I Nebuchadnezzar lifted up mine eyes unto heaven, and mine understanding returned unto me, and I blessed the Most High, and I praised and honored him that liveth for ever, whose dominion *is* an everlasting dominion, and his kingdom *is* from generation to generation. Wherefore, O king, let my counsel be acceptable unto thee, and break off thy sins by righteousness, and thine iniquities by showing mercy to the poor; if it may be a lengthening of thy tranquillity.

WATTS'S OAK.

DR. WATTS was in feeble health. His sacred songs had begun to attract attention. One day, he met, in old London, his good friend Thomas Abney. Mr. Abney was a rich London merchant. He had a fine country house in Stoke Newington. Near his house was the house of Lord Fairfax, where Cromwell spent the hot season; near this, Mrs. Barbauld lived and wrote, Howard the philanthropist dwelt, and De Foe wrote his Robinson Crusoe. Mr. Abney invited young Watts to visit the Abney house at Stoke Newington, and pass the night. Watts tells the rest: "I came to the house of my good friend Sir Thomas Abney to pass a single night. I have remained here thirty-six years."

The old mansion has been dismantled; the gardens have been changed. But one memorial of Dr. Watts abides. No gardens were more beautiful. The exquisite scenery afforded the sacred poet some of his finest imagery. Among others, "Sweet fields beyond the swelling flood."

The garden has been turned into a cemetery. In one corner is an ancient oak; it is guarded by an iron fence. On the oak is a sign, with this inscription, "Under this oak Dr. Watts often sat, and composed some of his most celebrated songs." But for the strong fence, the tree would be cut down and carried away as a memorial.

This oak was a sapling when Watts was young. One day, he sat at its root, meditating on the cross. With his knife he drew the sign of the cross on the smooth bark, and wrote:

"I'll carve my passions on the bark,
And every wounded tree
Shall drop, and bear some mystic mark
That Jesus died for me.

"The swains shall wonder when they read,
Inscribed on all the grove,
That Heaven itself came down to bleed,
To win a mortal's love."

CCLVIII.

CHRISTIAN MORALITY.

IN all things showing thyself a pattern of good works: in doctrine *showing* uncorruptness, gravity, sincerity, sound speech, that cannot be condemned; that he that is of the contrary part may be ashamed, having no evil thing to say of you. Remembering without ceasing your work of faith, and labor of love, and patience of hope in our Lord Jesus Christ, in the sight of God and our Father. Not purloining, but showing all good fidelity; that they may adorn the doctrine of God our Saviour in all things. For the grace of God that bringeth salvation hath appeared to all men. Teaching us that, denying ungodliness and worldly lusts, we should live soberly, righteously, and godly, in this present world.

LOVELY IN THEIR LIVES.

This is said of Saul and Jonathan. So sang David: "Saul and Jonathan were lovely and pleasant in their lives, and in their death they were not divided." "Behold, how good and how pleasant it is for brethren to dwell together in unity! It is like the precious ointment upon the head, that ran down upon the beard, even Aaron's beard: that went down to the skirts of his garments; as the dew of Hermon, and as the dew that descended upon the mountains of Zion: for there the Lord commanded the blessing, even life for evermore."

Two brothers belonged to the same church. They were united as Saul and Jonathan. Their boyhood friendship was undisturbed. In manhood, this friendship strengthened. One of them worked on a farm till he was twenty-one. He then took three thousand dollars, the portion allotted to him, put it in Western trade, and made half a million. The other was a trader in the city. The brothers made confidants of each other. The Western trader handed his brother ten thousand dollars, and said, "Put this in trade. Do the best you can with it, and we will divide." No memorandum was made of it, nor was it spoken of for more than six years. The brother who loaned the money sickened, and came near to death. His friend hastened to his bedside. "John, you remember that I have ten thousand dollars belonging to you. I have calculated the earnings, and found your portion to be sixty thousand dollars." The dying brother quietly replied, "All right, Charles. You will know what to do with it when I am gone." "Let brotherly love continue." "It is like the dew of Hermon on the mountains of Zion."

CCLIX.

JOY IN STRENGTH.

THE king shall joy in thy strength, O Lord; and in thy salvation how greatly shall he rejoice! Thou hast given him his heart's desire, and hast not withholden the request of his lips. Selah. His glory *is* great in thy salvation: honor and majesty hast thou laid upon him. For thou hast made him most blessed forever: thou hast made him exceeding glad with thy countenance. For they intended evil against thee: they imagined a mischievous device, *which* they are not able *to perform*. Therefore shalt thou make them turn their back, *when* thou shalt make ready *thine arrows* upon thy strings against the face of them. Be thou exalted, Lord, in thine own strength: so will we sing and praise thy power. Therefore will I give thanks unto thee, O Lord, among the heathen, and sing praises unto thy name. Great deliverance giveth he to his king; and showeth mercy to his anointed, to David, and to his seed for evermore.

VERY SMALL HELM.

The Bible recognizes the fact, that great excellences are neutralized by small defects. "Behold also the ships, which, though they be so great, and are driven of fierce winds, yet are they turned about with a very small helm, whithersoever the governor listeth." "Behold, we put bits in the horses' mouths, that they may obey us; and we turn about the whole body." "Even so the tongue is a little member, and boasteth great things." What is the strength, tonnage, beauty, and value of a ship, if the helm is not right! So the bit overpowers the strength and fleetness of a horse; and what is the beauty and completeness of an equipage, if the bit be not well adjusted?

Food, to do us good, must be well balanced. The same food that gives health and manly proportions can give us the dyspepsia, the rickets, apoplexy, and death. One part must be nourished at the expense of another. The rain and the snow that make the well-prepared ground fruitful, cover the neglected soil with briars and thorns. The sun that covers the gardens with fruits and flowers, hardens the barren earth. If men will come to the fullness of the stature of a perfect man in Jesus Christ, they must be well balanced and well developed.

One man is all emotion, and his piety is like the crackling of thorns under a pot; another is bold and proud—just, but stern. One is all action and zeal; another all doctrine and orthodoxy. Small matters detract from the value of an artist, a doctor, a pastor, a superintendent. Hundreds of men on the church-roll are of no account in the church, from some small defect. They are as a ship without a helm; a horse with no bit in his mouth.

CCLX.

AS IN MONTHS PAST.

OH that I were as *in* months past, as *in* the days *when* God preserved me; when his candle shined upon my head, *and when* by his light I walked *through* darkness; as I was in the days of my youth, when the secret of God *was* upon my tabernacle; when the Almighty *was* yet with me, *when* my children *were* about me. But as for me, my prayer *is* unto thee, O Lord, *in* an acceptable time: O God, in the multitude of thy mercy hear me, in the truth of thy salvation. Deliver me out of the mire, and let me not sink: let me be delivered from them that hate me, and out of the deep waters. Let not the waterflood overflow me, neither let the deep swallow me up, and let not the pit shut her mouth upon me. Hear me, O Lord; for thy lovingkindness *is* good: turn unto me according to the multitude of thy tender mercies. Wherefore laying aside all malice, and all guile, and hypocrisies, and envies, and all evil speakings, as newborn babes, desire the sincere milk of the word, that ye may grow thereby.

SUPERFLUITY OF NAUGHTINESS.

Worldly men are fond of talking about the insincerity of professors of religion. They are loud in their condemnation of men who clean the outside of the platter, and who whiten the outside of the sepulchre. We are told of professors who have been likened to wolves in sheep's clothing, and men who put on the livery of heaven with which to serve the devil.

It would be well if all the hypocrites were inside the church. But there are as many pretenders outside the church as there are in it. Strange enough, bad men in the church seem better than they are; but bad men outside seem worse than they are. Hence the exhortation, "Wherefore, my beloved brethren, let every man be swift to hear, slow to speak, slow to wrath. Wherefore lay apart all filthiness and superfluity of naughtiness, and receive with meekness the engrafted word, which is able to save your souls."

Seeming to be worse than one is. Naughtier in seeming than in fact. One man professes to find difficulties in religion, when he can map out a consistent Christian character; another professes to stumble at the many sects, while he knows that in answer to the question, "What must I do to be saved?" all agree. Another argues that a profession of religion has no advantage over a non-profession, when he condemns in Christians what he practices in his own life. Another serves the church in comparison with the characters of the age, while he knows that nine tenths of Christian charity is expended on people who malign religion and hate the Gospel.

CCLXI.

KING OF SALEM.

AND Melchizedek king of Salem brought forth bread and wine: and he *was* the priest of the most high God. And he blessed him, and said, Blessed *be* Abram of the most high God, possessor of heaven and earth: and blessed *be* the most high God, which hath delivered thine enemies into thy hand. And he gave him tithes of all. For this Melchizedec, king of Salem, priest of the most high God, who met Abraham returning from the slaughter of the kings, and blessed him; to whom also Abraham gave a tenth part of all; first being by interpretation King of righteousness, and after that also King of Salem, which is, King of peace; without father, without mother, without descent, neither having beginning of days, nor end of life; but made like unto the Son of God; abideth a priest continually. Now consider how great this man *was*, unto whom even the patriarch Abraham gave the tenth of the spoils.

KING OF CARTHAGE.

THERE is a passage in the history of Carthage which beautifully illustrates the loving-kindness and mercy of the Lord as displayed in the Gospel. The Carthaginians, at one time in their history, rose against their king. They dethroned him, and banished him from the country. The people, in their mádness, had neither pity nor compassion for any one connected with their late monarch. The wife and children of the king were driven beyond the gates to be carried captive by the hordes surrounding the walls, or to perish by neglect. The king wandered to a distant country. There he found friends. Mighty men of war enlisted in his behalf. An army was gathered, and led to the very gates of Carthage. It was resolved to raze the walls, and put the inhabitants to the sword. The people saw their danger, and resolved to submit. They selected their most honorable men; clothed them in sackcloth; put ropes about their neck; and barefooted and bareheaded, bearing the keys of the city, they were sent out to make terms with the offended sovereign. The king came forth to meet the suppliants. Addressing them, he said, "O Carthaginians, live. I have always loved Carthage. I am not your enemy, but your sovereign and your friend. I loved you when I reigned over you. I loved you when you drove me from my throne. I loved you when you did not spare my wife and children. I love you now. Be this a proof of my love: I pardon you; bid you open your gates, and receive your sovereign; and I will rule over you in affection and love." He entered the capital in triumph; his enemies were conquered by love, and the people shouted, "Long live the king!" A beautiful illustration of the mercy and compassion of our Lord, who says, "I loved you, O sinful ones, when in the bosom of my Father; when I appeared in the likeness of sinful flesh; when among you I was a homeless, houseless stranger: I suffered the agony of the garden, and the cruel death of the cross, that you might not perish. Receive me as your King, and you shall reign with me forever."

CCLXII.

CHRISTIAN VIRTUE.

AND besides this, giving all diligence, add to your faith, virtue; and to virtue, knowledge; and to knowledge, temperance; and to temperance, patience; and to patience, godliness; and to godliness, brotherly kindness; and to brotherly kindness, charity. For if these things be in you, and abound, they make *you that ye shall* neither *be* barren nor unfruitful in the knowledge of our Lord Jesus Christ. But he that lacketh these things is blind, and can not see afar off, and hath forgotten that he was purged from his old sins. Wherefore the rather, brethren, give diligence to make your calling and election sure: for if ye do these things, ye shall never fall: for so an entrance shall be ministered unto you abundantly into the everlasting kingdom of our Lord and Saviour Jesus Christ.

LION OF THE TRIBE OF JUDAH.

WHEN the mystery of redemption could not be unfolded, John wept; but the Lion of the tribe of Judah appeared, and was able to unloose the seals, and read the story of the cross. Our Lord sprang out of Judah, saith St. Paul, and was a high-priest after the order of Melchizedec, and not after the order of Aaron. Being of the tribe of Judah, our Lord took the symbol of that tribe, which symbol was that of a lion embroidered on a banner. As he lay on his death-bed, the patriarch Jacob called unto him his sons, and said, "Gather yourselves together, ye sons of Jacob, that I may tell you that which shall befall you in the last days." In vision, the father saw these twelve sons, strong and mighty as tribes. As in a division each regiment has its distinctive or regimental flag, so the banners to distinguish the twelve tribes were clearly set forth by the expiring sage. To Simeon was given the symbol of water. On the banner of Judah was to be emblazoned a lion rampant. Zebulun was a ship; Dan, a serpent; Gad, a troop; Joseph, a vine. Coming from the household of David and Solomon, our Lord had the name of the tribe from which he sprang, and was described from its symbol as the Lion of the tribe of Judah. It symbols his majesty; his power; his strength to save, and his strength to destroy. The Lion of the tribe of Judah unites in his gracious person the fulfillment of all the gracious prophecies and promises of the elder dispensation. When the babe of Bethlehem was born, and the angels heralded his birth, the prophecy of the old patriarch, uttered centuries before, was fulfilled. The Man of the house of David, who was to sit on David's throne and rule forever, had come. Mary was the last of the royal line. Out of all the tribes, Judah alone remained. Had it been prophesied that Jesus would come of any other tribe but that of Judah, the prophecy must have failed; for all the other families had passed away. And had not Christ been born of Mary in the city of David, or had Mary been gathered to the sepulchre of her fathers before the King of the Jews came to earth, all the predictions would have failed; for with Mary the royal line of David ran out, and the prophets would have been false witnesses before men. Well did the Saviour say, "All things must be fulfilled which were written in the law of Moses, and the prophets, and the psalms, concerning me."

CCLXIII.

CHRISTIAN KNOWLEDGE.

YEA doubtless, and I count all things *but* loss for the excellency of the knowledge of Christ Jesus my Lord: for whom I have suffered the loss of all things, and do count them *but* dung, that I may win Christ, and be found in him, not having mine own righteousness, which is of the law, but that which is through the faith of Christ, the righteousness which is of God by faith: that I may know him, and the power of his resurrection, and the fellowship of his sufferings, being made conformable unto his death; if by any means I might attain unto the resurrection of the dead. For we know that if our earthly house of *this* tabernacle were dissolved, we have a building of God, an house not made with hands, eternal in the heavens.

IN EXTREMITY.

THE directness of the prayers in the Bible is one of their marked peculiarities. The thing needed is asked for; the danger to be averted is stated; the blessing solicited is named. Among the extraordinary answers to prayer that are named at Fulton street, most of them have this direct feature about them. One day, a fine-looking gentleman, intelligent and earnest, took the floor. He was a cashier of a bank just out of the city; the business world was agitated by defalcations, embezzlements, and breaches of trust. Men who had stood high, and possessed public confidence for years, went under a cloud. In looking over the accounts of the bank, a discrepancy was discovered of several thousand dollars. The funds of the bank were in the sole charge of the speaker. If there was any error, he committed it; any mistake, it was his own; any defalcation, he must bear the blame. Do what he would, the account was against him. He was not conscious of any mistake. He knew he had not taken or used a dollar of the bank's money improperly. Again and again, he ran over the accounts. He passed whole nights in examining vouchers and trying to unravel the mystery. His sleep fled from him; his appetite departed. Heated, flushed, and nervous, disgrace stared him in the face. All the while, he was conscious of his integrity; yet the books were against him, and his accounts, read by strangers, would cover him with dishonor.

The next day, the bank was to be examined by officials. Stubbornly the error stood before him. A thousand temptations assailed him. Sometimes he resolved to fly and hide from disgrace. The morning dawned that was to settle his fate. The discrepancy in his accounts could not be hidden. But one thing was open to him: in his extremity he could call upon the Lord. He went down early to the bank; locked himself in. In the director's room, he threw himself on his knees, and asked God to deliver him. For one hour, he wrestled with God in prayer. When he arose, he was possessed of a calmness to which he had been a stranger for days. Guided by an impulse, he knew not what, he went to the safe, took out a blotter he had not seen for many a day, and laid it on the desk. It opened; and before his eyes lay the full account, complete in all its parts. He had neglected to copy the page. His light was as the noonday, and the darkness disappeared. He came to Fulton street to render thanks to the name of the Lord.

CCLXIV.

CHRISTIAN TEMPERANCE.

AND the king appointed them a daily provision of the king's meat, and of the wine which he drank: so nourishing them three years, that at the end thereof they might stand before the king. Now among these were of the children of Judah, Daniel, Hananiah, Mishael, and Azariah: but Daniel purposed in his heart that he would not defile himself with the portion of the king's meat, nor with the wine which he drank: therefore he requested of the prince of the eunuchs that he might not defile himself. Now God had brought Daniel into favor and tender love with the prince of the eunuchs. And the prince of the eunuchs said unto Daniel, I fear my lord the king, who hath appointed your meat and your drink: for why should he see your faces worse liking than the children which *are* of your sort? then shall ye make *me* endanger my head to the king.

"I AM DRUNK."

There are many temptations that beset social life. The drinking customs of society are perilous to the young. The fascinations of the wine-cup, when connected with fashionable life, lead many astray. People are cowards in morals as they are in war. Many a man faces the enemy in battle because bayonets are around him, and he must keep step or be shot. The first downward step of a dissipated life is taken in company. A lady moving in good society was invited by some friends to take a ride. She was a large-hearted woman, with a genial disposition, fond of company, and ready to take her share in the exhilaration of a pleasure-party. She was not initiated into the seductive power of fashionable drink. After the ride came the usual rest at a hotel, and fancy beverages were ordered. They were very sweet, very strong, and very exhilarating. While the gentlemen were getting their teams ready, the lady proposed to have another glass. Those better informed protested, but in vain. The second glass was enjoyed, and its effect was soon palpable. With great difficulty, the victim was taken into the coach. Reaching the hotel where the parties resided, the appearance of things attracted great attention. Supposing some one was injured, the entire force of the hotel came to the pavement. Coming to her feet with difficulty, she seized a colored waiter around the neck, exclaiming, "I am drunk; save me!" One such experience as this was enough. The lady resolved to give her influence to the cause of temperance. The kingdom would hardly induce her to undergo a repetition of the disgrace she suffered. Practically she knows the words of Holy Writ to be true, "Wine is a mocker; strong drink is raging, and whosoever is deceived thereby is not wise." "Look not on the wine when it is red; when it giveth its color in the cup. At last it biteth like a serpent, and stingeth like an adder."

Nārāyan Sheshāstri
Jalna and Indapūr
Via Bombay

CCLXV.

UTTERMOST PARTS.

AND he will lift up an ensign to the nations from far, and will hiss unto them from the end of the earth: and, behold, they shall come with speed swiftly: none shall be weary nor stumble among them; none shall slumber nor sleep; neither shall the girdle of their loins be loosed, nor the lachet of their shoes be broken; and in that day shall ye say, Praise the Lord, call upon his name, declare his doings among the people, make mention that his name is exalted. Sing unto the Lord; for he hath done excellent things: this *is* known in all the earth. Cry out and shout, thou inhabitant of Zion: for great *is* the Holy One of Israel in the midst of thee. For as the new heavens and the new earth, which I will make, shall remain before me, saith the Lord, so shall your seed and your name remain. And it shall come to pass, *that* from one new moon to another, and from one sabbath to another, shall all flesh come to worship before me, saith the Lord.

NARAYAN SHESHADRI.

Among the blessed influences flowing from the Evangelical Alliance was the bringing together of eminent Christians from all parts of the world. Even "the ends of the earth who had turned to the Lord" sent representatives. One of the most attractive speakers was Sheshadri, from Bombay. His Oriental garb, his turban and flowing robes, his clear and sharp-cut English, and his fervent religious spirit, created great enthusiasm at Fulton street. His speech was like "cold water to a thirsty soul." His message "was good news from a far country." Tough and unwelcome as was the soil which he tilled, the good seed of the kingdom had taken root, and brought forth precious fruits. Sheshadri represented the true Christian union that prevails in that far-off land. That union was embodied in an alliance which embraced a hundred and eighteen ministers of the gospel. At one meeting, thirty-two missionary societies, belonging to the United States, were represented ; thirty to Great Britain, and twenty from India herself. Among this company, there was but one spirit ruling in the hearts of all, and that was the spirit of the Lord Jesus Christ. The denominations present were, Baptists and Anabaptists, Independents and Presbyterians, Episcopalians and Congregationalists. These all working for the salvation of men. It was a fitting close to this meeting that the massive audience sang that world-wide hymn, "From Greenland's icy mountains."

CCLXVI.

CHRISTIAN PATIENCE.

TAKE, my brethren, the prophets, who have spoken in the name of the Lord, for an example of suffering affliction, and patience. Behold, we count them happy which endure. Ye have heard of the patience of Job, and have seen the end of the Lord; that the Lord is very pitiful, and of tender mercy. Choosing rather to suffer affliction with the people of God, than to enjoy the pleasure of sin for a season; esteeming the reproach of Christ greater riches than the treasures in Egypt: for he had respect unto the recompense of the reward. And the prayer of faith shall save the sick, and the Lord shall raise him up; and if he have committed sins, they shall be forgiven him. Confess *your* faults one to another, and pray one for another, that ye may be healed. The effectual fervent prayer of a righteous man availeth much.

WHITFIELD'S TROUBLES.

THE holiest and most devoted of men find life a pilgrimage, and its journey over a pathway dusty and often full of affliction. The prophet thought his troubles exceeded those of any who had gone before him. Paul had his thorn in the flesh, a messenger from Satan sent to buffet him. Whitfield had a popularity surpassing that of most men; his eloquence was unrivaled; his pathway was as brilliant as a meteor. He had the rare gift of captivating the cultivated, and drawing tears down the smutty faces of the ignorant miners at Kingswood. The humblest child of the Saviour sat at his feet with delight, and the haughty scientist who came to scoff under his ministry remained to pray. But Whitfield had his troubles. He was a man of many afflictions, and was often brought under the rod. He was especially fond of domestic life, and sighed for the comforts of home and the calm of a well-ordered Christian household. His marriage was not a happy one. There was no congeniality between himself and wife. He was too much in public life, too attractive, and surrounded by too many friends to suit the lady whom he had chosen as a companion. Leave his itineracy and sweep of labor he could not; to dwell amid contentions and domestic strife was not his duty. His usefulness would have been endangered, and his spirit chafed and harrowed. So a separation was agreed upon. Whitfield never blamed his wife for this want of domestic agreement. The pair were not fitted for each other, and, through constitutional infirmities, a change was impossible. The great preacher always spoke lovingly and generously of his wife. Once a man questioned him on the separation. "Was not your wife a good woman?" "Excellent; none better." "Do you not believe she is a Christian?" "Yes, she is an earnest, humble follower of the Lamb." "Why, then, could you not live with her?" "Because grace can live where I can not."

CCLXVII.

PRACTICAL GODLINESS.

ACCORDING as his divine power hath given unto us all things that *pertain* unto life and godliness, through the knowledge of him that hath called us to glory and virtue: whereby are given unto us exceeding great and precious promises; that by these ye might be partakers of the divine nature, having escaped the corruption that is in the world through lust. Then said Daniel to Melzar, whom the prince of the eunuchs had set over Daniel, Hananiah, Mishael, and Azariah, Prove thy servants, I beseech thee, ten days; and let them give us pulse to eat, and water to drink. Then let our countenances be looked upon before thee, and the countenance of the children that eat of the portion of the king's meat: and as thou seest, deal with thy servants. So he consented to them in this matter, and proved them ten days.

DYING TESTIMONIES.

BALAAM, the mad prophet, who loved the wages of unrighteousness, said, "I shall see him, but not now. I shall behold him, but not nigh. Let me die the death of the righteous." The Emperor Julian, the apostate, who, to falsify the Saviour's word, attempted to rebuild the temple, died in despair, shouting, "O Nazarene, thou has conquered!" "I shall go to hell, and you shall go with me," said Voltaire to his doctor. Paine, on his death-bed, alternated between blasphemous oaths and his piteous crys to the Lord for mercy. "Remorse, remorse!" were the last words of Randolph. "It is the last of earth; I die content," said John Quincy Adams, as he passed away. "This unworthy right hand," said Cranmer, as he thrust it into the flames. "Welcome this chain, for Jesus' sake; welcome, life everlasting," said Saunders, as he was bound to the stake. "Be of good cheer, Master Ridley," said Bishop Latimer, as he was burning in the flames. "I am dying," were the closing words of Whitfield. "Death can never take me by surprise," said Judson, as he was dying. "The best of all is God is with us," said John Wesley. His brother's testimony was, "I shall be satisfied with thy likeness." "The victory is won," said Payson. "I will now go to sleep," said Neander. Mozart wrote his requiem under the conviction that it was for himself. "I shall be saved as a pardoned sinner," said John Howe. "I am abundantly satisfied," said Calvin. Baxter said, "I have peace, I have peace." Humboldt exclaimed, "These rays beckon earth to heaven." "Die a man, die a man, Paine!" said one of his hardened associates, who saw the infidel shivering in his bed. Lord Byron said, "Come, come! no weakness! let's be a man to the last." It was Hobbe's wish that he might find a hole to creep out of the world at. The death to come is more bitter than this; the life to come more sweet. Polycarp, on the edge of martyrdom, said, "O Father of thy beloved son Jesus Christ, I bless thee that thou has counted me worthy of this day, to receive my portion in the number of the martyrs in the cup of Christ!"

CCLXVIII.

CHRISTIAN KINDNESS.

LET love be without dissimulation. Abhor that which is evil; cleave to that which is good. *Be* kindly affectioned one to another with brotherly love; in honor preferring one another. From whence *come* wars and fightings among you? *come they* not hence, *even* of your lusts that war in your members? Ye lust, and have not: ye kill, and desire to have, and can not obtain: ye fight and war, yet ye have not, because ye ask not. Ye ask, and receive not, because ye ask amiss, that ye may consume *it* upon your lusts. Ye adulterers and adulteresses, know ye not that the friendship of the world is enmity with God? One that ruleth well his own house, having his children in subjection with all gravity; (for if a man know not how to rule his own house, how shall he take care of the church of God?)

KINDNESS CONQUERS.

A COARSELY dressed man appeared in a country store. He was rugged, stoutly built, and had evidently been accustomed to rough it. He made inquiry for one who had long since been carried to the grave. He seemed shocked when he learned that his friend was dead. He asked to be shown to her burial-place. On reaching it, he threw himself on the green grass and wept bitter tears of sorrow. On coming to his feet, he said, "This person was the best friend I ever had. I was a boy, here, many years ago ; I was wild, rough, and unmanageable. Every body seemed to be against me. My father said I was a bad boy, and would go to ruin. Even my mother, kind and patient as she was, almost gave me over. Every body spoke ill of me except my Sunday-school teacher. She told me I could be a good boy if I would. She bore with my rudeness, and often stood between me and blame. Sometimes, when the school was closed, she would walk with me a little way, and urge me to be a good boy and love the Saviour. Even when every body cast me off, she stood my friend. Rough, wild, rude as I was, even then I would have given my life for my teacher. When the California fever broke out, I ran away and brought up on the California coast. For some years, I plunged into every kind of dissipation, and had a bad life of it. But everywhere I remembered my kind friend. When the fever held me to my rude couch, her gentle spirit seemed to pass before me. I could feel the touch of her soft hand, hear the tones of her pleading voice. Often I recalled the very words she spoke to me. We had no Sabbaths, no church, no minister. Our pastimes were gaming, drinking, and vice. Amid all these, I found the Saviour. And I ascribe my deliverance to the kindness, the gentleness, the faithfulness of her who sleeps beneath this sod. I have a little money, and I came home that I might see my kind friend, and tell her how thankful I was for her forbearance and faithfulness to me. We shall meet in a better land." Kindness always conquers. The loan of a pair of skates broke down prejudice of a colored boy at school. Isaac T. Hopper gained a friend by paying back a fine which he had imposed twenty years before as a magistrate.

CCLXIX.

CHRISTIAN CHARITY.

CHARITY suffereth long, *and* is kind; charity envieth not; charity vaunteth not itself, is not puffed up, doth not behave itself unseemly, seeketh not her own, is not easily provoked, thinketh no evil; rejoiceth not in iniquity, but rejoiceth in the truth; beareth all things, believeth all things, hopeth all things, endureth all things. Brethren, be not children in understanding: howbeit, in malice be ye children, but in understanding be men. For what glory *is it*, if, when ye be buffeted for your faults, ye shall take it patiently? but if, when ye do well, and suffer *for it*, ye take it patiently, this *is* acceptable with God.

THE HARVEST OF CHARITY.

At one period, there was a little unpleasantness between Wesley and Whitfield. Their work was the same, but their paths diverged. But they never lost confidence in each other, nor refused to bear an open testimony to the great work in which each was engaged. A small-hearted Christian attempted to ingratiate himself into the favor of Whitfield by condemning Wesley. And he asked, "Do you think we shall see John Wesley in heaven?" "Certainly not," said Whitfield; "John Wesley will be so near the throne, and you and I so far off, that we can not expect to see him." Lamartine tells of a Bedouin who found a poor sufferer at the roadside. "I am dying," he cried; "help me, and Heaven will reward you." The Bedouin got off his horse, and with great difficulty lifted the beggar into his saddle. The stranger proved to be a robber in disguise. Assuming his character, he put the horse to his mettle and galloped off. The Arab called after him, and begged him to stop for one moment. Safe from pursuit and attack, the robber drew up. "You have my horse," said the Bedouin, "but I conjure you never to tell any one how you obtained it." "Why not?" said the robber. "Because some man really ill and dying will ask help in vain." The words struck the robber with remorse. He returned the horse, embraced its owner, and promised to amend his life.

The Dutch Church was the original church of New-York. A handful of Episcopalians arrived, and founded the parish now known as Trinity Church. The Dutch gave the newcomers a warm welcome. They gave Trinity Church the use of their house of worship a part of the Sabbath, and when the first rector was instituted, the Dutch dominies lent a helping hand. Not to be outdone in liberality, Trinity parish, as it strengthened, presented their kind brethren with an elegant organ, which for years led the service of praise in the sanctuary.

CCLXX.

MODERATION.

LET your moderation be known unto all men. The Lord *is* at hand. Fools make a mock at sin: but among the righteous *there is* favor. And, ye masters, do the same things unto them, forbearing threatening: knowing that your master also is in heaven; neither is there respect of persons with him. Finally, my brethren, be strong in the Lord, and in the power of his might. The thoughts of the diligent *tend* only to plenteousness; but of every one *that is* hasty only to want. Forasmuch then as Christ hath suffered for us in the flesh, arm yourselves likewise with the same mind: for he that hath suffered in the flesh hath ceased from sin; that he no longer should live the rest of *his* time in the flesh to the lusts of men, but to the will of God. For the time past of *our* life may suffice us to have wrought the will of the Gentiles, when we walked in lasciviousness, lusts, excess of wine, revelings, banquetings, and abominable idolatries: wherein they think it strange that ye run not with *them* to the same excess of riot, speaking evil of *you*.

GIRARD AND HIS WORKMEN.

Stephen Girard had many excellent business traits. He was not a general giver; vagrants found little quarter in his house. But Girard was distinguished for his considerate conduct towards employees. If a man conformed to his whims, he would be his friend, and stand by him through all reverses. One day, a young man, just commencing business, wished to obtain of Girard a bill of goods on credit. "Have you brought a cart to take these goods with you?" "No," was the reply, "I prefer to save the expense; so I shall carry the goods home on my back." "You will succeed," said the banker, "if you don't drink. While you are sober and carry home your own goods, you can have all the credit you want." One day, a man came to him and wanted employment. "What do you want to do?" "I will do any thing that will give me an honest living." "I will give you a dollar a day," said Girard. "You take that pile of stones that you see in the end of that lot, and carry them to the other side and pile them up in the same manner that they are now." The job was completed, and the man took his money and went home. In the morning, he came for work. "Take that pile of stones," said the merchant, "and put them back where you found them; pile them up, and do it well." At night, the man came for his money. The next morning, he had to remove the stones again; and so he worked day after day for a week. On Saturday night, Girard complimented him on his industry, his attention to business, and the uncomplaining manner in which he went about his work. "I like you," said the banker; "there is no nonsense about you; you do what you are told to do. Many men would have objected to doing the work over and over again. You shall have work as long as I have any thing for any body to do."

CCLXXI.

GLUTTONY.

BE not among winebibbers; among riotous eaters of flesh: for the drunkard and the glutton shall come to poverty: and drowsiness shall clothe *a man* with rags. Whoso keepeth the law *is* a wise son: but he that is a companion of riotous *men* shameth his father. He that by usury and unjust gain increaseth his substance, he shall gather it for him that will pity the poor. The Son of man came eating and drinking, and they say, Behold a man gluttonous, and a winebibber, a friend of publicans and sinners. But wisdom is justified of her children. And they shall say unto the elders of his city, This our son *is* stubborn and rebellious, he will not obey our voice; *he is* a glutton and a drunkard. And all the men of his city shall stone him with stones, that he die: so shalt thou put evil away from among you; and all Israel shall hear and fear.

FAST YOUNG MEN.

THE premature old age of young men is one of the marked features of American trade. The old merchants and tradesmen of our cities who have seen sixty and even seventy winters are more vigorous and seem younger than the young men of the period. A man builds up a fine business; it has been the work of a lifetime; it has afforded a constant, healthful, and remunerative employ. The name of the house is of itself a capital. Its repute brings wealth into its coffers. How seldom the honor and business of a house descend to children! Sons commence where their fathers left off, and leave off where their fathers began. Down at eleven, off at two; on the road, with wines, swift horses, and gay company, they are illy prepared to maintain the position to which they are invited. The sons of porters, wood-sawyers, stevedores, and coal-heavers jostle the pampered children of luxury off of the path, and take the business and success of life into their own hands. It was ordered that young Daniel should have appointed to him daily provision of the king's meat, and of the wine which the king drank. He was to be trained in the learning and tongue of the Chaldeans. He was to dwell in the palace, and to be constantly in the society of the gay revelers of the king's household. This style of training was to last three years. Daniel at once saw the drift. He knew where he would be landed if he followed the course marked out for him. He purposed in his heart that he would not defile himself with the portion of the king's meat, nor with the wine which he drank. When the prince of the servants heard Daniel's request that he and his associates might live on the simple fare of their own country, and avoid the heating viands and enervating wines, he was afraid he would endanger his head. "Prove thy servants," said Daniel, "I beseech thee, ten days. Give us pulse to eat and water to drink, then let our countenances be looked upon." By temperance, industry, and intelligence, Daniel wore the purple robe and gold chain of a minister of state.

CCLXXII.

LET THEM SLIP.

THEREFORE we ought to give the most earnest heed to the things which we have heard, lest at any time we should let *them* slip. For if the word spoken by angels was steadfast, and every transgression and disobedience received a just recompense of reward; how shall we escape, if we neglect so great salvation. Not every one that saith unto me, Lord, Lord, shall enter into the kingdom of heaven; but he that doeth the will of my Father which is in heaven. Many will say to me in that day, Lord, Lord, have we not prophesied in thy name? and in thy name have cast out devils? and in thy name done many wonderful works? And then will I profess unto them, I never knew you: depart from me, ye that work iniquity. And some believed the things which were spoken, and some believed them not.

"*AS THY SERVANT WAS HERE AND THERE.*"

INATTENTION to small things is the ruin of men in trade. It is equally so in religious life. We bear our great troubles with fortitude, but the small annoyances are what disturb our peace and make us fretful and unmanly. A man comes home and makes a fuss about his tea and toast, who would hardly fret if the gable end of his house came down.

In the old times, when prisons were few and very insecure, a prisoner was put in charge of an officer who was to answer for the prisoner in his own person. If it was a capital offense, the jailer must answer with his own life. Thence the form of the case put by the prophet, " Thy servant went out into the midst of the battle: and behold, a man turned aside and brought a man unto me, and said, Keep this man; if by any means he be missing, then shall thy life be for his life, or else thou shalt pay a talent of silver. *And as thy servant was busy here and there he was gone.*"

Alas! what a type of life! " A price is put into the hands of a man to get wisdom." But he is busy here and there, and the opportunity is gone. The Holy Spirit calls a man to life. He is busy here and there, and the Spirit departs. In the midst of a revival, men resolve to fear the Lord. But they are busy, and the summer ends. Afflictions come, death smites, reverses sweep over the sons of men. Surely, now they will turn to God, so they say. But small inattentions creep in. " Thy servant is busy," and life is gone.

CCLXXIII.

DULL OF HEARING.

SAYING, Go unto this people, and say, Hearing ye shall hear, and shall not understand; and seeing ye shall see, and not perceive: for the heart of this people is waxed gross, and their ears are dull of hearing, and their eyes have they closed; lest they should see with *their* eyes, and hear with *their* ears, and understand with *their* heart, and should be converted, and I should heal them. Harden not your heart, as in the provocation, *and* as *in* the day of temptation in the wilderness: when your fathers tempted me, proved me, and saw my work. For there is no respect of persons with God. For as many as have sinned without law shall also perish without law; and as many as have sinned in the law shall be judged by the law; for not the hearers of the law *are* just before God, but the doers of the law shall be justified.

FAITH BY WORKS.

UNDER the eye of the apostle, men contended which was the greatest, faith or works. But St. James adroitly turns the argument by the statement, " One may say, Thou hast faith, and I have works : show me thy faith without thy works, and I will show thee my faith by my works." Two farmers might contend which was the most important part of a tree, the root or the branches. "You can have no sap," says one, " without the root." " You can have no fruit without the branches," says the other. Both are needed, else you have no tree. Action is important, as is the spirit to the body. When the new church was built at Quincy, John Adams, the second President, chose a pew. He was absent from home on public business, and the committee wrote to him that the pew he had chosen had a pillar in it, which somewhat hid the preacher. Mr. Adams replied, "Some one must occupy the pew, and you know that 'faith comes by hearing.' "

Men of the most fervent piety are usually men of the most intense action. When the fire glows richer the fervor reddens the face. Luther, Melancthon, Whitfield, Wesley, Hunt, Calvin, and other men of untiring labors, are illustrations. Those men who have built our colleges, institutions of mercy, houses of charity, homes for the dumb, and blind, and lame, who cast their bread on the waters by ship-loads, and who make donations to the Gospel large as the seas, these usually are men of intense faith and earnest piety. They show their faith by their works. "Faith cometh by hearing, hearing by the word of God."

CCLXXIV.

GOODNESS PASS BEFORE THEE.

AND he said, I will make all my goodness pass before thee, and I will proclaim the name of the Lord before thee; and will be gracious to whom I will be gracious, and will show mercy on whom I will show mercy. Thou shalt not bow down to their gods, nor serve them, nor do after their works: but thou shalt utterly overthrow them, and quite break down their images. And ye shall serve the Lord your God, and he shall bless thy bread, and thy water; and I will take sickness away from the midst of thee. At the same time my reason returned unto me; and for the glory of my kingdom, mine honor and brightness returned unto me; and my counselors and my lords sought unto me; and I was established in my kingdom, and excellent majesty was added unto me. Now I Nebuchadnezzar praise and extol and honor the King of heaven, all whose works *are* truth, and his ways judgment: and those that walk in pride he is able to abase.

GOODNESS A CHRISTIAN GRACE.

"YOU would not give a fellow a loaf of bread if he was starving, but you have got plenty of tracts to give away to them that can't read," said a rough-looking fellow to a lady who was tramping her rounds in one of the poorest wards of the city. "Do you know of any body who wants bread?" the lady quietly asked. "Yes, I want it; my wife wants it, and my child wants it. I hain't got no work, and nobody'll trust me. You come round here with yer prayers and yer good books, but why don't yer bring us something to eat?" "I will go with you," said the missionary; and the man turned his face homeward. The woman was one of a thousand who tread the lanes and alleys of sorrow, visit the chambers of want and suffering; who comfort the sick and console the suffering. A company who go not empty-handed. They have food for the hungry, clothes for the destitute, medicine for the sick, rent for the penniless, and coals for the shivering.

The man led the way toward a terrible neighborhood, full of crime, ignorance, and suffering; through dark alleys; through foul and unwholesome lanes; into an offensive neighborhood; up rickety and filthy stairways to an attic. A low moan came from a bed on which lay a little child. A woman, hardened and insensible by suffering and sin, sat stolidly on a box. There was no window and no chimney in the coarse black room. Every thing told of poverty, neglect, and suffering. The man was sullen, despondent, and ripe for crime. He told his story, and a sad one it was. "You shall not starve in a Christian city," the visitor said. She brought a substantial supper and kindlings to cook it. She spread the table, presided, and when she left, after promising to call again, said a word for the Master. A benevolent physician visited the child, nor did he overlook the mother. Ten days wrought a great change in that household. One day, the man said to his visitor, "What did you come here for? I can't pay you for your kindness." "I came," said the missionary, "in His name who had not where to lay his head. He does not need our service now, and he has bade us do good to others in his name. Won't you love him and serve him?"

CCLXXV.

GREEN OLIVE-TREE.

THE righteous also shall see, and fear, and shall laugh at him: Lo, *this is* the man *that* made not God his strength; but trusted in the abundance of his riches, *and* strengthened himself in his wickedness. But I *am* like a green olive tree in the house of God: I trust in the mercy of God forever and ever. I will praise thee forever, because thou hast done *it*: and I will wait on thy name; for *it is* good before thy saints. The sacrifices of God *are* a broken spirit: a broken and a contrite heart, O God, thou wilt not despise. Do good in thy good pleasure unto Zion: build thou the walls of Jerusalem. Then shalt thou be pleased with the sacrifices of righteousness, with burnt offering and whole burnt offering: then shall they offer bullocks upon thine altar.

UNSEEN ALLIES.

When the people of Israel were on the verge of defeat, and no hope seemed left to them, the prophet pointed his desponding friend to the mountains around, which were full of chariots and horsemen of fire. Christians are often despondent over obstacles that seem to threaten the ark of the Lord. The great and almost countless number of vagrant children brought up in ignorance, superstition, and sin, which abound in our large cities, would seem to imperil the commonwealth. A different phase is put on the matter when we count up our thousands of Sunday-school children, to which are to be added over a million educated and trained to virtue and honorable pursuits. It is believed that there are in the United States over half a million of children pledged to total abstinence.

A stranger, who should pass up the East River, from the Battery to Harlem, would be appalled at the thousands of Sabbath-breakers who spend the day in revelry. Five miles of dissipation greet the eye. Bowling, dancing, gunning, target-shooting, drinking, and boisterous revelry rule the hour. What can save New-York from the fate of Sodom if this tide of impiety increases? But we turn to our hundred pulpits, to our 140,000 Sunday-school children and their teachers; the hundreds of missionaries who are doing their work among the lowly; the mission chapels and stations dotted all over the neglected portions of the city; the great company of devoted women who give their time to mission work among the neglected; the reading-rooms, Refuges, homes for the friendless, refuges for the outcasts, and houses for those who wish to reform. These agencies are steadily at work resisting the evil. Like the hidden forces of nature beneath the frost and crust of winter, these are silently at work preparing for the outburst that will clothe the earth with fertility, and make the barren and neglected places beautiful as the garden of the Lord.

CCLXXVI.

SLOW TO WRATH.

A DOUBLE-MINDED man *is* unstable in all his ways. Let the brother of low degree rejoice in that he is exalted: but the rich, in that he is made low: because as the flower of the grass he shall pass away. If ye fulfill the royal law according to the Scripture, Thou shalt love thy neighbor as thyself, ye do well: but if ye have respect to persons, ye commit sin, and are convinced of the law as transgressors. Of his own will he begat us with the word of truth, that we should be a kind of firstfruits of his creatures. Wherefore, my beloved brethren, let every man be swift to hear, slow to speak, slow to wrath: for the wrath of man worketh not the righteousness of God. If any of you lack wisdom, let him ask of God, that giveth to all *men* liberally, and upbraideth not; and it shall be given him. But let him ask in faith, nothing wavering: for he that wavereth is like a wave of the sea driven with the wind and tossed. For let not that man think that he shall receive any thing of the Lord.

A TIGER FOR A PET.

HUNTING among the jungles of India, a traveler came upon a tiger's den. In it he found a young cub. He succeeded in bearing it away before the tigress returned. In the distance, he heard the howl of the bereaved mother. She filled the air with the rage of her loss. The young tiger soon became a pet on board of the ship. His captor proposed to train him, and bring him up as a pet. The cub had the run of the vessel, and was fed at the caboose. The voyage ended. The owner took the little animal into his own house. It became a favorite with all the household. It was playful as a kitten. Day by day, it developed its strength, and grew in symmetry and beauty. It learned to know its master, and watched for his coming. The cub was taught a great many tricks, and was thought to be thoroughly domesticated and trained. One well acquainted with the habits of the tiger said to the owner, "Give your pet cooked food; don't let him taste blood."

One day, the man was confined to his house. He had cut his hand, and the cloth wound round it was saturated with blood. He lay down to rest, and fell asleep. The young tiger, roaming round the house, came into the presence of his prostrate master. He cuddled up to him, as was his wont. The wounded hand attracted his attention., and he commenced licking the blood that saturated the cloth. In a moment, he was transformed; he was a tiger of the jungles, hungry for gore. Furiously he attacked his master, and lacerated his face in a dreadful manner. The man awoke in agony, and had strength enough to protect himself from the fury of a savage beast that gloated over him with eyes fierce with rage. His life was saved, though the man's face was terribly lacerated and disfigured.

What a type of concealed sin and secret wrong in the heart! No man is safe who nourishes secret faults, or makes a pet of hidden sin. How dishonesty bursts out of a sudden! A sudden temptation brings to light a long-cherished purpose of evil. The hidden love of drink, subdued in manhood, breaks out in age, and hurls one down to a drunkard's grave. The sins of the eye, a wanton imagination, and private indulgence of evil thoughts, are as dangerous as is a pet tiger for a plaything.

CCLXXVII.

KINGS BENDING.

THE kings of Tarshish and of the isles shall bring presents: the kings of Sheba and Seba shall offer gifts. Yea, all kings shall fall down before him: all nations shall serve him. And the Gentiles shall come to thy light, and kings to the brightness of thy rising. Lift up thine eyes round about, and see: all they gathered themselves together, they come to thee: thy sons shall come from far, and thy daughters shall be nursed at *thy* side. Thus saith the Lord, the Redeemer of Israel, *and* his Holy One to him whom man despiseth, to him whom the nation abhorreth, to a servant of rulers, Kings shall see and arise, princes also shall worship, because of the Lord that is faithful, *and* the Holy One of Israel, and he shall choose thee.

KINGS SHALL COME BENDING.

The king of the Sandwich Islands was made the subject of special prayer at Fulton street. A half century has rolled along since the Sandwich Islands was the home of cannibals, where idols were worshiped and men bowed down to stocks and stones. A few missionaries visited these islands of the sea. God gave them great favor with the people. Thousands have been turned to the Lord, and the largest Christian church in the world is gathered here, illustrating the power of Divine grace. The visit of the king of those islands, King Kalakaua, to New-York, created great interest in Fulton street. It was proposed especially to remember the king at one of the services. Eloquent and hearty prayers were offered that the king might bow at the footstool of His Throne who is the "blessed and only Potentate, who is the King of kings, and Lord of lords." The fact was mentioned that on the Sunday previous, King Kalakaua attended divine service in Park-street Church, Boston. In this church the missionaries were ordained who, under God, worked such marvelous results in the name of the King. The services so impressed his majesty that he refused himself that day to all callers, many of whom were in high official life, and many called for the purpose of showing him the city by a ride. The prayer of the Fulton-street meeting and the interest taken in his behalf were communicated to the king, and appropriately responded to.

CCLXXVIII.

MOCKINGS AND SCOURGINGS.

AND others had trial of *cruel* mockings and scourgings, yea, moreover of bonds and imprisonment: they were stoned, they were sawn asunder, were tempted, were slain with the sword: they wandered about in sheep-skins, and goat-skins; being destitute, afflicted, tormented; (of whom the world was not worthy:) they wandered in deserts, and *in* mountains, and *in* dens and caves of the earth. Then cometh he to his disciples, and saith unto them, Sleep on now, and take *your* rest: behold, the hour is at hand, and the Son of man is betrayed into the hands of sinners. Rise, let us be going: behold, he is at hand that doth betray me. These all died in faith, not having received the promises, but having seen them afar off, and were persuaded of *them*, and embraced *them*, and confessed that they were strangers and pilgrims on the earth.

ON THE BANKS OF THE MERRIMAC.

THE work of foreign missions was not popular at the start. It was thought better to convert sinners at home, than to spend time, money, and life to invade the domains of heathendom. Why disturb the Moslem, the devotees on the Ganges, or the dwellers in the mountains of cruelty, when thousands at our doors rejected Christ? Still the great commission rang in the ears of a few faithful souls, "Go ye into all the world, and preach the gospel to every creature." But this was supposed to be a commission only to men. The irreligious were startled and indignant when they heard that a frail girl from the banks of the Merrimac had offered her services to the Board. With her life in her hand, she proposed to go to India, and call the women of that great country to the Saviour. The secular press were loud in denunciation of the measure. It was a shame, it was an outrage, it was said, to work on the feelings of a simple-hearted maiden, and take advantage of her infatuation to do her a great wrong. Here was a delicate, sensitive, fragile girl to be exposed to all the atrocities of heathenism, and fling herself away on the soil of barbarism.

The offering, however, was accepted, and the devoted girl was sent to the field of her choice. She took with her the great heart of the church. The sympathies of all Christendom went with her. Her devoted life was crowned with the best results. Her name stands foremost among the brilliant and honored women of the world, who have served well their race. Her lonely grave in India, shadowed by the Hopia-tree, is as well known as is the mausoleum of Napoleon, the sarcophagus of Wellington, or the tomb of Frederick the Great. Her name is honored throughout the world. No ship-master, of any nationality, passes in sight of the grave of Miss Hazeltine without dipping his flag in honor of her memory. True it is, that man or woman who honors Christ, he will honor. They that lay down life, reputation, and wealth for the Saviour's sake, will receive in this world a hundred-fold, and in the world to come life everlasting.

CCLXXIX.

DWELLINGS OF THE WICKED.

SURELY such *are* the dwellings of the wicked, and this *is* the place *of him that* knoweth not God. He shall be driven from light into darkness, and chased out of the world. He shall neither have son nor nephew among his people, nor any remaining in his dwellings. They that come after *him* shall be astonished at his day, as they that went before were affrighted. He that oppresseth the poor, reproacheth his Maker: but he that honoreth him hath mercy on the poor. The wicked is driven away in his wickedness: but the righteous hath hope in his death. Unto thee will I cry, O Lord my rock; be not silent to me: lest, *if* thou be silent to me, I become like them that go down into the pit. Hear the voice of my supplications, when I cry unto thee, when I lift up my hands toward thy holy oracle. Draw me not away with the wicked, and with the workers of iniquity, which speak peace to their neighbors, but mischief *is* in their hearts.

SPURGEON'S FAITH.

LEAVING nothing undone that human skill, forethought, and industry can do, Spurgeon's faith in God is one of his marked traits. His piety is of a cheerful type. He is buoyant, clastic, and cheery. His first utterance when he stands before his great congregation, "Let us PRAY!" rings out like a clarion. It startles the worshipers like a bugle-blast. His prayer-meetings are elastic; full of spirit and fervor. He was to preach one day in the Surrey Gardens. The pressure of the week found him unprepared. The congregation was immense; but every thing like a sermon was gone from him. He was dry as the bones in Ezekiel's valley. All the ordinary resources of his mind seemed to desert him. He was at his wit's end. His finances were low, and he needed money to carry on his work. In his extremity, he retired to his little room to pray. He poured forth his desires in an impassioned manner. His prayer was, "O Lord! help thy servant. Give him a message to this people! O Lord, if thou wilt help thy servant in this extremity, and give me a sermon, I will put a colporteur into the field at once." This was about the greatest sacrifice he then could make. He had scarcely come to his feet, before a subject flashed through his mind. He grasped it, and went back to his platform. He preached with a power that surprised himself. His audience was swayed as the trees of the forest are by the winds. A great work of grace broke out, marvelous in power and extent. The service closed. A reaction took place during the singing. How was the pledge to be met? How could he put a missionary in the field when he had not money enough for present expenses? Before the hymn closed, a stranger handed him up a slip of paper. It covered a check of just the sum required to pay the salary of a missionary. Spurgeon was overwhelmed by the coincidence. It is one of his traits to note the providence of God. He deepened the excitement of the hour by stating in earnest simplicity the dealings of God with him that day. His embarrassment; his entire blank; his wrestling with the Lord; his covenant, and its marvelous fulfillment. "Praise the Lord!" he shouted, "praise the Lord!" and all the people said "Amen."

CCLXXX.

AXE AT THE ROOT.

AND now also the axe is laid unto the root of the trees: therefore every tree which bringeth not forth good fruit is hewn down, and cast into the fire. Deliver me from mine enemies, O my God: defend me from them that rise up against me. Deliver me from the workers of iniquity, and save me from bloody men. For, lo, they lie in wait for my soul: the mighty are gathered against me; not *for* my transgression, nor *for* my sin, O Lord. Whose fan *is* in his hand, and he will thoroughly purge his floor, and gather his wheat into the garner; but he will burn the chaff with unquenchable fire. For bodily exercise profiteth little: but godliness is profitable unto all things, having promise of the life that now is, and of that which is to come.

SPURGEON'S PRAYER.

AFTER a long and successful season of labor, Mr. Spurgeon's friends advised him to take a rest. The Tabernacle was to be completely overhauled, and Mr. Spurgeon resolved to go on the Continent. He was met in the street one day by a plain-looking man, who said, "Mr. Spurgeon, why don't you preach where we working-people can hear you? We can not get into the Tabernacle; and the poor people stand no chance." Instead of going on the Continent, Spurgeon resolved to spend his six weeks' vacation in preaching to the London masses. Three miles away from his church, on the other side of London, stood a huge building, known as Agricultural Hall, which was a miniature Crystal Palace. The interior was rough, whitewashed, and used for cattle-shows. The floor was tan. The rude gallery was covered with grotesque circus pictures, and the interior was fitted up with cattle-pens. The building would hold 25,000 people. This was the place selected by the great preacher for his services. Every body was astounded. Every body predicted a failure. No human being, it was said, could fill such a house. The day for the opening came. It was one of the rainiest of the season. A deluge of rain was borne on a fierce gale. The house was not only crowded to its utmost capacity, but thousands were turned away. The most remarkable thing about the service was the prayer of the preacher. He was evidently overwhelmed. He stood up and prayed a prayer of one of the old prophets. It was in the highest degree impassioned, and the preacher pleaded with God as a man would plead for the life of his friend. He said: "O Lord, come to the rescue of thy servant. Why have you brought this great multitude here, if this poor worm in the dust is to be left alone? Where is thy honor? where is thy glory? where is thy cross, if thou dost desert thy servant in such a time as this?" He went on, and reasoned and expostulated, appealing to the justice and honor of the Lord, and, like Jacob and the angel, refusing to let him go without a blessing. The effect was marvelous. The audience was overwhelmed and melted to tears, and was mowed down as the grass falls before the scythe.

CCLXXXI.

AVENGING OF ISRAEL.

PRAISE ye the Lord for the avenging of Israel, when the people willingly offered themselves. Hear, O ye kings; give ear, O ye princes; I, *even* I, will sing unto the Lord; I will sing *praise* to the Lord God of Israel. Lord, when thou wentest out of Seir, when thou marchedst out of the field of Edom, the earth trembled, and the heavens dropped, the clouds also dropped water. Judge me, O Lord my God, according to thy righteousness; and let them not rejoice over me. Let them not say in their hearts, Ah, so would we have it: let them not say, We have swallowed him up. Let them be ashamed and brought to confusion together that rejoice at mine hurt: let them be clothed with shame and dishonor that magnify *themselves* against me.

SKELETON IN SPURGEON'S HOUSE.

IN confidential moments, in the bosom of his family, Haman talked of all his greatness; of the glory of his riches; how the king had promoted him; how he had advanced him above the princes and servants of the king; how the queen did let no man come in with the king unto the banquet but himself. Yet in his house of greatness there was a skeleton. "All this availeth me nothing, so long as I see Mordecai the Jew sitting at the king's gate."

Among the princes of preachers in the old world, Spurgeon is chief. He built on no man's foundation. His church, when he took it, was on the eve of dissolution. He had no patron or great friend to recommend him. His style of preaching was not popular with the masses. The mission work, now so common, was then unknown. London lent an unwilling ear to his message. In his earnest indignation, the preacher shouted, "You shall hear me! If you will not hear me in a black coat, I'll make you hear me in a red one." The crowd received his message with jeers. *Punch* lampooned him. *The Times* thundered at him, till all London went to hear what eccentric things the boy-preacher was uttering.

Spurgeon fought the battle with the Londoners, and won. He built his great Tabernacle, and crowded it to excess. He was as popular abroad as he was at home. No place could hold the people where he was announced to speak. He established his college; founded his orphanage; ran his church-roll to an enormous count. His sermons entered nearly every hut and hamlet in the land. His fame ran over the seas. His income was princely. His style of living, whatever he chose to make it. A huge congregation; unparalleled success; with the largest regular congregation in the world; ample means, and the affection and love of the entire brotherhood throughout Christendom. What could Spurgeon want more?

Yet in his house was there a skeleton. "Let us tell our troubles," he said one day to his brethren in convention. "What are the hinderances to our success?" "You begin," was the response. "The bane of my life is to keep myself steady at my work. I often get discouraged, and think I should have done better at something else."

CCLXXXII.

VOICE OUT OF THE THRONE.

AND a voice came out of the throne, saying, Praise our God, all ye his servants, and ye that fear him, both small and great. And I heard as it were the voice of a great multitude, and as the voice of many waters, and as the voice of mighty thunderings, saying, Alleluia: for the Lord God omnipotent reigneth. Let us be glad and rejoice, and give honor to him: for the marriage of the Lamb is come, and his wife hath made herself ready. Let them shout for joy, and be glad, that favor my righteous cause: yea, let them say continually, Let the Lord be magnified, which hath pleasure in the prosperity of his servant. And my tongue shall speak of thy righteousness *and* of thy praise all the day long. Whoso offereth praise glorifieth me: and to him that ordereth *his* conversation *aright* will I show the salvation of God.

POWER OF PRINCIPLE.

When it was decided to build the Metropolitan Tabernacle, Mr. Spurgeon took it on himself to collect funds. He traveled far and near; preached at home and abroad. He lectured and made addresses in England, Scotland, Ireland, and Wales. Wherever he went, he had a contribution taken up for his great work. It is estimated that full 50,000 persons made contributions for the house of the Lord.

One Sunday was passed in Bristol. A great crowd was in attendance; the people of that ancient town did honor to the great metropolitan pastor. Mr. Spurgeon had accepted the hospitality of a poor but pious man who had some relations in the London church. A wealthy man of note prepared to entertain Mr. Spurgeon with a fine Sunday dinner. He had no doubt that to express his purpose to entertain Mr. Spurgeon would be all that was necessary. To his astonishment, not to say indignation, Mr. Spurgeon declined the elegant repast, and expressed his purpose to dine with his humble but pious friend. The rich man caused Mr. Spurgeon to know that the slight had cost the preacher five hundred pounds, the sum the gentleman proposed to contribute.

Mr. Spurgeon said nothing. In due time, the corner-stone was laid, and all contributors were invited to the solemn assembly. Among the number was the secretary of the Bristol merchant. He came, he said, to lay on the stone the sum of five hundred pounds, the gift of his master. It was a gift in honor of the steady principle of the preacher, who kept his word at his own loss.

CCLXXXIII.

NO VIOLENCE.

VIOLENCE shall no more be heard in thy land, wasting nor destruction within thy borders; but thou shalt call thy walls Salvation, and thy gates Praise. The sun shall be no more thy light by day: neither for brightness shall the moon give light unto thee: but the Lord shall be unto thee an everlasting light, and thy God, thy glory. Yet Michael the archangel, when contending with the devil he disputed about the body of Moses, durst not bring against him a railing accusation, but said, The Lord rebuke thee. Then judgment shall dwell in the wilderness, and righteousness remain in the fruitful field. And the work of righteousness shall be peace; and the effect of righteousness, quietness and assurance forever.

THE SWORD AND THE PRUNING-HOOK.

THE sword is an emblem of authority. The sword of the house of David represents, like the sceptre, a right to rule. It is an emblem of civil government, for the magistrate does not bear the sword in vain; without it, the business of life can not be carried on. In the days of Deborah, out of ten thousand men, there was neither sword nor spear. Bold, bad men trod the highway, and good men slunk in the by-paths. The business of life ceased. No furrow was turned; no one sowed or reaped; even women, who went to draw water for the midday meal, were shot by the treacherous archers. One battle under the banner of the Lord changed the whole nation, drove the desperadoes to the dens and caves, and brought good men to the front. The sword of the Lord and Gideon was the battle-cry that brought victory to the tents of Israel. The utterance of the Saviour, "The strong man armed keepeth his goods in peace," is as applicable to the security of nations now as it was eighteen hundred years ago.

The promise that the sword shall be beaten into plowshares, and the spears into pruning-hooks, does not indicate that the implements are evil, or the use of them wrong. It teaches that the time will come when men will not need these fierce incentives to duty, but will obey because prompted by divine love. The arid, thirsty, parched, barren earth, overrun with briers and thorns, nigh unto cursing, destined to be burned, can be transformed into a fruitful field, fragrant and pleasant as the garden of the Lord. So religion proposes to transform this earth, change the vile nature of men, with holiness to the Lord on the very bells of the horses of traffic. Then the sword can be safely beaten up; the implements of war transformed to implements of husbandry; and the men, being wholly righteous, shall learn war no more. On the shore of the South Sea, an American captain, with a friend, strayed away from their companions. Just across a little rivulet, he saw a party of savages approaching. He broke off a branch of the olive-tree, an emblem of peace since the days of Noah, and waved it toward the cannibals. In a moment, the savages broke branches from a similar tree, and waved their signal of friendly and pacific intentions.

CCLXXXIV.

A GOOD CONFESSION.

AND after this Joseph of Arimathea, being a disciple of Jesus, but secretly for fear of the Jews, besought Pilate that he might take away the body of Jesus: and Pilate gave *him* leave. He came therefore, and took the body of Jesus. And there came also Nicodemus, (which at the first came to Jesus by night,) and brought a mixture of myrrh and aloes, about a hundred pound *weight*. Then took they the body of Jesus, and wound it in linen clothes with the spices, as the manner of the Jews is to bury. And behold, *there was* a man named Joseph, a counselor: *and he was* a good man, and a just: (the same had not consented to the counsel and deed of them:) *he was* of Arimathea, a city of the Jews; who also himself waited for the kingdom of God. This *man* went unto Pilate, and begged the body of Jesus. And he took it down, and wrapped it in linen, and laid it in a sepulchre that was hewn in stone, wherein never man before was laid.

NICODEMUS IN COUNCIL.

OUR blessed Lord had few friends among the great and the mighty. The grand council of the nation professed to regard Jesus as an impostor; at the best, a madman; at the worst, as one possessed of a devil. Before this august body our Lord was on trial. He was arraigned for the highest crime known to the laws of his country, that of blasphemy. "He was a man," the people said, "and he made himself God. He was not yet fifty years old, and yet he had seen Abraham. He was a peasant of Nazareth, yet he made himself equal with the Father." So he was put on trial. It was resolved that he must die. Yet must he be put to death according to the forms of law. A crime must be laid to his charge. That crime must be proved and witnesses be produced.

In all the grand council that sat on the case of our Lord, there was but one friendly voice; but one man dared speak in his behalf: that man was Nicodemus. Once he was in awe of the Jews. He came to Jesus by night, that no prying eyes could look on his visit. He did not know enough of the Son of God to dare for him the rage and the malice of men. But that night-visit did wonders for him. He revealed to him the Messiah; it made him familiar with the plan of salvation. And when Jesus was put on trial, he was able to speak out in the august assembly and say, "Does our law judge any man before it heareth him?" So, like his Master before Pilate, "he witnessed a good confession."

CCLXXXV.

BE WARMED AND FILLED.

WHAT *doth it* profit, my brethren, though a man say he hath faith, and have not works? can faith save him? If a brother or sister be naked, and destitute of daily food, and one of you say unto them, Depart in peace, be *ye* warmed and filled; notwithstanding ye give them not those things which are needful to the body; what *doth it* profit? Even so faith, if it hath not works, is dead, being alone. Hearken, my beloved brethren; Hath not God chosen the poor of this world rich in faith, and heirs of the kingdom which he hath promised to them that love him? But ye have despised the poor. Do not rich men oppress you, and draw you before the judgment-seats? My brethren, count it all joy when ye fall into divers temptations; knowing *this*, that the trying of your faith worketh patience. But let patience have *her* perfect work, that ye may be perfect and entire, wanting nothing.

OPEN-HANDED HELP.

Franklin gave a dusty traveler a ride. "How can I pay you?" said the man. "Help the first person you find, who is in trouble; for good deeds, like money, should be kept in circulation."

Webster, when at Marshfield, looked more like a farmer than a statesman. With his slouched hat, heavy boots over his pants, and hatchet in his hand, he might easily be mistaken for the head workman on the place. "Will you carry me across the brook?" said a young man, in search of the great statesman. He was afraid of wetting his nice boots. Mr. Webster lifted the visitor across the little current. He handed him a piece of money. "Keep your money, sir; I don't want it. But never miss an opportunity to do a kind deed."

Dr. Watts, when ten years old, complained of the hymns sung in the chapel. "Don't find fault with what has done good service. Make better hymns, my son." Watts went to his chamber, and composed,

"Behold the glories of the Lamb."

A celebrated singer was told that his rival laughed at his singing. He replied, "Then I must learn to sing better."

The manner of aid is often quite as important as the thing done. Giving with cheerfulness is a divine command. Man, like the Lord, loveth a cheerful giver. A gruff, uncomfortable manner of complying is often as painful as rejecting. He that giveth, let him do it with simplicity. In one of our banks a young man gains more friends in denying a discount, than others do in granting them.

CCLXXXVI.

IN THY MOUTH SWEET AS HONEY.

AND I went unto the angel, and said unto him, Give me the little book. And he said unto me, Take *it*, and eat it up; and it shall make thy belly bitter, but it shall be in thy mouth sweet as honey. And I took the little book out of the angel's hand, and ate it up; and it was in my mouth sweet as honey: and as soon as I had eaten it, my belly was bitter. And he said unto me, Thou must prophesy again before many peoples, and nations, and tongues, and kings. How sweet are thy words unto my taste! *yea, sweeter* than honey to my mouth. Through thy precepts I get understanding: therefore I hate every false way. Moreover the profit of the earth is for all: the king *himself* is served by the field. He that loveth silver shall not be satisfied with silver; nor he that loveth abundance with increase: this *is* also vanity. When goods increase, they are increased that eat them: and what good *is there* to the owners thereof, saving the beholding *of them* with their eyes?

THE BOUNDING DEER.

"I HAD rather be a doorkeeper in the house of my God," said David, "than to dwell in the tents of wickedness." As the bounding deer panted for the water brooks, so he panted for the altar of praise. The Sabbath is not only a delight, but a necessity. The hart must drink or die. Men and nations perish without the Sabbath. Public worship does not sustain the Sabbath; the Sabbath sustains public worship. During the seventy years' captivity the people of Israel allowed the altar of the Lord to fall. The Sabbath was desecrated, and the merchants bought and sold on God's holy day. The people lost their language, lost their knowledge of the word of God, and became even as the heathen. Ezra, the scribe, stood upon his pulpit of wood, opened the book of the law in the sight of all the people; read distinctly, gave the sense, and caused the people to understand. This service overwhelmed the congregation with sorrow and shame. The Levites had to interfere: "Hold your peace, for the day is holy; neither be ye grieved."

God's day is the poor man's boon. The tyrant, the oppressor, and the avaricious would not bid one pause one day in seven; command the ledger to be closed, the hum of business to cease, and the hammer to lie still. Men who demand the Sabbath as a day of recreation for the poor, would take the Sabbath away from the laboring man. Even now, there are trades that demand that men shall work seven days or be discharged. The newspaper-offices, street-cars, boats for Sunday recreation, bands of music, restaurants and beer-gardens, are illustrations. In one of the great New-England mills, attending worship on Sunday was one of the conditions of employment. "Are all your stockholders religious?" said a visitor. "No, I don't know that any of them are." "Then why this rule?" "People are worth more to us as operatives who keep the Sabbath."

CCLXXXVII.

HOPE OF A TREE.

FOR there is hope of a tree, if it be cut down, that it will sprout again, and that the tender branch thereof will not cease. Though the root thereof wax old in the earth, and the stock thereof die in the ground; *yet* through the scent of water it will bud, and bring forth boughs like a plant. But man dieth, and wasteth away: yea, man giveth up the ghost, and where *is* he? Blessed *be* the God and Father of our Lord Jesus Christ, which according to his abundant mercy hath begotten us again unto a lively hope by the resurrection of Jesus Christ from the dead, to an inheritance incorruptible, and undefiled, and that fadeth not away, reserved in heaven for you. And hope maketh not ashamed; because the love of God is shed abroad in our hearts by the Holy Ghost which is given unto us.

POWER OF AN ENDLESS LIFE.

GOD as a rewarder is an indispensable element of reverence. He that cometh to God must believe that he is a rewarder. The power of future retribution on the conscience has been admitted, even by moralists, in all ages. Franklin was a rationalist. Paine showed him his foul attack on religion. "Throw it into the fire," said Franklin; "if men are so bad with religion, what would they be without it?" Voltaire's servant, who listened to his infidel discussions at the table, robbed his master. "How dared you do it," said Voltaire; "were you not afraid of the prison?" "You removed, sir, the greater terror, and I was willing to brave the less." Moffatt conversed with an African chief on the reality of the future life. "I have seen the ground thick with the dead and dying. Will these all come up at last?" "They will." "Will my father and mother live?" (He had killed them to get power.) "Yes, all the dead, small and great, will come forth." The cannibal African chief quailed before the power of an endless life.

The guilty king of Babylon gave a feast to his lords. To insult the God of the Hebrews, he called for the sacred vessels in the house of the Lord, which even his father had spared. In the midst of the drunken revelry, an armless hand wrote, in characters of light, the doom of the monarch. Neither the king nor the wise men of the court could read a word of the sentence. It would have been natural for the king to have interpreted the handwriting as an omen of good; that the gods had accepted the libation poured forth from the sacred vessel. Did the flaming letters promise light and health and a prosperous reign to the king? Not so. The monarch read his doom before a Daniel came to judgment. Ignorant of the sentence, ignorant of what the words meant, conscience already interpreted them as ominous to the guilty monarch. The power of an endless life took hold of him. His countenance changed; his joints were loosed; his knees smote one against another, and a certain fearful looking for of judgment took hold of him. Aaron Burr, when a young man, was troubled about his soul. It was a time of general revival. His minister said to him, "Young man, beware of fanaticism." Burr heeded the injunction. He dismissed the fear of future punishment from his eyes, and began that licentious career that will make his name famous in all times.

CCLXXXVIII.

GAINED THY BROTHER.

MOREOVER if thy brother shall trespass against thee, go and tell him his fault between thee and him alone: if he shall hear thee, thou hast gained thy brother. But if he will not hear *thee*, *then* take with thee one or two more, that in the mouth of two or three witnesses every word may be established. And if he shall neglect to hear them, tell *it* unto the church: but if he neglect to hear the church, let him be unto thee as a heathen man and a publican. Now it came to pass, when they spake daily unto him, and he hearkened not unto them, that they told Haman, to see whether Mordecai's matters would stand: for he had told them that he *was* a Jew. And when Haman saw that Mordecai bowed not, nor did him reverence, then was Haman full of wrath. And he thought scorn to lay hands on Mordecai alone; for they had showed him the people of Mordecai: wherefore Haman sought to destroy all the Jews that *were* throughout the whole kingdom of Ahasuerus, *even* the people of Mordecai.

BROTHERLY KINDNESS.

THE power of brotherly kindness can not be overstated. The elements of which it is composed are among the most valuable in practical life. Selfish, sordid, mean men rarely succeed. Men who gather in fortunes are usually large givers. A purely selfish man is rarely a successful man; he is one

> "Whom none can love, whom none can thank,
> Creation's blot, creation's blank."

The ferryman in California, who gave a poor miner a row across the river, did a good thing for himself. The poor fellow was dead-broke; he was anxious to return to San Francisco; he had no money. "Jump in," said the ferryman; "I am not the man to send a poor fellow adrift. I remember when I was little, and my mother a poor widow, we had no bread. A stranger gave mother a dollar, and that dollar made me all the money I have ever had. I am going to loan you five dollars on account of some poor sufferer whom you may relieve." The traveler found friends to help him, was successful in business, and sought out and rewarded the ferryman for his timely aid.

An Indian on the Shetucket River had a little hut at the foot of a long hill. One day, a man found his team set and unable to draw the load. He applied to the Indian for help. He went a long distance and caught his mustang, and with his aid drew the load to the top. "How much must I pay you?" was the question. "I don't charge any thing for helping a friend out of trouble," was the red man's reply. The word sank into his heart, for he was a churlish neighbor. He resolved to be a kinder man hereafter. He cut down a tree, and had a canoe made, which he presented to the noble-hearted Indian.

Good deeds run on and do their work after the author has passed away. An American, when in Egypt, was invited to see the unrolling of a newly discovered mummy. It was taken from a small stone tomb that had not been opened since the time of the Pharaohs. Yard after yard of the fragrant bandage was removed, and when near the body a single kernel of wheat was discovered. The American brought it to his native land. He planted the seed, and though it was 4000 years old, it bloomed, and a stock sprang up bearing the seven ears, as in the harvest of Joseph. To all the world it seemed lost; yet it had vitality, like a good deed in a naughty world.

www.ingramcontent.com/pod-product-compliance
Lightning Source LLC
LaVergne TN
LVHW021101110826
845150LV00001B/140

* 9 7 8 1 4 2 5 5 6 5 8 8 6 *